Other Guides in the Discovering Historic America Series

CALIFORNIA AND THE WEST

THE MID-ATLANTIC STATES

THE SOUTHEAST

Text:

Vicki Brooks
Michael Fiore
Martin Greif
Lawrence Grow

Design:

Frank Mahood
Donald Rolfe

Cover illustration: *First Church of Belfast, Maine; Historic American Buildings Survey, Cortlandt V. D. Hubbard, photographer.*

DISCOVERING HISTORIC AMERICA

NEW ENGLAND

General Editor: S. Allen Chambers

E.P. DUTTON & CO., INC. · *NEW YORK*
1982

Published in the United States by E.P. Dutton, Inc. 2 Park
Avenue, New York, N.Y. 10016

Library of Congress Catalog Card Number 82-71548
ISBN: 0-525-932-44-5 Volume I

Published simultaneously in Canada by Clarke, Irwin &
Company Limited, Toronto and Vancouver

10 9 8 7 6 5 4 3 2 1

First Edition

Contents

Introduction

EACH of the titles in the *Discovering Historic America* series brings together the rich and varied resources available to the traveler in an historic region of the United States. In whatever season of the year, the traveler may journey into a past that is alive today and not an ocean or oceans away from home. History may have begun on the other side of the Atlantic or Pacific, but it is abundantly and colorfully displayed in the highways and byways of rural and urban America, in historic homes, museum villages, state and national parks, inns and churches, courthouses and city halls, hotels and restaurants, museums and libraries, battlefields and archaeological sites, mills and manors.

This comprehensive guide to historic New England, organized state by state and from south to north, offers the traveler hundreds of opportunities to step away from the frenzied pace of everyday life — to enjoy the quiet of a picturesque wayside inn, to trace the path of Colonial forebears, to experience the delights of a ride in a horse and buggy or a steam-driven train, to discover our heritage in traditional arts and crafts. For families with small children *Discovering Historic America* provides useful information on activities which are not only entertaining but educational, whether on a day trip, weekend, or extended vacation. For every traveler there is a rich selection of historical treasures to be explored and enjoyed in almost every corner of the six tradition-rich states that make up New England.

Many of the places described in this book are listed in the National Register of Historic Places; some are also official National Historic Landmarks. These listings have been supplemented with historical museums, reconstructions such as museum villages, excursion railroad lines, traditional craft workshops, state parks, and monuments of historic interest. And there are, of course, hundreds of historic properties included here which have yet to reach the official listings in Washington or elsewhere.

For the traveler heading out from one of the major metropolitan areas, a one-volume guide which includes information on all of these features in addition to a selection of historic inns, hotels, and restaurants is of considerable value. Whether a trip is undertaken as a family activity or as a get-away-from-it-all escape for a weekend or a week, there is much pleasure to be gained in discovering the treasures of historic New England. Discerning travelers, dismayed by today's slick commercial tourism, will delight in the authentic and will find exploration of America's past a satisfying experience.

Dozens of people associated with New England's many historical societies, preservation organizations, and tourist authorities have provided generous suggestions and source material for this volume. In addition, the records of the National Register have been made available for checking facts. Although it is impossible to name everyone who has offered assistance, several people merit very special thanks. I wish particularly to thank Mrs. Colette Eady of the National Register staff for answering the many questions regarding the whereabouts of pertinent information on historic properties; thanks, also, to Peter D. Bachelder, vice president, information services, Maine Publicity Bureau; Charles Norwood, public information supervisor, Connecticut Dept. of Economic Development; and Leonard J. Panaggio, director, Tourist Promotion Division, Dept. of Economic Development, state of Rhode Island.

How to Use This Guide

Discovering *Historic America: New England* is a useful book to consult and a very easy book to use. It is organized by state, starting with Connecticut, and moves north through Maine. The states that make up New England, with the exception of Rhode Island, are further broken down into geographic regions. Connecticut, for example, is divided into southwestern, northwestern, central, and eastern sections. These smaller areas make the planning and execution of trips easier and enable the traveler to choose from a wide variety of historic sites and attractions concentrated within a self-contained geographic region. A state map, indicating the key regions within, appears at the beginning of each chapter of the book. The listings for each of these regions are broken down by town or city in alphabetical order.

Information on the historical, architectural, or other cultural significance of a place is given along with essential facts on hours of operation, address, telephone number, and admission fee if any. Some of the historic places listed and described remain in private hands, but are still accessible for viewing from the public way or are open on special days for group tours. These are so designated.

Special letter codes and symbols are used with many of the listings. **NR** means that the property has been nominated and accepted as an historic property by the National Register of Historic Places, National Park Service, Washington, D.C. **NHL** is the designation for a National Historic Landmark, an honor reserved by the National Park Service for properties or geographic districts of exceptional significance to the nation. All these landmarks are automatically included in the National Register. In New England a significant number of properties are administered and/or owned by the Society for the Preservation of New England Antiquities, located in Boston. The initials **SPNEA** are used to designate these listings. Places of special interest to families with children are marked with the symbol 👪 .

Listings of lodging and restaurants are included at the end of each state's entries. Only properties which can be considered historic to a significant degree have been included. In every case, modern improvements have been made, but these have been designed with consideration for the architectural integrity of the original building. Inns and hotels with restaurants open to the general public are designated with the symbol 🍴 .

The cost of lodgings has been rated on the following scale based on the average daily single room rate: **I** = inexpensive, $25 or under; **M** = moderate, $40 or under; **E** = expensive, over $40. The cost of meals has been rated on the following scale based on the average dinner price: **I** = inexpensive, $7.50 or under; **M** = moderate, $12.50 or under; **E** = expensive, over $12.50. Other abbreviations used in the lodging and dining sections are the following: **MAP** = modified American plan, **EP** = European plan, **AE** = American Express, **CB** = Carte Blanche, **D** = Diners Club, **M** = Mastercharge, **V** = Visa, and **PC** = personal checks accepted.

Although every effort has been made to insure the accuracy of addresses, telephone numbers, hours of operation, and admission fees appearing in this book, these are all subject to change over time. In planning a trip, it is always wise to call or write ahead for the latest information.

NEW ENGLAND

1. CONNECTICUT

DUTCH traders were the first to explore Connecticut's seacoast and inland waterways, but it was English Puritans from Massachusetts who first settled here in the 1630s, principally in Hartford, Wethersfield, and Windsor. In these and other settlements can be seen the strong sense of community which prevailed. The early towns were all planned around central commons, where stock was grazed, churches and schools built, and goods sold.

From its earliest days, Connecticut developed strong political and financial independence from Britain: its Fundamental Orders of 1639 established democratic principles of government based on the will of the people, giving rise to Connecticut's present nickname, The Constitution State. Many of the earliest residents exemplify that independent spirit—among them patriot Nathan Hale and Jonathan Trumbull, the only colonial governor to support America's cause in the Revolutionary War.

Education and the arts have been prominent in Connecticut for centuries. Yale University, one of only nine pre-Revolutionary colleges in the country, began in Clinton in 1701 with only one student before being transferred, finally, to New Haven. Judge Tapping Reeve founded the nation's first law school in Litchfield in the late 18th century. The landmark homes of Harriet Beecher Stowe and Samuel Clemens in Hartford, Eugene O'Neill's cottage in New Haven, and Noah Webster's birthplace in West Hartford are all present reminders of a strong literary heritage.

During the 17th century agriculture and trade were the primary sources of income, but limited farmlands led to the rise of manufacturing of all types. Along the coast, protected harbors and deep rivers proved ideal for shipbuilding. Mystic and New London were only two of the thriving port towns whose prosperity depended primarily on the shipyards, the fisheries, and the whalers. Many of the architectural masterpieces that survive along the Connecticut shore today, like those of New London's Whale Oil Row, were the very earthly rewards of diligently harvesting the fruits of the sea.

Connecticut's historic attractions, however, are by no means limited to the homes and businesses of her entrepreneurs. Visitors to any of the four regions suggested in the pages following will find museums, historic villages, and other entertainments of wide appeal. Southwestern Connecticut includes, besides the lovely old residential districts of Fairfield and New Haven counties, such educational amusements as the P. T. Barnum Museum in Bridgeport and the Branford Trolley Museum in East Haven. The Northwest, bounded by Litchfield County, contains some of the most beautiful old inns in the state, along with some of its most scenic lakes and hills.

The Central region, in addition to being the home of the state capital, Hartford, contains one of the most beautiful river valleys in the country. The lovely towns which dot the Connecticut River are, if possible, even lovelier when seen by rail aboard an old steam locomotive, or by river on an excursion boat.

Mystic and its famous seaport museum attract millions of visitors each year to Eastern Connecticut. Yet to miss the more northerly sections, well inland from the Atlantic, is to overlook a number of peaceful farming communities where time has virtually stood still for over a century.

Mystic Seaport Museum, Mystic, CT

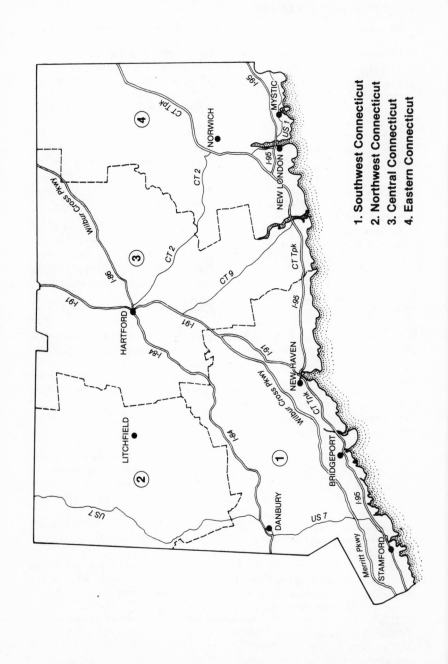

1. Southwest Connecticut
2. Northwest Connecticut
3. Central Connecticut
4. Eastern Connecticut

Southwest Connecticut

Branford

HARRISON HOUSE, 124 W. Main St., c. 1700. Some historians now call houses built in America before the 18th century "first-period" houses, and, if this is so, the Harrison house is one of the finest late "first-period" houses in this area. Built by Nathaniel Harrison, the 2½-story dwelling was home to three generations of Harrisons. Restored in the early 20th century, the house features an unusual stone chimney and is furnished with fine 18th-century pieces. Owned by SPNEA; operated by the Branford Historical Society. NR. Open June-Oct 15, W-Sa 12-5. Free. Donations accepted. 488-5771.

Bridgeport

MUSEUM OF ART, SCIENCE AND INDUSTRY, 4450 Park Ave. Since Elias Howe built his sewing machine factory in Bridgeport in 1863, the city has been known as a major manufacturing center, famous for its firearms, especially, and for its wares made of bronze, brass, iron, and steel. The museum features an astonishing range of goods made in 19th-century Bridgeport, which, taken together, are virtually a capsule history of 19th-century American industry. Featured, too, are fine collections of Indian artifacts, paintings, antique furniture, and circus memorabilia, Bridgeport having been the winter home of both Barnum and Bailey's Circus and Buffalo Bill's Wild West Show. Children whose interest in things historic has been sated will want to visit the museum's planetarium. Tu-Su 2-5, except F 10-5. $1 adults, 50¢ children, seniors, and students. No charge F. Closed M and national holidays. 372-3521. ♦♦

CAPTAIN JOHN BROOKS HOUSE, 199 Pembroke St., 1788. This clapboarded frame residence was originally a "half house"—with one room, two stories high, with a chimney at one end. Later additions made it into the fine example of a New England central-chimney house that it is today. Nicely furnished with period antiques, the house was built for Capt. John Brooks, a local merchant. Operated by the Museum of Art, Science and Industry. NR. Tu-Su 2-5. $1 adults, 50¢ children, seniors, students. 372-3521.

P. T. BARNUM MUSEUM, 820 Main St., 1891-92. Phineas Taylor Barnum, originator of "The Greatest Show on Earth" (1871), which merged with the Bailey Circus (1881) to form the Barnum and Bailey Circus, gave this exuberantly decorated late-Victorian structure to the citizens of Bridgeport for use as a scientific and historical museum, but financial troubles plagued the venture and the town eventually took over the building for use as a museum honoring the famous circus entrepreneur himself. The aesthetic pleasures of the building, including a large circular tower with a frieze constaining the busts of notable persons (including Barnum, naturally), are matched by the treasures within: circus memorabilia, highlighted by stores of material on Barnum's greatest stars, among them Tom Thumb and Jenny Lind. NR. Tu-Sa 2-5. $1 adults, 50¢ children. Closed M and holidays. 576-7320. ♦♦

Cheshire

LOCK 12 CANAL PARK, CT 42 (off CT

10), 1828-46. The Farmington Canal Company, chartered in 1822, was authorized to complete a waterway from New Haven northward to the Massachusetts line. Six years later a section of the canal was opened to traffic, but because of the advent of railroads the project was short-lived and closed in 1846. Lock 12 is a fine remnant of an impressive 19th-century engineering work. The park also includes replica blacksmith and carpentry shops and a picnic area. NR. Mar-Nov, daily 10-5; Su 1-5. Free.

FIRST CONGREGATIONAL CHURCH, 111 Church Dr., 1826-27. Situated at the end of a small village green, this is one of the finest churches in Connecticut and a perfect example of the neo-classical Adamesque style in America. Typical of the village churches of David Hoadley, the structure features a distinctive steeple that rises in two stages from a tower over the porch. The fanlights over the three doors have been much admired. NR.

Danbury

DANBURY SCOTT-FANTON MUSEUM AND HISTORICAL SOCIETY, 43 Main St., c. 1785. Part of this museum complex is the **John Rider House,** built for a local cabinetmaker in the late 18th century and one of the relatively few surviving examples of Colonial architecture in a town that was virtually destroyed by the British. The house, remarkably preserved and with its original hardware and stenciling intact, is a lovely setting for the museum's collection of 18th-century furnishings, woodworking tools, and crewel embroidery. A permanent exhibition on Danbury during the Revolution, an exhibit on the Danbury hatting industry, and a large library are among other features. NR. W-Su 2-5. Closed, M, Tu, holidays. Donations accepted. 743-5200.

Darien

BATES-SCOFIELD HOMESTEAD, 45 Old King's Hwy N., c. 1730. This classic example of an 18th-century Connecticut saltbox houses the Darien Historical Socie-

ty and features a massive center chimney, authentic local furnishings, magnificent crewel-embroidered curtains, and an excellent Colonial herb garden, among other amenities. A 900-volume library is available for those wanting to dip into New England genealogy. Tu, F 9:30-12:30; W, Th 9:30-12:30, 2-4; Su 2:30-4:30. Closed M, Sa, holidays. No charge. 655-9233.

East Haven

BRANFORD TROLLEY MUSEUM, River St. With its more than 90 classic trolleys, inter-urbans, and rapid-transit cars recalling an era of transportation all but lost in America, this is a perfect place for family entertainment and education. An informative guided tour of open car barns and restoration shops is offered, but the highlight is a three-mile trip aboard an antique trolley through the woods, hills, meadows, and trestles of the Connecticut shoreline. Picnic facilities available. Operated by the Branford Electric Railway Assoc. Apr, Su 11-5; May-mid-June, Sa, Su, holidays 11-5; mid-June-mid-Sept, M-F 10-5, Sa, Su, holidays 11-5; mid-Sept-Oct, Sa, Su, holidays 11-5; Nov, Su 11-5; Dec, Sa-Su 11-5. $2.50 adults, $1.25 children 5-11. Group rates. 467-6927.

Fairfield

FAIRFIELD HISTORICAL SOCIETY, 636 Old Post Road. The Society's museum maintains a fine collection of artifacts relating to the history of Fairfield and its environs, including exhibits of dolls, toys, costumes, woodworking and farm implements, clocks, portraits, and furniture. An 8,000-volume library is available to those researching New England genealogy. M-F 9:30-4:30, Su 1-5. Free. 259-1598.

OGDEN HOUSE, 1520 Bronson Rd., 1750. The home of Jane and David Ogden and their seven children, this saltbox farmhouse has been scrupulously furnished in keeping with a 1775 inventory listing items owned by the Ogdens. The result is an experience in living history that is both appealing and eye-opening, an 18th-century America far different from that pictured in Hollywood epics. For those who want to learn how a well-to-do Colonial family lived in a thriving, well-established port town, a visit to the Ogden House is recommended. The museum is famous for its 18th-century kitchen garden, planted, researched, and maintained by the Fairfield Garden Club. Owned by the Fairfield Historical Society. Mid-May–mid-Oct, Th, Su 1-4. $1 adults, 50¢ children. 259-1598.

FAIRFIELD HISTORIC DISTRICT, all buildings bordering the Old Post Rd. from its intersection with Turney Rd. (including buildings SE and NE of the Town Hall on both sides of Beach Rd. and the Old Burying Ground), 18th and 19th centuries. The Fairfield Historic District includes some 75 buildings in a variety of architectural styles. These range from the small number of pre-revolutionary homes that survived the burning of the town by the British to a Romanesque library built in 1890 and a variety of Victorian residences. All of the buildings taken together form a totality, the richness of which suggests a veritable history of American architecture over a period of 250 years. The district is significant from an historical point of view because it was the focal point of the first English settlement in the area and an important British target during the Revolutionary War.

Fairfield was settled at the end of the Pequot War (1637). Roger Ludlowe and a small band of Englishmen laid out the town along four squares of 25 to 30 acres each. These squares comprise the major part of the historic district. The **Town Hall** and **Town Green** are the focal point of the original squares. The Town Hall was rebuilt in 1794, remodeled a century later, and restored in 1936 to its 18th-century appearance. The **Rising Sun Tavern**, built in 1780 by Samuel Penfield and "home" to Fairfield's most prominent visitors of the past, is also on the green. The **Fairfield Academy** was moved from its original site to its present position SE of the Town Hall. The **Burr Mansion** (739 Old Post Rd.) was built in 1740 and remodeled in the Greek

Revival style a century later. A typical pre-revolutionary Connecticut saltbox (c. 1740) may be seen at 349 Beach Rd. The entire district, so rich in history, invites leisurely strolling.

SOUTHPORT HISTORIC DISTRICT, bounded generally by the old New York, New Haven & Hartford Railroad on the N; by Mill River and Southport Harbor on the S; on the W by Old South Rd. (including properties on both sides of the road); and on the E by Rose Hill Rd. (including properties on Church St. and both sides of Rose Hill Rd., but excluding commercial and industrial property along Pequot Ave.), 18th and 19th centuries. The historic district of Southport is significant because the area has always been the center of trade and commerce in Fairfield and because its history is typical of the development of commercial life in many New England ports in the 50 years following the Revolutionary War. The architecture of the district consists primarily of buildings constructed after 1779 when the British virtually destroyed Fairfield. It is a valuable concentration of Greek Revival and Victorian structures which were for the most part the homes of substantial men whose wealth came from their involvement in commerce, banking, and especially shipping.

Fairfield was founded in 1639, and shipyards and wharves sprang up along Mill River until 1831, when Southport was designated a separate borough by the Connecticut General Assembly (it remained so until 1854). The harbor was the focal point of local life in the past and, crowded with pleasure craft of every type, it should be visited as part of any walking tour of the area today. Noteworthy among the houses are **750 Harbor Rd.** (the Greek Revival house of ship-owner Oliver Perry); **780 Harbor Rd.** (Federal, 1830); **824 Harbor Rd.** (frame, c. 1766, the only known Southport house which escaped burning in 1779); **658 Pequot Rd., 385 and 418 Harbor Rd.** (all Victorian houses built between 1855 and 1870); and the **Pequot Library** (Richardsonian Romanesque, 1890s) at 720 Pequot Rd. **Trinity Church** (1862) at 651 Pequot Rd. is a particularly

fine example of mid-Victorian Gothic architecture.

Greenwich

THE BRUCE MUSEUM, Museum Drive. Although a general-interest museum featuring the fine arts, anthropological displays, and natural history, the museum is particularly rich in colonial artifacts that warrant its inclusion here. Municipally owned. Tu-Sa 10-5; Su 2-5. Closed M and holidays. $2 adults, $1 senior citizens and children. 869-0376.

PUTNAM HILL HISTORIC DISTRICT, E. Putnam Ave. (US 1) N and E of the central business area, 19th century. The district centers on the two major churches in the town of Greenwich in the last century and a cohesive selection of mid-Victorian estate houses. It includes what is perhaps the oldest structure in the town, **Putnam Cottage,** and contains the work of two major 19th-century architects, Calvert Vaux and Leopold Eidlitz. Putnam Hill was named for General Israel Putnam, a Revolutionary War hero who was able to evade pursuing British soldiers who had cornered him at **Knapp's Tavern** (now the **Putnam Cottage** museum). A D.A.R. boulder at

the top of Putnam's Steps in **Putnam Hill Park** records the event of February 26, 1779. This area was always considered a center of the town and was the site of the **Second Congregational Church** as early as 1702. By the time of the Civil War, Greenwich was becoming established as a rural resort town for influential New York City businessmen because of its rich scenery and proximity to both Long Island Sound and the metropolis. Greenwich, and particularly Putnam Hill, became the purlieu of such notable 19th-century individuals as "Boss" Tweed, the infamous New York City politican, and A. Foster Higgins, founder of the Johnson & Higgins insurance company of New York. (The Tweed Estate, which was located at the SE corner of Milbank and E. Putnam Aves., was demolished long ago, but its enclosing walls still stand.) Among the highlights of the Putnam Hill Historic District are:

Putnam Cottage, 243 E. Putnam Ave., c. 1692. Known as Knapp's Tavern during the Revolutionary War, this was the meeting place of several colonial leaders, including Genral Putnam who used it as his local headquarters in 1779, when in command of the Third Division of the Continental Army. The building's unusual features include scalloped shingles and huge fieldstone fireplaces connected by a unique pass-through in the large center chimney. Operated by the D.A.R. as a museum, Putnam Cottage houses many fine 18th-century furnishings, including local Greenwich pieces and a display of General Putnam memorabilia. NR. Daily, except Su, 10-5. $1 adults, no charge for children under 12. 869-9697. **⚘**

Second Congregational Church, 139 E. Putnam Ave., 1856. Designed by Leopold Eidlitz, the granite structure replaced an earlier church and features an impressive 220-foot corner spire with an open stone belfry and tower that dominates the important corner of E. Putnam and Maple Aves. The adjoining cemetery is worth exploring for its interesting studies in Victorian memorial sculpture.

Maple Avenue: Before continuing further on E. Putnam Ave., see the stately houses of Maple Ave. The **Solomon Mead House** at #48 was built in 1858 by a wealthy farmer and real estate developer in the Italiante style with an observatory tower to take in the views of Long Island Sound. **Dr. Hyde House** at #23 was built in 1906 and is among the few houses in the area to show the influence of the Prairie Style of architecture. The small **Park** on the NE corner of Maple and E. Putnam Aves. contains several monuments, including a Civil War memorial.

Tomes-Higgins House (now Christ Church Rectory), 216 E. Putnam Ave., 1861. Designed by Calvert Vaux (and illustrated as Design No. 29 in his *Villas and Cotttages*), this impressive mansion is one of the state's earliest to be built in the French style. Its unsurpassed arrangement of specimen trees attests to Vaux's genius as a Victorian "rural landscape" artist. Built for Englishman Francis Tomes as his country seat, the house was sold to New York financier A. Foster Higgins in 1877. (**Higgins Park,** on Park Ave. and Park Pl., was originally Higgins's vegetable garden.)

Christ Episcopal Church, 250 E. Putnam Ave., 1909. Designed by William S. Domenick, this English Gothic structure and its auxiliary buildings, along with its cemetery which dates back to the 18th century, combine to create a very convincing English effect. Of particular interest are the two signed Tiffany windows at the front of the nave.

U.S. TOBACCO COMPANY MUSEUM, 96 W. Putnam Ave. The impact of tobacco on American economics and culture can hardly be understated; hence this unusual museum wherein the history of tobacco on five continents is traced in a collection of pipes, snuff boxes, and other tobacco-related artifacts. Also represented are a collection of carved cigar-store Indians and a fascinating display of advertising graphics. Open year-round, Tu-Su 12-5. Free. 869-5531.

While in the Greenwich area, a visit to nearby Cos Cob is in order, particularly to the **Bush-Holley House,** 39 Strickland Rd. This 17th-century saltbox houses the Greenwich Historical Society, which furnished the house in 18th-century antiques. Originally built by a Dutch settler, Justus Bush, the expanded house became an inn

when Edward Holley bought it in 1882. Holley's daughter married the painter Elmer MacRae and attracted to the area such well-known artists as Childe Hassam, John and Alden Twachtman, and Louis Comfort Tiffany, and such writers as Willa Cather and Lincoln Steffens. Appropriately, the museum features works by many turn-of-the-century artists, as well as a collection of John Rogers sculptures. Tu-Sa 10-12, 2-4, Su 2-4. $2 adults, 50¢ children under 12. 622-9686.

Guilford

Guilford was first settled in 1639 by a group of English Puritans. The Rev. Henry Whitfield, leader of the group, constructed his stone house on what is now Old Whitfield St., and the house today, maintained as a museum (see listing below), is thought to be one of the oldest in America. The large central Green was established at this time, inspired by New Haven's Green, and has been maintained with only minor encroachments ever since. Although hopes to establish Guilford as a major mercantile port were unsuccessful, the town began its modest growth with an economy based on shellfishing and agriculture. Despite a minor boom between 1750 and 1812 in the shipbuilding industry and related maritime businesses, Guilford grew very little until the mid-20th century, a fact that is, no doubt, the principal reason for the preservation of its historic past.

GUILFORD HISTORIC TOWN CENTRE, bounded on the W by the West River, on the N by the CT Tpk (I-95), on the E by East Creek, and on the S by Long Island Sound, 18th and 19th centuries. This historic district covers an area of approximately four square miles and contains over 700 structures. More than a sturdy pair of walking shoes and "world enough and time" would be required to take in every interesting site of this beautiful and charming town. The first-time visitor, consequently, would do well to limit his excursion to the area around the focal center of the town, the **Guilford Green,** a 7.7 acre square of open space. Among the streets most worthy of exploration are:

Fair St. #20, **Spencer Foundry** (1872), a good example of Victorian industrial design; #63, **James Monroe House** (1850), built in the Gothic Revival style; #84, **Edwin Leete House** (1856), a rare octagonal house; #101, **Thomas Cook House** (1640), a very early Colonial building; #143 N., **Solomon Stone House** (1766), a later Colonial structure.

Broad St. #1, **Abel Chittenden House** (1804), built in the Federal style; #6, **Caleb Stone House** (1749), a Colonial structure; #29, an interesting Victorian barn, built in 1875; #29, **Abraham Coan House** (1808), a good example of Federal architecture; #76, **Jared Leete House** (1774), a Colonial structure; #122, **E.C. Bishop House** (1874), a Victorian mansion; the **First Congregational Church** (1829), on Broad at the Green.

Park St. #1, **John Redfield House** (1780), a Colonial building; #11, **Jared Redfield House** (1792), a central-hall Colonial with two chimneys; #37, **Heli Hoadley House** (1805), a Federal structure; **Christ Church** (1832), built in the Gothic Revival style; **Third Congregational Church** (1844), a Greek Revival building; #67, **Guilford Free Library** (1933), typical of the Federal Revival popular in public buildings during the Great Depression.

State St. Noteworthy are four Colonial houses, including three dating from the 17th century. #72, **Nathan Bradley House** (1655); #101, **Jabez Benton House** (1730); #138, **Kingsnorth-Starr House** (1640); #233, **Starr-Hall House** (1669).

Boston St. Recommended are five Colonial structures: #77, **Hyland House** (see separate listing below); #171, **Thomas Griswold House** (see separate listing below); #254, **Nathan Meigs House** (1787); #321, **Levi Hubbard House** (1761); #348, **Westal Scovil House** (1783).

Whitfield St. At Town Dock, **Lyman Beecher House** (1770), a Colonial structure; at end of Old Whitfield St., **Railroad Station and Octagonal Tower** (1852); on Old Whitfield St., **Henry Whitfield House** (see separate listing below); #20, **Joel Stone House** (1853), in the Italianate style; #21, **Dan Collins House** (1772), a Colonial building; #33, **Labodie House**

(1872), an Italianate structure; #161, **St. George's Church** (1876).

Other houses of interest in the immediate vicinity include: **Joseph Weld House** (1755), 108 Lovers Lane; **William Starr III House** (1826), 150 Church St.; **Samuel Shelley House** (1744), 1139 Boston Post Rd.; **Darius Collins House** (1769), 56 Union St.; **John Graves House** (1850), 17 Graves Ave.; and **George Hand House** (1850), 24 High St.

HENRY WHITFIELD HOUSE, Old Whitfield St., 1639. The oldest stone dwelling in New England, this is a unique example of English domestic architecture, furnished with 17th-century antiques. The home of the founder of Guilford, it also served as church and meeting hall for early settlers. Its exhibits include weaving equipment, an herb garden, and the first tower clock in the colonies (1726). Operated by the Connecticut Historical Commission. NR. Apr-Nov, W-Su 10-5; Winter, W-Su 10-4. Closed Thanksgiving, Dec 15-Jan 15. $1 adults, 50¢ senior citizens, 25¢ youth 6-18. 453-2457.

HYLAND HOUSE, 84 Boston St., 1660. This classic Colonial saltbox, home of early settler George Hyland, features 17th-century furnishings, including many local pieces; unusual interior woodwork; and five walk-in fireplaces, several outfitted for 17th-century cookery. Operated by the Dorothy Whitfield Historic Society. NR. June-mid-Sept, Daily (except M) 10-4; mid-Sept-Oct, Sa-Su 10-4. $1.50 adults, children under 14 free. 453-9477.

THOMAS GRISWOLD HOUSE, 171 Boston St., 1774. This saltbox with Georgian touches has been preserved as a museum of local history, displaying costumes, regional furniture, farm tools, books, and early photographs. NR. June-Sept, Tu-Su 11-4. $1 adults, children under 12 free. 453-3176.

Hamden

HAMDEN HISTORICAL SOCIETY, Mt. Carmel Ave. Housed in the **Jonathan Dickerman House** (1770), the society offers displays of 18th-century furnishings and artifacts, as well as a fine collection of books, land deeds, and early photographs for those engaged in historic research. June-Sept, Sa-Su 2-5. Free.

Meriden

HERITAGE HOUSE, 500 S. Broad St. (CT 5). Located on the grounds of the International Silver Company, the museum includes four rooms created to reflect 18th-century colonial life. Among the highlights are demonstrations by a silversmith and a pewterer showing early methods of production. M-Sa 10:30-3, groups by appointment. 634-2541.

MERIDEN HISTORICAL SOCIETY, 424 W. Main St. Housed in the **Moses Andrews House** (c. 1760), one of the few 18th-century houses remaining in Meriden, the society maintains displays of costumes, furniture, dolls, and items manufactured locally, as well as a fine collection of manuscripts, maps, and books. NR. Mar-June, Sept-mid-Dec, W and Su 2-4:30. $1 adults, children free, special group rates. 237-5079, 235-9790.

Milford

EELLS-STOW HOUSE (Milford Historical Society), 34 High St., c. 1685. This 2½-story, gable-roofed frame dwelling was built by Samuel Eells, a local magistrate, but its most illustrious owners were Captain Stephen Stow and Freelove Baldwin Stow. Together they nursed Revolutionary War prisoners who had contracted smallpox, until Captain Stow himself died of the disease. The house, now a museum, is furnished in period furniture and features an extensive collection of Indian artifacts. The Milford Historical Society also administers the **Ebenezer Downes House** (1785). NR. Memorial Day-mid-Oct, Su 2-5, holidays 12-5, and by appointment. $1 adults, senior citizens and children under 12 free. 874-2664. ♦

ST. PETER'S EPISCOPAL CHURCH, 71 River St., 1850-51. The Ecclesiological Movement in American church architecture was a major factor in the development of the Gothic Revival style, of which this church is an excellent example. Designed by Frank Wills, a leader of the movement, St. Peter's, the only remaining 19th-century building in downtown Milford, was constructed entirely of rough-cut brownstone blocks, massive in appearance, and topped by a two-stage tower with a simple spire at its apex. The windows on the east wall, and several along the north wall, contain original stained glass. Remaining windows are either of the plain leaded variety, thought to be original, or of figurative stained glass (along the south side of the nave), which seem to date from the early 20th century. The Parish Hall, of wood frame in an abbreviated Queen Anne style, was added in the mid-1890s; the brownstone choir room wing, in 1924; and the sacristy and church school, much later. NR.

New Canaan

NEW CANAAN HISTORICAL SOCIETY, 13 Oenoke Ridge. Certainly worth more than a quick glance, the New Canaan Historical Society's museum complex includes several fine old buildings offering a variety of interesting displays. The society's headquarters, an elegant town house, includes a costume museum, a replica of an early drugstore, and an extensive library. The adjacent **Hanford-Silliman House** is a fine example of the Georgian style, built c. 1764 by Stephen Hanford, who was to serve gallantly during the Revolutionary War. Purchased later by the Silliman family, the house was to remain the property of their descendants for more than two centuries. It is furnished with a number of early pieces, including a fine collection of pewterware. On the grounds are a print shop and tool museum, and the 1799 one-room **Rock Schoolhouse.** Open all year, W, Th, Su 2-4. $1 adults. 966-1776.

The nearby **John Rogers Studio** at 10 Cherry St., also administered by the New Canaan Historical Society, was moved from its original site. A two-story frame building of the Stick Style, with a gabled roof, overhanging eaves, and decorative

bargeboards, this was the home of American sculptor John Rogers from its construction in 1877 until his death in 1904. Rogers, largely self-taught, was an engineer and machinist before devoting his full time to his art. "Rogers' groups," as his sculptures are called, are of three basic types: the Civil War groups; studies of literary and dramatic figures; and genre groups, which depict contemporary everyday life. NR, NHL. All three are on display at the Rogers Studio. Open W, Th, Su 2-4. $1 adults. 966-1776.

New Haven

Originally called Quinnipiac after the Indian tribe from whom the land was purchased in 1638, New Haven is considered to be the first planned city in America. Laid out in nine squares by surveyor John Brockett, with the famed New Haven Green at its center, the original colony was founded and administered by the Rev. John Davenport, an English Puritan minister, and his followers, whose early constitution ignored allegiance to King and country in favor of the rigid laws of the Old Testament. Even after reluctantly joining the more democratic Connecticut colony in 1664, Davenport's parishioners strictly adhered to their church's teachings. Religious intolerance and persecution were widespread, and harsh punishment awaited the most minor infractions.

Although trade began only nine years after New Haven was founded, when first shoes and then beef were exported, it was the beginning of the 19th century before the city became an important commercial port. More than 100 ships regularly made oriental, West Indian and coastal voyages, and vessels arriving from England brought European goods. A number of the English ships seem to have used bricks for ballast, as many bricks, bearing their London imprints, have since been discovered during the demolition of period buildings.

To get a clearer idea of New Haven's prominence during the 19th century, and a different perspective on the city, you may wish to sail aboard the *Liberty Belle,* berthed at Long Wharf Dock, whose captain offers a variety of harbor cruises, with historic commentary. Call **Historic New Haven-Long Island Sound Cruises** at 562-4163 for information.

NEW HAVEN GREEN HISTORIC DISTRICT, bounded by Chapel, College, Elm, and Church Sts., 1812-16. At the heart of the original nine-square plan laid out in 1638, New Haven Green was originally set aside as common land for a daytime market and night pasture for stock. It has been the focal point of New Haven's development ever since. The first meeting house was built here in 1639, followed by a school, town jail, and early State House, all of which have long since vanished. Today the Green is a lush open space with three beautifully-proportioned churches facing it on the east.

Center Church, begun in 1812, is a superb example of the Georgian style. Its noted architect, Ithiel Town, is thought to have been influenced by James Gibbs's St. Martin's-in-the Fields, one of London's most famous churches. But with its solid red-brick facade, spanking white-columned portico, and graceful white steeple, Center Church has an unmistakably New England look about it. The lovely interior, with a three-sided gallery and vaulted ceiling, is highlighted by a great arched Tiffany window behind the pulpit which portrays John Davenport delivering his first sermon. Beneath the church is the **Crypt,** part of the original burying ground that was used from first settlement until the early 19th century. In 1821, that part of the cemetery outside the church walls was leveled, and the monumuents transferred to Grove Street Cemetery (see following). More than 100 ancient graves still lie beneath the church floor. Open Tu-F 9:30-12 and 1-4; Sa 10-12:45.

Trinity Episcopal Church, also designed by Ithiel Town, is vastly different in appearance and feeling. One of the earliest expressions of the Gothic Revival style in America, it was completed in 1816. Constructed of somber traprock with brownstone trim, Trinity originally was crowned by a squat wooden tower which was later rebuilt in stone. The interior, with groups of columns arranged in gracious proportions, is much less forbidding. Open M-F 10-3, Sa 10-12.

United Church (North Church), designed by David Hoadley, is a more typical example of early 19th-century Georgian architecture, with a three-stage central steeple and a simpler columned facade. The fine paneling and glass chandelier within are original to the church, and tablets dedicated to Roger Sherman, New Haven's first mayor and famous American statesman; architect Hoadley himself; and other local dignitaries are ranged about the walls. Open Tu-Th 10-4:30.

All three churches welcome visitors to Sunday services as well as during stated hours. NR, NHL.

New Haven City Hall

In addition, you may rent cassettes for self-guided tours of the Green and nearby points of interest at the **New Haven Visitors' Information Center,** 155 Church St. Two doors down from the Center, at 161 Church, is the imposing **New Haven City Hall,** designed by Henry Austin in brick and stone, and completed in 1861. One of the first High-Victorian Gothic buildings to be constructed in America, it is famous for its elaborately detailed 3½-story facade and tall corner clock tower (reconstructed in 1976). NR.

YALE UNIVERSITY, 1702. Just off New Haven Green, at the corner of Elm and College Sts., is **Phelps Gate,** which marks the entrance to Yale's old campus. Guided tours of the campus originate here. One features the oldest sections, including **Connecticut Hall** (see following), contrasted by the modern **Beinecke Rare Book Library,** whose transluscent marble walls protect such treasures as a Gutenburg Bible and Audubon's original bird prints; and **Sterling Memorial Library,** designed by James Gamble Rogers, which houses more than four million volumes of the University's collection. A second tour covers **Hillhouse Ave.,** said by Charles Dickens, who visited New Haven in 1846, to be "the most beautiful street in America." The homes of Yale's president and secretary are here, and the University's famous Steinert Collection of musical instruments. Tours are scheduled daily from 9:15-3 M-Sa and at 1:30 and 3 on Su. No charge.

One of John Davenport's dreams was to found a college in the New Haven colony, but it was after his death, in 1701, that a group of Connecticut clergymen met at the home of the Rev. Samuel Russell of Branford to discuss the formation of a "collegiate school." The first student began studies in 1702 in Clinton (then Killingworth), and in 1707 the classes were transferred to Saybrook. It was not until 1716 that the college was formally—and permanently—moved to New Haven and named after Elihu Yale, a successful entrepreneur with the East India Company, whose generous donation to the school resulted in the honor.

Yale's reputation for educational excellence is legendary. Among its distinguished early alumni are Nathan Hale, Noah Webster, Vice President John C. Calhoun, Samuel F. B. Morse (inventor of the telegraph), President William Howard Taft, and unsuccessful presidential candidate Samuel J. Tilden.

The Old Campus, bounded by Chapel, High, Elm and College Sts., has been the nucleus of campus life since the early 18th century. Connecticut Hall (1752), where

Nathan Hale lived and studied, is the oldest of the extant early buildings and the only remaining pre-Revolutionary structure. The lone survivor of "Brick Row," a group of Georgian brick buildings, the Hall was originally three stories tall. A fourth story with dormer windows was added in 1796. NR, NHL. Private. As you stroll through the old campus, you'll notice a variety of architectural styles, which taken together give Yale its unique character. The earliest buildings are basically of the sedate Georgian style, while late 19th- and early 20th-century buildings show a preference for the more ornate and towering collegiate Gothic. Ivy, of course, is everywhere. Harkness Tower, on High St., with narrow pointed windows and a soaring, multifaceted tower, is probably the best, and certainly the most conspicuous, example.

At the north edge of the original campus (end of High St. at Grove) is the Grove Street Cemetery, a park-like retreat containing the graves of many prominent figures in New Haven's and New England's history, among them Lyman Beecher, abolitionist and father of Harriet Beecher Stowe; Noah Webster; and Ithiel Town. Original headstones bearing legends and history from the 1600s have been moved

here from the Green. The Egyptian Revival archway at the entrance was designed by noted New Haven architect Henry Austin.

The New Haven Colony Historical Society, 114 Whitney Ave., while not a part of the University, is on the way to Yale's Peabody Museum further up the road, and is certainly worth a long visit. Established in 1862, the society has an extensive library with over 25,000 volumes and many manuscripts devoted to the history of New Haven from the Colonial period to the present. The Decorative Arts Collection contains furniture, silver, pewter, ceramics, and glass produced in the area over three centuries, as well as handsome materials imported on New Haven ships. The Industrial Collection includes the patent model for Eli Whitney's cotton gin—an invention which profoundly altered the history of agricultural production in the United States. Other inventors represented are Ithiel Town and Samuel F. B. Morse. Special attention is given to school children, hundreds of whom visit the museum each year. Open all year, Tu-F 10-5; Sa-Su 2-5. No charge. ($1 for library). 562-4183.

Further north still, at 170 Whitney Ave., is the Peabody Museum. Not far from picturesque Hillhouse Ave., it is the largest natural history museum in New England, with many exhibits sure to delight children, ranging from mammoth dinosaur skeletons to butterflies to amazingly lifelike stuffed animals placed in simulated natural settings. Open all year, M-Sa 9-4:45, Su 1-4:45. $1 adults, 50¢ children. 436-0850.

Marsh Hall, (1876), 360 Prospect St., was originally the home of Othniel C. Marsh, America's first professor of paleontology, who collected much of the material now in the Peabody Museum. Of graceful Queen Anne design, the hall is now operated by the Yale School of Forestry. The adjacent Botanical Garden contains many rare trees and shrubs. NR.

Further information about Yale and its many treasures is available from the Yale Visitor's Information Office. 436-8330.

NEW HAVEN HARBOR AREA. One of

the busiest harbors in New England is also the site of one of New Haven's earliest extant buildings, an historic fort, and a fine early lighthouse. The harbor area is about five miles south of downtown New Haven, off I-95 at the Townsend Ave. exit.

Fort Nathan Hale (Black Rock Fort), south end of Woodward Ave., 1775. Commanding the eastern shore of New Haven Harbor, Fort Nathan Hale, as it is now known, was constructed four times between 1649 and 1863. The earliest fortification was an earthwork erected to defend the New Haven colony. A second defense work, a log fort constructed in 1775, was successfully attacked by a British force on July 5, 1779, and all defenders taken prisoner. Early in the 19th century the federal government purchased the site and constructed a brownstone and brick fort which was manned during the War of 1812. At this time the fort was named for patriot Nathan Hale. The second Fort Hale was built between 1863 and 1866. It consisted of five concrete buildings, of which three remain, enclosed and covered by earthworks. NR, NHL. Recently restored, the fort is open all year. An information center operates from Memorial Day-Labor Day, daily 10-5. No charge. 467-1409.

Lighthouse Point Park, at the end of Lighthouse Rd., is an 80-acre recreational area crowned by an 1840 lighthouse. An extensive park renovation program is currently under way which will include restoration of a turn-of-the-century carousel. A fine place for picnicking and swimming. Open Memorial Day-Labor Day, daily 9-dusk. 25¢ adults, 10¢ children (parking $1). 🏛

Pardee-Morris House, Morris Cove, 18th century. Captain Amos Morris built this frame house with stone ends c. 1750 on land acquired nearly 100 years earlier by Thomas Morris, one of New Haven's original settlers. Burned to the ground during the British invasion in 1779, the dwelling was subsequently rebuilt in its original form on the remaining foundations. The Morris family occupied the house until 1915. Restored and furnished to represent the later years of Amos Morris's occupancy, with grounds featuring both herb and formal gardens, Pardee-Morris House is owned and operated by the New Haven Colony Historical Society. Open June-Aug, Tu-Su 1-4. Donations accepted. 467-0764.

Norwalk

LOCKWOOD-MATHEWS MANSION MUSEUM, 295 West Ave., 1864. An eclectic Victorian mansion, featuring a magnificent octagonal rotunda surrounded by 60 spacious rooms, this ostentatious landmark home was designed by Detlef Lienau for financier LeGrand Lockwood. Of granite and brick, with an irregular facade and full-width south veranda, the mansion is perhaps most famous for its richly-decorated interior. Artists and artisans were brought from Europe to create the wide variety of gilt, fresco, marble, wood, and etched-glass decorations found throughout. Lockwood, who was treasurer of the New York Stock Exchange, lived here until his death, and in 1876 the mansion was purchased by Charles D. Mathews, whose family maintained ownership until 1938. Since then it and its stone outbuildings have been operated by the City of Norwalk. NR, NHL. Open all year, Tu-F 11-3, Su 1-4. $3 adults, $2 children. 838-1434.

Redding

PUTNAM MEMORIAL STATE PARK, CT 58, 1778-79. During the winter of 1778-79 a contingent of Continental troops under the command of Major General Putnam wintered on this site, which was selected because the soldiers could defend southeastern Connecticut and easily reach the Hudson River or Long Island. Within the 250-acre park are firebacks once part of the soldiers' houses, foundations of an oven and a powder magazine, and a reconstructed barracks. A **Revolutionary War museum**, built in 1921, houses a collection of relics of the period. Operated by the state. NR. The park is open all year; the museum Memorial Day - mid-Oct, daily 9-5. No charge. 938-2285.

Ridgefield

KEELER TAVERN, 132 Main St., 1772. This 2½-story frame landmark was operated as an inn from its construction in 1772 to 1907. During the Battle of Ridgefield, in April, 1777, it served as headquarters for the patriots and was hit by British cannon fire. A ball remains imbedded in a wall of the building and accounts for its other name—the Cannonball House. Administered by The Keeler Tavern Preservation Society, the building is furnished with early pieces. Open all year, W, Sa, Su 2-5 and by appointment. $1.50 adults, 50¢ children. 438-5485.

Stamford

HOYT-BARNUM HOUSE, 713 Bedford St., 1699. This simple frame farmhouse with a native stone chimney is little changed from the 17th century. Three sides of the exterior are clapboard, the fourth shingle. An open porch on the north side, incorporated under the main roof, shows Dutch origins. Samuel Hoyt, a blacksmith, built the house for his bride, Susannah, on land that had been granted to his father at a town meeting in 1668. In this small house, Hoyt's thirteen children by Susannah and his second wife, Mary Weed, grew up. The building changed hands only once before David and Betsey Barnum and their descendants occupied it—from 1826 until 1922. Now the headquarters of the Stamford Historical Society, the sturdy building exhibits 17th and 18th-century Americana, including farm implements, needlework, quilts, dolls, and household equipment. NR. Open all year, M-F 10-3, Su 1-4. Donations accepted. 323-1975.

Stratford

CAPTAIN DAVID JUDSON HOUSE, 967 Academy Hill, 1723. Located on Stratford's 17th-century town common, and on the site of an earlier house, this simple frame building was originally the home of David Judson, auditor of the colonial Connecticut records and deputy of the General Assembly. Faithfully restored and furnished by the Stratford Historical Society, its exhibits include, decorative arts, costumes, antique furniture, toys, and textiles. NR. Open Apr-Oct, W, Sa, Su 11-4. $1.50 adults, 75¢ children. 378-0630.

Woodbridge

THOMAS DARLING HOUSE AND TAVERN, 1907 Litchfield Tpk., c. 1765. Thomas Darling was a Congregational minister, Yale tutor, judge, and merchant who operated this 1½-story gambrel-roofed frame house as a drovers' stopover on the early Litchfield turnpike. Occupied by the same family until 1973, the house is furnished with early pieces, including cooking implements, account books, clothing, and furniture. Administered by the Amity and Woodbridge Historical Society. Open all year, F 7-9, Su 2-5. No charge. 387-2823.

Northwest Connecticut

Kent

SLOANE-STANLEY MUSEUM, at the Kent Furnace site, CT 7. The ruins of the **Kent Iron Furnace,** which began production of pig iron in 1826 and operated for nearly 70 years, can be seen just below this museum of fine early American tools. Clearing the undergrowth surrounding the outbuildings and the millrace which once diverted water from the Housatonic River is planned as part of the overall development. The massive granite blocks and Gothic arch of the furnace are clearly visible. NR. The adjacent museum, in addition to its collection donated by Connecticut artist and writer Eric Sloane, displays a diorama of the Kent furnace as it appeared in the late 19th century, along with educational exhibits depicting the operation of a blast furnace of the period and the process of smelting pig iron. Operated by the Connecticut Historical Commission. Open early May - Oct 31, W-Su 10-4:30. $1 adults, 25¢ children. 566-3005. 🏛

Kent vicinity

BULL'S BRIDGE, Bull's Bridge Rd., late 19th century. One of only three covered bridges remaining in Connecticut, Bull's Bridge, with its wood shingled roof and vertical planking sides, spans the scenic Housatonic River south of Kent. The bridge is still in use and is maintained by the town. NR.

Litchfield

With its broad streets, stately shade trees, and graceful early homes fronting a central green, Litchfield is one of New England's best surviving examples of an 18th-century town. Its first settlers arrived in 1720, establishing the community as an outpost and trading center for the northwest frontier. Fear of Indian attack prompted the construction of palisades around five of the early houses, but even with occasional harrassment from local tribes, agriculture flourished, mills were built near neighboring streams, and iron was forged for tools, chain, and anchors.

At the beginning of the Revolutionary War, many of Litchfield's militia were sent to Bunker Hill or served other prominent roles in military and government activities. Oliver Wolcott became a member of the Continental Congress, and Aaron Burr, who had been studying law at his brother-in-law Tapping Reeve's home, enlisted and served in Benedict Arnold's Quebec expeditionary force. Because of its protected inland site and productive farmlands, Litchfield became a focal point for army stores and workshops. After the war, private enterprise, stimulated by the Revolutionary activity, flourished until late in the 19th century, when the newly developed railroads bypassed the town, resulting in the eventual demise of most local industry. Thus was maintained the tranquil country setting so admired today by summer vacationers and weekenders alike.

LITCHFIELD HISTORIC DISTRICT, east and west sides of North and South Sts., to Prospect St. on the north and Gallows La. on the south. Late 18th-19th centuries. Early maps of Litchfield show the streets located substantially as they are today: four main thoroughfares stretch towards the cardinal points of the compass, with the central common, now called The Green, at their intersection. Around this central core the town gradually developed, and there remain fifteen houses,

Julius Deming House

located on North and South Sts. and on the northeast side of The Green, that were erected in the last half of the 18th century, along with three early 19th-century landmarks. Interspersed among the most important Colonial structures are a number of later homes which are typical of the mid-19th-century fondness for the Greek Revival and late-Federal styles. The historic area is small and best admired on foot. Most of the homes are private, but all can be easily seen from the street. Among the most notable of the early buildings are **Sheldon's Tavern** (North St.), built in 1760 and remodelled in the Georgian style about 1790 by William Spratt, a British army officer taken prisoner with Burgoyne's army at Saratoga, whose success with his wartime architectural commissions convinced him to stay on in Connecticut after the Revolution. Diagonally across North St. is the **Julius Deming House,** designed by Spratt in 1793, a magnificent example of the late Georgian style, with a colonaded entrance portico, hip roof, and four tall chimneys. At the northeast corner of The Green stands the **Congregational Church,** an imposing, gracefully-proportioned building with a columned facade and two-stage steeple, which has had a somewhat checkered history since its construction in 1829. In the 1870s it was moved from the site by townspeople who didn't appreciate its classic styling and was replaced by a more exotic Gothic building. Until well in-

to the 20th century it served variously and ignominiously at its new location as an armory, dance hall, and movie house, but it was finally restored to its original site and use when wiser heads prevailed. Near the church is the **1781 Apothecary Shop,** unusually positioned with its gabled end facing the street, and **Collins House,** built in 1782 as an inn by the son of Litchfield's first parson. It is a large, two-story frame building with an overhanging roof. South of the common on South St. is the **Oliver Wolcott, Sr., House,** one of the earliest extant buildings in Litchfield (1753), a large, two-story frame landmark with its central porch supported by four Ionic columns. Wolcott, a state senator, delegate to the Continental Congress, and signer of the Declaration of Independence, served as governor from 1796 until his death the following year, and lived in this house for 44 years. NHL. Maintained by the Wolcott Library and Historical Society, the house now contains offices and is open during library hours.

The **Tapping Reeve House** (1773) and **Law School** (1784) stand opposite the Wolcott House. The tiny one-story frame school, founded by Judge Reeve, was the first law school in the United States. Among its graduates were Vice Presidents Aaron Burr and John C. Calhoun, three justices of the United States Supreme Court, 90 members of the House of Representatives, and 26 senators. Because of the

Tapping Reeve House

prominence of its alumni, the school significantly influenced the development of American law. It and Reeve's two-story frame home have been restored and furnished by the Litchfield Historical Society. NHL. Open May 15-Oct 15, Tu-Sa 11-5. 567-5862. $1.50 adults, 50¢ children.

At the corner of East and South Sts., facing the Green, is the two-story red-brick **Litchfield Historical Society and Museum.** Open from mid-Apr to mid-Nov, Tu-Sa 11-5, the Society has many exhibits of local historic interest which help to explain Litchfield's development. Free. 567-5862. As an indication of Litchfield's historic prominence, the entire district has been designated a National Historic Landmark.

Norfolk

Surrounded by the beautiful hills of northwestern Connecticut which attract the winter sports enthusiast as well as the more sedentary vacationer, and famed for the trout fishing in its Blackberry River, the town of Norfolk has been a popular resort area since the late 19th century. Its first settlers were farmers who cleared the land and established their community around what is now the Village Green. Sawmills fed by the surrounding lush forests, gristmills, and smithies followed, but it was basically the enterprise of one man that led to Norfolk's greatest period of development in the early 19th century. Joseph Bat-

tell, proprietor of the local general store, was such an influential and capable merchant that Norfolk became *the* trading center for neighboring communities, and many mills and manufactories sprang up along the river banks, producing linseed oil, hats, scythes, woolens, silk thread, hoes, and guns for both local sale and transport to other markets. While these industries declined during the latter half of the century, the development of the Connecticut Western Railroad made the area accessible to vacationers, and it emerged as the popular resort it remains today.

NORFOLK HISTORIC DISTRICT, surrounding the Village Green, 19th century. The **Church of Christ,** with its tall steeple and impressive columned facade, dominates the Green. Built in 1814, it was designed by David Hoadley. Next door is **Whitehouse,** now the principal building of the Yale Summer School of Music and Art, built in 1799 as the residence of Joseph Battell. The imposing three-story landmark, with a stately circular portico supported by four soaring columns, has been much enlarged over the years, but the original central section is easily identifiable.

On the Green opposite Whitehouse is an unusual directional sign (see illustration). Made by Raymond Dowden of the Yale Summer Art School, it is a copy of the early original, now in the Historical Society

Museum, which has been attributed to an itinerant painter. The **Historical Society Museum** itself, on the east side of the

Green, shows decorative arts, costumes, folklore, maps, early manuscripts, and farm tools among its displays. Open June 16-Sept 14, Sa 10-12, 2-5; Su 2-5. Free. 542-5761. On the south end of the Green stands the **Eldridge Fountain** (formerly the Joseph Battell Memorial Fountain), designed by famed architect Stanford White. The **Norfolk Library,** a massive stone building which dates from 1888, flanks the Green on its north side.

Riverton

THE HITCHCOCK MUSEUM, 1829. The landmark Old Union Church is now the setting for a wide variety of antique painted furniture, including not only the

work of Lambert Hitchcock, whose famous chairs were manufactured nearby, but that of other 18th- and 19th-century craftsmen. Hitchcock became America's most successful chairmaker during the early 1800s, and his original factory, restored immediately following World War II, is a short walk from the museum on the bank of the Farmington River. Craftsmen demonstrate weaving, woodworking, rushing, and stenciling in the Hitchcock showrooms. The museum is owned by the Hitchcock Chair Company. Open June 1-Oct 30, Tu-Sa 10-5; Nov 1-May 30, Sa 10-5. Free. 379-1003.

The tiny village of Riverton has changed little since the 18th century. While you're in the area, you might enjoy dining at its 185-year-old inn, or browsing in its antique shops and general store.

Salisbury

Perhaps Salisbury's greatest claim to fame these days is its lovely old inn, The White Hart, complemented by its younger brother, the Ragamont Inn. (See Lodging.) Should you choose to spend some time in the area, you will be captivated by the charm of the town itself, which is arranged along a neat main street bordered by old homes and shaded by great maple trees.

Torrington

TORRINGTON HISTORICAL SOCIETY, 192 Main St., c. 1890. The elegant late-Victorian **Hotchkiss-Fyler House,** built by a local politician influential in state government, is now home for the local society's collection. Many of the mansion's original furnishings are on view. The parquet floors, mahogany paneling, and delicate stenciling have been carefully protected, and a period greenhouse and carriage house remain on the grounds. Early glassware, china, and silver are displayed, along with costumes, industrial and commercial artifacts, and local memorabilia. Open all year, M-F 8-4. No charge. 482-8260.

Washington

AMERICAN INDIAN ARCHAEOLOG-
ICAL INSTITUTE, off CT 199, Curtis
Rd. Interpretive exhibits covering 12,000
years of prehistory and history in North
America are displayed at the Institute's
visitors' center. A simulated archaeological site, a reconstructed longhouse, and
Connecticut's most complete mastodon
are among the wide variety of objects on
display. The work of the Institute in exploring Indian cultures and achievements
is pursued by full- and part-time staff,
volunteers, and students who analyze, interpret, and publish archaeological find-
ings for the lay person as well as the
specialist. Open all year, M-Sa 10-4:30, Su
1:30-4:30. $2 adults, $1 children. ⋔
868-0518.

Located on the Washington town green is
the **Historical Museum of the Gunn
Memorial Library,** housed in a late 18th-
century building. Its collection includes
general Americana, Civil War and World
War I memorabilia, and American Indian
artifacts. Open all year, Tu, Th 2-5, Sa
12-3. No charge. 868-7756.

West Cornwall

WEST CORNWALL BRIDGE, CT 128,
1841. In continuous service as a span
across the Housatonic River since its construction, this frame covered bridge is
thought to have been designed by Ithiel
Town, inventor of the truss system which
supports it. Maintained by the state. NR.

Woodbury

WOODBURY HISTORIC DISTRICTS
#1 AND #2, 17th-20th centuries. The
town of Woodbury was founded in 1673.
Its peaceful main street, bordered by many
fine old homes of the Colonial period, is
shaded by beautiful old trees. Many of the
town's early residents fought with Ethan

Allen's force at Fort Ticonderoga, and two
noted Civil War generals, Grant and Sherman, were descended from Woodbury
families.

The primarily residential historic districts contain a variety of styles—from
Federal and Greek Revival to the more ornate Victorian—reflecting the changing
tastes of succeeding generations. Most are
painted white and reflect the restraint and
simplicity typical of rural New England
communities.

By far Woodbury's most famous landmark is **Glebe House;** a simple 2½-story
frame dwelling on Hollow Road, it is now
renowned as the birthplace of the American Episcopal Church. Built in 1690, and
much enlarged in the mid-18th century, it
became a minister's house, or glebe, in
1771, when the town's first Anglican
minister, John Rutgers Marshall, moved
in. Marshall, a confirmed Tory, stymied
his patriot neighbors during the Revolutionary War by constructing a secret
passage within the house that allowed him
access to a tunnel running into the hills.
Just two weeks after American independence was secured, a group of clergymen
met secretly at the Glebe House to discuss
the fate of the Church of England in the
new nation. Samuel Seabury, one of their
number, was elected as bishop and crossed
the Atlantic to receive consecration by
English archbishops. Refused in England,
he was accepted and consecrated in Scot-
land, thus becoming the first American
bishop of the Episcopal Church in a step
which assumed both the separation of
church and state and religious toleration in
the infant democracy. Carefully maintained today by the Seabury Society for the
Preservation of Glebe House, this important landmark retains much of its original
paneling and furnishings. Displays of
historic documents relating to Seabury and
his associates, and early prints, paintings,
and books are on view. NR. Open all year,
Sa-W 1-5. $1 adults. 263-2855.

Central Connecticut

Avon

AVON CONGREGATIONAL CHURCH, 6 W. Main St., 1818-19. Designed by David Hoadley, this Federal landmark is a frame structure with a graceful three-stage bell tower. The entrance is defined by four fluted Ionic pilasters, while the interior contains a three-sided gallery with five windows at both the first- and second-story levels of the side walls. It does not demean this beautiful building to say that it is virtually everybody's idea of a picturesque New England church. NR. Open M-F 9-3 except July and Aug.

Bristol

AMERICAN CLOCK AND WATCH MUSEUM, 100 Maple St. The 1801 **Miles Lewis House,** a handsome 2½-story frame residence, houses the principal part of the museum's extensive collection. The front parlor displays horological memorabilia, such as the 19th-century accounting desk of famous clockmaker Eli Terry, Jr., as well as a fine collection of clocks of all shapes and sizes. The summer kitchen displays small Connecticut shelf clocks produced in the Bristol area between 1840 and 1860, while the adjacent Ebenezer Barnes Wing, completed in 1955, contains a large display room and the museum's extensive library. Paneling in this wing is from the Ebenezer Barnes House, the first permanent residence in Bristol (1728), which was razed in the early 20th century. This is one of the most extensive horological collections in the country, graced by its stately setting. Open Apr 1-Oct 31, daily 11-5. $2.50 adults, $1.25 children. 583-6070. ⚤

LAKE COMPOUNCE CAROUSEL, Lake Avenue, 1890. Located in **Lake Compounce Amusement Park,** established in 1846 and thought to be one of the oldest such parks in the country under continuous operation, the carousel, with its early 20th-century Wurlitzer band organ, is a favorite

with children. Sixteen rows of horses, three abreast, are painted and carved in numerous ways, with two chariots and a goat for variety. NR. The park itself offers many diversions. Open Easter-mid-June, Sa-Su; mid-June-Labor Day daily. $1 parking. 582-6333. ⚤

Coventry

NATHAN HALE HOMESTEAD, South St., 1776. Richard Hale, father of Nathan whom the British hanged as a spy on September 22, 1776, built this unadorned 2½-story frame home for his family and moved in one month after his son's death. The Hale family lived here until 1832, running a farm, while Nathan's brother David taught school, and Richard, who was also Justice of the Peace, held court. The homestead has ten rooms, all completely furnished as they might have been when inhabited by the Hales, with many pieces original to the house. Family memorabilia, such as Nathan's silver shoe buckles and boyhood fowling piece; his sister Joanna's china, pewter, and brass kettles; and his father's desk, are also displayed. Operated by the Antiquarian and Landmarks Society. NR. Open May 15-Oct 15, daily 1-5. $1 adults, 25¢ children. 742-6917.

East Granby

OLD NEW-GATE PRISON AND COPPER MINE, Newgate Rd., 1707. The celebrated Simsbury copper mine, later known as New-Gate Prison, was first worked in 1707. While the output was excellent and the ore of good quality, most work at the mines had ceased by 1773 because of the imperfect state of mining knowledge and machinery, and the expense of shipping the ore to England for smelting. The colony of Connecticut first used New-Gate (named after the notorious London prison) as a place of confinement late in 1773. Designated as a place of confinement for burglars, horse thieves, robbers, and counterfeiters, it was later used for Tories and prisoners of war. At first the prisoners were required to mine the copper, but when this proved unprofitable, their efforts were turned to nail and shoe making, among other trades. New-Gate gained a reputation for great strength and security, and in October, 1776, it became the first state prison in the country. During its forty-two years of operation, over 800 prisoners were committed to the subterranean cells. The Connecticut Historical Commission plans to restore the Guardhouse to house a museum of interpretive exhibits. A note of caution: the mine tunnels are narrow and headroom is limited. Sturdy shoes are recommended, along with a sweater, as even on the hottest days the subterranean temperature rarely climbs above the mid-40s. NR, NHL. Open mid May-Oct 31, W-Su 10-4:30. $1.50 adults, 50¢ children. 566-3005.

East Haddam

GOODSPEED OPERA HOUSE, Norwich Rd., 1876-77. Many successful Broadway productions have had their beginnings in this glistening white landmark on the banks of the scenic Connecticut River. Thought to be one of the tallest wooden structures along the river, the Opera House was built for William H. Goodspeed, banker, shipbuilder, and ferry operator. It was designed for passenger and freight service at the basement water level, with a store, office, and the theatre on the upper levels. Interior furnishings and hangings, many of which remain, were elaborate for their time. The theatre auditorium occupies the two upper floors, with a horseshoe balcony and boxes, both originally featuring gold leaf rococo designs. The theater season runs from April to November, and the house is famed especially for its musical productions. NR. 873-8664.

Nearby, on Main St., is the **Nathan Hale Schoolhouse,** where the patriot taught for a year before the Revolutionary War. Displays in its single room include local history and memorabilia, and a few Hale possessions. Open Memorial Day-Labor Day, Sa-Su 2-4. Admission 25¢. In front of the schoolhouse is **St. Stephen's Church,** which is said to house the oldest bell in Christendom — cast in Spain in 815.

Essex

A scenic old Connecticut River town, Essex grew to prominence as a shipbulding center in the 1840s. Main St., which leads down to the docks, is lined with picturesque sea captains' homes and is the site of one of Connecticut's most historic inns, **The Griswold** (see Lodging), which has been welcoming travelers since 1776.

CONNECTICUT RIVER FOUNDATION AT STEAMBOAT DOCK, Main St. The Steamboat Dock at the foot of Main St. was built in 1848 to service passenger and freight boats on the river. An 1879 wooden warehouse now displays the collection of this fine maritime museum; its extensive library is housed in the nearby chandlery of Captain Richard Hayden, which was completed in 1813. Open all year; winter, Sa-Su 1-4; summer, W-Su 1-5. No charge. 767-1564. 🏃

PRATT HOUSE, 20 West St., 1740. Pratt House, a center-chimney Colonial typical of Essex's many fine old homes, many of which are still privately owned, has been carefully restored and furnished by the Essex Historical Society. It contains the Griswold Collection of early American furnishings, and the adjacent colonial herb garden is lovingly tended by the Essex Garden Club. Open all year, Tu-Th, Su 1-5. $1.50 adults. 767-8201.

THE VALLEY RAILROAD, Essex Depot. Faithfully-restored vintage coaches, pulled by old-fashioned steam locomotives, roll through the scenic Connecticut River valley, past brooks and back roads, meadows and marshes, to Deep River. Here a century-old train connects with one of several river boats for a tranquil cruise on the river, past famous **Gillette Castle.** Open daily, May 9-Sept 7; Tu-Th, Sa, Su, Sept. 8-Nov 1. Train only during Dec. $3.75-$7.75 adults, $2-$5 children (depending on choice of train only or train

and cruise), group rates. 767-0103. 🏃

Farmington

FARMINGTON HISTORIC DISTRICT, both sides of Main St.; Colton and High Sts., 17th-20th centuries. Settled in 1640, Farmington had grown to be the 10th largest community in the American colonies by the Revolutionary War. Its growth was due in large part to the enterprise of Farmington merchants whose ships came upriver as far as Middletown, where their cargos of sugar, molasses, rum, and indigo were unloaded and carted in for distribution to newer settlements. Business flourished in the village, enriching its tinsmiths and silversmiths, hat makers, leatherworkers, and makers of muskets, buttons, and carriages. A canal, still partly in evidence, was a vital part of this commerce, as was Farmington's position on the old stage route between Hartford and Litchfield.

Within the Farmington Historic District and contiguous areas are concentrated more than 100 houses dated prior to 1835, most still in use as private residences. The centerpiece of this lovely old residential area is the **First Church of Christ** at 75

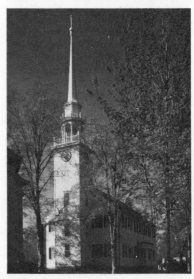

Hill-Stead Museum

Main St., probably the only original Congregational church in the state with its entry at the side. Designed by Judah Woodruff, with a square clock tower topped by an open belfry and steeple, the frame and clapboard building is particularly interesting as a transitional structure between the simple square meeting house of the Colonial period and the more ornate Greek Revival style. NR, NHL. Open all year, M-F 9-4. Donations accepted.

Miss Porter's School, an internationally known private girls' academy, is an integral part of Farmington life. Founded in 1844 by Sarah Porter, sister of Yale's eleventh president, the school is housed in some of the town's most striking old buildings. The **Union Hotel** on Main St., an 1830 Federal brick landmark with white Doric columns and a central cupola on its roof, now serves as Miss Porter's Administration Building. "**Colony House,**" a 1799 frame Federal mansion, and the **Deming-Lewis House,** also designed by Judah Woodruff in 1740, are both school properties, along with many other landmarks of the 18th and 19th centuries ranged along Main and High Sts. and Mountain Rd.

The **Hill-Stead Museum,** 671 Farmington Ave., 1901. Situated on top of a hill about half a mile from the center of Farmington, the museum is housed in a graceful Colonial Revival mansion designed for industrialist Alfred Pope by Stanford White. Completely furnished as it was when a private home, the house is full of fine examples of period furniture, prints, sculpture, and ceramics. Pope's major collection of superb French Impressionist paintings remains: Manet's *The Guitar Player,* Degas's *Jockeys,* and Monet's *Boats Leaving the Harbor* are only three of the priceless paintings collected by this farsighted man at a time when these artists were little-known and unappreciated. Open all year, W, Th, Sa, Su 2-5. $1.50 adults, 75¢ children. 677-9064.

Stanley-Whitman House (Farmington Museum), 37 High St., c. 1660. Representative of those few surviving frame houses built in 17th-century New England, the Stanley-Whitman House has a central chimney plan with a second story overhang. The lean-to at the rear was added some time after 1700. The narrow casement windows are typical of a period when glass had to be imported from Europe, making it expensive and sparingly-used. This carefully-restored landmark, one of the oldest and best-preserved frame houses in the state, is furnished with many period pieces and historic artifacts. NR, NHL. Open Mar, Apr, Nov, Dec, Su 1-4; May-Oct 31, Tu-Su 1-4. $1 adults, 50¢ children. 677-9222.

Hadlyme

GILLETTE CASTLE STATE PARK, off CT 148, 1919. Perhaps the best way to reach this intriguing fieldstone mansion overlooking the Connecticut River is via the **Chester-Hadlyme Ferry,** second oldest in the country. (Fare 75¢ per car and driver, 25¢ each additional passenger). The state park entrance is just north of the ferry slip, and the trip affords a superb river view of the looming medieval-style home designed by, and for, actor William Gillette. One of the great figures of the American stage, whose portrayal of Sherlock Holmes brought him international fame, Gillette purchased 122 acres of land overlooking the river in 1913, and spent the next six years overseeing the construction and finishing of his castle. Each detail—from the thick granite walls to the hand-hewn oak trim and stout doors of the interior—was fashioned to his exacting specifications. Twenty-four rooms are scatterd about in a bewildering lack of uniformity. Portions of the man-sized railroad he had built on the grounds are still in evidence. Cat lovers will enjoy the many feline images which decorate the rooms—Gillette was said to have kept more than 15 cats (along with goldfish and two pet frogs), and their status is reflected in carved doorstops, mantle decorations, and ceramics. Operated by the state. Open Memorial Day-Columbus Day, daily 1-5. $1 adults. 526-2336. ♦♦

Hartford

Hartford is a city of superlatives. Connecticut's largest city and its state capital, it is home to many of the world's largest insurance companies, boasts the country's oldest state house, and one of its most prestigious colleges, Trinity. Situated on the west bank of the wide, meandering Connecticut River, Hartford attracted its first English settlers as early as 1635, and its permanent name (after an English community) only two years later. Early resident Roger Ludlow authored Connecticut's famous Fundamental Orders in 1639. Radical for their time, they set forth the principle that "the foundation of authority is the free consent of the people," thus becoming the basis of a democratic government and constitution that were not to be formally established until more than a century later.

By the middle 1600s the Hartford colony comprised more than a dozen towns which were united with six New Haven settlements under the jurisdiction of a general legislature. The legislature met alternately between Hartford and New Haven until 1875, when Hartford's dominance was finally established.

Early settlers found the surrounding valleys excellent for farming, and it wasn't until the latter part of the 18th century that shipbuilding and foreign trade gained a prominent role. Maritime commerce never recovered from the depression following the War of 1812, but the development of industry, with an emphasis on machinery and transportation, filled the gap. The insurance industry which plays such a large part in Hartford's economy today began as an outgrowth of the early financial institutions so vital to the trade of a flourishing river port.

Hartford today is a sprawling, bustling city whose modern skyscrapers are often cheek by jowl with its most historic sites. To facilitate tours of the city, three arbitrary divisions have been assigned: Downtown, including the capitol buildings; The western area (not to be confused with West Hartford, which is treated separately further on); and the southern area. Comfortable shoes and plenty of time are advised.

DOWNTOWN HARTFORD, roughly bounded by Broad, Commerce, Park and Morgan Sts. This is the most important and bustling area of the city, since it includes the capitol complex as well as the headquarters for many of America's largest insurance companies.

The **Amos Bull House,** 59 S. Prospect St., 1788. One of the few 18th-century structures remaining in the city of Hartford, this 2½-story brick dwelling is home to the Connecticut Historical Commission, which moved it from Main St. to its present site and undertook restoration in 1971. It probably stood originally on a narrow lot with adjacent or attached two-story buildings on either side, as indicated by the absence of side windows on the first two floors. Bull, first owner of the house, operated a drygoods business here and sold the property around 1820. The plain regularly-placed windows of the second floor are thought to be original, as are the three dormers above them and much of the brickwork. The paneled wainscoting, cornices, and fireplace trim of the second-floor interior are also believed to date from the home's construction. NR. Open all year, M-F 8:30-4:30. No charge. 566-3005.

Bushnell Park, bounded by Elm, Jewell, and Trinity Sts., 1868. This sprawling urban park, designed by landscape architect Jacob Weidenmann, was advocated by theologian Horace Bushnell as an open space for the enjoyment of downtown workers. Numerous statues and monuments, most notable being the 1885 **Soldiers and Sailors Monument,** are spread throughout the grounds. A restored 1914 **carousel,** with intricately-carved wooden horses and a period Wurlitzer, is housed in an elegant pavillion. The carousel operates Sa and Su in Apr, May and Sept; Tu-Su in June, July and Aug, from 11-5. 20¢ per ride. 525-1618.

Butler-McCook Homestead, 396 Main St., 1782. The oldest part of this historic landmark is the restored kitchen that was once the 1747 blacksmith shop of William Hooker. When Dr. Daniel Butler bought the shop and property in 1782, he converted the existing building into a kitchen to serve his new home, a large, rambling 2½-story frame building. All of the furnishings in the kitchen, as well as in the other nine rooms in the museum, were family possessions, including a set of Windsor chairs, early pewter plates, fireplace equipment and china. At the rear of the property, the 1866 carriage house now contains a museum of old family bicycles, sleds, military uniforms, and sports equipment. The restored rear garden and expansive lawn form a quiet oasis in the midst of downtown industry. Operated by the Antiquarian and Landmarks Society. NR. Open daily May 15-Oct 15, 12-4; Oct 16-May 14, Tu, Th, Sa, Su 12-4. $1 adults, 25¢ children. 247-8996 or 522-1806.

Cheney Building (G. Fox Building), 942 Main St., 1875-76. Designed by Henry Hobson Richardson, the Cheney Building is considered an important milestone in architectural history, part of the evolution of the modern skyscrapers which have drastically altered American city life. Rough-faced blocks of Berea limestone give the seven-story exterior a rugged appearance, which is softened somewhat by the five broad arched openings at street level. Multiple series of arches punctuate the upper facade, with bands of Portland brownstone used for ornamentation. NR. Private.

The **Connecticut State Capitol,** Capitol Ave., 1872. A three-story marble and granite edifice highlighted by a tall central dome, end pavilions with corner turrets, and a projecting center pavilion with four-story corner towers, the capitol is a striking example of High-Victorian Gothic. Designed by Richard Upjohn, it is situated in a prominent location at the edge of Bushnell Park. Marble statues of famous Connecticut citizens adorn all sides of the building, and there are 12 figures crowning the pillared buttresses of the 12-sided gold-leafed dome.

The interior consists of three towering sky-lit wells enclosed on three levels by connecting balconies. The resulting courtyard effect is enhanced by hand-painted columns, stenciled beams, and Italian marble flooring. The capitol houses a good deal of historical memorabilia, including the battle flags of Connecticut's Civil War regiments, a replica of the Liberty Bell, and a bronze statue of one of the state's earliest heroes, Nathan Hale. The State House of Representatives is located at the second level, with the upper house, or State Senate, at the third. Both are accented with fine carved paneling and rich carpets. Guided tours are available, and are recommended, as there is much here to see. NR, NHL. Open all year, M-F 9:00-3:30. No charge. 566-3662.

First Church of Christ (Center Church), Gold and Main Sts., 1807. This graceful Georgian brick meeting house is dominated by a two-story columned portico on its main facade, and a four-tiered bell tower with Ionic columns, a frieze, and a balustrade ornamented by urns at each level. Tucked behind it is **The Ancient Burying Ground,** whose earliest graves date from 1640. For almost two centuries it was the only community burial place in Hartford, and it contains nearly 400 headstones and memorials commemorating residents of state and local prominence. Hartford's founder, the Rev. Thomas Hooker, is believed to be buried under or near a corner of the present church, which replaced an 18th-century building. NR. Open all year, daily 12-4. No charge. 728-3201.

Museum of Connecticut History, 231 Capitol Ave. Located in the imposing Connecticut State Library and Supreme Court Building opposite the State Capitol, the Museum displays the historic Fundamental Orders of 1638, the 1662 Charter, and Constitutions of 1818 and 1965. The Charter was purportedly hidden inside an oak tree when agents of England's King James II sought to retrieve it in 1687. Portraits of Connecticut governors hang in the museum's Memorial Hall. An outstanding collection of Colt firearms and memorabilia, an early Selden automobile, invented by a local resident in 1877, and a collection of fine Connecticut clocks are also displayed. The massive State Library collection is also open to the public. Open all year, M-F 9-5, Sa 9-1. No charge. 566-3056.

Old Statehouse (Connecticut Statehouse), 800 Main St., 1793-96. First of the public buildings designed by Charles Bulfinch,

the Old Statehouse, in addition to its architectural distinction, was the first such ediface constructed in the nation. The first written constitution in the world was signed here. It was the scene of the Hartford Convention of December 1814, which voiced New England opposition to the War of 1812 and resulted in great embarrassment and political harm to the Federalist party. From 1879 to 1915 the statehouse served as the Hartford City Hall. Gilbert Stuart's famous portrait of George Washington hangs in the Senate Chamber. On permanent loan from the state, it is the only Stuart portrait in the country that can be seen in its original commissioned setting. Of brownstone and brick, the three-story landmark, with its central domed cupola (added in the 1820s), is one of the best surviving examples of Federal architecture and one of the most important historic sites in America. NR, NHL. Open all year, M-Sa 10-5, Su 12-5. 50¢ adults, 10¢ children. 522-6766.

Second Church of Christ (South Church), 277 Main St., 1825-27. Designed by William Hayden and Nathaniel Woodhouse, this two-story Federal landmark is the third oldest public building in Hartford. Of harmonious proportions and fine detailing, it is noted for its Flemish-bond brickwork and its five-stage steeple. The interior boasts a magnificent domed and vaulted ceiling. NR.

Wadsworth Atheneum, 600 Main St., 1842. A Gothic Revival design of cream-colored granite, with crenelated towers and diamond pane windows, this major

Second Church of Christ

primarily industrial district includes an arms factory, single and multiple-family workers' housing, and the 114-acre **Colt Park.** Dominant is the 3½-story brick **armory,** with a cross-gabled roof and central blue onion-shaped dome supported on a ring of white columns. The armory was founded by Samuel Colt, who in addition to his success as an inventor also pioneered in mass production processes and provided housing and recreational facilities for his employees and their families. The 2- and 3½-story brick and frame residences, with Italianate and "chalet-style" elements, are prominent in the area. NR.

museum was designed by Ithiel Town. Its extensive art collection covers every major American period. Painting, sculpture, porcelain, silver, glass, firearms, textiles and furnishings are displayed in what is one of the oldest public museums in the country. NR. Open all year, Tu, W, F 11-3; Th 11-8; Sa-Su 11-5. $2 adults, $1 children (free Th). 278-2670.

SOUTHERN HARTFORD, roughly bounded by Park St., Vandyke Ave., Brown and Zion Sts. Industry and education take center stage here, dominated by the inventiveness of Samuel Colt, father of the automatic revolver.

The **Church of the Good Shepherd and Parish House,** 155 Wyllys St., 1867-94. Architect Edward T. Potter was commissioned by Elizabeth H. Colt to design this High-Victorian Gothic landmark in memory of her husband Samuel and son Caldwell. Both church and parish house are of rock-faced brownstone. The church sports a bell tower with corner turret, corner buttresses, and an open belfry, and a lavish wooden interior. NR.

Colt Industrial District, roughly bounded by Wawarme, Wethersfield, Hendricxsen, and Van Dyke Aves. and Stonington, Masseek and Sequassen Sts., 1848-75. This

Nearby at 80 Wethersfield Ave. is Colt's residence, **Armsmear,** an ornate Victorian mansion built in 1857 which is now a residence for retired Episcopalian churchwomen. NR.

Trinity College, based on Summit St. just west of the Colt area, was founded in 1823. Its 90-acre campus contains some of the oldest and most striking Gothic buildings in the country, chief among which is the **Trinity College Chapel.** Although not constructed until 1932, it is considered to be the most beautiful Collegiate Gothic building in the state. The soaring tower, buttressed by towering corner pinnacles, dominates the campus. The interior is cathedral-like, with clustered columns rising to a vaulted ceiling, and rich stained glass windows at either end.

WESTERN HARTFORD, roughly bounded by Asylum, Laurel, and Park Sts. and

Prospect Ave. This area, part business and part residential, has been the home of some of America's most famous artists. Mark Twain and Harriet Beecher Stowe (see following) lived here, as did one of the preeminent women of the theater and cinema, Katharine Hepburn.

The **Connecticut Historical Society,** 1 Elizabeth St. A rich assortment of objects relating to Connecticut's past and peoples is exhibited here. Paintings and prints by local artists, photographs and scenic views, documented examples of Connecticut furniture, and a wide range of products resulting from early industry and craftsmanship are on display. An extensive collection of furniture from the Colonial and Federal periods is especially noteworthy. Special exhibitions on a wide variety of themes are offered from time to time. Open all year, M-F 1-5. No charge. 236-5621.

Nook Farm, Farmington Ave. at Forest St., 19th century. Three homes and two carriage houses are all that remain of a mid-19th century neighborhood that was to nurture a number of famous Americans. John Hooker and Francis Gillette, who purchased Nook Farm and began to subdivide it in 1853, had a wide range of interests, and they made their neighborhood a cultural center and a mecca for distinguished visitors during the next fifty years. Among the notables who lived here were Isabella Beecher Hooker, a suffragist leader; Charles Dudley Warner, author and editor of the *Hartford Courant*; Joseph R. Hawley, Civil War general and U. S. senator; and William Gillette, actor and playwright.

The **Mark Twain House,** 351 Farmington Ave., was designed for Samuel Clemens ("Mark Twain") and his wife Olivia by Edward T. Potter, who incorporated many of their suggestions in his plans. Clemens and his family had moved to the Nook Farm area in 1871, first leasing the house which belonged to John Hooker and his wife Isabella, Harriet Beecher Stowe's half sister, and they were to live in their new house from its completion in 1874 until the early 1890s. Many of Clemens's most famous books, including

Life on the Mississippi, The Adventures of Tom Sawyer, and *The Adventures of Huckleberry Finn,* were written here. The whimsical design of the house, which combines Queen Anne, Victorian Gothic, and Stick Style elements, is very much in keeping with Clemens's writing style. The porch resembles the deck of a Mississippi

River steamboat, as do the many balconies which ornament all sides of the building.

Interior walls throughout the house are stenciled in various rich designs by Louis Comfort Tiffany and his associates, Candace Wheeler and Lockwood de Forest. In the dining room, an unusual window over the fireplace enabled the family, in Clemens's words, to "watch the flames leaping to meet the falling snowflakes." Many of the rooms contain original Clemens family pieces, and a museum room in the basement, which was formerly a series of coal bins, displays such oddities as

Clemens's Russian sleigh and his bicycle. Operated by the Mark Twain Memorial. NR, NHL. Open all year; Sept 1- May 31, Tu-Sa 9:30-4, Su 1-4; June-Aug, daily 10-4:30. $2 adults, $1 children. 525-9317.

Harriet Beecher Stowe House, 73 Forest St., 1871. The author and her husband, Professor Calvin Stowe, bought this simpler Victorian house in 1873, two years after it was built. A 2½-story brick structure, it is lavishly trimmed in wood. A variety of porches and a steep hip roof ornament the exterior. Much of the interior wall covering has been exactly reproduced from early photos of the period, and many of the Stowes' furnishings remain, placed as they were originally, including the drop-leaf mahogany table on which parts of *Uncle Tom's Cabin* were written. Even the gardens have been restored as exactly as possible. Operated by the Stowe-Day Foundation. NR. Open at the same times as The Mark Twain House, and at the same admission rates. Combination tickets for both houses may by purchased as well: $3.50 adults, $1.75 children. 525-9317.

The third Victorian mansion in the Nook Farm area, the **Day House** (1884), 77 Forest St., contains the **Nook Farm Research Library,** a comprehensive collection including manuscripts and photographs concentrating on both the lives of local residents and the architecture, decorative arts, history, and literature of the latter half of the 19th century. Hours same as Twain and Stowe Houses. No additional charge. 525-9317.

The Nook Farm neighborhood is a part of **Asylum Hill Historic Resources,** a late 19th-century residential area which was originally part of a larger real estate development, **Imlay Farm.** One of the most interesting buildings, now an architect's office, is the **Perkins-Clark House** at 49 Woodland St. Built in 1861, and designed by the Hartford firm of Octavius J. and Augustus Jordan, this stucco Gothic Revival building is surrounded by six acres of land. NR.

Manchester

CHENEY BROTHERS HISTORIC DISTRICT, bounded by Hartford Rd. and Laurel, Spruce and Campfield Sts., 18th-20th centuries. The silk industry in America dates from the early 17th century, when James II encouraged its beginnings in Virginia. In subsequent years entrepreneurs attempted to produce silk in almost every colony, but it was not until 1827 that the nation's first successful mill was built, near Mansfield, Connecticut. It was three of eight Cheney brothers, descended from a clockmaking and farming family in Manchester, who were responsible for building the large mill community, with its many factories and workers' homes, which grew to be one of the most successful silk-producing complexes in the country.

The historic district which bears their name covers 175 acres of land, and includes the 18th-century family homestead, several later mansions built by the brothers and their descendants, two dozen mill buildings, several schools and churches either built by the Cheneys or situated on land donated by them, and more than 200 individual and multi-family mill houses either built by the Cheneys or purchased by them for use by their employees. The Cheney Brothers Manufacturing Company felt a deep responsibility towards the welfare of the community, which is reflected even today in the park-like atmosphere of the area — not at all what one would expect of a 19th-century mill town.

The Cheney Homestead at 106 Hartford Rd. was built about 1780 by Timothy Cheney, father of the entrepreneurs. The oldest house in the area, it is a 2½-story gable-roofed white frame building on a stone foundation. Now owned by the

Manchester Historical Society, it serves as its headquarters and is furnished with period antiques. Several family pieces are included, among them a clock that Timothy Cheney built into the east wall of the living room. A reconstructed one-room school, the **Keeney Schoolhouse,** sits on the property. Open all year, Th, Su 1-5. 50¢ adults. 643-5588.

Further along Hartford Rd., at #48, is the **Mary Cheney House,** a 2½-story Victorian brick residence built in 1870 for the daughter of Frank Cheney, one of the original brothers. At #21 is the **George W. Cheney House,** completed about 1860, a frame dwelling distinguished by its tall red brick chimneys and one-story balustraded porch. At #20 is the **Frank Cheney Jr. House,** a red brick neo-Colonial residence designed by Charles Adams Platt at the turn of the century.

Immediately east of the George Cheney House is the mansion of **Clifford D. Cheney,** a 1904 pink stucco landmark with a one-story columned portico, situated on a wide expanse of lawn. On Forest St. and Hartford Rd. are half a dozen other Cheney homes, dating from the mid-19th to early-20th centuries.

The **Cheney Mills** form the center of the historic district and reflect the general appearance of the manufacturing complex about 1916. Sixteen mills and several support buildings, mostly of red brick with green-painted window, door, and roof trim, remain; they date from 1886 to 1916.

Also noteworthy are the **Spinning Mills** (63 Elm St.), a complex of three three-story brick buildings, and the **Velvet Mills** (60 Elm St.), built in 1886 and 1901 respectively.

Many other mill buildings and workers' houses complete the complex. A stroll through the neighborhood is recommended as the best way to capture the flavor of this century-old mill community.

Middletown

Settled by Puritans from Hartford and Wethersfield in 1650, Middletown was named because of its location halfway between the capital and Saybrook. Its long, wide main street parallels the stately Connecticut River, running up a gradual hill, at whose summit lies historic **Wesleyan University,** the focal point of the community.

Middletown was an important port in its early years, shipping both lumber and farm products to the West Indies. Simeon North, first official gun maker to the United States Government, built an arms factory here during the Revolution and is credited with inventing assembly-line production in 1813. Many other industries, past and present, have contributed to the community's prosperity, notable in the broad, shaded streets and lovely old homes.

Wesleyan University was founded in 1831 by the Methodist Conference, but has always operated as a nonsectarian school under a charter which prohibited religious teaching. Its campus is a comfortable mix of early brownstone and later brick structures and more modern dormitories and classrooms. Among the most noteworthy of its early buildings are:

RUSSELL HOUSE (The Honors College), Washington and High Sts., 1827-29. Designed by Ithiel Town, Russell House has the form and appearance of a Greek temple. It was the home of the Russell family, china trade merchants, before being acquired by the University. Rectangular in shape, the two-story dwelling has a front portico with six giant Corinthian columns supporting a heavy entablature. Sidelights and the overdoor light contain frosted glass etched with floral patterns. A centrally-located double stairway leads to the garden entrance. NR. Open Sept-June, M-F 9-5. No charge. 347-9411.

ALSOP HOUSE (Davison Art Center), 301 High St., 1840. The design of this Greek Revival house has been attributed to Ithiel Town, although without firm authentication. A wrought-iron porch surmounted by a balcony runs across the facade, whose most unusual feature is the painted oil on plaster decoration repeated within. The exterior trompe l'oeil painting includes three sunken panels which resemble niches containing life-size statues. Exterior stucco has been painted pink, and the eaves and ceiling of the porch are blue. Inside, the stairway has been lined and painted to simulate marble, while walls of two parlors are painted to look like paneling. Other painted decoration includes dancing girls, angels, cherubs, birds, and insects, and the house is furnished in part with fine antiques. NR. Open Sept-May, Tu-F 12-4, Sa-Su 2-5. No charge. 347-9411.

Moodus

AMASA DAY HOUSE, Moodus Green, 1816. This late Federal-style house is considered to be one of the earliest structures built in the town and was named for a local businessman who purchased it in 1843 and lived there until his death more than 50 years later. Furnished almost entirely with three generations of Day family heirlooms, it has been restored to the period. Much of its unusual stenciling is still visible in two first-floor rooms, on the front stairs, and in the upstairs hallway. Operated by the Antiquarian and Landmarks Society. NR. Open May 15-Oct 15, daily 1-5. $1 adults, 25¢ children. 247-8996.

Old Saybrook

GENERAL WILLIAM HART HOUSE, 350 Main St., 1767. Hart was a successful merchant and Revolutionary War officer, who, when only 21, built this 2½-story frame Georgian home for his new bride. An elegant residence, unusually roomy for its time, it reflects the prosperity of the owner. A large parlor opens off each side of the central hall; to the rear is a spacious drawing room and original kitchen with walk-in fireplace and Dutch oven. The house has eight corner fireplaces, the one in the library decorated with Staffordshire tiles illustrating Aesop's Fables. Administered by the Old Saybrook Historical Society, the Hart House is furnished throughout with period pieces and interesting memorabilia. NR. Open mid-Apr-mid-Oct, Th, F, Su 11-3; also Sa in June, July and Aug. No charge. 388-2622.

Within walking distance of the Hart House are a number of other historic sites, includ-ing the 1840 **Congregational church** next door. Across the street is **Trivet Green,** named for its unusual shape, at one corner of which stands the **Humphrey Pratt Tavern** (1785), once an important stage stop between New Haven and Boston. On College St. is the site of the **Collegiate School,** founded in 1701, which was moved to New Haven to become Yale University. General William Hart's grandfather, John Hart, was the first student to receive a B.A. degree from this institution. General Hart is buried in the adjoining cemetery.

Simsbury

MASSACOH PLANTATION (Captain Elisha Phelps House), 800 Hopmeadow St., 1771. The 18th-century house at the center of this complex of early buildings is typical of New England architecture of the period, with a gambrel roof, center chimney, and unadorned facade. Also on the property are the first **Simsbury School House** (1740), the first **Meeting House** (1683), a mid-19th century Victorian carriage house, and the 1795 **Hendrick Cottage.** The extensive collections of historic artifacts and memorabilia, administered by the Simsbury Historical Society, include three centuries of tools and furnishings, including antique sleighs and carriages, and the Higley Coppers, the first copper coins struck in America. NR. Open May-Oct, daily 1-4. $3 adults, $1.50 children. 658-2500.

Storrs

GURLEYVILLE GRISTMILL, Stone Mill Rd., 1830s. Constructed on the foundations of an earlier wooden structure, the Gurleyville mill is the only stone gristmill in Connecticut. Except for its stonework, however, it is typical of the many gristmills which served the small rural farming communities throughout New England. Corn, rye, barley, and wheat were ground here. Lumber and shingles were produced at an attached sawmill now gone. In the mid-1800s the mill was operated by Samuel Cross, father of Wilbur Cross (four-term governor of the state and a renowned scholar of 18th-century English literature). It contains a complete system of perfectly preserved milling equipment illustrating the changing industrial technology of the 19th century. Operated as a museum by Joshua's Tract Conservation and Historic Trust. NR. Open May 3-Oct 25, Th and Su 1-5. No charge. 429-2637 or 456-2221. The mill is located within the **Gurleyville Historic District**, a 19th-century residential and industrial area. 🏃

Nearby, at 954 Storrs Rd., is the **Mansfield Historical Society Museum**, housed in the former Mansfield town office building, with collections of household equipment, farm machinery, costumes and furniture. Open May-Oct, Th and Su 1:30-4:30. No charge. 429-9789.

Storrs is primarily famous as the home of the **University of Connecticut**, a school whose modern campus dominates the town. It was founded in 1881 as an agricultural school, as were most state universities. An information center is located at the main campus on CT 195. 486-2000.

Suffield

HATHEWAY HOUSE, 55 S. Main St., 1760. The main part of this stately frame structure was extended when its second owner, Oliver Phelps, added a north wing in 1795. Phelps, who had been a delegate to the Massachusetts constitutional convention, was a wealthy land speculator and merchant. His taste for luxury is evident especially in the north wing, which contains original handblocked wallpapers of the 1780s, in addition to fine plasterwork decoration. One of the wing's rooms is signed and dated, most unusual in houses of the period. Restored and elegantly furnished by the Antiquarian and Landmarks Society, its collection represents the best of 18th-century taste. NR. Open May 15-Oct 15, daily 1-5. $1 adults, 25¢ children. 668-0055.

Hatheway House is the centerpiece of the **Suffield Historic District**, a fine residential area which reflects the fortunes made from the area's tobacco industry. The American cigar business was born here in the early 1800s, and 16 million

were produced in 1860 alone. Also part of the district is **Suffield Academy**, founded in 1833. The campus of this excellent prep school contains many fine Victorian buildings, some of which were "Colonialized" in the early 20th century.

Warehouse Point

THE CONNECTICUT ELECTRIC RAILWAY, CT 140. A museum of vintage trolley cars from the early 1890s to 1947 includes three miles of scenic track over which several of the trains may be ridden. Thirty trolleys, plus several steam and electric locomotives and other historic railway equipment, are included. Open all year; Memorial Day-Labor Day M-Sa 10-4, Su 12-6; otherwise Sa, Su and holidays 12-5. No charge for the museum. Rides: $2.00 adults, $1 children. 623-7417.

West Hartford

NOAH WEBSTER BIRTHPLACE, 227 S. Main St., c. 1676. Webster, the famous lexicographer and spelling book author, was born in this two-story frame farmhouse in 1758. His various literary achievements include the publication of textbooks, histories, and dictionaries. Best remembered for his *American Dictionary of the English Language,* the basis of today's most popular dictionary, Webster was one of Yale's distinguished alumni, and went on, in the course of his 85 years, to become a schoolteacher, lawyer, editor, legislator, and lecturer. He wrote on many subjects, including farming, economics, disease, science, and history; was one of the founders of Amherst College in Massachusetts; and created some of the first American copyright laws. His boyhood home is an excellent example of a typical Connecticut farmhouse of the period, erected around a massive central chimney, with a cavernous fireplace dominating the kitchen. The simple interior is authentically furnished. Operated by the Noah Webster Foundation and Historical Society. NR, NHL. Open all year, Su and Tu 1-4, Th 10-4. $1.50 adults, 75¢ children. Group rates. 521-5362.

Wethersfield

OLD WETHERSFIELD HISTORIC DISTRICT, bounded on the N and W by the New Haven Railroad tracks, on the E by I-91, and on the north by Wethersfield Cove, 17th-18th centuries. Wethersfield is one of the oldest and best preserved areas of settlement in Connecticut. A group of adventurers from the Massachusetts Bay Colony led by John Oldham, acquired land here in 1634. The community joined with other area towns in adopting the famous "Fundamental Orders" in 1639 which became a model for the U.S. Constitution. The town grew rapidly and was, until 1700, the head of navigation on the Connecticut River. Ships built here engaged in extensive trade with Europe, the West Indies, and Atlantic ports. From the earliest days of settlement, Wethersfield's wage earners depended on the river and the Atlantic for their livelihoods. More than half of the able-bodied men were shipowners or sailors at least part of the time. Through warehouses such as the one remaining on Wethersfield Cove, local products, including a famous flat red onion known as the "Wethersfield Red," were shipped abroad. The variety is still grown, and seeds are sold throughout the world.

The large historic district comprises nearly 1,200 buildings of all ages, about 100 of which date from the 17th century. Wethersfield's green, along which many of the most historic old homes are arrayed, is a slender diamond shape nearly half a mile long, partly shaded and part open. Around the corner from the green is the **community church,** a well preserved brick building

(1761) which has been recently restored.

There are many types of Colonial and Federal buildings in the district, some of which originated as one-room structures, and some two-story residences with two rooms on each floor. There are frame and brick houses of all types, with one, two, and four chimneys, most retaining their original appearance, except for the color of the frame dwellings, now predominantly white, which were at first painted with dull reds, greens, yellows, and blues. Although by far the majority of the homes are still private residences, there are six landmarks, each unique and historically important, which are open to the public. All have been restored with painstaking care, and taken together they present the real flavor of this early New England community:

Buttolph-Williams House, 249 Broad St., 1692. The oldest restored dwelling in Wethersfield, this two-story frame landmark was constructed by David Buttolph on land willed to him by his father who had moved to Wethersfield in 1676, where he established himself as a glovemaker and trader. After more than 250 years of continuous occupancy, the house was restored to its original 17th-century condition in the 1940s. Operated by the Antiquarian and Landmarks Society, it is furnished with a superb collection of period pieces, including pewter, delft, fabrics and furniture. The 17th-century kitchen is considered to be the most completely furnished of its type in New England, with a fine collection of early woodenware, wrought iron, twin highchairs and other accessories. NR, NHL. Open daily May 15-Oct 15, 1-5. $1 adults, 25¢ children. 529-0460.

The Silas Deane House, 203 Main St., 1764. Deane, a lawyer, merchant and politician, was a delegate to the First Continental Congress who was commissioned in 1776 to travel abroad to develop Franco-American trade. His activities in France became suspect, he fell from favor, and Congress refused to pay his back salary. He spent his last years in unsuccessful attempts to clear his name and never returned to his home. The 2½-story frame house he built after his marriage has an un-

usual hallway with an elaborate staircase. Portraits of Deane hang in the elegantly-furnished front parlor. Furnishings in the house date from before 1775, the year in which Deane left for the last time. Many distinguished guests called here, among them John Adams and, it is thought, General George Washington. Open all year Tu-Sa 10-4; also Su 1-4 May 15-Oct 15. Operated by the Webb Deane Stevens Museum. NR. NHL. $1.50 adults, special rates for children and three-house tour (Joseph Webb House, Isaac Stevens House, and Silas Deane House). 529-0612.

Captain James Francis House, 120 Hartford Ave., 1793. Operated by the Wethersfield Historical Society, this early landmark remained in the same family for 170 years, and it has been restored and furnished to reflect the changing tastes of its occupants over that time. Open June 15-Oct 15, Sa 10-4, Su 12-4. 75¢ adults, 25¢ children. Group rates. 529-7656.

Isaac Stevens House, Main St., 1788. Stevens, a leather tanner and saddler by trade, built this house for his bride, Sarah. His account book and leather fire buckets are on display, along with many furnishings owned by the family, representing the accumulation of several generations of inhabitants. Two Connecticut clocks, a collection of caps, and examples of early 19th-century needlework are among the furnishings. One of the second-floor chambers retains its original blue paint on the fireplace wall, and much of the early paneling and flooring remains. Operated by the Webb-Deane-Stevens Museum. NR. Open all year, Tu-Sa 10-4; also Su 1-4 May 15-Oct 15. $1.50 adults, special rates

for children and three-house tour of the Webb, Deane, and Stevens houses. 529-0612.

Joseph Webb House, 211 Main St., 1752. In the spring of 1781 General George Washington and the Count de Rochambeau met at the home of this prosperous Wethersfield merchant to lay plans for a joint offensive against the English. The meeting marked the implementation of the

Franco-American military alliance, resulting in the two armies being united for a push southward, timed to coincide with the arrival of a French fleet from the West Indies. The south parlor of this two-story gambrel-roofed frame house has traditionally been identified as the conference room in which was held the four-day meeting leading to the final campaign of the Revolutionary War and the defeat of Cornwallis at Yorktown. The bedchamber where Washington slept is still decorated with the original red-flocked wallpaper hung in honor of his visit. Also on view are fine examples of the work of early Connecticut cabinetmakers and silversmiths, as well as a large collection of early American needlework. Among the pieces on display which were owned by the Webb family are portraits by Charles Willson Peale and William Verstile. Operated by the Webb Deane Stevens Museum. NR, NHL. Open all year, Tu-Sa 10-4; also Su 1-4 May 15-Oct 15. $1.50 adults, special rates for children and three-house tour. 529-0612.

Wethersfield Historical Society, 150 Main St. The **Old Academy,** a long plain brick building with a bell-shaped cupola, was built in 1801 as a public school and later served as the local library. The historical society's collection of local history, maritime lore, genealogy, tools and crafts, furniture, and the decorative arts is now housed here. The society administers several other landmark structures, among them the **Cove Warehouse** (1690), **Captain John Hurlbut House,** an early 19th century building opposite the Webb House, and the **James Francis House** previously described. NR. Its main museum is open May 15-Oct 15, Tu, Th, Sa 1-4. Donations accepted. 529-7656.

Windsor

OLIVER ELLSWORTH HOMESTEAD (ELMWOOD), 778 Palisado Ave., c. 1740. The original section of the Ellsworth Homestead was built in the first half of the 18th century and consisted of a single rectangular section with a central entrance sheltered by a columned portico. Two chimneys define the early end walls, and the entire house is frame covered with clapboards. Ellsworth added the south ell with its two-story colonnade in 1783, and another wing extends eastward from the rear of the house. A U.S. senator and chief justice of the Supreme Court, as well as a member of the Continental Congress, Ellsworth lived here from 1782 until his death in 1807. Family heirlooms as well as many period antiques are on display throughout the house. One unusual piece is a Gobelin tapestry presented to Ellsworth by Napoleon as a token of his esteem. Operated by the Connecticut D.A.R. NR. Open Apr 1-Nov 1, Tu-Sa 1-5. $1 adults. 688-8717.

Down the road at 96 Palisado Avenue is the **Fyler House,** one of the oldest surviving frame houses in Connecticut (c. 1640), which has been carefully restored and furnished by the Windsor Historical Society. Its adjoining **Wilson Museum** contains rare historical and genealogical materials. Open Apr 1-Dec 1, Tu-Sa 10-12 and 1-4. $1 adults, 25¢ children. 688-3813.

Windsor Locks

BRADLEY AIR MUSEUM, Bradley International Airport. As a change of pace, and certainly a treat for the children, have a look at this collection of 25 aircraft — vintage World War II and later — both on display and under restoration in an outdoor setting. Special exhibits cover the history of aviation. Open all year, daily 10-6 (weather permitting). $2 adults, $1 children. 623-3305.

Eastern Connecticut

Chaplin

CHAPLIN HISTORIC DISTRICT, 19th century. When CT 198 was laid out in the early 20th century, its planners bypassed the small agricultural village of Chaplin, leaving its 43 original buildings intact. And so it remains today, totally free of modern intrusions. Chaplin was incorporated in 1822, and by the '30s was a thriving light-industrial community noted especially for its silk production. The comfortable, solid homes of wealthy former residents, mostly late-Federal and Greek Revival in style, line the main street. The 1814 **Congregational Church,** with high stone basement and pedimented front, and the **Gurley Tavern** (1822), with recessed porch, pilasters, and Palladian window are also nearby. All of the village's properties were constructed between 1815 and 1840, and it is as though time has stood still since, leaving Chaplin as an excellent example of how northeastern Connecticut's early mill towns appeared nearly 150 years ago.

East Lyme

THOMAS AVERY HOUSE (Smith-Harris House), Society Rd., 1845. Originally part of a farm of more than 140 acres, this imposing 2½-story frame Greek Revival home at the end of a rustic lane has been recently restored by the Smith-Harris Commission. Many of its early features survive, partly because no plumbing or electricity was installed until 1970. The working model farm on which the house is located is an important illustration of an early agricultural settlement. Call for information, 739-0761.

Groton

Just across the Thames River from historic New London (see description following), Groton is best known for its huge U.S. Naval Submarine Base, and as the home of the General Dynamics plant where many of the submarines, including the first diesel-powered and first atomic-powered models, were built. The USS *Nautilus*, first of the atomic subs, was launched in early 1954, made her maiden voyage the following year, and remained on active duty until just two years ago, having achieved fame for her unprecedented ability to circumnavigate the globe, submerged, at comparitively high speeds. Plans call for the *Nautilus*, recently entered on the National Register, to be available for tours in the near future. In the meanwhile, you can visit the World War II sub *Croaker,* whose interior has been restored to its original combat-ready condition. It is berthed on the river adjacent to 359 Thames St. Open daily all year, Apr 15-Oct 15 9-5, Oct 16-Apr 14, 9-3. $2 adults, $1 children. 448-1616. Tours of the submarine base itself are available only by special bus. For information call 449-4779.

FORT GRISWOLD, bounded by Baker Ave., Smith St., Park Ave., Monument Ave., and the Thames River, 1775-19th century. Constructed between 1775 and 1778 to defend the shore of Groton and New London, Fort Griswold was the site of a major Revolutionary War battle in 1781, when British forces commanded by Benedict Arnold attacked the American garrison, successfully stormed the fort, slaughtered the small band defending it,

and set fire to most of neighboring New London. It was garrisoned during the later War of 1812, the Spanish-American War, and World War II. As constructed, the fort had stone walls about twelve feet high and was surrounded by a ditch. The star-shaped earthen outlines of the fort remain, along with a 19th-century stone house used for storing powder, rifles, and ammunition, and a brick hot shot house (1812) where cannonballs were heated prior to firing.

On the grounds you may visit the **Revolutionary War Museum**, whose exhibits detail the heroic actions of area residents during this bloody but triumphant, period in history. Open Memorial Day-Columbus Day, daily 9-5. The nearby **Ebenezer Avery House** (1750), a center-chimney Colonial structure with period furnishings throughout, served as a temporary hospital and shelter for the wounded after Arnold's takeover of the fort. Open June-Aug, Fri-Su 2-4 and by appointment. NR. The fort itself, operated by the state, is open year-round from 8-sunset. Free. 445-1729. ♠

EASTERN POINT HISTORIC DISTRICT, 19th-20th centuries. Located primarily along the bank of the Thames River, the district comprises a significant group of late 19th- and early 20th-century summer residences, including examples of the Queen Anne, Colonial Revival, and Shingle styles. At the turn of the century, Eastern Point was a fashionable gathering place for middle- and upper-class vacationers. Many of the houses, particularly those on the water, are built on a grand scale in the manner of the more famous "cottages" of Newport and Watch Hill, Rhode Island, reflecting the increasing importance of leisure as an element of status and also indicating the wealth of the summer crowd. Since the 1940s, the district has changed in character, and is now primarily residential. Private, but well worth a stroll or drive along Thames St.

Lebanon

JONATHAN TRUMBULL HOUSE, The Common, c. 1735. Built for Connecticut's

Open May 30-Oct 1, Sa 1:30-5. Donations accepted.

Both the War Office and the nearby Trumbull residence are located within the **Lebanon Green Historic District,** whose 17th- and 18th-century buildings surround a broad, tree-shaded common. Most imposing among the graceful old landmarks is the **Congregational Church** (1807), designed by artist John Trumbull of brick, with four white-painted brick columns framing a recessed porch, and a three-stage wooden spire topping the whole.

Revolutionary War Governor, the only colonial governor who supported the war for independence, this two-story frame landmark with pedimented central entrance and matching windows was the scene of many conferences among America's most notable founding fathers, including Benjamin Franklin, George Washington, and the Adamses. Governor Trumbull's son John, famed for his sketches of Revolutionary War scenes, and for his portraits of prominent leaders, was born here in 1756. He was commissioned by the federal government to paint the four Revolutionary War scenes which adorn the rotunda of the Capitol Building in Washington D.C., the first American artist to be so honored. Owned and maintained by the Connecticut Daughters of the American Revolution, the Trumbull House is furnished with period antiques, including some of the Trumbull family possessions. NR, NHL. Open May 15-Oct 15, Tu-Sa 1-5. $1 adults. 642-7558.

WAR OFFICE (Captain Joseph Trumble Store and Office), West Town St., c. 1732. Shipping entrepreneur and wealthy town resident Joseph Trumble built this small gambrel-roofed structure with a central chimney as his retail outlet and office. His shipping business was eventually taken over by his son Jonathan, who changed the spelling of the family name to Trumbull. During the Revolution, Governor Trumbull met with his War Council here when the General Assembly was not in session to discuss all aspects of the campaign. NR.

Ledyard

MAIN SAWMILL, Iron St., 1869. A reminder of the early lumbering industry which played a vital part in the development of Ledyard, the Main Sawmill is probably the only surviving vertical sawmill in the state, with a wide opening across the front of its single board-and-batten story through which logs could be rolled for placement upon the wooden saw carriage inside. The third such structure on its site, the mill has been restored and contains nearly all of its original equipment. Sawing demonstrations are given, and the museum contains shingle making, ice harvesting, and blacksmithing exhibits. Operated by the Connecticut Historical Commission. NR. Open Apr-May, Oct-Dec, Sa 1-4. Free. 464-8740.

NATHAN LESTER HOUSE, Vinegar Hill Rd., 1793. Typical of Connecticut farmhouse construction, the Lester House is unusual because of its excellent condition and because it remained in the Lester family until the early 20th century. The 100-acre grounds include many original buildings and a farm museum containing many early implements and machinery. The house is overshadowed by an ancient tree known as the Ledyard Oak, a favorite subject of local legend. Municipal. NR. Open Memorial Day-Labor Day, Tu and Th 2-4, Sa-Su 1-4:30 and by appointment. Free. 464-2401.

Mystic

An old maritme community of trim white homes and warehouses along the picturesque and irregular Mystic River (actually a tidal outlet of Long Island Sound), Mystic is justly famous for its major attraction, the **Mystic Seaport Museum.** Certainly you'll want to spend hours, or even days, on the grounds of the museum itself, but to overlook the attributes of the surrounding community would be a mistake. The village of Mystic, situated between the towns of Stonington and Groton, and jointly governed by them since 1705, is divided by the river into two distinct, and somewhat different, areas. Main Street (US 1) connects the **Mystic Bridge Historic District** on the east and the **Mystic River Historic District** on the west, in both of which most of the important 19th and 20th century landmarks are located. The western bank is primarily residential in feeling, while the eastern contains more shipyards and factories and less substantial housing. Prior to the 19th century, this was a sleepy river town. Its growth was due in large part to its protected harbor, several miles inland from the rough Atlantic waters, which afforded an excellent site for the shipbuilding so critical to the burgeoning transportation and commerce of the 1800s. Once launched, the many ships born here could be easily dispatched to coastal and foreign ports, and so Mystic became home not only for those who built the ships, but for those who sailed them. After the beginnings of the gold rush in 1849, the industry peaked as carpenters and joiners rushed to turn out ever faster and sturdier vessels. Many records were set and broken by Mystic ships on the arduous voyage around Cape Horn to the California mines.

The yards were also instrumental in providing wooden steamers for the Civil War, the shipbuilding activity being financed in part by proceeds from sealing and then whaling voyages launched from the port.

Toward the end of the 19th century, shipbuilding declined because the river did not provide the deep water necessary for construction of modern steel-hulled ships. This form of commerce was replaced to some degree by increased manufacturing: at one time the village had a soap works, iron works, numerous textile mills, and a distillery (for witch hazel). Such industry is largely gone today, but if you walk the residential streets it will be easy to imagine yourself transported back to the 19th century. The broad avenues, the architecture of the houses (largely Greek Revival and Federal, with some later Italianate and Queen Anne), the nearness of the river and the spacing and relationship of all these elements to each other create an atmosphere difficult to duplicate elsewhere.

Not in either historic district, but well worth a visit, is the **Denison Homestead** (Pequotsepos Manor) on Pequotsepos Ave., a two-story shingled landmark built in 1717, which was owned by the Denison family until 1941. Its first owner, Captain George Denison, was a founder of Stonington, and his forebears had lived on the site of the house since 1654. Because of the unusually long and unbroken family history associated with the house, it has been possible to furnish various rooms to reflect different eras in its development. Five distinct periods are represented, ranging from early 18th century (kitchen) to the early 20th (parlor). Eleven generations of Denison family heirlooms are displayed, and it would be difficult to find a more convenient way to demonstrate the widely divergent styles of interior decorating popular at various stages of New England's history over more than 250 years. Operated by the Denison Society. NR. Open May 15-Oct 15, Tu-Su 1-5. $1.25 adults, 50¢ children. 536-9248.

MYSTIC SEAPORT MUSEUM, Greenmanville Ave. (CT 27), 18th-20th centuries. For most of the 19th century, the seventeen acres along the Mystic River now occupied by this superb museum were part of the Greenman shipyards. The area was known as Greenmanville, and its main street still carries the name. A textile mill operated by the Greenman family also stood on the site, and some of its buildings remain as part of the museum complex.

From their shipyards, the Greenman brothers launched nearly 100 vessels between 1838 and 1878, including the

famous clipper *David Crockett*. It was against this historic background that the Mystic Seaport Museum, then the Marine Historical Association, was founded in 1929 by Dr. Charles K. Stillman, Edward E. Bradley, and Carl C. Cutler. During the ensuing years, it has grown from a single building and a small collection to more than 70 buildings, ships, and formal exhibits painstakingly and beautifully arranged along the waterfront, and has become a major interpretive center of American maritime history.

There is something here for every member of the family, from exhibit buildings filled with all manner of scrimshaw, marine paintings, and curiosities to a planetarium, a children's museum, a fully-stocked 19th-century general store, and a working shipyard where craftsmen demonstrate the maintenance and refurbishing of many types of vessels. In addition to boarding the training ship **"Joseph Conrad,"** a graceful square-rigger, or the world famous **"Charles W. Morgan,"** the only surviving 19th century wooden whaler, which is now a National Historic Landmark, you may cruise the Mystic yourself on the 1908 coal-fired steamboat **"Sabino"** (May to October only). One note of caution is in order: partly because of its wide appeal, and partly because of its accessibility to New England's summer resort areas

via I-95, the Seaport can become extremely crowded, most notably during July and August. Since the museum itself and most of its exhibits are open year-round, you may have a more rewarding visit by planning your trip for an off-peak time. Both spring and fall are lovely seasons along the New England coastline, and the stark beauty of winter could be to your particular taste. No matter what time of year you choose to visit here, be sure to allow plenty of time to explore.

Within the museum grounds, between Greenmanville Ave. and the river, there are eleven buildings indigenous to the area, and nearly thirty original landmarks with historic associations that have been moved to the site. The balance has been constructed by the museum with great care to blend in with its historic surroundings.

Among the indigenous buildings are three built for the Greenman brothers in 1839, '41 and '42, all on the west side of Greenmanville Ave. Similar in style, they are all 2½-story, three-bay Greek Revival homes with ells towards the south. Two have identical, elaborate arcaded Eastlake porches on the front and side. The original iron fence runs along in front of these houses and in front of the museum administration buildings.

The **Edmundson House** (1860), originally the shipyard foreman's home, now houses the **Pugsley Clock Shop.** It is similar in style to those of the Greenman brothers.

Several of the original buildings once part of the textile mill now house exhibits, among them the former power house (1890), now the **Packard Exhibit,** an oblong brick industrial structure; the **Wendell Building** (1890), once a machine shop; a square, three-story mill of Georgian design, now the **Stillman Building** (1865); an 1841 workshop which contains the **Children's Museum;** and a barn of the same vintage which is now the **Nantucket Cooperage.** Greenmanville's original church, too, remains as it was more than a century ago: a solid, Greek Revival clapboard building with a square, two-stage belfry, which was completed in 1851.

Among those buildings moved to the museum from elsewhere in Connecticut and environs, perhaps the most spectacular is the **New York Yacht Club Building** (1845) from Hoboken, NJ, attributed to Andrew Jackson Davis. Its 1½ stories are capped by a gable roof and flared eaves, which are trimmed with a continuous row of drop finials. Its double doors and windows are diamond glazed and surrounded by vertical wood siding. The **New Shoreham Lifesaving Station** from Block Island (1874) is of similar size and proportions in the Stick Style.

Probably the oldest landmark in the museum is the **Buckingham House** from Old Saybrook, CT, a 2½-story Colonial which dates from 1760, in striking contrast to its neighbor, the **Mystic Bank,** a granite two-story Greek Revival building with stone pediments.

Quite dramatic in appearance, and the longest building in the Seaport, is the Plymouth Cordage Company's **Ropewalk,** whose grey, shingled sides and rows of double-tiered windows date from 1824.

All of the buildings, both original landmarks and reconstructions, are connected by streets and walks of cobblestone, paving, and flagstone, and by dirt paths, many of them edged with old anchor chain. In some cases the buildings are arrayed along a street to form a convincing early town, with many homes open for touring. The Seaport's fourteen wharves, piers, and docks are an integral part of the scene, harboring such diverse vessels as a fishing schooner, oyster sloop, Noank smack, and cutter. The entire complex is part of the Mystic Bridge Historic District. NR. Open daily except Christmas Day; Mar-Nov 9-5, Dec-Mar 9-4. Grounds open until 8 from early May-late Sept, with selected exhibits open evenings during July and Aug. $7.50 adults, $3.75 children. Group rates. 536-2631. ♔

New London

The good harbor provided by the Thames River estuary attracted settlers as early as 1646, when John Winthrop, Jr., founded New London on its west bank, and maritime activities played a key role in the community's development from its infancy. Bank St., running along the river, provided a convenient location for warehouses and for the homes of their owners. Shipbuilding and coastal and international trade flourished until the Revolution, when the excellent port facilities made New London a center of military action.

Under Benedict Arnold's direction, much of the city was burned during a raid in 1781, and thus the oldest extant buildings in the port area date from the late 18th century. After the War of 1812, whaling became a key industry, and it was during the second quarter of the 19th century that New London became the country's second largest whaling port (behind New Bedford, MA). The prosperity resulting from the catches of the great fleets made possible the construction of many impressive homes, most in the popular Greek Revival style, a number of which remain today (see Whale Oil Row, following).

New London has not aged altogether gracefully in the intervening years, and parts of the city, as is typical of many once-flourishing ports, have deteriorated badly. Recently, however, great efforts have been made to restore and refurbish many of the historic buildings, and there is much to see that is well-interpreted and proudly offered.

DOWNTOWN NEW LONDON HISTORIC DISTRICT, roughly bounded by Captain's Walk, Bank, Tilley and Washington Sts., late 18th-20th centuries. A variety of architectural styles is represented in the district, and especially along Bank St., whose configuration follows the curve of the river it fronts. Most of its buildings are three or four stories tall, and on both sides of the street the facades are basically continuous. The **Lawrence Hospital Building** (c. 1790) at 60-64 Bank is of red brick with a hip roof. Dating from the same period is the **Bulkeley House** at 109-115, built as a five-bay frame residence, but altered as a store in the 1880s, and the **Gurley House** at 99-107, which has undergone greater alterations, including the addition of a new first floor with two store fronts in the early 20th century. The **New London Customhouse** at 150 Bank was built to serve the city in its heyday as a port (1833), a solid Greek Revival landmark of light and dark gray granite, with massive granite pilasters at its corners, and an imposing flat-roofed entrance portico.

Starr St., whose buildings remain basically free of alterations, is a good example of a modest 19th century neighborhood which owed its existence to the activity of the port. Generally Greek Revival in style, and dating from the 1830s and 40s, the houses along the street once belonged to a whaling agent, captain, doctor, tavern keeper, marble polisher, soap factory worker, plumber, blacksmith, and, later in the century, a railroad clerk and engineer. At the edge of the district, on Captain's Walk (formerly State St.), stands the imposing **New London Railroad Station**, designed in 1886 by Henry Hobson Richardson, a large 2½-story red brick landmark with a hipped roof and graceful central archway. Its main waiting room has a full-height ceiling punctuated by exposed wooden beams.

Further up Captain's Walk is the **Nathan Hale Schoolhouse**, a simple one-room structure where Hale taught prior to enlisting in Washington's Army in July, 1775. Open Memorial Day-Labor Day, M-F 10-3. Free. 443-2861.

Captain's Walk has played a major role in downtown New London's revitalization program. During the late 19th century it became the main thoroughfare of the area,

and the middle two-block section has recently been converted to a cobblestone pedestrian mall as part of the general effort to spruce up the center city.

On Eugene O'Neill Dr., just north of Captain's Walk, are buildings for a bank and a newspaper, the **Savings Bank of New London** and **The New London Day**. The facades of both structures are slightly curved to conform with the curve of the street. The center section of the bank was constructed in 1870, the two wings in 1890, and the entire facade brought to its elaborate rococo appearance in 1905. The simple design of the newspaper building (1906) serves as a wonderful foil.

One of the earliest extant buildings in the downtown district is the **New London County Courthouse** at 70 Hunting St., designed by Issac Fitch in 1784. The Georgian-style frame building, moved from its original site, has served numerous functions, as a hospital for the treatment of yellow fever (1798), site of the Peace Ball following the War of 1812, and as a community meeting place.

FORT TRUMBULL, Fort Neck, 18th-19th century. One of Connecticut's most important defenses during the Revolutionary War, Fort Trumbull fell into disrepair during the early part of the 19th century, although there were troops stationed here during the war of 1812. The construction of the present fort was begun in 1839, and completed in 1850. Within the tall granite walls is a military complex containing many stern granite buildings. Unusual Egyptian detailing can be found at the entrance to Building #32. The oldest extant building on the grounds is a 1790 blockhouse. From 1910-33 the U.S. Coast Guard Academy, now based nearby, was housed here. NR. Operated by the Federal Government. Open occasionally.

JOSHUA HEMPSTEAD HOUSE, 11 Hempstead St., c. 1678. One of the state's oldest dwellings, and one of the few houses in New London that escaped burning by the British in 1781, the 2½-story frame landmark has a very medieval look characterized by its irregular shape and projecting two-story gabled entrance pavilion. The house has a rare, well-documented early history, as Joshua Hempstead's son kept a careful diary from 1711 until his death in 1758. Painstakingly restored in the 1950s by the Antiquarian and Landmarks Society, it is furnished with many of its original pieces and family possessions. NR. Open Tu-Su, 1-5. $1 adults, 25¢ children. 247-8996.

NATHANIEL HEMPSTEAD HOUSE (Huguenot House), corner of Jay, Hempstead, Cort, and Truman Sts., c. 1759. Now completely covered with ivy, the Nathaniel Hempstead house is unusual for its time and place because it is built of stone. Local legend attributes its construction to Huguenots, but records do not substantiate the claim. Its design and construction are similar to those of the Shaw Mansion (see listing following), and therefore it is thought that the same craftsmen may have been responsible for both. Located directly in front of the Joshua Hempstead House, and also operated by the Antiquarian and Landmarks Society, the house has seven of its rooms completely furnished with period pieces. NR. May 15-Oct 15, daily 1-5. 247-8996.

LYMAN-ALLYN MUSEUM, 625 Williams St. Located on the Connecticut College campus, the museum contains an outstanding collection of doll houses, doll furniture, and toys, along with displays of American art, furniture, silver, and costumes. The neighboring **Deshon-Allyn House** at 613 Williams, built by a prominent whaling captain in 1829, is operated by the museum. The sturdy 2½-story

granite residence exhibits both late Federal and early Greek Revival features, most notably the simple frieze beneath the carved cornice. The interior, with a center hall plan and four rooms on each floor, is furnished with many original Federal pieces. Both the house and museum are on the National Register, and the house itself is a National Historic Landmark. Both open Tu-Sa 1-5, Su 2-5. Free. 443-2545.

MONTE CRISTO COTTAGE (EUGENE O'NEILL HOUSE), 325 Pequot Ave., 1888. Considered one of America's outstanding dramatists, Eugene O'Neill spent most of his early summers here and lived at the cottage sporadically between 1911 and 1914. The simple two-story frame house with wrap-around porch was the setting for two of O'Neill's most famous plays, *Ah Wilderness,* and *Long Day's Journey into Night.* NR, NHL. The house is currently being restored, but may be toured by appointment. 443-0051.

SHAW MANSION, 11 Blinman St., c. 1756. An impressive three-story granite dwelling of Georgian design, the Shaw Mansion was built within sight of the harbor by successful sea captain Nathaniel Shaw and now houses the collection of the New London County Historical Society. During the Revolutionary War, Shaw's son was named Marine Agent, and the mansion became Connecticut's Naval Office. As such it welcomed such notables as George Washington, Lafayette, and Nathan Hale for strategy sessions. The current displays include many of the Shaw family's furniture and mementos, along with Revolutionary War artifacts and the balance of the Society's fine collection. NR. Open all year, Tu-Sa 1-4. $1 adults, 50¢ children. 443-1209.

UNITED STATES COAST GUARD ACADEMY, 20th century. The academy was founded in 1876 to provide training for Coast Guard career officers and moved into its present 125-acre facility in the early 1930s, after more than 20 years at Fort Trumbull. The spacious tree-shaded grounds on the banks of the Thames just north of New London proper are open to visitors year-round, and the **U.S. Coast**

Guard Museum is well worth a visit if you want to learn about the service and its predecessors. Ship and airplane models, paintings, and artifacts are on display. You may also tour the training ship, the bark *Eagle,* when she's in port. Open M-F 8-4, Sa-Su 10-4. Free. The Academy itself is open from 9-sunset every day.

WHALE OIL ROW, 105-119 Huntington St., c. 1835-45. Perhaps the best indication of New London's prosperity during the mid-19th century is to be had by a visit to these four imposing Greek Revival buildings which were constructed as private homes by successful entrepreneurs of the time. All four have similar facades, highlighted by two-story porticos with spanking-white fluted Ionic columns. Three of the four have been converted to offices, and the last now houses the **Tale of the Whale Museum,** whose single-minded collection includes everything you'd ever want to know about whales and whaling. NR. Open all year, Tu-Su 1-5 50¢ adults, 25¢ children. 442-8191.

Niantic

LITTLE BOSTON SCHOOL and THOMAS LEE HOUSE, Romagna Ct., 1734 and 1660, respectively. The East Lyme Historical Society operates these two early landmarks. **Lee House** is one of the state's oldest wood frame houses. It is furnished with early English and Colonial pieces, and many of the structural framing details are still visible. The **Little Boston School** was the first district school established in the area between New York and Boston. Its one room was used to conduct classes until 1922. Open Memorial Day-Columbus Day, M, W-Su 10-5. $1 adults, 25¢ children. 739-6070.

Norwich

A busy industrial city at the junction of the Yantic and Shetucket Rivers, which flow into the tidal estuary known as the Thames River, Norwich was founded in the 1600s, and the community developed from a "Nine Mile Square" of land deeded by Uncas, chief of the Mohegan tribe. Because the surrounding lands were rocky and unsuitable for extensive farming, Norwich's early residents turned to trade and shipbuilding for their livelihoods. By 1760 seven Norwich ships plied the route between New England and the West Indies, and by the late 18th century the port area had become the focal point of the business district.

LITTLE PLAIN HISTORIC DISTRICT, a downtown residential area with houses arranged around Little Plain Park and Huntington Place, demonstrates a variety and quality of architecture indicative of Norwich's prosperity during the 18th and 19th centuries. Examples of all major architectural styles popular between 1775 and 1875 cluster around the park and the narrow green of Huntington Place. Specific examples worthy of mention are the Georgian-style **Deacon Jabez Huntington House** at 181 Broadway, the Federal **Hezekiah Perkins** and **Dewitt-Sigourney** houses at 185 and 189 Broadway, and, at 167 Broadway, the stately Greek Revival **Woodhull.** Those who appreciate the Greek Revival style will not want to miss **Slater House,** 352 Main St.,

built in 1827 for John Slater, an early cotton manufacturer. It now houses the Elks

Club. The district also contains a few late 19th- and early 20th-century Shingle Style homes. All are private, but easily seen as you stroll through the neighborhood.

NORWICHTOWN HISTORIC DISTRICT, town green and radiating streets, 17th-20th centuries. The Norwichtown District, northwest of the town proper and its Little Plain District, is the site of the first settlement in the area. The pattern and features of that settlement are still apparent in the great number of early structures remaining. The triangular green is surrounded by closely spaced structures, most of which were built in the 18th century. Several outstanding buildings are the **Joseph Carpenter Silversmith Shop** at 71 E. Town St. (1772), a 1½-story rectangular frame structure with one brick chimney in its southwest corner that was originally intended as a forge; **Dr. Daniel Lathrop's School**, at 69 E. Town (1782), identical in scale, size, and color to the Joseph Carpenter shop next door, but of brick with a wooden belfry on the roof; and the **Bradford-Huntington House** at 16 Huntington Lane, built in several stages from 1691 to 1740. The latter house is L-shaped, and each wing contains a central chimney and a gambrel roof.

None of the preceding landmarks is open to the public, but you can visit the **Leffingwell Inn,** one of the town's oldest and most famous buildings, which uniquely demonstrates the evolution of a simple, sturdy 17th-century style into an affluent mid-18th century town house, with exhibits arranged to give a fascinating picture of the area's development and historical importance. The Leffingwell Inn, at 348 Washington St., was originally a simple frame saltbox home built in 1675 by Stephen Backus, son of one of the original settlers of Norwich. In 1700 the house was sold to Ensign Thomas Leffingwell who was granted a coveted innkeeper's license the following year. In the early 18th century an addition was made to what is now the tavern room by fastening a separate building onto it. That "new" building became what is now the entrance hall and south parlor. Most of the original sash (c. 1720) is intact. The third and last stage of construction (c. 1730-65) resulted in the addition of a kitchen and north parlor. Christopher Leffingwell, who added the later section, was a leading citizen, prosperous industrialist, and ardent patriot. By 1770 he had established the first paper mill in Connecticut, along with many other small industries. His businesses were a dependable source of supply for the Continental Army, and in 1775 he was appointed one of the Committee of Correspondence, reporting to his community

news of the battles of Lexington and Concord. The Tavern Room, with its heavily shuttered windows which afforded privacy, was the scene of many Revolutionary War conferences.

The Inn today has been faithfully and carefully restored, and it contains many pieces which originated in or were associated with early Norwich.

The Tavern Room, contains furnishings dating from the 17th and early 18th centuries, including early pewter and other serving pieces. Proudly displayed is a carved wooden succotash bowl made by the Mohegan Indians over 300 years ago. When Christopher Leffingwell enlarged the Inn about 1760, he added wall paneling in this room, but still visible inside the paneled cupboards are the original 17th-century corner posts, beams, and wainscoting.

The George Washington Parlor, where Leffingwell entertained Washington during April of 1776, is elegantly furnished with Oriental carpeting and Chippendale chairs. A grandfather clock, made by a local clockmaker and silversmith, stands in its original 18th-century position.

The kitchen contains various early implements and utensils assembled around its working fireplace. Also displayed are a sawbuck table and ladder-back chairs, and a cupboard painted with an odd mixture of brick dust and sour milk.

The Great South Parlor, the most formal room in the house, is papered in an elaborate gray and white design copied from an early pattern, and furnished with fine 18th-century pieces, including Queen Anne chairs, a Queen Anne tea table set with valuable export china and Chippendale chairs surrounding it, and a Massachusetts blockfront chest-on-chest. Operated by the Society of the Founders of Norwich. NR. Open late-May and Labor Day-Oct 15, Tu-Su 2-4; June 1-Labor Day, Tu-Su 10-12 and 2-4; Oct 16-May 15, Sa-Su 2-4 and by appointment. $1.50 adults, 50¢ children. 889-9440.

Old Lyme

OLD LYME HISTORIC DISTRICT, Lyme St. from Shore Rd. to Sill La., Old Boston Post Rd. from Sill La. to Rose La., 18th-19th centuries. The heart of this tree-shaded coastal village, steeped in the seafaring tradition, is lined with the graceful old homes of sea captains and their descendants. Settled in about the mid-17th century, Old Lyme became an important shipbuilding center, and the predominantly Colonial, Federal, and Greek Revival homes of its wealthy residents are remarkably unchanged, making the district one of the best in Connecticut for its depiction of early community life.

Samuel Belcher, a noted master builder and architect, designed several of Old Lyme's more memorable buildings, including the **First Congregational Church** on Lyme St., in the second decade of the 19th century. The church was destroyed by fire later in the century, but an exact duplicate was constructed in 1908-9, and it remains today as one of the area's most prominent buildings.

The **Florence Griswold House** at 96 Lyme St. (1817) was also designed by Belcher in the imposing late-Georgian style, with four massive columns across its facade enclosing a grand portico. Bought from its original owner by wealthy sea captain Robert Griswold in 1841, the house remained in his family until well into the 20th century. Griswold's daughter, Florence, transformed the family home into an artist's retreat at the end of the century, and many painters lived in its attic, bedrooms, and parlors, using studios in old barns by the river, and thus making the residence into one of the best known art colonies in the country. The Lyme Historical Society is now headquartered here, and its exhibits are wide-ranging, including as they do fine collections of early furniture, needlework, and paintings, local history, and a superb collection of Victorian toys. The spirit of the art colony remains, both in the numerous oils and watercolors which grace the walls, and in the many landscapes painted directly on door panels and on the dining room walls. Across the mantel the artists painted a caricature of themselves which remains today as an amusing footnote.

Next door to the Griswold House is the

Marvin Huntley House, a traditional center-chimney, one-story home built in Laysville in 1794, and recently moved to its present site. It currently serves as a staff residence and meeting area for the society. NR. Open all year; summer, Tu-Sa 10-5, Su 1-5; winter W-F and Su 1-5. Free. 434-5542.

Stonington

STONINGTON HISTORIC DISTRICT, 18th-19th centuries. The borough of Stonington, privately situated on its own small peninsula, is a well-preserved coastal village of tightly-spaced homes and shops, which since its settlement in 1752 has been closely linked with the sea. Originally a humble fishing village, Stonington became a prosperous maritime center, building and outfitting whaling and sealing ships, and sending out fleets of cod fishermen. Throughout much of the 19th century Stonington was the western terminus for the New York, Providence and Boston Railroad. Passengers en route from Boston to New York connected at Stonington, picking up steamships which carried them on to New York. By the mid-19th century, the small peninsula the borough occupies had developed as a snug community of two-story frame houses, primarily in the Federal and Greek Revival styles, with commercial buildings lining Water St., and the stylish mansions of sea captains and wealthy shipowners along Main St. Little has changed today. In fact, of some 450 buildings within the district, only 63 date from the 20th century. Notable are the **Thomas Ash House** (c. 1780) at 5 Main St., a snug gambrel-roofed cottage; the **Nathaniel Eells House** (1785) at 53 Main St., a two-story house with a handsome entry topped by a molded entablature and leaded transom, and the **Ira H. Palmer House** (1847), a massive Greek Revival landmark with Italianate touches. Among the town's finest and purest examples of the Greek Revival style is the **Peleg Hancox House** (1820), 33 Main St. Built for a wealthy shipfitter, the house features a temple front with four fluted Ionic columns, flat corner pilasters, a wide unadorned frieze, and a simple lunette in the

pediment. The foregoing are private homes, but there are many early buildings housing shops which welcome visitors.

The **Stonington Harbor Lighthouse** at 7 Water St. was built in 1840 and is reputed to be the first Federal lighthouse in Connecticut. This octagonal stone building, with an adjacent 1½-story granite keeper's house, played an important role in Stonington's 19th-century commercial harbor activity. Now a museum displaying early portraits, whaling and fishing gear, and military artifacts, the lighthouse's beacon has been dark since 1889. Operated by the Stonington Historical Society. NR. Open July-Labor Day, Tu-Su 11-4:30. $1 adults, 50¢ children. 535-1440.

WHITEHALL MANSION, CT 26, c. 1720. Moved to its current site and restored by the Stonington Historical Society, this early gambrel-roofed house exhibits paintings, furniture, and furnishings from the 17th and 18th centuries, along with local historic artifacts. Note the rare brick "trimmer arch" on the fireplace. NR. Open May 1-Oct 31, Su-F 2-4 and by appointment. 75¢ adults, 25¢ children. 536-2428.

Uncasville

TANTAQUIDGEON INDIAN MUSEUM, 1819 Norwich-New London Tpk. Reproductions of an early wigwam, long house, and stockade are arranged on the grounds here, displaying the craftmanship of the Mohegan Indians and other early New England tribes. Open May-Oct, daily 10-6. Donations accepted. 848-9145.

Windham Center

WINDHAM CENTER HISTORIC DISTRICT, Bricktop Rd., Windham Center Rd., Plains Rd., The Green, and Weir Ct., 18th-19th centuries. Once the most important and thickly-settled early area of Eastern Connecticut, and the county seat form 1726 until 1820, Windham is a quiet settlement of old homes grouped about a picturesque village green. Among the earliest houses are the **Eliphalet Dyer House** and the **Colonel Jedidiah Elderkin House,** both dating from the first part of the 18th century, which stand side by side on Bricktop Rd. Much more imposing is **St. Paul's Episcopal Church** (1833), a large Gothic Revival structure on Plains Rd.

The **Dr. Chester Hunt Office** on Windham Center Rd. is a Federal-style commercial building constructed on a miniature scale about 1800, and used as an office and dispensary by a local doctor during the middle years of the century. Its original purpose is not known. The two-story frame structure has a gambrel roof and tall, narrow windows with many lights on the ground floor. There is elaborate stencil work on some of the interior plaster, and the only second-story window has Gothic decoration. Operated by the Windham Free Library Association.

Woodstock

HENRY C. BOWEN HOUSE (ROSELAND COTTAGE), CT 169, 1846. Located in the extreme northeastern corner of the state, the most sparsely-populated settlement and perhaps the least accessible, is the small town of Woodstock, surrounded by scenic lakes and small working farms. Facing its shaded, quiet town green is an architectural anomaly for the time and place: one of the most important surviving examples of a Gothic Revival "cottage" in the country. Built for Henry C. Bowen, an influential publisher and founder of *The Independent,* which boasted Henry Ward Beecher as its editor for a time, the mansion and its complementary outbuildings were the site of annual Fourth of July celebrations, at which all successive presidents from Grant to McKinley were guests. Perhaps the most distinguishing feature of the "cottage" is its pink board and batten exterior, with contrasting dark red trim, a tradition established by the original owner and contiued by his descendants, who occupied the premises until the SPNEA acquired the property in 1970.

Roseland's main double parlor still contains the furniture designed for it by the architect Joseph Wells, which repeats in its carved decoration the ornate quatrefoils and arches of the exterior trim. Many of the mansion's other rooms, too, are decorated as they were more than 100 years ago, with massive, ornate furniture and accessories, heavily embossed wallpapers and intricate paneling.

Among the outbuildings is a bowling alley, containing all its original equipment, which was tried out by President Grant during a July 4th gala. Thought to be one of the earliest examples in the country, the bowling alley is attached to the gabled car-

riage house, which has ornamental bargeboards echoing those of the mansion, and the same pink and dark red color scheme. NR. Open June 1-Sept 15, Tu-Su 12-5; Sept 15-Oct 15, F-Su 12-5. $2 adults, $1 children. 928-4074.

Lodging and Dining

THE tradition of warm hospitality in Connecticut's inns is hundreds of years old. Many of its taverns served first as stopping points for wayfarers en route between New York and Boston. Some of the fine inns and restaurants listed below have been in continuous operation for two centuries. The care and ingenuity with which these early buildings have been restored and maintained speak well of the respect for history which is found throughout the state. From a Victorian fieldstone mansion overlooking Long Island Sound to a 225-year-old hostelry in the beautiful northwestern hills, there are accommodations of genuine historic interest to suit every taste and budget. Choice of fare ranges from hearty country meals served family style to the finest in Continental cuisine and, of course, the incomparable fresh seafood to be found all along the New England coast.

Cornwall Bridge

CORNWALL INN, US 7, 06754. (203) 672-6884. Beatrice Dennehy. An early 19th-century colonial-style inn with later addition. Patio overlooking gardens and fields. 8 rooms. Moderate. D, CB, MC, V. ⑪

East Haddam

GELSTON HOUSE RESTAURANT, Goodspeed Landing, 06423. (203) 873-9300 or 873-8257. Ronald Williams & family. Open all year; closed M in Jan & Feb. Originally a 1736 tavern called River Side Inn, the Gelston House was first refurbished in 1826. The Goodspeed Opera House is next door. Lunch and dinner. Moderate. AE, D, MC, V.

Essex

THE GRISWOLD INN, 48 Main St., 06426. (203) 767-0991. William G. Winterer. Open year-round except Christmas Eve and Christmas Day. Opened to serve travelers in 1776, the lovely old Griswold has been in the business ever since. In more than 200 years of continuous operations, the inn has been owned by just five families. Famous for its fine cuisine, the building is furnished with rare antiques, and many prints and mementos grace its charming rooms. 21 rooms. Pets welcome. Public restaurant. Moderate. AE, M, V, PC. ⑪

Glastonbury

BLACKSMITH'S TAVERN, 2300 Main St., 06033. (203) 659-0366. Peter T. Tripp. Open year-round for lunch and dinner. An 18th-century tavern filled with antiques, and overlooking the historic town green. Moderate. AE, D, CB, MC, V.

Greenwich

HOMESTEAD INN, 420 Field Point Rd., 06830. (203) 869-7500. Mrs. Lessie B. Davison & Mrs. Nancy K. Smith. Open year-round for lunch and dinner except major holidays and M. A private residence dating to 1788 with early 20th-century additions. Moderate. AE, D, CB, MC, V.

Guilford

SACHEM COUNTRY HOUSE, Goose Lane, 06437. (203) 453-5261. Mr. and Mrs. N.

Horsandi. Open all year for lunch and dinner except major holidays and M. A private residence dating to 1788; early 20th-century additions. Moderate. AE, D, CB, MC, V.

Hartford

36 LEWIS STREET, 36 Lewis St., 06103. (203) 247-2300. Alan J. Frankey. Open year-round for lunch and dinner. Built as a sea captain's house, c. 1845; recently restored. NR. Moderate. AE, D, MC, V.

Ivoryton

IVORYTON INN, Main St., 06442. (203) 767-0422. Jean & Doug Neumann. Open all year. Parts of this old inn, which began taking in travelers in the early 1800s, date from even earlier. 27 rooms. Moderate. AE, MC, V, PC.

New Preston

HOPKINS INN, Hopkins Rd., 06777. (203) 868-7295. Beth & Franz Schober. Open May-Oct. Parts of the building, which has always been an inn or summer guest house, date from 1789, with additions in 1847 and 1867. 9 rooms. Moderate. PC. ⑪

INN ON LAKE WARAMAUG, Lake Shore Rd., 06777. (203) 868-2168. Richard Bonynge Combs. This 1795 home has been a guest house since 1860. Some of the 25 rooms feature working fireplaces. Expensive. AE, D, MC, V, PC. ⑪

Newtown

NEWTOWN INN, 160 S. Main St., 06470. (203) 426-9351 or 426-2325. Nino De Nicola. Open for lunch and dinner daily. A 1787 colonial inn with low-beamed ceilings and central fireplace. Moderate. PC.

Norfolk

MOUNTAIN VIEW INN, CT 272, 06058. (203) 542-5595. Pamela & Joseph Quirinale. Open all year. An 1875 Victorian country inn which has served as a piano tuning school and a boarding house in the past. 7 rooms. MAP. Expensive. MC, V.

Old Lyme

OLD LYME INN, 85 Lyme St., 06371. (203) 434-2600. Kenneth & Diana Milne. Open year-round except Christmas week. Restored 1850s mansion in Old Lyme's historic district, with a recent addition in keeping with the original. 5 rooms. Pets welcome. Moderate. AE, D, CB, MC, V, PC. ⑪

Old Saybrook

THE CASTLE INN AT CORNFIELD POINT, CT 154, Hartland Dr., 06475. (203) 388-4681. David Garfield. Open all year. Victorian (1900) fieldstone mansion overlooking Long Island Sound. 20 rooms. Moderate.

Redding Ridge

SPINNING WHEEL INN, CT 58, 06876. (203) 938-2511. Bob & Margaret Butler. Open Tu-Su for dinner, year-round; lunch from Mar-Oct. This 1742 structure was originally a toll house on an historic turnpike. Moderate. AE, D, CB, MC, V, PC.

Ridgefield

THE INN AT RIDGEFIELD, 20 West Lane, 06877. (203) 438-8282. Henry H. Prieger. Open daily for lunch and dinner. This 1810 New England colonial, decorated in French country style, has been a restaurant for more than 30 years. Expensive. AE, MC, V.

Salisbury

RAGAMONT INN, Main St., US 44, 06068. (203) 435-2372. Rolf Schenkel. The c. 1830 Ragamont has been an inn since 1853, and has been recently restored. 14 rooms. Moderate. 🍴

WHITE HART INN, Village Green, 06068. (203) 435-2511. W.R. Harris & John Harney. Built as a store and private home in 1800; an inn since 1867. Located in the historic and lovely town center. 20 rooms. Pets welcome. Moderate. AE, D, CB, MC, V, PC. 🍴

Simsbury

CHART HOUSE, 4 Hartford Rd., 06070. (203) 658-1118. Open for dinner year-round except Christmas Day. This former tavern (1786) boasts five working fireplaces and its own resident ghost. Moderate. AE, D, MC, V.

Stafford Springs

CHEZ PIERRE, 179 W. Main St., CT 190, 06076. (203) 684-5826. Pierre E. Courrieur. Open year-round for dinner only. The restaurant is housed in an 1830 home with French country inn decor, and offers fine Continental cuisine. Expensive. AE, MC, V, PC.

West Cornwall

THE DECK RESTAURANT, CT 128, 06796. (203) 672-6765. David Michels. Apr-Oct for lunch and dinner. Former town hall and general store (c. 1820) offers outdoor dining overlooking a waterfall and brook. Moderate. MC, V.

Westport

THE THREE BEARS, CT 33, 333 Wilton Rd., 06880. (203) 227-7219. Stephen C. Vazzano. Open for lunch and dinner except M. and Christmas. Originally a colonial tavern (1799). Offers a large display of antique glass. Moderate. AE, D, CB, MC, V.

Woodbury

CURTIS HOUSE, 506 Main St. S., 06798. (203) 263-2101. Garwin D. Hardisty. Open all year. Reputed to be Connecticut's oldest inn, Curtis House was built c. 1734 and has been an inn since 1754. 18 rooms, including 4 in a former carriage house. Moderate. MC, V. 🍴

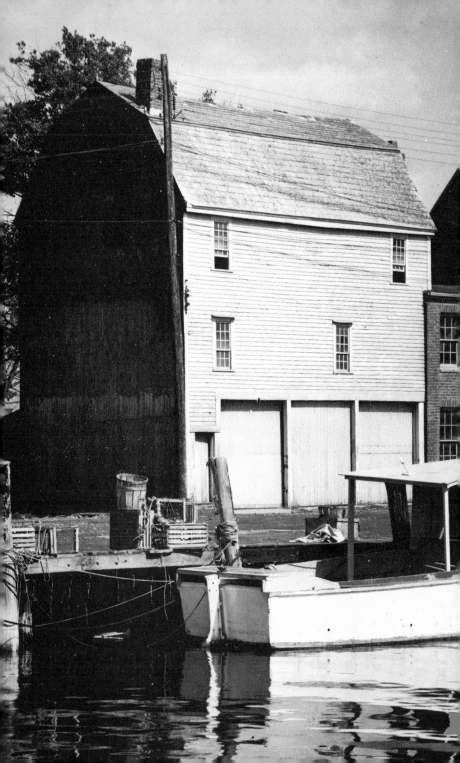

2. RHODE ISLAND

WITH an ultimate length from north to south of only 48 miles and a width of merely 36 miles, Rhode Island and Providence Plantations, as the Ocean State is officially called, is certainly the smallest state in the union and the one with the largest name. The history of "Little Rhody" and the exploits of its citizens, however, loom large indeed. Founded by Roger Williams and a group of independent-minded settlers from Massachusetts in 1639, Rhode Island proved to be the home for feisty individualists who refused to allow their native England to dictate policy or conscience. That spirit of independence and individuality is visible today throughout the state in many forms, from Slater Mill Historic Site in Pawtucket, the birthplace of American industry, to the incredible mansions of Ocean Drive in Newport, where the nation's millionaires came to play in their off hours.

As was the case with other New England seacoast colonies, Rhode Island's early trade depended to a great extent on the skill of its carpenters and shipwrights who supplied the vessels so necessary to whaling, fishing, and international commerce. As the Industrial Revolution made the great sailing ships obsolete, the artistry that had created them did not vanish but was transferred to recreational craft. The Herreshoff Marine Museum in Bristol displays models and artifacts from world-famous yachts, some of which successfully defended the classic America's Cup.

The textile industry which began at the Slater Mill in 1793 soon became vital to Rhode Island's prosperity and development. One of America's oldest mill villages is in Slatersville, near the Massachusetts border, and everywhere in the state one finds examples of the mills, workers' homes, and artifacts associated with the craft. Several Rhode Island antique shops still display old wooden mill spools once used to wind thread; many a visitor has taken home a pair or two to be reincarnated as candle holders.

The atmosphere of religious tolerance engendered by Roger Williams and his followers in the early days made possible the development of communities populated by settlers of various faiths. The two oldest Quaker meeting houses in America are located in Rhode Island—at Newport and Portsmouth. North Kingstown's Old Narragansett Church is among the earliest Episcopal landmarks in the nation, while Newport's Trinity is one of its most beautiful. The first Baptist congregation in the country was begun by Roger Williams in Providence in 1638. Nearby on College Hill are Brown University, chartered in 1764, and the Rhode Island School of Design, more than a century old, which together contribute greatly to the state's reputation for educational excellence.

Because of the relatively small size of Rhode Island, the listings of historic sites that follow are not divided by geographic area. Although it is a relatively simple matter to cross the state by car in an hour or two via Interstates 95 and 295, the traveler for whom time is not pressing should consider leaving the main routes and wandering the back roads instead. For example Route 1 and its offshoot 1A wind along the coast from Westerly eastward, offering scenic vistas of ocean and saltmarsh, and connecting with RI 138 to Newport. Surprises abound throughout the state, from the quaint, colorful carousel at Watch Hill to the inventive sculptures in the topiary gardens at Green Animals in Portsmouth.

Bowen's Wharf, Newport, RI

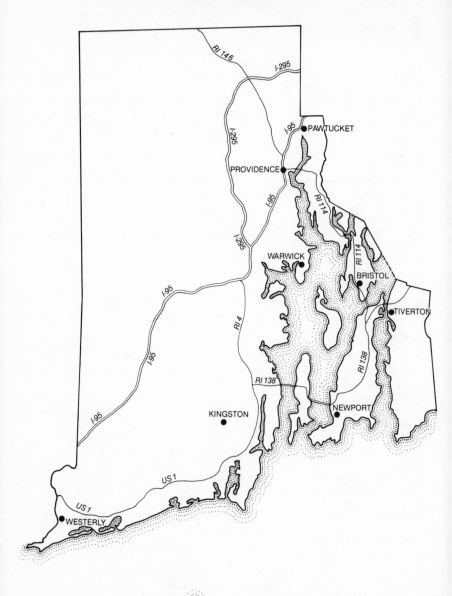

RI 146

I-295

I-95 PAWTUCKET

PROVIDENCE

RI 114

I-295

I-95

RI 114

I-295

WARWICK

BRISTOL

I-95

TIVERTON

RI 4

RI 138

I-95

RI 138

KINGSTON

NEWPORT

US 1

US 1

WESTERLY

BLOCK ISLAND

Block Island

OLD HARBOR HISTORIC DISTRICT, encompasses the town of New Shoreham in the vicinity of the Village Sq., 18th-19th centuries. While Block Island had been settled as early as 1661, it wasn't until the construction of the breakwater on the eastern coast between 1870 and 1876 that the Old Harbor area began to experience a development boom. The government breakwater meant that large steamships could now make the island a stopping place, thus paving the way for the influx of vacationers which would transform this sleepy settlement village into one of the leading coastal resort areas in the U.S. by the late 19th century. Although fire has ravaged many of the district's famous old Victorian hotels, including the grand old Ocean View, several fine structures still remain.

The **Spring House** (1852) was considerably expanded during the early 1870s. Three stories high with a flared mansard roof, cupola, and full-length veranda, it is an excellently preserved example of a Victorian resort hotel on the island.

The **Hotel Manisses**, an 18th-century structure set back from the shore on High St., was rebuilt to its present appearance in 1882 and is considered one of the most finely furnished of the island's hotels. Its main block was just completely restored to Victorian elegance. "Manisses," incidentally, was the name the Narragansett Indians gave to Block Island; it meant "Manitou's Little Island."

The picturesque **Surf Cottage** on Dodge St. dates from 1876 and features an elaborate mansard interrupted by three large Gothic dormers. Also on the corner of Dodge St. and Corn Neck Rd. is the **Woonsocket House,** originally a typical boarding house built in the 1870s, and now owned by the **Block Island Historical Society.** The Society itself is located on the corner of Old Town Rd. and Ocean Ave. A good source of information about the history of the Old Harbor district, it is open mid-June-Sept, M-F. 50¢ adults, 25¢ children. 466-2481.

BLOCK ISLAND NORTH LIGHT, Sandy Point, off N end of Corn Neck Rd., 1867. Built of granite imported from Connecticut and hauled to the site by oxen, the lighthouse was one of four lights which flashed their warning beacons to protect sailors from the treacherous seas along the New England coast. Three previous lights had been rendered useless by gale winds and shifting sands, but the present structure remained in active duty until it was abandoned in 1970. Located on a 28-acre tract of land maintained as a wildlife refuge, it has been saved by an organizaton called the North Light Commission, currently in the process of restoring the original clock mechanism and burner and eventually intending to found a maritime museum on the site. NR.

Bristol

BLITHEWOLD GARDENS AND ARBORETUM, Ferry Rd., 1907. The late-Victorian summer estate of Marjorie Van Wickle Lyon includes 33 acres of beautifully landscaped grounds extending to Bristol Harbor and overlooking Narragansett Bay. The original mansion of 1895 was built for the wealthy coal magnate Augustus Stout Van Wickle and was destroyed by fire. The present 45-room house, though not as elaborate as the estates of Newport, was designed in the style of an English manor by the Boston architects Kilham and Hopkins. Mrs. Lyon bequeathed the entire estate to the Heritage Foundation of Rhode Island in 1976, and today the mansion and gardens are open to the public. The beautiful grounds feature exotic trees and shrubs from Europe and the orient, labeled for the visitor's convenience. A giant sequoia, measuring over 90 feet tall, is a rare and surprising sight on the eastern seaboard. Of course, the breathtaking flower gardens located throughout the grounds are Blithewold's featured attraction. The original landscaping was done by John DeWolf, who designed Prospect Park in Brooklyn, New York. NR. Grounds: Jan-Dec, Tu-Su 10-4; $1.50 adults, 50¢

children. Mansion: May-Oct, Tu-Su 12-4; $1 adults, 50¢ children. 253-8714.

BRISTOL COUNTY JAIL, 48 Court St., 1828. Built of stone ballast from Bristol sailing ships, the 2½-story structure with gabled roof was constructed to replace an earlier frame jailhouse built in 1792 on the same site. Practically devoid of emebellishment, the exterior features material reused from the original structure, including the old red cedar clapboards which were split and used for laths. Today the old jail houses the library and collections of the **Bristol Historical and Preservation Society,** including a children's museum, costumes, Indian artifacts, war relics, and portraits and objects from the 18th and 19th centuries. The Society offers a very complete guide to historic Bristol with several suggested walking tours. NR. Apr-Dec, W 2-5 and by appointment. $2 for library use. 253-8825, 253-5705. ⚓

BRISTOL WATERFRONT HISTORIC DISTRICT, Bristol Harbor to E side of Wood St. as far N as Washington St. and S to Walker Cove, late 17th-20th centuries. Over 400 historic buildings are included in this largely residential district. Bristol's town plan is unique among the state's communities, having originated as a commercial venture with planned community, residential, and commercial spaces. The historic homes in the district reflect Bristol's rise from a colonial seaport to a leading New England maritime center, and none more interestingly than the ten remaining houses designed by one of the state's most brilliant architects, Russell Warren. Warren's work spanned many of the 19th century's most popular styles. Notable are the magnificent **Linden Place** (1810) at 500 Hope St., designed in the Federal style for Gen. George DeWolf; the **Dimond-Gardner House** (1838) at 617 Hope St., one of four great Greek Revival homes which once lined Hope St.; and the **Wyatt House** (1848) at 89 State St., an early Victorian stone mansion with Italianate detailing. Warren, however, was not the only famous architect practicing in town. James Renwick, architect of St. Patrick's Cathedral in New York, designed "**Seven Oaks**"

(1873) for Gov. Augustus O. Bourn on the corner of Walley and Hope Sts.

Of course, not all of the district's noteworthy buildings are residential. The

Bristol County Courthouse on High St. was built in 1817, possibly by Warren, and features a two-stage wooden tower supporting an octagonal belfry. Originally erected as a State House, where sessions of the General Assembly were held from 1819-52, the building has been used since as a courthouse, and the upstairs courtroom is particularly worth a visit.

Bristol's later fame can be attributed to the accomplishments of the Herreshoff Manufacturing Company, designers and builders of numerous "America's Cup" defenders between 1893 and 1934. The **Herreshoff Marine Museum** at 18 Burnside St. exhibits a collection of the company's yachts along with photos and memorabilia of the golden age of yachting. May-Oct, W and Su 1-4. Free. 253-6660.

COGGESHALL FARM MUSEUM, located off RI 114 in Colt State Park. This 18th-century working farm features several original farm buildings enhanced by reconstructions. The Coggeshall farmhouse, an original, though modest, mid-18th-century dwelling, can be found amid a reconstructed blacksmith shop, barn, and pottery shed. Like other living museums of its kind, the complex contains animals, vegetable gardens, orchards, hayfields, and craft demonstrations. Operated by the Coggeshall Farm Museum, Inc. July-Aug, Sa-Su 1-5. $1 adults, 50¢ children. 253-9062.

Chepachet

CHEPACHET VILLAGE HISTORIC DISTRICT, both sides of US 44, 18th-19th centuries. One of the early settled communities in the state, the village continues as the town center for the surrounding Glocester area. All of the historic buildings in the district are of wood frame construction except the **stone mill** (1814), the last remaining vestage of the town's reliance on water power. The district also contains two frame **churches** from the early 1800s and the **Masonic Hall,** used for its original purpose since 1802.

Taverns appear to have served an interesting role in the history of this country town, as they did in other places in old New England. The **Stage-Coach Tavern** (c. 1800) served as the military headquarters for the "Dorr Rebellion," led by a young lawyer, Thomas Wilson Dorr. Dorr had championed more liberal suffrage in the state, and in 1842 planned an armed revolt which never materialized. NR.

Charlestown

HISTORIC VILLAGE OF THE NARRA-GANSETTS, bounded by US 1 on the S and RI 91 on the N, 1790-c. 1930. This is the site of a major village of the Narragansett Indian tribe and includes a simple granite **Indian church** in the Greek Revival style which replaced an earlier wooden structure in 1859. Within the immediate area, the ruins of over 25 houses and their outbuildings are discernible by their dry masonry stone lines and foundations. In the woods about a half-mile NW of the church are the **Child Crying Rocks,** an outcropping where tradition relates the Indian custom of destroying weak infants at birth. Even today as the wind plays through the rocks some imaginative visitors still claim that they hear the wailing of the dying infants. Follow signs to the **Indian Burial**

Ground where a twenty-acre plot marks the burial place of the Narragansetts.

While in the area, take some time to investigate the remains of **Fort Ninigret** on Fort Neck Rd. At the head of Fort Neck Pond stands what's left of a small earthwork fort, probably built by Dutch traders in the first half of the 17th century. Legend suggests that the fort was later held by the Niantic Indians who had been driven from Connecticut by the Pequot tribe. NR. ♟

Coventry

GEN. NATHANAEL GREENE HOME-STEAD, 40 Taft St., 1774. The general designed and built this two-story clapboard dwelling so typical of 18th-century New England farmhouses. Greene was most noted as the commander of the Army of the South during the Revolution, having replaced the famed Gen. Horatio Gates in 1780. He occupied this house until his move to Newport in 1783. NR, NHL. Dec-Feb, W, Sa-Su 2-5 and by appointment. 50¢ donation. 821-8630.

While in the area, visit the **Paine House** (c. 1700), 1 Station St., Washington Village. This former inn is now the museum of the Western Rhode Island Civic Historical Society. Open Apr-Oct, Sa 1-4:30 and by appointment. Donations accepted. 397-7589.

East Greenwich

EAST GREENWICH HISTORIC DISTRICT, roughly bounded by Division, Peirce, and London Sts., Greenwich Cove, and Dark Entry Brook, 17th-19th centuries. Because of the town's protected location along Narragansett Bay, East Greenwich became a prosperous port in the 18th century and by 1750 became the county seat.

The **Armory of the Kentish Guards,** on the corner of Armory and Peirce Sts., stands as a reminder of the town's involvement in the Revolution. While the armory itself is a Greek Revival structure dating to 1842, the volunteer militia unit known as the Kentish Guards proudly traces its organization back to 1774, making it the fifth oldest chartered military company in the United States.

Also notable within the district are the **Col. Micah Whitmarsh House** (1767-71) and the Georgian **Kent County Courthouse** (1803), both located on Main St. Of

especial interest is the **Gen. James Mitchell Varnum House** (1773), 57 Peirce St. The handsome two-story frame clapboard structure was the home of the first colonel of the Kentish Guards. The interior paneling and wallpaper are exceptional. Washington, Lafayette, and Thomas Paine were guests in this fine old Georgian mansion which is currently operated as a private museum featuring period furniture, colonial and Victorian children's playrooms, and an 18th-century garden. NR. June 1-Labor Day, Tu-W, F-Su 1-4. $1 adults, 50¢ children. 884-4312.

NEW ENGLAND WIRELESS & STEAM MUSEUM, Frenchtown and Tillinghast Rds. As a pleasant change of pace, especially for tired dads and cranky children, visit this delightful museum and enjoy its exhibits of early radio, telegraph and telephone equipment, and stationary steam, hot-air, gas, and oil engines. Technology is as much a part of America's history as periwigs and period furniture. Open June-Sept, Su 1-4 and by appointment. $2 adults, 50¢ children. 884-1710.

Foster

FOSTER CENTER HISTORIC DISTRICT, Killingly and Foster Center Rds., 18th-20th centuries. The rural character of this small village off RI 94 is its chief attraction; it has remained largely unchanged for many years and is worth a visit to drink in the simplicity and careful workmanship that define its architectural character. Such pastoral settings are becoming increasingly rare in 20th-century America. The village is small, consisting largely of about a dozen houses on the right of the main road. The most outstanding building in the district is the **Town House** (1796), a large two-story structure with a gabled roof and a small brick chimney. It served as a Baptist church until 1841 and is still actively used as a public meeting place. NR. Tours available by appointment. 397-7771.

Jamestown

JAMESTOWN WINDMILL, North Rd., off RI 138, 1787. Here's an opportunity to observe the workings of an early gristmill. The great cogged wheels still rumble and creak as raw grain is poured down a chute and ground between two huge stones. Introduced by the Dutch settlers of New Amsterdam, these windmills once dotted the Northeast, though few survive. The three-story Jamestown Windmill stands on Conanicut Island and overlooks the east passage of Narragansett Bay; it was restored to operating condition by the Jamestown Historical Society. NR. June-Labor Day, Sa-Su 2-4. Donation requested. ⚐

In the vicinity of the windmill is the **Friends Meeting House** (1786), North Rd. and Weeden Ln., a small place of worship notable for its simplicity and adherence to Quaker architectural principles and completely unchanged for two centuries. Other places of interest in the area include the **Sydney L. Wright Museum,** North Rd. off RI 138, rich in Indian and colonial artifacts (and one of the rare museums with both day and evening hours); the **Beavertail Lighthouse** (1856) at Beavertail Point;

the **Fire Department Memorial Building** on Narragansett Ave., featuring antique fire fighting equipment (Tu-Sa 9-4); and the **Jamestown Museum** on Narragansett Ave., a converted 19th-century schoolhouse with exhibits on the town's old ferry boats (June-July, Tu-Sa 1-4).

Johnston

DAME FARM, Brown Ave. off US 6 in Shake Den State Park. Built around a 1789 farmhouse, this living museum—still in use as a dairy farm—shows how the farm evolved over a period of 150 years. The silos are two of the few left in the state. Also featured are farm and kitchen equipment used from 1870 to 1915. Apr 15-Nov 15, Sa-Su tours at 2, and weekdays by appointment. 949-3082, 934-1548. ♦♦

While in the area visit the **Clemence-Irons House** (c. 1680), 38 George Waterman Rd., a classic 17th-century stone-ender, operated as a museum by the SPNEA. Admission by appointment only. Call (617) 227-3956.

Kingston

KINGSTON VILLAGE HISTORIC DISTRICT, along Kingston, Mooresfield, North, and South Rds., 18th-19th centuries. Originally the site of the hunting and agricultural grounds of the Narragansett Indians, the Kingston area in the 18th century developed a society which was an anomaly in New England, indeed which was more akin to the plantations of the South. With a cultural affinity to Newport, an economy based on slaves, and a freedom from the religious restrictions of the other New England colonies, a wealthy, even flamboyant, life of leisure flourished. While the other Rhode Island towns had been built around ports, basing their economies on the commerce of trade, Kingston was the cultural and professional center of a great agricultural district.

The village was for nearly a century and a half the county seat, and the **Court House** itself (1775) was for fifteen years one of the five state houses of Rhode Island. Besides the Court House, **Records**

Office, and **Jail,** there were taverns and inns, stores, schools, offices, a church and even a stagecoach barn. Unchanged by the Industrial Revolution of the 19th century, this heritage comes down to us today nearly intact. For of the 44 structures within this small village district, fully three quarters predate 1840.

Visitors to Kingston can best acquaint themselves with the town by visiting the **Washington County Jail** (1790), now the headquarters of the Pettaquamscutt Historical Society, whose collections include furnishings and artifacts of the 18th century to the present related to the history of this picturesque village. Open Apr-Dec, Tu, Th, and Sa 1-4 and by appointment. 50¢ adults, 25¢ children. 783-1328.

Fayerweather Craft Center (c. 1830) was the home of village blacksmith George Fayerweather, a black whose descendants continued to run his business for many years. The house is now owned by a craft guild of the same name that sponsors weekly demonstrations of its art during the summer months. Open May-Dec 24, Tu-Sa 11-4. No charge. 789-9072.

Helme House, built in 1802, is now home to the South County Art Association. Open Tu-Su 2-5 during exhibitions (usually the first two weeks of the month). No charge. 783-2195.

Little Compton

WILBOR HOUSE AND BARN, West Main Rd., 17th-19th centuries. This sprawling house, with sections built over three centuries, is the home of the Little Compton Historical Society and features collections of 17th- and 18th-century furniture. The barn contains over 1,000 traditional New England farming items, including tools, utensils, and vehicles. On the grounds is the Little Compton **Friends Meeting House** (1800). Open late June-mid-Sept, Tu-Su 2-5. $1.50 adults, 50¢ children. 635-4559.

Middletown

PRESCOTT FARM, West Main Rd. (RI 114), 1715-1812. This group of restored farm buildings includes Gen. Richard

Prescott's **guardhouse** (c. 1730), now a museum featuring furniture dating from the Pilgrim period; a c. 1715 **country store**, once a ferry master's house; and an 1812 **windmill** in working condition. Gen. Prescott was the commander of the British forces in Rhode Island during the Revolution, but is perhaps best known as the victim of one of the boldest exploits of the war, carried out by a group of 40 colonists on the night of July 9, 1777. Surprised in his sleep, Prescott was hurried away unclothed through a thorny field of blackberry bushes. The general was later exchanged for the American Major-General Charles Lee. Operated by the Newport Restoration Foundation. NR. Mar-Dec, daily 10-5. Jan and Feb by appointment. $1.50 adults, 75¢ children and students. 847-6230.

WHITEHALL, 311 Berkeley Ave., 1729. Dean George Berkeley, Irish patriot, philosopher, and Anglican bishop, landed in Newport in 1729 when his ship bound for Bermuda — where he intended to found a college for the training of missionaries — was blown off course. Berkeley eventually founded a Rhode Island philosophical society which became the basis for the famed Redwood Library in Newport. This two-story house, built shortly after his arrival in Rhode Island, is distinguished by its central chimney, high hipped roof, and long lean-to, all painted in the old Spanish-brown common to dwellings of this period. At one time Whitehall was a public house, run by a Mr. Anthony whose daughter would become the mother of the American painter Gilbert Stuart. In 1899 the Colonial Dames of Rhode Island secured a 999-year lease and began restoration of the building, now

operated as a museum. NR. June and Sept, Sa-Su 2-5; July-Aug, daily 10-5 and by appointment. $1.75 adults, 50¢ children. 846-3790.

Narragansett

THE TOWERS, Ocean Rd., 1883-85. These rock-faced granite towers are the only remaining portions of the famed Narragansett Casino, built by the architectural firm of McKim, Mead, & White. The original rambling wooden casino was once the summer haven for the fashionably rich and provided the Newport Casino across the bay with some healthy competition. The Towers originally served as one of the entrances to a complex of dining, gaming, and guest rooms, and a bridge across the coastal highway to the seashore. Though the casino burned in 1900, the remaining stone towers have become the visual focal point of Narragansett, and one can still drive beneath the massive granite arches. NR.

Newport

Marble House. The Breakers. Hammersmith Farm. These names and others conjure up a vision of late 19th-century Newport as a fabulously wealthy, exclusive summer colony catering to the cream of society, who constructed their opulent summer "cottages" on the cliffs overlooking the Atlantic, competing among themselves to produce the most lavish vacation homes and to entertain there in the most outrageous style. Though Newport's popularity as a summer resort has continued, today the extravagance of that era is largely gone. The mansions, however, remain — a number now open to display the results of fortunes gained during America's post-Civil War economic coming of age.

Newport is also famous as the home of the America's Cup races. Usually run every four years, the superb yachting competition brings together outstanding sailors from every corner of the globe. Australian, French, and British teams often are top contenders for the historic silver trophy which has remained the property of the

United States since it was first won by the yacht *America* more than a century ago.

The notoriety engendered by twelve-meter yachts and elegant mansions can overshadow the humbler, but no less important, beginnings of this lovely harbor town. Settled in 1639 by a small group of families from Boston, Newport, along with Providence, became an early haven to those for whom the tenets of individual liberty and separation of church and state were indisputable. The group welcomed all religions: in the 1650s the first Jewish emigrants arrived from Holland, attracted both by the liberal beliefs of the first settlers and by the protected harbor and productive lands the area afforded.

History notes that the first wharves were constructed within a year of settlement. By 1680 Newport was a bustling center of commerce, with mills, breweries, shipyards, shops, and inns arrayed along its streets. It quickly became one of the principal trading centers of the young colonies and was to remain so until the Revolutionary War, when the British overwhelmed the community. For nearly three years, from 1776 until 1779, they were to retain command, during which time many buildings were destroyed and the population cut nearly in half.

Newporters rallied, however, and in the early 19th century a new period of building and growth began. It was after the Civil War that the wealthy began to be attracted to the area, initiating the construction of the incredible mansions so popular among today's visitors.

It is largely through the efforts of the Preservation Society of Newport and the Newport Historical Society that so much of the town's early history has been preserved or restored. Perhaps nowhere else in the country has there been such a concerted program to ensure architectural and archival permanence. The historic attractions are legion — and span three centuries. Most of Newport is contained within one or another district assigned by the National Register, and many individual buildings are listed as well. In addition, the wharf and Ocean Drive areas have been designated National Historic Landmarks. The **Preservation Society of Newport,**

whose main offices are located at 118 Mill St. (847-1000) administers many of the most historic sites and has available a broad selection of material explaining their significance. The Society offers special combination tickets at discounted rates to many of its buildings. The **Newport County Chamber of Commerce,** 10 America's Cup Ave., is open daily throughout the year and offers advice on attractions and tours by bus and boat. 847-1600.

For the convenience of the reader of this book, Newport has been divided into two arbitrary districts: the downtown or wharf area (see detail map), much of which is accessible on foot; and the southern peninsula, featuring famed Ocean Drive and outer Bellevue Avenue, where transportation is advisable.

As is the case with so many of New England's most popular resorts, Newport has a tendency to become somewhat overcrowded during the summer months. Those desiring a quieter visit might plan an off-season vacation.

DOWNTOWN NEWPORT. To limit one's tour of Newport to just the mansions along Ocean Drive is to bypass 200 years of history. The prosperity which the town enjoyed in its early years is reflected in the many Georgian buildings which dominate its heart. Much of the design for these early landmarks can be attributed to master carpenter Richard Munday or noted colonial architect Peter Harrison. Their buildings rank among the most advanced and sophisticated of any erected in the colonies. Newport's unique character is not dependent upon the residences of its wealthy merchants alone, however: it can be seen in the modest shops and houses which dot the old sections of the community.

The Art Association of Newport, 76 Bellevue Ave. A small, choice art collection is housed in **Swanhurst,** an elegant Stick Style residence designed by Richard Morris Hunt in 1851. Open all year, Tu-Sa 10-5, Su 2-5. No charge. 847-0179.

Artillery Company of Newport Museum, 23 Clarke St., 1835. While this two-story Greek Revival building is a mere 150 years

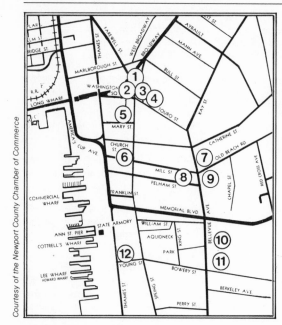

Newport (detail)

1. Hazard House
2. Old Colony House
3. Touro Synagogue
4. Historical Society
5. Artillery Company Museum
6. Trinity Church
7. Redwood Library
8. Mystery Tower (Old Stone Mill)
9. Art Association and Gallery
10. Tennis Hall of Fame
11. Newport Automobile Museum
12. Samuel Whitehorne House

Courtesy of the Newport County Chamber of Commerce

old, the company which it sheltered was chartered in 1741, making it the oldest active military organization in the country. The museum features over 100 foreign military pieces and a substantial collection of American and foreign uniforms. Open Apr-Sept, Tu-Su 10-3:30; Sept-Mar, Sa 1-3:30 and by appointment. Donations accepted. 846-8488. 🕴

Brick Market, Long Wharf and Thames St., 1762-72. Designed by Peter Harrison, who already had to his credit Newport's Redwood Library, Boston's King's Chapel, and Christ Church in Cambridge, Brick Market was constructed as a trading center and granary. Originally its ground floor was an open arcade, and the upper floors contained shops and offices. It was later used as a town hall and theater. Rotating exhibits now feature artifacts and collectibles. NR, NHL. Open Apr-May 20, daily 10-6; May 21-Dec 30, M-Sa 10-9, Su 10-6. No charge. 849-3441.

Friends Meeting House, Marlborough and Farewell Sts., 1699. This and the Portsmouth Meeting are considered to be the two oldest such buildings in the country.

Restored and enlarged in the 18th and 19th centuries, the Friends Meeting House is a superb example of Colonial architecture and construction. NR. Open early June-Labor Day, M-Sa 10-5 and by appointment. $1 adults, 50¢ children. Group rates. 846-0813.

The International Tennis Hall of Fame (Newport Casino), 194 Bellevue Ave., c. 1880. The architectural firm of McKim, Mead and White designed the Newport Casino in their now-famous Shingle Style during Newport's heyday as a summer resort. Stores and restaurants, separated by brick piers, were located on the ground floor, with clubrooms above. It was just over 100 years ago that this landmark was the site of the first National Lawn Tennis championships, which were held here until moved to Forest Hills in 1915. Exhibits include a Davis Cup room, a collection of tennis art, halls resplendent with trophies and tennis memorabilia, and special displays relating to the history and manufacture of tennis equipment. In addition, the Casino's twelve beautifully-tended grass courts are the only ones in the country accessible to the general public. NR. Open May-Oct, daily 10-5; Nov-Apr daily 11-4. $3 adults, $2 children. Group rates. 846-4567.

Edward King House, Aquidneck Park (Spring St.), 1845-47. One of the earliest summer homes in Newport was designed by Richard Upjohn in the sytle of an Italian villa, representing a notable break with the more symmetrical houses popular during the period. Its smooth red-brick walls convey a feeling of weight and mass, while variations in roof height create a fancifully irregular form. The interior decoration is plain and heavy, with floors of inlaid wood. Built for Edward King, who made his fortune in the China trade, this landmark was a refreshing early attempt to create a picturesque, whimsical summer home in the days before Newport's architects strove to outdo each other with monumental reproductions of European castles and palaces. NR, NHL. The villa currently houses a Senior Citizens' Center. Visitors are welcome all year, M-F 9-4. No charge. 846-7246.

Naval War College Museum, Coasters Harbor Island, 1819. Founders Hall, the original site of the Naval War College, now houses art, manuscripts, artifacts and prints describing the history of naval warfare, with specific emphasis on the operation of the Navy in the Narragansett Bay region. NR, NHL. Open Jan-May, M-F 9-4; June-Aug M-F 9-4, Sa, Su 12-4; Sept M-F 9-4, Sa 12-4. No charge. 841-4052.

Newport Automobile Museum, Casino Terrace at Bellevue Ave. The largest collection of antique and classic automobiles, gas engines, and brasses in New England is housed here. Open all year, daily 10-7 (winter, 10-5). $3 adults, $2 children. Group rates. 846-6688. 🏢

Old Colony House (Old State House), Washington Sq., 1739. Certainly one of the most distinguished public buildings dating from the Colonial period, this gracious 2½-story structure, designed by Richard Munday, represents one of the earliest applications of brick in the city. The facade is accented by a double-doored entrance topped by a second floor balcony

from which the Declaration of Independence was first read on July 20, 1776. Although the building was erected to house the deliberations of the General Assembly, it has been used for public meetings, religious and social functions throughout its long history. Both the British and French used it as a hospital during the Revolution, and General Washington was welcomed here by the French General, Count de Rochambeau. The first floor interior is handsomely designed with great paned windows, wide sills, and broad window seats. NR, NHL. Open all year, July-Sept 6, daily 9:30-12 and 1-4; Sept 7-June, M-F 9:30-12, 1-4. Guided tours available. No charge. 846-2980.

Old Stone Mill, Touro Park, c. 1673. It is fun to speculate, as locals have for over a century, that this stone ruin might be the remains of a Norse church built nearly seven centuries ago. The general consensus, however, still favors the traditional claim that Governor Benedict Arnold was responsible for building the round arcaded structure—probably to serve as a windmill. Regardless of the tower's origin, the masonry of the mill suggests strong ties with the early "stone-ender" homes which are the hallmark of Rhode Island's early building heritage. Open all year. No charge. 846-9600.

Redwood Library, 50 Bellevue Ave., 1748. The nucleus of this fine library's collection can be traced to a generous contribution by Abraham Redwood in 1747. Designed by Peter Harrison, the building features a Greek temple portico whose classical feeling probably antedates Jefferson's influence in the colonies. The library, one of the oldes in continuous operation in the United States, features a large group of early paintings in addition to its rare book collections. A charming park surrounds the building. NR, NHL. Open all year, M-Sa 10-6 (Aug, 10-5). No charge. 847-0292.

Seventh Day Baptist Church, 82 Touro St., c. 1729. By 1729 the first meeting place of the Sabbatarians, about a mile north of Newport proper, had outgrown its usefulness. The small two-story clapboard building which took its place on Barney Street was moved to its present location in the early 20th century. The church features the typical meeting house plan of its period, with the door on the long side and the pulpit opposite. The interior detailing is particularly reminiscent of Newport's Trinity Church, although the twisted balusters of the pulpit stairway were not a usual feature, but one which would reappear in many of the town's colonial houses. Original furnishings abound, including the fine clock made by William Claggett in 1731 which still occupies a prominent position on the gallery opposite the pulpit.

Operated by the Newport Historical Society, whose newer museum building stands adjacent and houses collections of glass, silver, pewter, and documents relating to local history. Open all year, Tu-F 9:30-4:30, Sa 9:30-12 (Sa 9:30-4:30 in summer). Donations accepted. 846-0813.

Touro Synagogue, 85 Touro St., 1763. By the mid-18th century, the combined Newport community of Sephardim and Ashkenazim Jews from Europe was in desperate need of a place to worship. When sufficient funds were raised, architect Peter Harrison was commissioned to design this Georgian masterpiece, which stands today as a monument to Rhode Island's promise of religious tolerance.

Harrison's design was necessarily, to accommodate the Sephardic rituals, a slight modification of the traditional Georgian style. The synagogue, inconspicuously located on a quiet street, stands diagonally on its small plot so that worshippers face eastward towards Jerusalem. The austere brick exterior gives little indication of the richness to be found within. Twelve Ionic columns, representing the tribes of ancient Israel, support a gallery, with five massive brass candelabra hanging from the ceiling. NR, NHS. Guides of the Society of Friends of Touro Synagogue are available to lead tours during visiting hours. Open late June-Labor Day, M-F 10-5, Su 10-6; Su 2-4 and by appointment the rest of the year. No charge. 847-4794. A short walk up Touro Street is the old burial ground, where many famous members of Newport's Jewish community were laid to rest.

Trinity Church, Spring and Church Sts.,

1725-26. This Georgian frame church built under the direction of Richard Munday is one of the finest examples of colonial religious architecture in the country. The wooden steeple, composed of a square tower, arcaded belfry, lantern, and slender spire, is modeled closely after the Old North Church in Boston. The interior features box pews and the only three-tiered wine-glass pulpit remaining in America. The organ is thought to have been tested by Handel before it was sent from England. The church presently serves an active Episcopal congregation. NR, NHL. Open summer daily, 10-4; M-F afternoons by appointment the rest of the year. Donations accepted. 846-0660.

Wanton-Lyman-Hazard House, 17 Broadway, c. 1695. The oldest restored house in Newport illustrates the transition from 17th to 18th-century styling. While its simple frame construction recalls early New England architecture, the sophisticated ornamentation heralds the more urbane Georgian style which followed. The dwelling was once owned by Richard Ward, who became Governor of the Rhode Island colony in 1740. It was damaged during the 1765 Stamp Act riots, and its Tory owner was forced to flee aboard the British sloop of war *Cygnet*. Shortly thereafter John Wanton purchased the house at public auction. His daughter, Polly, was well known among the French officers of the day—a window pane from the house bears the inscription "charming Polly Wanton," no doubt a remnant of a romantic rendezvous. NR, NHL. Operated by the Newport Historical Society, the house also features a tidy colonial garden and exhibitions of 18th-century cookery. Open June-Labor Day, M-Sa 10:30-5. $1.50 adults. Group rates. 846-0813.

Samuel Whitehorne House, 414 Thames St., c. 1800. This three-story Federal home was built for Samuel Whitehorne, a prosperous Newport merchant. Its location, facing the harbor and waterfront businesses, is typical of high-style residences of the day. Housed within are exquisite examples of furniture, silver, and pewter fashioned by early Newport artisans. NR. Open Apr-Nov, daily 10-5; Dec-Mar by appointment. $2 adults, $1 children. 847-2448.

THE SOUTHERN PENINSULA. To the south of the town of Newport itself are the residential areas made famous by the cream of 19th-century American society, whose sprawling mansions and occasionally modest homes were built here between 1830 and the early 1900s. The genteel character of these neighborhoods, with wide streets, well-kept lawns, and old shade trees, sets them apart from Newport's other summer attractions. Scientists and professors, authors, physicians, businessmen, and artists were attracted by the ocean views and tranquil setting, making it the center of the community's Gilded Age.

The most spectacular mansions are lined up along the eastern peninsula facing the ocean. You may drive along Ocean Drive and other boulevards for a front view of these splendors, or stroll along **Cliff Walk**, a footpath which begins at Memorial Boulevard and winds along the crest of the cliffs, with the pounding surf below and the gardens and spacious lawns of the estates to the west. Originally a fisherman's trail, the walk was once the center of a court battle between the estate owners and the public. When the owners erected barriers to obstruct the viewing of their properties, natives of the town objected—and won back their right to an unobstructed path around the island. The spectacular views along Cliff Walk have become an integral part of any visit to Newport. NR. Among the many landmarks are the following:

Beechwood Museum, Bellevue Ave., 1855. The summer home of Mr. and Mrs. John Jacob Astor was a focal point for lavish entertaining, although it is not as sumptuous as some of Newport's other famous oceanside dwellings. Today, in Beechwood's library, guests are treated to an audiovisual presentation which shows American society from pre-Revolutionary times until the 20th century. NR, NHL. Operated by the Beechwood Foundation. Open all year, daily 9:30-7. $4.50 adults. 846-3774.

Belcourt Castle, Bellevue Ave., 1891. The visitor entering this large estate is im-

mediately reminded of the palaces of Europe. Richard Morris Hunt, the architect, employed the finest craftsmen and artists from the Continent and spent nearly three-million (19th-century) dollars to fashion a masterpiece in the style of Louis XIII's palace in France. Each room is decorated in a different period of French, English, or Italian design. The Grand Stair is an authentic reproduction of one found in the Musée de Cluny in Paris, and was carved completely by hand. The largest private collection of stained glass in America is housed within, as well as the Harold B. Tinney Family collection of antique furnishings, including paintings, rugs, and furniture and highlighted by an extensive armor collection. The Royal Arts Foundation exhibits its exquisite collection of French furniture and silver here—and a gold coronation coach weighing four tons. NR, NHL. Open Apr-Dec, daily 10-5. $3 adults, $2 students, $1.25 childen. 846-0669.

The Breakers, Ochre Point Ave., 1895. Cornelius Vanderbilt hired Richard Mor-

ris Hunt to create this magnificent estate modeled after northern Italian Renaissance palaces. The interior is richly decorated, much of it with mosaics and carved stone, alabaster and marble. The Grand Salon was designed in France and reassembled on the site; and the variety of materials and colors present in the dining room offers the ultimate in wealth and extravagance. A child's playhouse, lavish in its own miniature scale, is open on the grounds. NR, NHL. Operated by the Preservation Society of Newport County. Open Apr-Oct, daily 10-5; W and Su until 8 from July-Sept. $3.50 adults, $1.25 children. Group rates and combination tickets available. 847-1000.

Chateau-Sur-Mer, Bellevue Ave., 1852. Originally built for William S. Wetmore, this three-story granite Victorian mansion remained in the Wetmore family until the 1960s. The original structure, designed by Seth Bradford, was extensively remodeled in the early 1870s by Richard Morris Hunt, who added a mansard roof and opened the main hall through all three

stories. A large stained-glass window designed by John La Farge lights the main stairwell. The carved walnut ceilings and woodwork of the library and dining room are particularly ornate and elegant. Maintained by the Preservation Society of Newport County. NR, NHL. Open May-Oct, daily 10-5; July-mid-Sept, F until 8; Nov-Apr, Sa and Su 10-4. $3 adults, $1.25 children. Group rates and combination tickets available. 847-1000.

The Elms, Bellevue Ave., 1901. Imagine a French chateau built by a famous Philadelphia architect for a wealthy coal magnate; only in Newport would such circumstances fail to raise an eyebrow. Commissioned by Edwin J. Berwind, Horace Trumbauer modeled this elaborate limestone rectangle after the Chateau d'Asnieres near Paris. The ornate statuary, consoles, and cartouches surrounding the window and door openings are neo-classical, but the effect is French throughout—from the interior decor to the informal sunken garden. Maintained by The Preservation Society of Newport County. NR, NHL. Open May-Oct, daily 10-5; July-mid-Sept, Sa until 8; Nov-Apr, Sa and Su 10-4. $3 adults, $1.25 children. Group rates and combination tickets available. 847-1000.

Fort Adams State Park, Harrison Ave., 1824. In 1799 Major Louis Toussard dedicated the first permanent fortification on this site to John Adams. Originally constructed to protect the entrance to Narragansett Bay, the fort became one of the largest seacoast fortifications in the country. Its longevity provides a visual chronicle of American military history from the early 18th century to the end of World War II. Found to be inadequate defense during the War of 1812, Fort Adams was rebuilt in 1857, with walls of granite shipped by schooner from Maine, along with shale and brick quarried locally. NR, NHL. The park is open all year, 6-11, but entrance to the fortification is by guided tour only. Tours leave the jail every fifteen minutes from 11:30-4:30 W-Su during the summer. Modest admission fee.

A reproduction of the sloop-of-war **Providence,** the first authorized ship of the Continental Navy, is moored here. The original 12-gun, 65-foot ship was the first command of John Paul Jones. Open May-Sept, daily. 846-1776. 🚶

Hammersmith Farm, Harrison Ave. (Ocean Dr.), 1887. John W. Auchincloss built this 28-room Shingle-Style cottage in which four generations of his family have spent their summers. The 50 rolling acres surrounding the house were first farmed in 1640 by William Brenton and today remain the only working farm in Newport. Hammersmith was the setting for Jacqueline Bouvier's debut and the reception after her wedding to Senator John F. Kennedy. The house and grounds, including the formal gardens designed by Frederick Law Olmstead, are open for guided tours. NR, NHL. Mar and Nov, Sa, Su; Apr-May 25 and Sept 2-Oct, daily 10-5; Me-

Newport   *Courtesy of the Newport County Chamber of Commerce*

1. Hunter House
2. Kingscote
3. The Elms
4. Continental sloop Providence
5. Fort Adams State Park
6. Hammersmith Farm

7. Chateau-sur-Mer
8. The Breakers
9. Rosecliff
10. Beechwood Museum
11. Marble House
12. Belcourt Castle

morial Day-Labor Day, daily 10-8. $3 adults, $1.50 children. Group rates. 846-7346.

Hunter House, 54 Washington St., 1748. This simple frame house was originally constructed for Deputy Governor Jonathan Nichols and is known to have passed to one of his successors, Joseph Wanton, Jr., a Loyalist who fled to New York during the Revolution. In the summer of 1780, Admiral Chevalier de Ternay of the

French navy made his headquarters here. The sophisticated interior features a special grouping of Townsend-Goddard furniture, silver, and period portraits. Operated by the Preservation Society of Newport County. NR, NHL. Open May-Oct, daily 10-5 and by appointment. $3 adults, $1.25 children. Group rates and combination tickets available. 847-1000 or 847-7516.

Kingscote, Bellevue Ave. and Bowery St.,

Hunter House

1839. Generally acknowledged as the nation's first summer "cottage," this irregular frame residence was designed by Richard Upjohn for George Noble Jones of Savannah, Georgia. It features a celebrated dining room added by McKim, Mead and White in 1881, complete with Tiffany glass wall and cork ceiling. There are fine exhibits of Townsend-Goddard furniture and Chinese export porcelain. Operated by the Preservation Society of Newport County. NR, NHL. Open May-Oct, daily 10-5; July-mid-Sept, Th until 8. $3 adults, $1.25 children. Group rates and combination tickets available. 847-1000.

Rosecliff, Bellevue Ave., 1902. Dazzling, but still the least intimidating of the extravagant Newport mansions, Rosecliff was built for Herman Oelrichs by McKim, Mead and White. The exterior facing is of polished white terra cotta, with the overall design modeled after the Grand Trianon at Versaille. The bright, airy ballroom—the largest in the area—forms the "bar" of this cottage's unique H-shaped plan, an arrangement which affords spectacular views of the coastine from almost any window. Operated by the Preservation Society of Newport County. NR, NHL. Open Apr-Oct, daily 10-5; July-mid-Sept, M until 8. $3 adults, $1.25 children. Group rates and combination tickets available. 847-1000.

Marble House, Bellevue Ave., 1888. The most orante of Richard Morris Hunt's designs of the late 19th century, this mansion, faced with white Vermont marble, was commissioned by William K. Vanderbilt. The stately main entrance features a projecting portico supported by four Corinthian columns. The interior design is dazzling: walls and ceilings of marble, crystal, and gold; a master bedroom suite of carved black walnut with padded silk walls; priceless furnishings. The **Harold S. Vanderbilt Memorial Room** features yachting trophies and memorabilia.

On the grounds is the **Chinese Tea**

Rosecliff

House, a romanticized American version of an Oriental pavilion, built in 1913 for Mrs. Vanderbilt. Operated by the Preservation Society of Newport County. NR, NHL. Open Apr-Oct, daily 10-5. $3.50 adults, $1.25 children. Group rates and combination tickets available. 847-1000.

North Kingstown

WICKFORD HISTORIC DISTRICT, roughly bounded by Tower Hill and Post Rds., N. to Mill Cove and S. to Lindley Ave., 18th-20th centuries. The small harbor village of Wickford, now part of North Kingstown, began in the 1640s with the establishment of a trading post by Richard Smith, an associate of Roger Williams.

In addition to farming, the early settlers became active in milling, shipbuilding, trading, banking, and finally tourism, but Wickford manages to maintain its village atmosphere. Throughout the district are a variety of 18th- and 19th-century residential, public, and waterfront structures; common among these are two-story five-room 18th-century dwellings, each with a central chimney; small clapboard houses with hooded center entrances; and later, more elaborate, Victorian vacation homes. Among the most interesting buildings are:

Old Narragansett Church (St. Paul's Episcopal Church), 60 Church Ln., 1707.

A simple 2½-story frame meeting house with rounded arched windows and a gabled roof, this landmark was moved to its current site in 1800. The interior features box pews, a wine glass pulpit, and a gallery. Queen Anne communion silver is on display. NR. Open July and Aug, F, Sa 2-4 and by appointment. No charge. 294-9331 or 294-4357.

Built to replace the Old Narragansett Church in 1847 was **St. Paul's Church** at 76 Main St., designed in the Romanesque Revival style by Rhode Island architect Thomas A. Tefft. A frame structure, it is graced by a three-story clock tower with an open, arcaded belfry and spire. The front entrance is recessed in a round, arched opening, which is repeated in the round arched windows of the side walls. NR. Open for Sunday services.

The house on Pleasant St. built by Lodowick Updike's grandson, John, in 1745 is typical of Wickford's early building period. A wooden two-story center chimney house with a gable-on-hip roof, it relates to many important pre-1750 Newport houses. More typical of the plainer early homes is the **Cyrus Northrop** house at 90 Main St., built in 1803. The excellent pedimented fanlight doorway is indicative of the more sophisticated carpentry of the 19th century. NR. Both houses are privately owned, but may be seen from the road.

North Kingstown vicinity

SMITH'S CASTLE, 1½ miles north of Wickford on US 1, 1678. This frame and clapboard 2½-story residence was built to replace Richard Smith's original trading post, on the same site, which was burned during King Philip's War. The L-shaped center-chimney landmark became a social and political center during the 18th century. It is believed to be the only extant building in which Roger Williams stayed, and from which he preached to the Indians. The restored house contains a large doll collection, and an 18th-century garden has been reconstructed on the grounds. NR. Open Apr 15-Nov 1, M-W, F, Sa 10-5, Su 1-5. $1 adults, 50¢ children. 249-3521.

SOUTH COUNTY MUSEUM, Quaker Ln. and Stony Ln. (off RI 2). Exhibits concentrate on early Rhode Island rural life and industry, with displays of tools, farming implements, utensils, appliances, and mechanical devices. Open summer, W-M 11-5; fall Sa-Su 11-5; $1 adults, 50¢ children. 295-0498.

Pawtucket

CHILDREN'S MUSEUM OF RHODE ISLAND, 58 Walcott St. Housed in the mid-19th century **Pitcher-Goff Mansion,** the museum's exhibits are specially arranged to appeal to children under twelve. Exhibit areas include the Mini Fire House, Grandmother's Kitchen, Quiet Room, and Ocean Room, all incorporating a "hands-on" approach. Open all year (except the first two weeks in Sept), Tu, Th, Sa, Su 1-5. $1 per person, maximum $4 per family. 726-2590.

SLATER MEMORIAL PARK, Armistice Blvd., US 1-A. The oldest and largest park in the city of Pawtucket, Slater Park covers 197 acres. The bulk of the land, formerly known as Daggett farm, was purchased by the city in 1894, with the acquisition of two extra parcels in the early 20th century. Miles of paths meander through the park and around its three ponds, leading to a wide variety of attractions with appeal for all ages and interests. There are formal gardens and fountains designed by John C. Olmstead (nephew of Frederick Law Olmstead); an early 20th-century carousel housed in a quaint 10-sided wooden building; a sunken garden; a small zoo; and a neo-classical domed bandstand.

The most significant historic attraction is **Daggett House,** a 2½-story plank-walled farmhouse built in 1685, with 18th- and 19th-century additions. The house is thought to have consisted originally of two rooms with a central fireplace and chimney. Administered by the Pawtucket Chapter of the DAR, it has been furnished with antiques, including colonial pewter, early china, and household tools. NR. The house is open during July and Aug, Su 2-5 and by appointment. 75¢ adults, 25¢ children. 434-8195, or

722-2631. Slater Memorial Park is open year-round, daily 7:30 a.m.-10 p.m.; the zoo 8-4. No charge.

SLATER MILL HISTORIC SITE, Roosevelt Ave., 1793. Here, in the late 18th century, Samuel Slater founded the cotton textile manufcturing industry in the United States. While serving as an apprentice in a mill in England, Slater had committed to memory the plan of such an establishment, which he transferred to his new home in America. He is credited with introducing to this country not only the textile industry, but also the factory system of manufacturing.

Located on the Blackstone River, the Slater Mill Historic Site includes the original mill, the 1810 **Wilkinson Mill,** the 1758 **Sylvanus Brown House** (owned by a skilled millwright and carpenter who worked at the mills), the Slater Mill **dam and power canal,** and over two acres of riverfront park. The site's buildings and exhibits explore the transition of American manufacturing from handcraft to machine production, interpreting the history of the industry and living conditions surrounding it. NR, NHL. Open June 1-Sept 5, Tu-Sa 10-5, Su 1-5; March 1-May 31 and Sept 6-Dec 22, Sa, Su 1-5 and weekday appointments for groups only. $2 adults, 75¢ children, group rates. 725-8638.

Portsmouth

GREEN ANIMALS TOPIARY GARDENS, Cory's Ln. off RI 114. Spacious grounds are the setting for 80 sculptured trees and shrubs shaped in animal forms.

Espaliered fruit trees, rose arbors, and formal flower beds afford riotous color during the summer months. In addition to being delighted by the giraffes, elephants, lions, and other animal shapes in the gardens, children will want to see the **Victorian Toy Museum** on the grounds. Open May 1-Sept 30, daily 10-5; Sa, Su and holidays in Oct. $2.50 adults, $1.25 children. Operated by The Preservation Society of Newport County. 847-1000.

PORTSMOUTH FRIENDS MEETING HOUSE, PARSONAGE, AND CEMETERY, 11 Middle Rd., c. 1700. This plain two-story shingled frame building sits near the crest of Quaker Hill, from which there are impressive views across the rolling fields of still partially-rural Portsmouth. Behing the meeting house is the **cemetery**, which has occupied the same site since about 1706, although its earliest extant markers date from the 1830s. North of both stands the **parsonage**, built in 1891 when the meeting hired its first pastor.

The Portsmouth meeting house was one of the first such Quaker buildings in the American colonies; it and the meeting house at Newport, built at the same time, are the oldest ones in existence today and the oldest religious structures in Rhode Island. NR. Open for Sunday meeting.

PORTSMOUTH HISTORICAL SOCIETY, 807 E. Main Rd. The former **Christian Sabbath Society Meeting House** (1865) houses the Society's collection of early household articles, farm implements, furnishings and, toys. Julia Ward Howe, author of "The Battle Hymn of the Republic," is known to have preached here. A monument on the grounds marks the site of the Battle of Rhode Island on August 29, 1778.

The Historical Society also maintains the nearby **Old School House** (c. 1716), one of the oldest in the nation. On display are antique school desks, school bells, and a variety of early textbooks. Both the museum and school are open Memorial Day-Labor Day, Sa, Su 2-5 and by appointment. Donations accepted. 683-3858.

Providence

The colony of Rhode Island and Providence Plantations was founded in 1636 by Roger Williams, a young English minister whose opposition to his established, tradition-bound church resulted in his emigration to the colonies in 1631. He first settled in Boston, where he was originally welcomed as a "goodly minister," but his firm — and for the times, radical — belief in freedom of conscience went against the strict Puritan ethic, and he was banished several years later.

The site for Rhode Island's future capital was selected, after one false start nearby, in order that Williams and his followers could establish a community totally outside the jurisdiction of the Bay Colony and Plymouth where his guiding principle, that "no man should be molested for his conscience," could form the basis of an experimental community in which settlers of all faiths and political backgrounds would be welcome.

By 1643, settlements based on Williams's tenets existed in Newport, Portsmouth, and Warwick as well. Faced with internal squabbles and external threats from other colonies, particularly Massachusetts Bay and Connecticut, Williams sailed for England to obtain a patent for the area and, with the help of influential allies in Parliament, was granted a charter for the Providence Plantations in Narragansett Bay. The charter assured the new colony of Rhode Island independence "conformable to the laws of England" and liberty of conscience. Twenty years later efforts were made to rescind the document, and Williams, with John Clarke of Newport, returned to England once more, where King Charles II was persuaded to grant Rhode Island a favorable new charter "to hold forth a lively experiment that a most flourishing civil state may stand and best be maintained with full liberty of religious concernments."

It is against this historic background that Providence should be viewed today, for many reminders of Williams are present. The official name for the state is still "State of Rhode Island and Providence Plantations." Many of the streets which

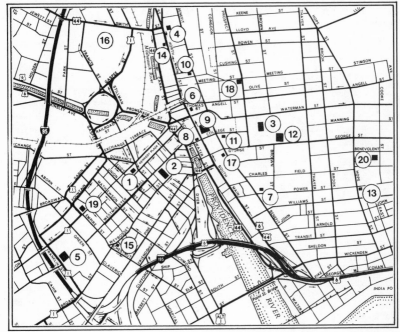

Courtesy of the State of Rhode Island

Providence

1. City Hall
2. Arcade
3. Brown University
4. Cathedral of St. John
5. Cathedral of SS. Peter & Paul
6. First Baptist Church
7. John Brown House
8. Market House
9. Museum of Art, R.I. School of Design
10. Old State House
11. Providence Athenaeum
12. John Carter Brown Library
13. Rhode Island Historical Society Library
14. Roger Williams National Memorial and Spring
15. Beneficent Congregational Church
16. State House
17. Stephen Hopkins House
18. Woods-Gerry House
19. Trinity Square Repertory Company
20. Aldrich House, Museum of R.I. History

Williams named remain: Benefit, Hope, Benevolent, Friendship. Rhode Island was declared the first free and independent republic in America by act of the House of Deputies in May, 1776 — two months prior to the Declaration of Independence (see **Old State House**, following).

As the town grew, early reliance on farming was replaced by an increased maritime trade, and then by industry, a pattern that repeated itself in many New England coastal settlements. First known for its textile manufacture, Providence today is famous for its silver and jewelry industries.

The variety of historic attractions to be found here is staggering: as is the case with so many major cities, time is always too short. To supplement the suggested list which follows, a visit to the **Greater Providence Convention** and **Visitors Bureau** at

10 Dorrance St. (274-1636) is recommended.

THE ARCADE, 130 Westminster St. and 65 Weybosset St., 1828. One of the few surviving examples of an early 19th-century shopping arcade built in America, this is a monumental Greek Revival building with huge granite columns and a three-story skylighted interior mall. A wide variety of shops and restaurants are contained here. NR. Open all year, M-W, Sa 9:30-6, Th, F, 9:30-9, Su 12-6. Restaurants open until 1 a.m. except Sunday.

BENEFICENT CONGREGATIONAL CHURCH (Round Top Church), 300 Weybosset St., 1809. Originally designed by Barnard Eddy as a two-story rectangular stone building with a hip roof, the church was remodeled in 1836 by James Bucklin, who added Greek Revival elements, including a columned portico. He enlarged the dome to form a stuccoed octagon, topping it with a wooden replica of an Athenian monument. The dome was gilded in 1857. NR. Open all year, M-F 8:30-4:30; Sa-Su 9-1. No charge.

CATHEDRAL OF SAINTS PETER AND PAUL, Cathedral Square, 1878-86. This recently-renovated neo-Gothic church stands on the site of the first Roman Catholic church in Providence (1838). Its interior boasts a huge Cossavant organ. Open daily 6:30 a.m.-5 p.m. 331-2434.

CITY HALL, Kennedy Plaza, (Dorrance and Washington Sts.,) 1875. Designed by Samuel F.J. Thayer, this is an imposing Second Empire building, three stories tall, with a round arched entrance portal. The interior is highlighted by a grand marble staircase and much original plaster, brass, and woodwork. NR. Open all year, M-F 8:30-4:30. No charge.

COLLEGE HILL HISTORIC DISTRICT, bounded by Olney and Hope Sts., Cohan Blvd., and the Providence and Moshassuck Rivers, c. 1730-1880. Within this huge area to the east of the Providence River are located a majority of the key historic landmarks in the city. College Hill is steep, and few businesses have chosen the location, so its appearance, with the exception of Brown University and the Rhode Island School of Design, is predominantly residential. It contains most of the original area settled by Roger Williams and his followers in the 17th century, plus 300 later buildings, the most accessible of which are described following. College Hill is especially noteworthy for its great concentration of intact early buildings—thought to be the largest such district in the United States. Among the highlights are:

John Brown House, 52 Power St., 1786-88. Designed by the noted colonial amateur architect Joseph Brown for his wealthy merchant brother, this large three-story Georgian mansion has four exterior chimneys, massive brick walls, and interior brick partitions. The four rooms on each floor are divided into pairs by a wide central hall that extends through the house. Restored by the Rhode Island Historical Society, complete with the duplication of

lavish French wallpapers and the original paint colors, the Brown house is furnished with fine examples of Rhode Island cabinetmaking, including many early family pieces. NR, NHL. Open Mar-Dec, Tu-Sa 11-4, Su 1-4; Jan-Feb, Sa-Su 1-4 and by appointment. $2.50 adults, $1 children, group rates. Combination ticket available with Aldrich House (see Hope-Power-Cooke Streets Historic District).

Brick School House, 24 Meeting St., 1769. This two-story frame and brick Georgian building was one of the first free schools in the country and housed early Brown University classes during the American Revolution. It is now the headquarters of the Providence Preservation Society, which offers literature and information about many local sites of interest. NR. Open all year, M-F 9-4:30. No charge. 831-7440.

Brown University, College and Prospect Sts., 1764. Founded as Rhode Island College, and renamed for a major benefactor, Brown is the seventh-oldest university in

the United States. The later **Pembroke College for Women** (1892) was merged with Brown in the early 1970s. Among the many historic collections and/or buildings on the campus well worth a visit are: **John Carter Brown Library,** George St., noted for its superb collection of early American history. Open Sept-May, M-F 8:30-5, Sa 9-12; June-Aug M-F 9-5. 863-2725. **Annmary Brown Memorial,** 21 Brown St., features 17th-19th century American manuscripts, Brown family heirlooms and correspondence, and Civil War memorabilia. Open all year, M-F 9-5. No charge. 863-2429. **Corliss-Brackett House** (1875-82), Prospect and Angell Sts., is an ornate Victorian mansion that now houses Brown's admission office, where guided tours of the campus are available at specified times. Call for information 863-2378. **John Hay Library,** Prospect and College Sts., contains one of the world's leading Abraham Lincoln collections. Open all year, M-F 9-4:30. 863-2146. **University Hall,** (1770-71), Brown's oldest building and a late Georgian four-story landmark, is the only extant structure closely associated with Horace Mann, who was instrumental in establishing the first normal school in the United States in 1839. University Hall now serves as Administrative Headquarters. NR. NHL. Open during business hours.

Cathedral of St. John (King's Church), 271 N. Main St., 1810. The original wooden King's church, one of the earliest Episcopal parishes in Rhode Island, was replaced by this early Gothic Revival landmark. Its adjoining graveyard contains monuments to

many prominent early residents. Open all year, M-F 8:30-4, Su 8:30-11:30. No charge.

First Baptist Church (Meeting House), 75 North Main St., 1774-75. Joseph Brown designed this two-story Georgian frame building, using as his model an unexecuted design for St. Martin's-in-the-Fields, London. Its two tiers of roundheaded windows are an unusual feature. The origins of the church date from the establishment of the first Baptist organization in America by Roger Williams in 1639. NR, NHL. Open Apr-Oct, M-F 10-3, Sa 10-12; Su tours at 12 year-round, and by appointment. No charge. 751-2266.

Governor Stephen Hopkins House, 15 Hopkins St., 1707. The early 18th-century frame house, when acquired by Hopkins in 1742, was a small dwelling consisting of two ground floor rooms and an attic. It was incorporated as an ell in Hopkins' new home, a 2½-story frame Colonial. Hopkins, a signer of the Declaration of Independence and member of the first and second Continental Congresses, was ten times governor of the state and chief justice of the Rhode Island Superior Court. Furnished with antiques of the period, the house and its adjacent 18th-century garden are administered by the state. NR, NHL. Open Apr-Dec, W, Sa 1-4 and by appointment. No charge. 831-7440.

Old State House (Sixth District Courthouse), 150 Benefit St., 1760-62. This solid brick structure with rustic stone trim served as Rhode Island's capitol from 1776 until 1900. Architect Thomas Tefft altered and enlarged the building in the mid-19th century by constructing a new entrance pavilion on the west front and surmounting it with an adaptation of the old wooden cupola. Only one room, on the second floor, retains its original appearance, although all restoration has been done with a view to maintaining the building's 18th-century ambience. The extensive portrait, furnishings, and furniture collections of the Rhode Island Historical Preservation Commission are housed here. NR. Open all year, M-F 8:30-4:30. 277-2678. No charge.

Providence Athenaeum, 751 Benefit St., 1753. One of the oldest libraries in the United States, where Edgar Allan Poe courted Sarah Williams, the Athenaeum houses a fine art collection in addition to its extensive library. NR. Open all year, M-F 8:30-5:30, Sa 9:30-5:30 (closed Sa in summer). No charge. 421-8670.

Rhode Island School of Design, College St. Founded in 1877, this is one of the most prestigious art schools in the country. On the campus, at 224 Benefit St., is the superb **Museum of Art.** The **Pendleton House** collection of American furniture, silver, china and decorative arts occupies its own buiding — an early 20th-century replica of the Georgian mansion in which its benefactor lived. Charles Leonard Pendleton was a successful Providence lawyer whose interest in antiques became a life's avocation. In 1904 he donated his entire collection to the school, on condition that a new building, designed as nearly as possible along the lines of his residence, be constructed to house it. The rest of the museum's extensive holdings of painting, sculpture, and decorative arts is in an adjacent building. Open Sept 1-June 15, Tu, W, F, Sa 10:30-5, Th 1-9, Su and holidays 2-5; June 16-Aug 31, W-Sa 11-4. $1 adults, 25¢ children. 331-6363 or 331-3511. At 62 Prospect Street is the **Woods-Gerry Gallery,** an 1860 town house designed by Richard Upjohn which now houses the University's administration offices and exhibition galleries with student art displays. NR. Open all year, Tu-Sa 11-4, Su 2-4. No charge. 331-3511. On

Market Square is **Market House,** a late 18th-century building, once the focal point of trade in colonial Providence, which contains the University's design department.

Roger Williams National Memorial, bounded by North Main, Canal, Smith, and Haymarket Sts., 1636. Site of the old town spring once used by the Williams family, whose house stood across North Main St., this national park, with exhibits on city and state history, encompasses four acres of gardens and lakes. NR. Open all year, daily 9-5. No charge. 528-4881.

HOPE-POWER-COOKE STREETS HISTORIC DISTRICT, bounded by Angell, Governor, Williams and Brook Sts., 19th-20th centuries. This primarily residential district, just east of College Hill, features a number of excellent 19th-century landmarks, among them two museums:

Nelson W. Aldrich House, 10 Benevolent St., 1821-27. Aldrich, one of the most powerful men in the United States Congress during his thirty years as a Rhode Island senator, who fought successfully to maintain the conservative, pro-business stance of Congress during his tenure (1881-1911), lived in this three-story frame Federal mansion for nearly forty years. The Rhode Island Historical Society now administers a **Museum of Rhode Island History** here. NR, NHL. Open all year, Tu-Sa 11-4, Su 1-4. $1.50 adults, 50¢ children (or combination ticket available with John Brown House). 331-8575.

Rhode Island Historical Society Library, 121 Hope St., 1873. The society's collection of books, pamphlets, early newspapers, and manuscripts can be found here. Open Sept-May, Tu-Sa 10-5; June-Aug, M 1-9, Tu-F 10-5. No charge. 331-0448.

While you're on Hope St., have a look at the **Governor Henry Lippitt House** at #199, a three-story brick landmark which is an excellent example of the Renaissance Revival style. NR, NHL.

RHODE ISLAND STATE HOUSE, 90 Smith St., 1895-1900. The distinguished architectural firm of McKim, Mead and White designed this imposing state capitol, with a huge central dome flanked by four smaller domes supported on columns. Two long wings extend east and west from the center and are topped by glass saucer domes. The exterior is faced and decorated with white Georgia marble, and on the south facade is a central arcade below a two-story loggia. A statue by George T. Brewster, "Independent Man," stands atop the central dome. Inside are the governor's offices, the legislative chambers, the State Library, and Rhode Island's original charter from 1663. The State Archives, including manuscripts and other artifacts pertaining to Rhode Island history, are housed here. NR. Open all year, M-F 8:30-4:30. Guided tours available. 277-2311. No charge. 🛉

ROGER WILLIAMS PARK HISTORIC DISTRICT, 950 Elmwood Ave., 19th-20th centuries. The 450 acre spread of this public park was once part of the territory obtained by Roger Williams from the Indians. A descendant, Betsy Williams, was the first to donate land for this, the city's first public park. Formal landscaping, waterways, drives, and walkways connect numerous special facilities. The 1773 **Betsy Williams Cottage,** a small gambrel-roofed house, contains colonial furniture and other items of historic interest. Open all year, M, T, F, Sa 10-4, Su 1-4. No charge. Also within the spacious grounds are a **Museum of Natural History,** the **Roger Williams Park Zoo,** and other recreational attractions. NR. Open all year, daily 7 a.m.-9 p.m. No charge. 421-3300. 🛉

Saunderstown

SILAS CASEY FARM, US 1A, (off RI 138), c. 1750. This mid-18th-century homestead, in a picturesque rural setting, still functions as a working farm. Surrounded by fields, barns, and high stone walls, the house overlooks Narragansett Bay and Jamestown Island. The Casey family, prominent in Rhode Island affairs, occupied the building for over 200 years, bequeathing it to the SPNEA in 1955. The farmhouse contains family paintings, prints, china, furniture, and documents from the 18th through 20th centuries. NR.

Open June 1-October 15, Tu, Th, Su 1-5. $1 adults. (617) 227-3956.

GILBERT STUART BIRTHPLACE, Gilbert Stuart Rd., 1751. Best known for his portraits of George Washington, Stuart was among the outstanding American painters of his time. After studying for four years in England under Benjamin West, he continued painting portraits, some of his most notable subjects being John Adams, John Quincy Adams, Thomas Jefferson, and James Madison. His boyhood home is furnished to the period, and on the grounds are an 18th-century snuff mill, the first in America, and a 1755 gristmill. NR, NHL. Open all year, Sa-Th 11-5. $1.25 adults, 50¢ children. 294-3001.

Slatersville

SLATERSVILLE HISTORIC DISTRICT, bounded by Main, Green, Church, and School Sts. and Ridge Rd., 19th-20th centuries. This was the first textile mill village in the state of Rhode Island, established in 1805 by Samuel Slater and the firm of Almy and Brown, that had introduced textile production to America in the late 18th century (see Pawtucket). Two stone mills are located here, along with the early residences, church, and stores which sprang up to accommodate employees. NR.

South Kingstown (see Kingston)

Tiverton

TIVERTON FOUR CORNERS HISTORIC DISTRICT, Main Rd., 18th-19th centuries. Two miles south of the town of Tiverton, the Four Corners area became a focal point during the Revolutionary War, as it intersected the main north/south road from Stone Bridge to Little Compton and the east/west highway leading from the Fogland Ferry to Dartmouth. Dorcas Soule, one of the early residents, is known to have captured a British spy in her kitchen (see Soule-Seebury House, following). After the war, whaling became the predominant industry of local residents. The **Chase-Cory House** (c. 1730) was long owned by whaling men and their descendants. Logbooks, harpoons, shells, and whale vertibrae are all part of the Cory family memorabilia. Now operated by the Tiverton Historical Society, the house is open May-Sept, Su 2-4:30, oftener for special exhibits. 624-4013.

The **Soule-Seabury House** (c. 1760) was enlarged by Captain Cornelius Soule in 1809. Soule was employed both in the China trade and in John Jacob Astor's scheme to build a fur empire in the Pacific Northwest. In 1811 he sailed the *Beaver,* pride of Astor's fleet, from New York to the mouth of Oregon's Columbia River. Mementos from his many voyages are among the exhibits now open to the public in his early Georgian home. May 1-Columbus Day, Sa, Su and holidays 1-5 and by appointment. $1 adults, 50¢ children. 624-3076.

Warren

WARREN WATERFRONT HISTORIC DISTRICT, bounded roughly by the Warren River, Belcher Cove, and the old town line (includes Main St. to Campbell St.) 17th-19th centuries. Warren was acquired by the English from the Wampanoag Indians in the Sowams Purchase of 1653. The town developed around shipbuilding, merchant service, and trade until the mid-19th century, when textile manufacturing so vital to other parts of the state became prominent. The district includes the oldest sections of Warren, with a wide variety of religious, public, commercial, and domestic buildings in many styles reflecting the changes from economic growth to stabilization and then depression.

The **James Maxwell House**, 59 Church St., c. 1743, is among the earliest homes in the district. Built of brick, with a massive central chimney featuring two beehive bake ovens (which are periodically demonstrated), it is currently undergoing restoration and is open by appointment only. 245-5077. For further information about other historic sites of interest in the area, call the Bristol County Chamber of Commerce (in Warren) at 245-0750.

Warwick

JOHN WATERMAN ARNOLD HOUSE, Roger Williams Avenue, c. 1760. Stephen Arnold, one of the first settlers in the area, bought the land on which the present house stands from the Indians in 1660, and it was passed down from father to son for six generations. Among the early features which still remain of this typical colonial house are a beehive oven, paneled doors with H and L hinges, and the fireplace paneling in the dining room. A colonial garden blooms during the summer months. Operated by the Warwick Historical Society. NR. Open Mar-Dec, Su 2-4 and by appointment. No charge. 467-7647.

WARWICK MUSEUM, Kentish Artillery Armory, 3259 Post Rd. Here is housed a collection of local artifacts and exhibits explaining Warwick's development from the 17th century onwards, including the role played by native son Nathanael Greene, commander of the American Army of the South during the Revolutionary War. (See also East Greenwich.) Open all year, Tu-F 11-4. $1 adults, 50¢ children. 737-0010.

Watch Hill

FLYING HORSE CAROUSEL, Bay St., c. 1876. One of the two oldest carousels in the United States (along with that at Oak Bluffs, Martha's Vineyard) stands about 200 yards from Watch Hill's lovely town beach. The intricately carved and painted horses have survived more than a century of abuse both by children and by nature; after the infamous hurricane of 1938, they were discovered, scattered and buried in the sand, and were carefully restored. Originally the carousel was powered by a real horse that spent its summers walking in circles, and music was provided by a hand organ. Now electricity powers the wooden horses and provides the accompaniment. Because of the age and fragility of the horses, only children under 12 are allowed to ride. NR.

As you drive through town, be on the lookout for the wonderful late-19th century stone or weathered frame "cottages" which line the hill overlooking the water. Watch Hill is somewhat of a miniature Newport—a still popular summer resort town which has remained largely unspoiled. 🏃

Westerly

BABCOCK-SMITH HOUSE, 124 Granite St., c. 1750. Westerly's first post office was established in the Georgian home of Dr. Joshua Babcock, first physician in the area. He was appointed postmaster by Benjamin Franklin, a frequent visitor. Babcock's two-story frame house has been restored and furnished to its original period. NR. Open May, June, Sept, Oct, Sun 2-5; July-Aug, W, Su 2-5 and by appointment. $1 adults, 50¢ children. 596-5704.

WILCOX PARK HISTORIC DISTRICT, 18th-20th centuries. Located in the heart of bustling Westerly is a quiet, well-maintained park. Its 18½ acres separate the residential and business sections of the town, and it is rimmed with homes and public buildings constructed during a span of more than 200 years. Facing the park is the **Westerly Public Library,** an 1892 Richardsonian Revival building which, in addition to its book and magazine collection, houses a small historical museum. Civil War artifacts, dolls, toys, furniture and paintings are included. Open all year, M-W 8 a.m.-9 p.m., Th 8-5, F-S 8-2. No charge. 596-2877.

Lodging and Dining

THE Ocean State's inns, lodgings, and hotels naturally cluster near the sea. As far back as the 19th century vacationers and weekend travelers ventured north from New York or south from Boston to escape the oppressive heat of the cities in the summer. While Newport's famous Cliff Walk is dotted with the Victorian mansions of the rich, the state's breathtaking coastal views can be enjoyed by all, even today.

From an elegant country inn housed in a 100-year-old Cape, to the splendor of the restored Providence Biltmore, Rhode Island has accommodations to match any fancy. Interested in history? Then hoist a few in the oldest operating tavern in America. Interested in fine cuisine? Then savor Newport's elaborate restaurants. If you're just interested in quiet times, then take the ferry out to Block Island where you can relax on the veranda of an old Victorian hotel, bicycle past sand dunes, or simply watch the waves from the window of a quiet inn.

Block Island

SPRING HOUSE HOTEL, Box 206, 02807. (401) 466-2633. Douglass Mott. This lovely inn, the oldest and largest on the island, is located on a hill overlooking the Atlantic and within easy access to "The Village." 75 rooms. MAP, expensive. AE, PC. Open mid-June to Labor Day. ⟨¶⟩

THE SURF HOTEL, on the beach, 02807. (401) 466-2241. Ulric & Beatrice Cyr. This Victorian hotel, built in 1876, is appropriately provided with period furnishings which contribute to the antique charm. 45 rooms. Moderate. PC. Memorial Day-Columbus Day.

THE 1661 INN/THE MANISSES HOTEL, Spring St. (P.O. Box 367), 02807. (401) 466-2421. Joan & Justin Abrams. Antique colonial furniture and braided rugs adorn each room of The 1661 Inn; shuttle service to the beach. The Abramses have reopened the restored Manisses Hotel, built in 1874, for the first time in 40 years. 26 rooms. Moderate. AE, M, V, PC. Inn open year-round. ⟨¶⟩

Jamestown

BAY VOYAGE INN, Conanicus Ave., 02835. (401) 423-0540. Frederick & Ann Coleman. Built in 1860; Victorian flavor and a spectacular view of the bay. Quiet setting within minutes of Newport. 20 rooms. EP, expensive. AE, M, V, PC. Open year-round.

Newport

THE CLARKE COOKE HOUSE, Bannister's Wharf, 02840. (401) 849-2900. David W. Ray. Located in the heart of Newport's waterfront district, this restored 18th century manor house offers a unique blend of past and present. 9 rooms. Expensive. AE, D, CB, M, V.

INN AT CASTLE HILL, Ocean Drive, 02840. (401) 849-3800. Paul McEnroe. Mansion-inn on the edge of Narrangansett Bay, located on Newport's famous Ocean Drive. 34 rooms. EP, expensive. MC, V. Dining room closed Jan 2-Easter; guest rooms open all winter.

THE INNTOWNE, 6 Mary St., 02840. (401) 846-9200. Betty & Paul McEnroe. An elegant colonial inn in the heart of historic Newport; authentic furnishings and decorative accessories add to this inn's colonial charm. 17 rooms. Expensive. M, V, PC. Open year-round.

LA FORGE CASINO RESTAURANT, 186 Bellevue Ave., 02840. (401) 847-0418. Michael F. Crowley. This fine restaurant is located in the famous Newport Casino, built in the 1880s by Stanford White. Adjacent to the International Tennis Hall of Fame. Moderate. AE, D, CB, M, V. Open 7 a.m.-10 p.m.

LA PETITE AUBERGE, 19 Charles St., 02840. (401) 849-6669. Roger & Martine Putier. Stephen Decatur's birthplace, built in 1714. Early American and French decor; cafe with brick floor and fireplace. Expensive. AE, D, M, V. Open for dinner, 6-10.

WHITE HORSE TAVERN, Marlborough and Farewell Sts., 02840. (401) 849-3600. Built in 1673; the oldest operating tavern in America. AE, CB, D, MC, V. Expensive. Open 11:30-3, 6-10. Su brunch, 12-3.

North Kingston

RED ROOSTER TAVERN, 7385 Post Rd., 02852. (401) 295-8804. Normand J. LeClair. An elegant country inn housed in a 100-year-old Cape decorated with antiques and collectibles. Expensive. AE, D, CB, M, V, PC with I.D. Dinner served Tu-Sa from 4:30; Su from 2:30

Providence

BILTMORE HOTEL, Kennedy Plaza, 02903. (401) 421-0700. Completed in 1922, this recently restored hotel is a key visual landmark in downtown Providence. Though largely unadorned, classically derived detailing is found throughout. 350 rooms. Expensive. AE, CB, D, MC, V. ⑪

Watch Hill

OCEAN HOUSE, Bluff Ave., 02891. (401) 348-8161. An imposing white-columned resort built by George Nash in 1868. Features include wide verandas and a ballroom. 59 rooms. Expensive. Open July-Labor Day. ⑪

Old Slater Mill, Pawtucket

3. MASSACHUSETTS

ALTHOUGH other parts of the eastern seaboard were explored and settled earlier than the Massachusetts coast, it is generally believed that America began at Plymouth in 1620 with the landing of the Pilgrims. Although a sunnier clime down the coast in Virginia had been their aim, the rocky shores of Massachusetts may actually have been better suited to the dissenting English spirit. Just how well the Pilgrims and their Puritan brethren did is well documented in such communities as Boston, Ipswich, Newburyport, Plymouth, Duxbury, Sandwich, Salem, New Bedford, and Fall River, all of which lie along the coast. A remarkable number of 17th-century buildings employing medieval construction techniques exist in these early settlements. They have been preserved together with the magnificent Georgian and Federal mansions of the merchant and shipping families of the mid-18th to mid-19th centuries.

Citizens of Massachusetts are proud of these possessions from the past and munificently support them through such institutions as the Society for the Preservation of New England Antiquities, the Trustees of Reservations, various antiquarian societies, and governmental bodies. No other state has so many buildings of historic value open to the public on a regular basis.

Boston, the Puritan's "city on the hill," was meant to be a beacon to all the nations. In the 19th century the city was in every way America's Athens—the national educational, literary, and musical center. To emulate the Boston style in architecture and in art—from Bulfinch to Richardson and from Copley to Sargent—was a national pastime.

Interior Massachusetts was more slowly settled during the 17th and early 18th centuries than was the coast. The physical environment is a naturally beautiful one with great broad river valleys, gently rolling hills, and numerous glacial lakes. Despite the intensive development of the land for industry of every sort, much of the countryside has not been spoiled. Education has always been one of the important "businesses" in Massachusetts, and such towns as Amherst, Deerfield, and Williamstown have profited culturally and economically from the presence of preparatory schools and colleges.

The flavor of old Massachusetts is perhaps best acquired on the relatively isolated islands of Nantucket and Martha's Vineyard and along the remote estuaries of the southeast, including parts of the Cape. Here fishing is still a way of life for some residents, and framing a house in the Colonial style or building a skiff are talents handed down from generation to generation. Antiques are not treasures, but objects for everyday use and enjoyment. Museums which celebrate this way of life are scattered everywhere throughout the region.

Massachusetts' historic properties are presented in the following pages from the western area of the state to the eastern, beginning with the Berkshires (area 1), continuing through the central Connecticut River valley (area 2) to Boston and surrounding communities (area 3), on to the maritime towns north of Boston (area 4), and finally to the old Plymouth colony, the Cape, and the islands (area 5).

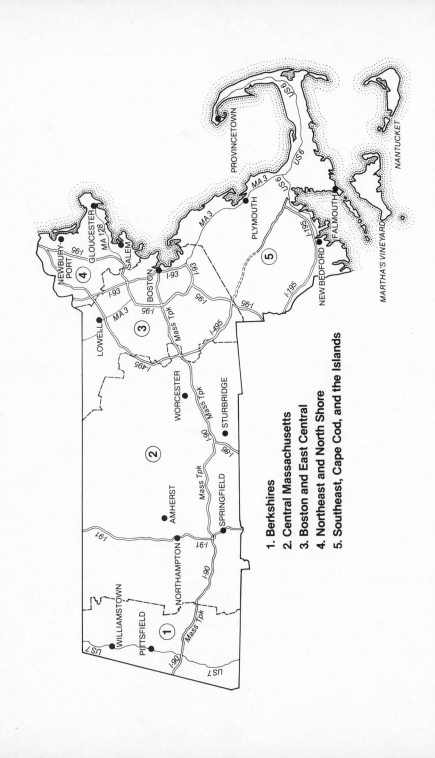

1. Berkshires
2. Central Massachusetts
3. Boston and East Central
4. Northeast and North Shore
5. Southeast, Cape Cod, and the Islands

Berkshires

The Berkshires—always spoken of as if the hills and the surrounding countryside are one and the same—is probably America's most patrician country area. There are industrial towns in Berkshire county—Pittsfield and North Adams being the most developed in this respect—but the overall impression of the hilly landscape is of a gentlemanly province of summer and weekend retreats that peacefully coexist with ancestral abodes. The actress Fanny Kemble came here in the 1800s, as did Matthew Arnold. The English felt as much at home as that most aristocratic of American novelists, Edith Wharton. Since the late 19th century, the Berkshires have been considered a congenial setting for the work of artists, musicians, and writers. "The wild and the cultivated," one writer observed more than forty years ago, "are close companions in our country, and we are happy in the companionship." The past is close by, too, in the graceful old homesteads, lofty meeting houses, and town halls.

Adams

SUSAN B. ANTHONY BIRTHPLACE, corner of East Rd. and East St., Bowen's Corner section, 1810. The most famous of American suffragettes spent her first five years in this village in the shadow of Mt. Greylock. The clapboard house was built by her father ten years before his daughter's birth. It is a private residence but can be viewed from the road.

QUAKER MEETING HOUSE, Maple Street Cemetery, 1781-84. This area of the county was settled by Rhode Island Quakers in the late 18th century. Their frame meeting house has the typical separate entrances for men and women and an interior layout which provided for segregation by sex. Presumably, Susan B. Anthony did not find the setting congenial, even as a child. The building has survived over 200 years in an almost unaltered state. NR.

Ashley Falls

BARTHOLOMEW'S COBBLE, Weatogue Rd. via Rannapo Rd., off MA 7A. Bordering on the peaceful Housatonic River is one of America's first "National Natural Landmarks." A cobble is an English term for a stone outcropping. Mark Van Doren, a frequent visitor to the 200-acre reservation, has described it best: "It is a small but precious eminence, a little marble mountain upon whose sides grow trees of ancient origin and plants of unimaginable age." The Bailey Natural History Museum on the grounds features photographs of wildflowers and bird nests and eggs. The cobble was part of a land grant to Col. John Ashley whose home is also located here. NR, NNL. Guided tours available. $1.50 adults, 50¢ children. 229-8600.

COL. JOHN ASHLEY HOUSE, Cooper Hill Rd., 1735. The colonel's house is the oldest in the county and is now open to the public. It is furnished with 18th-century antiques. The 2½-story center-chimney frame house was moved a half mile and restored in the 1930s. Privately administered. NR. Open June 1-Oct 15, W-Su 1-5. Admission $1.50 adults, 50¢ children 6-16. (413) 229-8600.

Dalton

CRANE MUSEUM, Housatonic St., 1844. Papermaking is one of the oldest New England industries, and Crane & Co. has been in the Dalton area since 1801. How fine papers were first made by hand and then by machine is explained in a series of permanent exhibits housed in what is known as the Old Stone Mill. Open June-Sept, M-F 2-5. Free. (413) 684-2600.

Florida and Savoy vicinity

MOHAWK TRAIL, along the bank of the Cold River for approximately 4 miles in Mohawk Trail State Forest, 17th-19th centuries. The historic path followed first by Indians traveling from the Connecticut and Deerfield valleys of west central Massachusetts to the Hudson and Mohawk valleys of New York has been almost completely obliterated. To some extent MA 2 takes this route over Hoosac Mountain but, except in the state forest, the natural setting has been lost. There are public facilities in this deeply wooded area. NR.

Lenox

THE MOUNT (Edith Wharton Estate), S of Lenox on US 7, off Plunkett St., 1902. Lenox lies almost at the geographic center of Berkshire county and was until recent years the undisputed social headquarters for the country gentry. Mrs. Wharton's residence, modeled after "Belton," an English Georgian manor house, was one of several dozen estates created in the late 1800s and early 1900s by summer residents. It was here that she wrote *Ethan Frome* (1911), a novel set in rural New England. The estate is now in the lengthy process of restoration by Shakespeare and Co., a performing and training school for professional actors. NR, NHL.

Other buildings in Lenox which are well worth viewing or visiting are the **Lenox Library** (originally the county Court House), 1816, on Main St. and across from it the **Lenox Academy**, 1803. Further up Main St. is the **Church on the Hill** (Congregational), a sturdy Federal-style clapboard building with a formidable square clock tower and a double octagonal bell tower. The clock is said to have been given by summer resident Fanny Kemble.

North Adams

MONUMENT SQUARE-EAGLE STREET HISTORIC DISTRICT, 19th century. The heart of this old industrial town has changed very little in the 20th century. Along Eagle St. are both clapboard buildings from the first half of the last century and red brick commercial structures from the second half. In the 1870s foreign workers by the hundreds poured into town to work in the many mills. As late as 1939, the author of the WPA guide to the Berkshires could write of the town's "constant hum of noise and a confusion of tongues: French-Canadian, Italian, nasal Yankee, and the upper New York twang characteristic of northern Berkshire." In contrast to the quiet hills, he added, "North Adams is nervous with the energy of twentieth-century America." It has been a much quieter place since World War II. Fortunately, urban renewal projects have not robbed the town of its character and past. The **Blackinton Mansion,** built by the leading 19th-century manufacturer in 1869-72, still stands on the east side of Monument Sq. and has served as the Public Library since 1897. Nearby, is the **First Congregational Church** (1863-64), a red brick Romanesque building in style not unlike the area's woolen mill. The change from clapboard to brick for public and commercial buildings in the small New England industrial cities during the mid-1800s is perhaps nowhere as graphically illustrated as in North Adams.

Pittsfield

BERKSHIRE MUSEUM, 39 South St. The county historical room at the museum houses a sizeable collection of materials on the region's past. It is open Sept-June, Tu-Sa 10-5, Su 1-5; July-Aug, M 10-5. Free. (413) 443-7171.

PARK SQUARE HISTORIC DISTRICT, at junction of North, South, East and West

Sts., 18th-19th centuries. Pittsfield has lost some major buildings in the 20th century, and the fight to retain and restore the best from the past is being waged almost daily. Most of the principal buildings around the centrally-located city park are still standing. Among these are the **Old Town Hall,** the **Berkshire County Court House,** the **Berkshire Athenaeum,** the **Berkshire County Savings Bank Building, The First Church of Christ** (Congregational), and **St. Stephen's Church** (Episcopal). Of these, the first three buildings are of special interest to the visitor.

The **Old Town Hall,** 43 East St., 1832, is Pittsfield's oldest surviving civic building and from 1891 to 1968 served as the City Hall. When the Berkshire Agricultural Fair, the oldest in the country, was held in the park opposite, the building also provided space for the exhibition of household crafts. As the Town Hall, it was an important meeting place during the Civil War recruiting campaigns. Since the 1970s the dignified two-story Federal-style landmark has been completely restored as a branch facility for the Berkshire County Savings Bank.

The **Berkshire County Court House,** 1872, is in the monumental Romanesque style favored for civic buildings in the post-Civil War era. It was designed by Louis Weisbein of Boston and executed in marble from the Sheffield region of the county.

The **Berkshire Athenaeum** is one of the most unusual New England libraries. Like the athenaeums of St. Johnsbury, Boston, and Providence, it began as a private institution in 1871. It has since become the public library. And, like the other distinguished institutions, it is housed in a fine building. In the case of Pittsfield, the style is Venetian Gothic with Great Barrington bluestone embellished with red Missouri granite and red Longmeadow freestone; iron cresting is found on the roof ridges. The alternation of the red and the lighter color creates the "Venetian" effect. The building went up in 1876 and was designed by William Appleton Potter of New York. Today the Athenaeum's most important collections are those which relate to the life of Herman Melville whose home is also in the Pittsfield area. Open winter months,

M,W,F-Sa 10-5, Tu, Th 10-9; summer months, W,F 10-5, Tu, Th 10-9, Sa 10-1.

ARROWHEAD (Herman Melville House), 780 Holmes Rd., 1780. Melville's large Colonial-period home was his refuge during the years 1850 to 1863. Here he wrote his most famous novel, *Moby Dick,* as well as such other works as *Typee* and *Billy Budd.* The Berkshire County Historical Society is headquartered at Arrowhead, and its collections include far more than Melville memorabilia. This is a study center for Berkshire county history and a place to exhibit area-related artifacts. NR, NHL. Open June 1-Oct 1, M-Sa 10-5, Su 1-5; Nov 1-May 31 by appointment only. $1.50 adults, $1 senior citizens, 50¢ students. (413) 442-1793.

Pittsfield vicinity

HANCOCK SHAKER VILLAGE, US 20 (Pittsfield-Albany Rd.), 5 miles S of Pittsfield, 1790-1960. Formally closed in 1960, Berkshire county's Shaker community — the third to be founded in the country — is thriving today on a very different basis, but with much the same spirit as in the past. One thousand acres are left from nearly 3,000, and twenty buildings are found in place today, most of which have been restored. Practicing Shakers no longer live at Hancock, but students of this inspired tradition are here to interpret it for the outside world. Among the most interesting of the buildings which are found on the neatly landscaped grounds bordering each side of US 20 are the following:

The stone **Round Barn,** believed to have been the first round farm building built in America, was constructed in 1826. The building's superstructure is 12-sided, and above this perches an octagonal cupola. An octagonal air shaft runs from the base of the building through to the cupola and was designed to provide ventilation for hay storage. The building was restored to its original state in 1968.

The **Main Dwelling House** is a 3½-story brick building which was added to the community in 1830 and has been painstakingly restored. It was a residence for 100 brothers and sisters and now includes

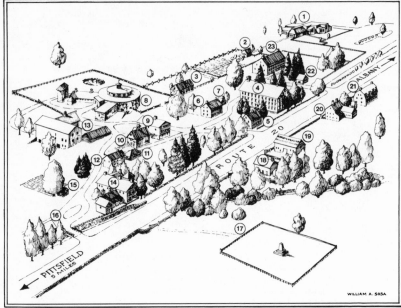

Courtesy of the Shaker Community, Inc.

Hancock Shaker Village

1. Visitor's Center and Village Office
2. Garden Tool Shed and Herb Garden
3. Poultry House (Library and Exhibit Hall)
4. Brick Dwelling
5. Brethren's Shop
6. Sister's Dairy and Weaving Shop
7. Ministry Wash House
8. Round Stone Barn
9. Tan House
10. Ice House
11. Brick Garage
12. Hired Men's Shop and Printing Office
13. Barn Complex
14. Trustee's Office and Store
15. Trustee's Office Privy
16. Trustee Office Sheds
17. Cemetery
18. Schoolhouse
19. Horse Barn (Educational Center)
20. Ministry Shop
21. Meeting House
22. Garage
23. Laundry and Machine Shop

period rooms which tell much about the domestic ways of the Shakers. Found here, too, are the sect's communal rooms—dining room, kitchen, storage rooms, etc.

The **Meeting House** is the second on this site, the first having been demolished in 1938. Both buildings were designed by Moses Johnson and have both the clapboarded frame construction technique and the gambrel roof form in common. The present building was brought to Hancock from Shirley, MA, in 1962 where it had been part of another Shaker community. The interior walls are painted white and the woodwork a deep blue, this in accordance with the group's aesthetic rules. The meeting house has separate entrances—as was customary—for men and women.

The **Sisters' Dairy and Weaving Shop** was the center for important women's work. Everyone, of course, worked in this utopian community, and sisters produced

tion of the community and the interpretation of its history. Craft programs are held from time to time on the grounds, and these relate to the imaginative Shaker tradition in the arts. Guided tours, lectures, films, and gallery talks are also offered. NR, NHL. Open June-Oct, daily 9:30-5. $4.50 adults, $1 children. ⁛ (413) 443-0188.

Stockbridge

CHESTERWOOD, MA 183, 1897, 1900-01. Daniel Chester French's home is one of a handful of culturally significant properties maintained by the National Trust for Historic Preservation. Open to the public is the 2½-story Georgian Revival home designed by Henry Bacon, French's sculpture studio, a barn gallery, and what is probably best of all—the landscaped gardens which include moving examples of this classic artist's work. French is best known for the brooding Lincoln figure enshrined in the Memorial in Washington, D.C., but from Chesterwood one gathers a greater appreciation of the scope of his work. NR, NHL. Open May 1-Oct 31, daily 10-5. $2.50 adults, $2 senior citizens, $1 students and children, $2 for

extemely useful domestic items for their own benefit as well as for sale to the outside world. Their herbs and herb remedies were particularly renowned.

Shaker Village, Inc., is a non-profit corporation dedicated to the careful restora-

members of adult groups of 10 or more. (413) 298-3579.

MERWIN HOUSE (TRANQUILITY), 39 Main St., c. 1825. The Federal brick mansion house is one of the most handsome architectural types of dwellings built in America. Tranquility is typical of this sort of early town residence. A Shingle-Style ell was added later in the century, but this does not detract from the cool composure of the residence. It is well furnished with period antiques and is open as a museum through the support of the Society for the Preservation of New England Antiquities. June 1-Oct 14, Tu, Th, Sa-Su 12-5. $1.50 admission. Call (617) 227-3956 for further information.

MISSION HOUSE, Main St., 1739. Few buildings in western MA are as full of history as Mission House. This was an outpost in the wilderness during the early 18th century and provided the Rev. John Sergeant, missionary to the Stockbridge Indians, with room for tutoring his charges. A special entrance and long hallway through which the noble savages could reach the minister's study can still be seen. Although the Rev. Jonathan Edwards, Sergeant's successor in the 1750s, did not live in this house, he was surely a frequent guest there. The building was superbly restored by members of the Choate family (see Naumkeag) some years ago. The antique furniture is of exceptional quality and includes some Sergeant family pieces. Operated by the Trustees of Reservations. NR, NHL. Open Memorial Day-Columbus Day, T-Sa 10-5, Su and holidays 11-4. $1.50 adults, 50¢ children and students 6-16. (413) 298-3383.

NAUMKEAG, Prospect Hill Rd., 1866. The Choate family, which has done so much for Stockbridge and the Berkshires over the years, lived here summers until 1959. The house is a comfortably sprawling Shingle-Style mansion of the type popular in the late 1800s. It was at this time that Joseph Hodges Choate served as U.S. Ambassador to the Court of St. James's. The grounds were handsomely landscaped, and are well maintained today. The Chinese Garden, including a pagoda, is a favorite of visitors. Operated by the Trustees of Reservations. Open May 23-June 21, Sa 10-5, Su 11-4; June 28-Sept 1, Tu-Sa, 10-5, Su and holidays 11-4; after Sept-Oct 13, Su and holidays 11-4. Admission to house and garden, $2.50 adults; 75¢ children 6-16. Admission to house only, $2; gardens only, $1.25. Special group rates. Reservations should be made by mail: c/o P.O. Box 115, Stockbridge, MA 01262. (413) 298-3239.

THE OLD CORNER HOUSE, Main St., c. 1800. Norman Rockwell is part of the Berkshire tradition, too, and many of his paintings and sketches are preserved here at the headquarters of the Stockbridge Historical Society. The Georgian residence is a bit fancy for Rockwell, but nonetheless representative of traditional New England.

STOCKBRIDGE CASINO (Berkshire Playhouse), E. Main St. at Yale Hill Rd., 1887-88. This is one of Charles McKim's inspired Georgian Revival designs. Once a social club, it is best known for its summer theater. It is now the home of the Berkshire Public Theater. NR. (413) 458-8146.

Stockbridge vicinity (Interlaken)

OLD CURTISVILLE HISTORIC DISTRICT, 3 miles NW of Stockbridge center, MA 183, Willard Hill Rd. and adjoining roads, 19th century. There are few areas in which one can get a better glimpse of what village life must have been like during the early 1800s. The railroad bypassed the crossroads in the 1830s, and ever since that time — except for a brief flurry of interest in papermaking — nothing much has happened in what is known as Interlaken. The village's stone bridge, dams, and raceways are still in place along the Larrywang Brook. All the buildings to be seen today are private, but almost all lie close to the road. Most date from the 1820s or '30s and were carefully built in the Federal or Greek Revival styles. The **Congregational Church** (1826) and **Citizens Hall** (1870) are especially noteworthy and face each other on Willard Hill Rd. The Second Empire Citizens Hall was the last structure of importance to be built in the area. It has been skillfully restored in recent years. Lovers of early American folk art will be interested to learn that Curtisville was the home of Ammi Philips (1788-1865), an itinerant portrait artist whose works are now highly prized.

Williamstown

WILLIAMS COLLEGE, US 7 and MA 2, 1790s-1900s. Williams is Williamstown, and vice versa. For preppies, it is paradise. Academically, it is hard to beat if a small college suits one's temperament. The campus is handsomely arranged on each side of MA 2 and the buildings are largely Georgian Colonial in spirit. The Museum of Art is housed in the 1846 **Lawrence Hall,** an Ionic rotunda. The **Sterling and Francine Clark Art Institute** is the best known Williamstown institution and houses one of the great collections of French Impressionist paintings. It is open year-round, Tu-Su 10-5, and is free. (413) 458-8109.

Central Massachusetts

Central Massachusetts is not as hilly and heavily forested as Berkshire county, but it is every bit as beautiful. The heart of the state is crossed from north to south by the pastoral Deerfield and Connecticut River valleys; in the northeast and central sections of Worcester county there are numerous reservoirs and small lakes nestled in the gently rolling landscape. A step back in time — to a colonial village green or an elegant row of Victorian town houses — is never very far away in central Massachusetts.

Amherst

Massachusetts has many towns distinguished as centers of learning. As the home of both Amherst College and the University of Massachusetts, Amherst is among the most prominent. The most famous resident of the town was not a student or a teacher, but a recluse from much of everyday life — the poet Emily Dickenson. Her father served as the college's treasurer and her grandfather was a founding father.

AMHERST COLLEGE CAMPUS, on the Common, 19th century. Since 1821 students have been attracted to the handsomely designed campus in the center of town for a first-rate private education. Sharing a "Little Ivy League" tradition with Williams (see Williamstown listing) and Wesleyan (see Middletown, CT listing), Amherst remained, like the other two colleges, a men's school for most of its years. The buildings are primarily nononsense red brick monuments to the Georgian Colonial style. **South College** and **North College** are among the earliest buildings (1820s) and have been described as being like army barracks. They stand to each side of the impressively porticoed **Johnson Chapel.**

DICKINSON HISTORIC DISTRICT, Main St., Lessey St., Triangle St., Tyler Pl., 19th century. The **Emily Dickinson Home** (1813), 280 Main St., lies at the center of the district and in an area of other family residences. Most of these buidings, however, date from the mid-1800s and are Italianate or Italian Villa-style houses. The Dickinson Home is a 2½-story brick residence in the Federal style. Amherst College

now owns the building, and it is open to the public for tours. These are held on Tu and F at 3, 3:45 and 4:30, by appointment. (413) 542-2321.

While visiting in this area, there are several other homes of special interest to see. The **William Austin Dickinson House** (1856), 214 Main St., was built by Emily's father and is a fine Italian Villa-style dwelling with a three-story square tower. The twin **Hills houses,** at 360 Main St. were built for Leonard M. Hills, a palm hat manufacturer, in the early 1860s. He was a founder of Amherst's other major educational institution, U Mass, which began life as the Massachusetts Agricultural College.

UNIVERSITY OF MASSACHUSETTS, MA 116 N of the center of town, 19th-20th centuries. Founded in 1863, U Mass, as it is invariably called, is better known for its modern buildings than for those from the past. Hugh Stubbins & Associates, Marcel Breuer and Herman Beckhard, and Kevin Roche/John Dinkeloo & Associates established a fine architectural tradition in the 1960s-70s which should stand up for generations.

NEHEMIAH STRONG HOUSE, 67 Amity St., 1744. This is the oldest house in town and has been entrusted to the care of the Amherst Historical Society. The clapboard and frame building has a central chimney and a simple columned entry porch. The society displays period furnishings and historical memorabilia. Open Memorial Day-Labor Day, T, Th, F 1-4.

Barre

BARRE COMMON DISTRICT, around the Common, 19th century. Barre's town common is a spacious fifteen acres and provides space for memorials, fountains, and, most important, an octagonal bandstand. The present version dates only from 1831 but it is the third on the site, and concerts held there during the summer months help Barre to retain its reputation as the "Band Concert Town of New England."

Surrounding the Common is a fine assortment of buildings dating from the 1830s and '40s and designed in the Greek Revival style of the early American republic. The **Barre Historical Society building** (1836), on the south end of the Common, was designed by a talented local architect, Elias Carter, for Spencer Field. Antique objects of local historical interest are kept here. Open May-Sept, Th and Su 2-5. Free.

Cummington vicinity

WILLIAM CULLEN BRYANT HOMESTEAD, 1½ miles S of MA 9, Bryant Rd., 1783. The "Old Homestead" is a colonial-period structure which was redressed in Victorian garb in 1856. The home is a charming one and houses many objects associated with this famous poet's career and travels. Also on the grounds is a barn where antique farm implements are displayed. Bryant lived here during his boyhood and returned in his later years after serving as editor of the New York *Evening Post.* Maintained by the Trustees of Reservations. NR, NHL. Open June 26-Sept 1, F, Sa, Su and holidays 1-5; Sept 1-Oct 12, Sa, Su and holidays 1-5. $1.50 adults; 50¢ children; under 6, free. (413) 634-2244.

Deerfield

HISTORIC DEERFIELD, The Street, 17th-20th centuries. Of the Deerfield countryside, Benjamin Silliman wrote in 1819: "Just at evening, we drove over to Deerfield, a distance of three miles, through the most luxuriant and beautiful country, that we had anywhere seen in our whole journey. Even now, in the latter part of October, the grass is most vividly green, thickly matted, and rich as the shag of velvet. The remains of the crops of corn, evinced also great productiveness, and seemed almost to realize the fables of the golden ages. We were comfortably lodged in a good inn, just in time to visit, before dark, a very interesting antiquity in this town."

It would seem that Deerfield was always a special place. It is certain that it is today one of the best preserved and interpreted of 18th- and early-19th century villages. The pace has been slow in Deerfield for at least 200 years and the crassly commercial is kept well beyond arm's length. Historic Deerfield, established in 1952 by Henry and Helen G. Flynt as a non-profit educational venture, is by no means the only cultural enclave in town along The Street (known earlier and more prosaically as Old Deerfield St.), but the complex is the most important and absorbing of present-day Deerfield institutions. It encompasses twelve historic buildings open to the public, the **Deerfield Inn** (see Lodging), and the **Henry N. Flynt Library.** These buildings may be toured separately or as part of a combination visit. Anyone wishing to visit the village may profit by writing ahead for information regarding special lectures, tours, and other events which might be taking place at the time of the proposed visit. Information may be secured by writing Historic Deerfield, Box 321, Deerfield, MA 01342, or by calling (413) 773-8689.

Deerfield was the northernmost outpost on the Massachusetts frontier during the mid- to late-17th century, and barely survived the aptly named Bloody Brook Indian massacre of 1675 and the great Deerfield raid of 1704. The only one of the historic buildings to predate—in part— the latter disaster is the **Frary House** located on the Common. It was added to later in the 1800s and first restored in 1890. It once served as a tavern and boasts an elegant ballroom. Historic Deerfield has provided a "touch-it" room which helps to bring history alive for children. $1.50 adults, 50¢ children 6-14.

Other buildings which are original to the village and which may be toured as part of Historic Deerfield are: the **Asa Stebbins House** (1799-c. 1810), a late Georgian Colonial brick mansion with handsome French wallpapers, wall painting, and appropriate furnishings of the period. ($2.50 adults); **Allen House** (c. 1720), a center chimney saltbox with a very beautiful collection of antique furnishings and accessories ($2.50 adults); the **Parker and Russell Silver Shop** (1814), which houses an extraordinary collection of English and American silver, a silversmith's workshop, and a Federal period country parlor ($1.50 adults); the **Helen Geier Flynt Fabric Hall** (1872), formerly a barn, containing examples of antique American, English, and European needlework, textiles, and costumes ($1.50 adults); the **Wright House** (1824), a Federal-style brick dwelling furnished with fine Chippendale and Adams-style furniture and other elegant appointments ($1.50 adults); the **Wells-**

Thorn House (1717, 1751), which includes 18th-century room settings and furnishings ($1.50 adults); the **Wilson Printing Office** (1816), a restored frame building which also includes a cabinet-maker's shop ($1 adults, 50¢ children 6-14); the **Sheldon-Hawks House** (1743), featuring the Potter collection of Boston and Connecticut valley furniture and domestic antiques ($1.50 adults); and **Ashley House** (c. 1730), the meticulously restored former residence of Deerfield's Tory minister during the American Revolution ($1.50 adults).

Buildings from other areas of the state

which complement the landmarks original to the village have been saved and brought to Deerfield. The first building which the visitor is likely to enter, **Hall Tavern** (c. 1760), once stood in Charlemont, MA, in the Berkshires. It now serves as an information center and gift shop and includes a seven-room museum complex ($1 adults).

The **Dwight-Barnard House** (c. 1725), is a very fine early Georgian Colonial residence from Springfield, MA. Seven rooms—including a doctor's office and a parlor—are devoted to elegant period furniture and accessories from Boston and the Deerfield area ($1.50 adults).

Combination tickets for entrance to three buildings are available for $3.50 for adults during the summer months. There is also a special admission price of $12 for a tour of eleven buildings. Admission is by guided tour only, and each house requires 30-45 minutes. Only six persons are taken by a guide at a time, thereby insuring that neither the visitors nor the facilities are overtaxed. Historic Deerfield's properties are included in the Old Deerfield Village Historic District and have been designated as part of a National Historic Landmark. The museum houses are open all year except Thanksgiving, Dec. 24-25, and New Year's Day, M-Sa 9:30-4:30 and Su 1-4:30. (413) 773-8689 or (413) 774-5218.

Special tours known as "tours-by-appointment" can also be arranged at Historic Deerfield. This affords the visitor a special opportunity to linger for awhile over some special interest—whether it be silver, textiles, or antique furniture. This program also encompasses four special

buildings not otherwise seen by the visitor—the **Sheldon-Hawks Shed** (toy collection), the **Wapping Schoolhouse** of 1839, the **Frank L. Boyden Collection of Carriages and Buggies,** and the **Museum of Architectural Fragments.** Morning, afternoon, and all-day tours can be arranged for two to six persons by writing Historic Deerfield at the previously given address or by telephoning (413) 774-5218.

POCUMTUCK VALLEY MEMORIAL ASSOCIATION LIBRARY and THE HENRY N. FLYNT LIBRARY OF HISTORIC DEERFIELD, INC., Memorial St., are jointly administered by the regional historical society and the museum village. The Pocumtuck collection was organized in 1870 and includes, books, manuscripts, and other printed material and photographs which document the cultural life of the area and its leading families. The Flynt collection is devoted primarily to the decorative arts and essential documentary material relevant to the Connecticut Valley of Massachusetts. The Memorial Libraries, as they are jointly designated, are open M-F 9-4:30. (413) 772-0882.

MEMORIAL HALL MUSEUM, Memorial St., 1798. This was Deerfield Academy's first building and is among the many Massachusetts buildings designed by the gifted Asher Benjamin. The Pocumtuck Valley Memorial Association has maintained an historical museum here since 1880, and it is said that this institution was the first to install permanent period rooms—a kitchen, parlor, and bedroom—to show off the artifacts of pioneer settlers. The collections are quite remarkable and include the famous "Indian House Door," a badly battered reminder of the 1704 Indian raid on Deerfield, and the sole surviving relic of the 1698 Sheldon house. Open May 1-Oct 31, M-F 10-4:30, Sa-Su 12:30-4:30; by appointment Apr and Nov. $1.50 adults, $1 students, 50¢ children 6-12; $3.50 family rate. (413) 773-8929.

DEERFIELD ACADEMY, off the Common and the Albany Rd., 1797-20th century. Memorial Hall was the first of the important academy buildings. Those most visible today which serve the exclusive boys' school are much more recent and are primarily built of brick in the Georgian Colonial Revival style. Also located in the village is the **Bement School**, a coeducational institution.

THE BRICK CHURCH (Meeting House), off the Common, 1824. The Unitarian church is a formal neo-classical building worthy of such a learned town. It is located next to the Post Office and fits in well with the Deerfield Academy complex.

INDIAN HOUSE MEMORIAL, and BLOODY BROOK TAVERN, c. 1700, Main St. (The Street). These two buildings occupy the same site and have a curious history. The Memorial is a reconstruction of a building of the same name which survived the 1704 onslaught. Only the door, housed in Memorial Hall, remains from the original building destroyed in 1848. The Deerfield Historical Society decided that history had to be put back together again and raised anew a fortress-like timbered house with framed overhangs on the second and third floors. Bloody Brook Tavern was moved here some years ago from South Deerfield, presumably to save it from destruction. On exhibit in these two buildings are decorative objects, antique furniture, and displays of looms and weavings. NR. Open May 1-Oct 31, M, W-Sa 1-5, Su 1-5, holidays 9:30-12 and 1-4. $1.50 adults, $1 students 12-16, 50¢ children 6-12. (413) 772-0845.

Grafton

WILLARD HOUSE AND CLOCK MUSEUM, INC., Willard St., 1718. Anyone with the slightest interest in clocks and timepieces will enjoy visiting this museum. The house itself is of historical importance as it is one of the earliest homes remaining in the area. The work of the Willard family —Benjamin, Simon, Ephraim, and Aaron —is celebrated in portraits, tools, letters, furniture and, of course, in the timepieces so finely crafted by members of this family from the 1770s through the first decades of the 19th century. Open all year, Tu-Sa

10-4, Su 1-5, holidays 1-4. $1.50 adults, 75¢ children. (617) 839-3500. 🚻

Hadley

HADLEY FARM MUSEUM, 147 Russell St., 1782. A restored barn houses agricultural and domestic objects as well as sleighs and a stagecoach. Open May 1-Oct 15, Tu-Sa 10-4:30, Su 1:30-4:30. Free. (413) 584-8297. 🚻

PORTER PHELPS HUNTINGTON HISTORIC HOUSE MUSEUM, 130 River Dr., 1752. Furnishings which have descended through generations of three prominent area families have been gathered in this handsome mansion house. The grounds are similarly well disposed and there is a carriage house and corn barn for inspection., The most accomplished resident was Bishop Frederick Dan Huntington (1891-1904) of the Episcopal diocese of Central New York. The museum is the site of colonial-period teas in July and August, a concert series in August, and story-telling sessions in September. Open May 15-Oct 15, Sa-W 1-4:30, and other times by appointment. $1 adults, 50¢ for children under 12. (413) 484-4699.

Harvard

FRUITLANDS MUSEUMS, Prospect Hill Rd., 18th-19th centuries. There are four major buildings at Fruitlands, but the most important is the c. 1750 **farmstead** which served as the center of Bronson Alcott's ill-fated experiment with communal living in 1843-44. The ideal "Con-Sociate" family community was called New Eden. No one was to eat meat or to exploit the labor of another creature. Even silkworms—brought in to spin—were excused from work. The members tried to pull their own plows across the stony fields. Alcott's daughter, Louisa May, remembered the whole nutty scene in a piece entitled "Transcendental Wild Oats." Today the house stands as a museum of the Transcendental movement as understood by Alcott, Emerson, Thoreau, Margaret Fuller, and others. By no means were all the experiments they undertook quite so impractical.

Also on the grounds is **Shaker House,** a 1970s office moved to Fruitlands from nearby Harvard Shaker village; the **American Indian Museum,** with exhibits of Indian art and artifacts; and the **Picture Gallery** which focuses on the work of primitive American artists and the painters of the Hudson River School of the mid-19th century. NR, NHL. Open June-Sept, Tu-Su 1-5. $2 adults, 50¢ students 7-16; free for children under 6. (617) 456-3924.

HARVARD SHAKER VILLAGE, 1 mile S of MA 2A on Shaker Rd., 1790s-late 19th century. The Shakers began their Harvard experiment in the 1790s after Mother Lee—the divine founder—had planted missionary seeds in this rather barren ground. The community, however, prospered and by the 1820s there were nearly 200 members and 1,800 acres of well-tended farmland. The community slowly dissolved in the late 1800s and in 1918 was sold off for other purposes. Unlike Hancock Shaker Village in the Berkshires, no non-profit institution came to the rescue when the community closed. The Fruitlands Museums, however, have saved many pieces of furniture, artwork, and other artifacts. Some of the remaining buildings are in good shape and these include the **meeting house** (1791); the **Ministry's shop** (1847); **Square House** (Shadrach Ireland House) (1769); **tailors' shop** (c. 1800); and **Trustees' office** (c. 1835). All of these buildings are to be found on the east side of Shaker Rd. Each one has been altered in some manner during the past 150 years and is by no means a perfect period example of Shaker architecture. All of these buildings were part of the "Church Family" group. Those that were part of a second gathering within the Harvard fold, the "South Family," were sold off in 1899. Unfortunately, nearly half of these buildings along S Shaker Rd. have been demolished; the remainder are in a deteriorating condition.

Although in private hands, all of the remaining Shaker buildings can be viewed from the road.

Holyoke

WISTARIAHURST, 238 Cabot St., 1848, 1878, 1913, 1927. A mansion originally built for the Skinner family, it has grown like Topsy over the years. The house first stood in Williamsburg, MA, where William Skinner's silk mill was located. After a flood in 1874, house and business

Ministry's shop, Harvard Shaker Village

were relocated in Holyoke. The town is a rather gritty industrial one, but Wistaria-hurst is living proof that at least on the right side of the tracks life could be pleasant. A conservatory and music hall were added in 1913 and a two-story main hall in 1927. Since 1959 the mansion has served as a municipal museum and is furnished with Victorian antiques. NR. Open all year, Tu-Sa 1-5, Su 2-5. Free. (413) 536-6771.

Lancaster

FIRST CHURCH OF CHRIST (Congregational), the Common, 1816. This is the fifth meeting house to have been raised in Lancaster, and there are few finer in New England. Charles Bulfinch was the architect, and the soaring red brick edifice with a great portico and two-stage tower is acknowledged as one of his greatest works. Inside there is a gallery on three sides; the interior was decorated in the style of Bulfinch's MA State House in 1900. The nearby 1785 parsonage can also be visited. NR, NHL. Open all year, Su 11-12; other times by appointment. (617) 365-2427.

Northampton

This ancient city on the Connecticut River has given the world the Graham cracker

and many thousands of Smith College graduates. It has also been the home of Calvin Coolidge as he made his slow way to the White House, and, much earlier, that of the Rev. Jonathan Edwards of hell and damnation fame. It is not the most attractive of the commonwealth's old industrial towns, but it may be among the most interesting. An active and imaginative historical society can be credited with bringing the past alive in a meaningful way.

BRIDGE STREET AREA, including the **Isaac Damon House**, #46 (1812); the **Cornet Joseph Parsons House**, #58 (1658); and the **Pomeroy-Shepherd House and Barn**, #66 (1792), 17th-19th centuries. The headquarters of the Northampton Historical Society is found in the Parsons dwelling, and here the visitor can arrange to visit the three historic museum houses. One of the best costume collections in New England is carefully displayed at the Isaac Damon House; the Parsons House features a typical 18th-century parlor with fine period antiques and Connecticut valley paintings; the Shepherd House contains the 19th-century furnishings of a distinguished local family. Open all year, W, F, Su 2-4:30, and by appointment. $1 adults for each house, 50¢ for children under 12. (413) 584-6011.

Not in this part of town, but worth a special visit if you are a Coolidge groupie is the rather dumpy **Calvin Coolidge House**, 19-21 Massasoit St., 1900-01. This became Coolidge's home after leaving Vermont. A simple frame and clapboard structure, it symbolizes the homely virtues which marked Coolidge's rise from mayor of Northampton and state legislator to governor and the presidency. NR. Private but viewable from the street. The Northampton house he moved to after leaving the White House, **The Beeches**, off High St., is a mansion and cannot be viewed easily.

DOWNTOWN HISTORIC DISTRICT, principally the buildings along Main St., 19th century. It would have been unthinkable ten years ago to recommend that anyone take a stroll along Main St. Not in the slightest degree "quaint," somewhat down-at-the-heels, and clearly commercial, the central business area of Northampton is light years away from the village greens of Sturbridge or Lexington. We are merely displaying our advanced age, however, when scoffing at mid- to late-Victorian architecture and design. Most of the buildings in this area are a century old, and some of them have been rediscovered and refurbished for today's enjoyment. Starting from the railroad bridge, among the most interesting are: the **Smith Charities Building,** 51 Main St. (1865), a Renaissance Revival cube of ashlar masonry; the **Hampshire County Courthouse** (1886), a very fine Richardsonian Romanesque granite monument trimmed in brownstone and marble; the brownstone **First Church of Christ** (Congregational), 129 Main St., designed by the Boston architects Peabody and Stearns in 1877 with glowing Tiffany windows and colorful Victorian interior decoration; and the **Northampton City Hall** (formerly the Town Hall) (1848-49), with turrets, pendants, and Tudor windows.

Not on Main St., but close by on Pleasant, is the **Dr. Sylvester Graham House,** #111. The cracker was only one of Dr. Graham's health interests.

SMITH COLLEGE CAMPUS, Elm St., adjoining streets and avenues, Paradise Rd., 19th century. Sophia Smith established one of the world's most famous women's colleges in 1875. Included on the campus are a sprinkling of very early buildings along Elm St. — including the **Sessions (Jonathan Hunt) House,** #109 (c. 1700); the **Hankins House,** #197 (1730); and the **Elizabeth Drew House,** #84 (1789). The large number of commodious private homes which were available for the college's use precluded the design and building of a stylistically consistent and appealing campus. Rather, Smith's new academic buildings are distinguished more for their utility than their charm. Most fall into that category known as Georgian Colonial Revival. **College Hall,** at the intersection of West and Elm Sts. (1874), is an exception. Peabody and Stearns of Boston, de-

signers of the First Church, executed this interesting Victorian Gothic structure.

Royalston

ROYALSTON COMMON HISTORICAL DISTRICT, around the Common, 19th century. There are no great buildings in town, but a fine collection of Federal and Greek Revival public and private structures. Their arrangement around the triangular-shaped Common presents a very handsome picture of New England town planning at its best. Of special interest to the visitor is the **Bullock Mansion,** on the west side (1807), a large two-story Federal residence with a main entrance that incorporates both a fanlight and sidelights. The Gothic Revival style balustrade is a later 19th-century addition. The **Columns,** just off the Common at the intersection of Main St. and MA 68 (1838), is a pure Greek Revival temple. So, too, is the **Congregational Church** on the east side of the Common (1851). NR.

Shrewsbury

GENERAL ARTEMAS WARD HOMESTEAD, 786 Main St., 1727, 1785. Ward was one of the great figures of the Revolution. His home, originally part of a 100-acre estate on the outskirts of town, has been carefully preserved by Harvard University. The rooms in this two-story clapboard house contain handsome wainscoting and such early features as sliding solid shutters. Ward family furnishings — furniture, china, pewter, portraits — appear throughout the house. NR. Open Apr 15-Oct 31, Tu-F 10-12 and 1-4, Sa 10-12 and 1-5, Su 1-5; Nov, Sa 10-12 and 1-5, Su 1-5. Free. (617) 842-8900.

Springfield (see also West Springfield)

Springfield has been the industrial and commercial center of western and central Massachusetts since the early 19th century. With the establishment of the federal Armory in 1794, the town's future importance was assured. The deactivation of the arsenal in 1968 was as graphic a symbol of the city's decline as a manufacturing center in the 20th century as any act could be. The city, however, remains a vibrant and a significant source of historical riches. Springfield's impressive public buildings and the establishments and residences of the wealthy manufacturing and trading families provide a superb foundation for the building of a more prosperous future. Few "Sun Belt" cities can claim such superb public facilities and institutions.

SPRINGFIELD ARMORY NATIONAL HISTORIC SITE, Armory Sq., 1794. George Washington and Henry Knox chose this site above the Connecticut River for one of two national armories in the 1790s, the other being at Harper's Ferry, VA. Springfield quickly became renowned for the skill and speed with which the gunsmiths assembled arms. A system of interchangeable parts made on a mass production basis was well established by the early 1800s. A museum displaying what is the world's largest collection of small arms is

located in the 1847 **Main Arsenal** building. NR, NHL. Administered by the National Park Service. Open all year, daily 8-4:30. Free. (413) 734-6477.

AMES HILL/CRESCENT HILL HISTORIC DISTRICT, bounded by Central, Maple, Mill, and Pine Sts., Crescent Hill, Ames Hill Dr., and Maple Ct., 19th-early 20th centuries. Just about any style of dwelling fashionable among the wealthy in America from the 1820s through the 1930s can be found in this fascinating residential area. There are great Italianate, Italian Villa, Shingle Style, Queen Anne, Colonial Revival, and Tudor Revival houses spread out over two hills which form a ridge SW of the central business district. Among the noteworthy buildings are these on Maple St.: **David Ames House**, #141 (1826), a transitional Federal-Greek Revival design executed by Asher Benjamin in white painted brick; the **Walter Wesson House**, #302 (1882), an eccentric Queen Anne turreted mansion with a facade employing half-timbering, shingling, brownstone and brick; the **Julius Appleton House**, #313 (1886), a Stick Style residence of brownstone and shingling with the type of twisted woodwork in balustrades and porch which typify the style.

Another fascinating group of homes is found along Crescent Hill. The **Mills-Stebbins Villa**, #3, is the oldest (1849), an acknowledged masterpiece of the Italian Villa style. Henry A. Sykes was the architect of this two-story brick home with a three-story square tower that incorporates a loggia.

COURT SQUARE HISTORIC DISTRICT, bounded by Main, State, and Pynchon Sts., Broadway, and City Hall Pl., 19th-20th centuries. Many of Springfield's principal public buildings are found within this area. The oldest (1819) is the **First Church of Christ** (Congregational) at 50 Elm St., designed by Isaac Damon in a neo-classical style. The church is situated on the west side of **Court Square Park** (1812), a refreshing green space in the midst of government buildings. The **Hampden County Courthouse** (1871) is also located on Elm St. It was one of Henry Hobson Richardson's early commissions in his distinctive granite Romanesque style with tall arches forming the entrance and the openings in the medieval-looking bell tower. The building was remodeled by the firm of Shepley, Rutan and Coolidge in 1906. Few buildings that went up in the 1920s can be rated as landmarks, but the **Municipal Group,** as it is called in Springfield, is of a special class. Situated on the NW side of Court Square are the **Administration Building, Auditorium Building**

(Symphony Hall), and a 300-foot **campanile** — all elements in a Classical Revival composition. The tower is fitted with an elevator which will whisk one up to view the Connecticut River valley; the Auditorium, recently refurbished, is said to have superb acoustics and seats 4,000.

Springfield's principal museum buildings are located on State and Chestnut Sts., east of the Court Square district. The **Connecticut Valley Historical Museum,** 194 State St., exhibits regional Americana, including paintings, furniture, pewter, glass, and other decorative arts. Period rooms may be seen; the archives are rich in histor-

ical materials from the period 1650-1940. Open all year, Tu 12-9, W-Su 12-5. Free. (413) 732-3080.

Sturbridge

OLD STURBRIDGE VILLAGE, junction of MA Tpk, I-86, US 20, and MA 131. The Northeast's largest museum village comprises over 100 buildings, both old and modern copies, which recreate life in rural New England between 1790-1840. Try to make your visit in any season but summer. The Village draws more visitors than any other single-site tourist attraction in the commonwealth. Sturbridge can be a visual delight in almost any season. In the spring when there are 25,000 bulbs blooming one wants to linger on forever. The well-landscaped grounds are one of the special delights of the Village; so, too, are the agricultural exhibits which are a natural expression of the working farm program so authentically carried out at Sturbridge. The complex will never be placed on the National Register of Historic Places because it is, in effect, a recreation. As such, it is extraordinarily faithful to the past and skillful in its interpretation. Among the most interesting of the buildings are those antique structures which have been brought to this site from nearby areas or other locations in New England.

Tours are begun at the Visitor Center. Here you can receive much useful information on special programs for the day, especially those of interest to children. The Village is open from Apr 1-Oct 24, daily 9:30-5:30, and from Oct 25-Mar 30, M-F 1-4, Sa-Su 9:30-4:30. $7 adults, $3 youth (6-15), free for children under 5. Admission is for all buildings. (617) 347-3362.

Among the most interesting and authentically restored buildings brought to the Village are the following:

The **Hervey Brooks Pottery Shop,** built in Goshen, CT, c. 1815, was moved to Sturbridge in 1961. It includes a reproduction kiln, potter's wheel, and mill for grinding glazes.

The **John Fenno House,** built in Canton,

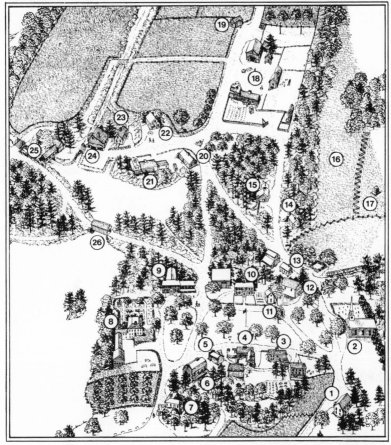

Courtesy of Old Sturbridge Village

Old Sturbridge Village

1. Quaker Meetinghouse
2. Village Meetinghouse
3. Fenno Home
4. Fitch Home
5. Bank
6. Grant Store
7. Printing Office
8. Towne Family Home
9. Tavern
10. Parsonage
11. Law Office
12. Knight Store
13. Shoe Shop
14. District School
15. Pottery
16. Freeman Farm Fields
17. Powder House
18. Freeman Farmstead
19. Cooper Shop
20. Tin and Broom Shop
21. Farmer's Nooning
22. Blacksmith Shop
23. Carding Mill
24. Grist Mill
25. Saw Mill
26. Covered Bridge

MA, c. 1704, is furnished to represent the home of a newly-married couple of the early 1800s.

The **Asa Knight General Store** was built in Dummerston, VT, 1811, and has additions made in 1820 and 1830. Exact reproductions of the kinds of goods available for sale in the early 19th century are displayed.

The **Pliny Freeman Farm complex** includes a farmhouse built in Sturbridge, c. 1801; a New England-style barn; the Moses Wilder blacksmith shop, c. 1810, from Bolton, MA; and the James Nash cooperage, c. 1840, from Waldoboro, ME.

The **Village Meeting House,** built in Sturbridge town in 1832, served the Baptist congregation. It is a typical Greek Revival

building. At its side is a reconstructed cemetery or burying ground. Only the gravestones, however, were removed from their original resting places elsewhere. They were replaced with modern stones.

The **General Salem Towne House** is a residence in the Federal style built in Charlton, MA, in 1796. It has been furnished and landscaped to represent the residence of a community leader. The garden, orchard, and barn complex are also interesting to explore.

The **Isaiah Thomas Printing Office,** built in Worcester, MA, c. 1780, was the workplace of one of America's early leading book and periodical publishers, and author of *A History of Printing in America* (1801). This is probably the Village's most historically important building.

The **Thompson Bank** was opened in Thompson, CT, in 1835. The Greek Revival banking house symbolizes the developing commercial and industrial activity in the early 19th-century New England village.

Uxbridge vicinity

FRIENDS MEETING HOUSE, MA 146, 1770-76. The building has been restored in recent years and two outbuildings—a horse shed and shed for oxen—have been reconstructed. Quakers from Rhode Island settled this corner of the Puritan commonwealth at the time the meeting house was built. It is unusual in being of brick. The interior is as simple as other Quaker meeting houses, with a moveable partition dividing the space set apart for men and women. There is also a primitive second-floor gallery. NR.

West Springfield

JOSIAH DAY HOUSE (Ramapogue Historical Society), 70 Park St., 1754. Brick saltboxes were rarely built in the 18th century and the Day House is an even rarer survivor. It is furnished with period furniture and accessories, including some Day

Storrowton Village

family pieces. NR. Open May-Nov, Sa-Su 1-5. $1 adults, 50¢ children. (413) 734-8322.

STORROWTOWN VILLAGE, 1503 Memorial Ave., Eastern States Exposition Grounds. This museum village was established in 1929, nine years before the founding of Sturbridge and only three years after Colonial Williamsburg. The Springfield-area complex is by no means as ambitious an undertaking as either of these other major institutions, but Storrowtown should not be overlooked. Among the 18th- and 19th-century buildings which can be toured in the company of a costumed interpreter are the **Eddy Law Office** (1810), which once served the needs of Zechariah Eddy, a colleague of Daniel Webster; the **Chesterfield Blacksmith Shop** (1825), brought here from Chesterfield; the **Union Meeting House** (1834), from Salisbury; a **one-room schoolhouse** (1810), from Whatley; the **Gilbert farmhouse**, built in 1794, and found in West Brookfield; the **Potter Mansion** of North Brookfield (1789); and what is termed **Aunt Helen's Herb Garden.** There is also a general store and tavern (for dining) on the grounds. Craft demonstrations and workshops are among the most popular Village activities. Open mid-June-Labor Day, M-Sa 1-5; Labor Day-June 23, M-F 1-5 for tours by appointment and scheduled programs. $1.50 adults, 75¢ children 6-16, free for children under 6. (413) 736-0632. 👫

Wilbraham

ACADEMY HISTORIC DISTRICT, Main and Faculty Sts., late 18th-early 19th centuries. The **Old Academy building** (1825), a Federal style structure, has well served Wilbraham Academy (now known as Wilbraham and Munson). The **Old Meeting House** (1793) relates to the secondary school. Both were centers of the development of the Methodist Church in New England. NR.

Williamsburg

HAYDENVILLE HISTORIC DISTRICT, Main and High Sts., Kingsley Ave. in Haydenville neighborhood, 19th century. The Hayden family dominated the village named after them from the early 1800s until at least the end of the century. This industrial southeast section of the town of Williamsburg had as its primary business the making of brass objects. The second **Hayden factory** of 1875 is still standing on Main St. and replaced the original 1808 building. Also on Main St. are the two Hayden brothers **twin mansions**, each a striking Greek Revival landmark in the area. Both houses display columned porticoes. The clapboard residence dates from 1839 and its brick twin, 1828. NR.

Worcester

Worcester's cultural institutions are almost as well known as those of Boston. The Art Museum is world famous; the American Antiquarian Society has more important documents and books dealing with the development of the United States than almost any other research facility in the country. Many families made great fortunes in Worcester during the 19th and early 20th centuries, and they have richly endowed the city with the perquisites of a civilized society. This tradition has been kept alive today in the handsomely restored and newly appointed downtown Common area. The past is still respected in Worcester and given a significant role to play.

THE AMERICAN ANTIQUARIAN SOCIETY, 185 Salisbury St., was founded in 1812 and lodged in this building in 1910. It is a library containing 650,000 volumes of original source material on American history up to 1877. Of special note is the society's collection of American newspapers (1670-1820), fiction (1774-1850), and imprints before 1820. It is, like the Library of Congress in Washington, a

place for serious research. Guided tours are available, and there are exhibitions and lectures. Open M-F 9-5. Free. (617) 755-5221.

WORCESTER HISTORICAL MUSEUM, 39 Salisbury St., is situated on the same street as the Antiquarian Society. Decorative objects, costumes, and militariana are featured in the displays. Open Tu-Sa 1-4. Free. (617) 753-8278.

MECHANICS HALL, 321 Main St., 1855-57, has been completely restored in the past few years as part of the downtown renovation. It is a superb Renaissance Revival building with a facade of cast and galvanized iron and mastic-covered brick. A music hall is located on the second floor level, and this facility played host to some of the great artists and public figures of the Victorian era. NR. (617) 752-5608.

TIMOTHY PAINE HOUSE (The Oaks), 140 Lincoln St., 1774-78. The Col. Timothy Bigelow Chapter of the D.A.R. has taken good care of this Colonial-style mansion. The original owner, a prominent and ardent Tory, has probably turned over in his grave several times at the thought of the ladies of the American Revolution tending his ancestral home. It remained in family hands until early in this century and survived amazingly well. It is now furnished with some original pieces of furniture; the D.A.R. chapter has restored the slate and marble fireplaces dating from the mid-19th century. Alterations were made throughout the 1800s, but the late 18th-century appearance was respected. NR. Open by appointment only. (617) 755-3207.

SALISBURY HOUSE, 61 Harvard St., 1836-38, was built by the second member of this distinguished Worcester family to bear the Christian name of Stephen. It is now the headquarters of the American Red Cross chapter, and much that was stylish in the early 1800s has been retained. The style of the exterior is Greek Revival and the house was designed by Elias Carter, a master builder, in imitation of the even fancier clapboard frame mansions of the coastal cities of the commonwealth. The interior contains large airy rooms; a graceful spiral staircase winds its way through the central hall. NR.

SALISBURY MANSION and STORE, 30 and 40 Highland St., 1772, 1790. Stephen Salisbury I, a Bostonian and the father of the owner of the previously described residence, began a successful hardware business in Worcester in 1767. Both buildings were originally located on Lincoln Square and were moved by their then owner, the Worcester Art Museum, to the present location to save them from demolition in 1929. The Mansion is a two-story clapboard and frame building of traditional colonial design; a neo-classical portico was added in 1819. The interior rooms contain most of the original elegant woodwork. The Mansion is now rented to the Worcester Girl Scouts Council.

The Salisbury Store was restored in the 1930s. The two-story clapboard structure contains the original hoist and interior loft. This building is even more elegant than the Mansion, with a central second-story Palladian window and bull's-eye windows at each end of this floor. The store is also now used as offices. NR.

Boston and East Central

As one travels toward the eastern shore of Massachusetts, reminders of the historic past are encountered more and more frequently. The patriotic enclaves of Concord and Lexington are as close to being sacred national shrines as any in the country. And clustered in the towns and villages surrounding Boston in a wide semi-circle are hundreds of colonial and early 19th-century historic sites which are the settings for important chapters in American economic, social, and military history. Nearly every town is a living historical museum, and costumes and playacting are not needed to give the settings an air of authenticity. Like tidewater Virginia, eastern Massachusetts is aristocratic to the bone, and the relics and memories of yesterday remain vital to the enjoyment of the present. Perhaps nowhere is this more true than in Boston, "the city on the hill" of the Puritan fathers.

Boston

The city of Boston, including such historic neighborhoods as Charlestown, Dorchester, and Roxbury, is treated separately from surrounding Middlesex and Norfolk county communities.

The average traveler is accustomed to making his way quite easily in cities laid out in a regular grid pattern. Boston is not so easy. Traveling around the city can be a confusing experience as the streets are often very narrow and do not follow a straight line. Touring on foot is somewhat easier than attempting to navigate the crooked lanes by private car. The visitor can follow a twisting path called the Freedom Trail which will bring him to most of the important patriotic sites, but it will not lead him to many other Boston landmarks of equal or even greater interest. The best way to understand and to experience historical Boston is to approach it on a neighborhood by neighborhood basis.

BACK BAY, extending from the Public Garden and Arlington St. to Massachusetts Ave., and from the Charles River Embankment to Huntington Ave., 19th century. This area was reclaimed from a swampy beginning in the 1850s. For the most part, the streets conform to a straight line as city planners were able to work their master plans at a relatively late date in Boston history. The north-south streets are named in alphabetical order, starting with Arlington and ending with Hereford. Despite the penchant for Anglophilia in the naming of streets, there is a Continental air about the area. This is most clearly seen on Commonwealth Ave. where great town houses in the Second-Empire style were built. Arlington St. also presents a handsome picture, especially when viewed from the Public Garden. As described by one historian, "the majestic, harmonious, mansard blocks of Arlington Street constitute a splendid frontispiece to the Back Bay. . . ." Many of Boston's great cultural and religious institutions are located in this area, and the buildings in which they are housed coexist gracefully with private residences, landmark hotels, club houses, shops, and stores.

Arlington Street Church, Arlington and Boylston Sts., 1859-61. The creation of the master planner of Back Bay—architect Arthur Gilman—this church is among the most famous Unitarian parishes in America. It was the pulpit of the abolitionist William Ellery Channing in the mid-1800s, and more recently served as a center of anti-Vietnam War resistance. The style of the building is basically Georgian, but has Italianate overtones. The elaborate steeple is modeled on that of St. Martin-in-the-Fields, London. NR.

Boston Public Library, Copley Sq., 1888-95. This building is a great monument to late-19th century architecture and to the central role of the literary life in Boston. The massive granite walls of the Renaissance Revival building are decorated with friezes and other detailing; massive arched windows handsomely define the second story. Charles McKim of the firm of McKim, Mead and White was the architect responsible; unfortunately, his sure hand is all too obviously missing on the Boylston St. addition (1969-72). NR. Open M-F 9-9, Sa 9-6. (617) 536-5400.

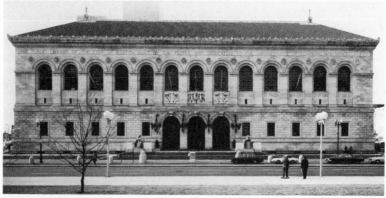

Boston Public Library

Copley Plaza Hotel, Copley Sq., 1910-12. This distinguished hotel—the last of the great Renaissance Revival palaces to be built in the city—strikingly complements the Public Library across the way. The massive limestone facade is curved in an elegant manner; the interior spaces are similarly sophisticated in composition and layout. The design is by Henry Hardenburgh, architect of New York's Plaza Hotel and the Dakota Apartments. The hotel has been completely restored in recent years. For further information, see listing under Lodging and Dining.

Crowninshield House, 164 Marlborough St., 1868-70. There are many handsome town houses and apartment buildings along Back Bay's avenues and streets and the four-story, red-brick Crowninshield House—named for one of the area's great families—is a particularly distinguished residence. It was designed by Henry Hobson Richardson and was his first domestic architectural commission. NR. Privately owned, but visible from the street.

First Baptist Church (Brattle Square Church), Commonwealth Ave. and Clarendon St., 1872. H.H. Richardson was the designer of this major landmark with a 176-foot corner tower tucked in between the nave and transept. A massive tower frieze was modeled by Frederic Auguste Bartholdi, the artist better known for his design of the Statue of Liberty. The frieze with four gigantic angels blowing gilded trumpets has led the edifice to be called "The Church of the Holy Bean Blowers." NR.

Bonwit Teller (formerly Museum of Natural History building), 234 Berkeley St., 1862. Few department stores are as serenely housed. The elegant classical building was designed by William G. Preston. NR.

Massachusetts Historical Society, 1154 Boylston St.. The building which the society occupies is a relatively new one by Boston standards, only dating from 1899, but the collection it houses is venerable. The society itself is the oldest in the United States. Rare objects are the subject of temporary and permanent exhibitions. NR, NHL. Open M-F 9-4:45. Free. (617) 536-1608.

New Old South Church, 645 Boylston St., 1874-75. The church sits at one corner of Copley Sq. Its campanile—towering 235 feet—is the most distinctive element in the Victorian Gothic design from the architectural firm of Cummings and Sears. The facade is richly textured and the interior displays a wealth of fine woods. NR, NHL.

Symphony Hall, 1900, and **Horticultural Hall,** 1901, both located at Massachusetts and Huntington Aves., in the SW corner of Back Bay. This area was among the last to be built upon in the 1890s and early 1900s. Every attempt was made to harmonize these two major public buildings, the first having been designed by McKim, Mead and White, and the second by the firm of Wheelwright and Haven. Each is in the Renaissance Revival style and is of red brick trimmed with granite or limestone. Symphony Hall is the home of the famous Boston Symphony Orchestra and is renowned for its acoustical excellence; it is also the site of the nationally-known "Pops" concerts. NR.

Trinity Church, Copley Sq., 1874-77. Appearing much like a cathedral, Henry Hobson Richardson's most famous church dominates Copley Sq.; even the nearby John Hancock Tower seems to shrink somewhat in size by comparison. The great square central tower rises 211 feet above the Romanesque structure of Dedham granite and Longmeadow freestone. John La Farge was responsible for the murals inside the Episcopal Church as well as some of the stained glass windows. Trinity is unique in almost every aspect of its design, a monument to its builder as well as to the faith it celebrates. NR, NHL.

Trinity Rectory, Clarendon and Newbury Sts., 1879-80. Trinity Rectory was built for Phillips Brooks, rector of the church and later bishop of Massachusetts. Like the church, this brick building, trimmed with brownstone, was designed by Henry Hobson Richardson in his interpretation of the Romanesque style. NR.

BACK BAY—THE FENWAY. Extending in a southwesterly direction from the main residential section of Back Bay is the Fenway—a combination of park and parkway. It is one of the most pleasant places to visit during the warmer months and nearby are some of Boston's major cultural institutions, of which one—the Museum of Fine Arts—is of special interest to every serious student of American civilation.

Museum of Fine Arts, Huntington Ave. The collections of early American decorative arts are perhaps unequalled in the country. Some of the most important pieces of furniture are displayed in period rooms as well as in special displays. The museum is especially renowned for its

church silver, including many works by Paul Revere. Open Tu, Th-Su 10-5, W 10-10; West Wing, Th-F 5-10. $3 adults, $2 senior citizens, no charge for children under 16; no charge Sa 10-12; West Wing, $2 adults.

BEACON HILL. The streets surrounding Charles Bulfinch's famous gold-domed State House are those which really delineate Beacon Hill. These are Charles, Chestnut, Beacon, Spruce, Walnut, Joy, Mt. Vernon, and Pinckney. Here is found the largest concentration of prim red brick Federal-style town houses which are the neighborhood's hallmark. But beyond these boundaries—on the other side of Charles St. toward the river, down the back slope of the hill to Cambridge St.—are houses often similar in style to those of Beacon Hill proper. Taken altogether, the area is one of the most unusual in the United States and among the earliest sophisticated "old town" neighborhoods to be rediscovered and treasured in the 20th century. To stroll up and down the lanes of Beacon Hill is almost always a pleasure. The neighborhood has remained amazingly residential and free of the cute boutiques that plague other fashionable districts.

Headquarters House, 55 Beacon St. (1806), is typical of the Federal-style residences built in the early years of the republic. It is four-stories tall, of red brick, and was designed by Asher Benjamin. At one time it was the home of the eminent historian of the Americas, William H. Prescott. The house is now maintained by the National Society of Colonial Dames in

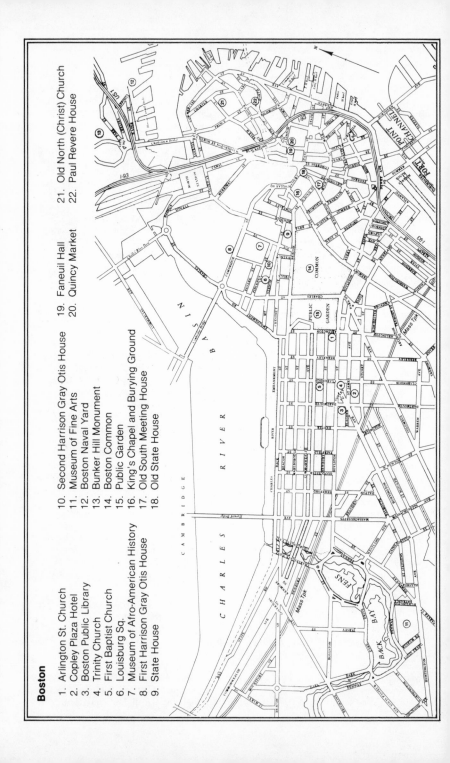

Boston

1. Arlington St. Church
2. Copley Plaza Hotel
3. Boston Public Library
4. Trinity Church
5. First Baptist Church
6. Louisburg Sq.
7. Museum of Afro-American History
8. First Harrison Gray Otis House
9. State House
10. Second Harrison Gray Otis House
11. Museum of Fine Arts
12. Boston Naval Yard
13. Bunker Hill Monument
14. Boston Common
15. Public Garden
16. King's Chapel and Burying Ground
17. Old South Meeting House
18. Old State House
19. Faneuil Hall
20. Quincy Market
21. Old North (Christ) Church
22. Paul Revere House

Massachusetts. Open M and W 10-4 and by appointment. (617) 742-3190.

Louisburg Square, between Pinckney and Mt. Vernon Sts., 1826-44. This most famous and attractive of Boston's residential squares is lined with brick town houses in the late Federal and Greek Revival styles. The scale has been kept low—not more than three or four stories—and many of the facades are elegantly curved in a bow-shape. Among the famous who have lived here are Louisa May Alcott, William Dean Howells, and Jenny Lind. NR.

Museum of Afro-American History, Smith Court, 1806. Smith Court is tucked away off Joy St. on Beacon Hill's downward slope toward Cambridge St. Here is found the African Meeting House, the oldest extant black church in America. Boston's first abolitionist organization—the New England Anti-Slavery Society—was founded here in 1832 by William Lloyd Garrison. Exhibits illustrate the history of New England's black community. The museum also makes available a brochure on Boston's "Black Heritage Trail" which is available by writing to Dudley Station, Box 5, Roxbury, MA 02119. NR. Open Su-F 11-5. Free. Guided tours of the Black Heritage Trail are available at a cost of $5 adults, $2.50 children. (617) 445-7400.

Nichols House Museum, 55 Mt. Vernon St., 1803-04. Charles Bulfinch was responsible for the Federal design of the row houses at 43-49 and 51-57 Mt. Vernon St., a thoroughfare which crosses Beacon Hill at its highest point. The tall brick residence at #55 and its adjoining neighbors were built for speculation and are crowded right up to the sidewalk. They served as models for other homes built during the next 30 or 40 years in the area. The building is now maintained as a museum and is furnished with antiques from throughout the world. Open M, W, Sa 1-5. $1 adults. (617) 227-6993.

First Harrison Gray Otis House, 141 Cambridge St., 1796. A major residential landmark, this first home designed by Charles Bulfinch for the Otis family lies just outside

the Beacon Hill area, but relates very much to it and to the second house built on Mt. Vernon St. for Otis. As the headquarters for the Society for the Preservation of New England Antiquities, the first dwelling has been treated with exceptional care. Of special interest to anyone concerned with the decorative arts are the period drawing room and the dining room. The fabrics, paints, and papers used are superb reproductions appropriate for early 19th-century interiors, and are based on documented sources. The furnishings have been chosen with concern for suitability and availability in the home of this sort and period. The building originally stood much closer to Cambridge St., but was moved in 1926. NR, NHL. Open daily, M-F 9-5 and for guided tours at 10, 11, 1, 2, 3. $2 adults, reduced rates for children. (617) 227-3956.

The Second Harrison Gray Otis House, 85 Mt. Vernon St., 1800-2. Otis was one of a group of wealthy real estate speculators who bought up the pasture land west of the new State House on the hill. Each agreed to build a mansion house along Mt. Vernon St. which would serve as a model for others to follow. Architect Charles Bulfinch was also a partner and built for himself a double house at 87-89 Mt. Vernon, a large house for Jonathan Mason (demolished), and the Second Harrison Gray Otis House. It is the only house on the hill which illustrates Bulfinch's original scheme for the neighborhood. Each house

was to be set well back from the street and
to be free on each side of its neighbors. It is
a superbly proportioned and detailed Federal brick residence which has survived
almost unaltered. Each of the three floors
builds upon the other in a graceful formal
manner, with arches, bays, and pilasters
defining the windows. A wooden balustrade decorates the hip roof and the latter
is surmounted by an octagonal wood
cupola. NR.

David Sears House, 42 Beacon St., 1816.
Architect Alexander Parris was one of the
masters of the Federal style. Although
greatly altered over the years, the scale of
this town house is still monumental. The
walls are made up of carved granite panels.
NR, NHL.

State House, off Beacon St. between Joy
and Bowdoin Sts., 1795-98. Massachusetts' capitol building is considered one of
Charles Bulfinch's masterpieces. The great
gold dome which rises above this part of
the city has been copied again and again in
other public buildings. Bulfinch was made
the first architect of the U.S. Capitol in
1817, and the parallels between that building and the State House are obvious to any
viewer. Although there have been major
additions and alterations over the years,
the essential and commanding Bulfinch
Federal design is still effectively projected.
Inside are the Senate Chamber and its
former space, now the Senate Reception
Room. Both retain the neo-classical elegance that was the mark of Bulfinch's style.
Memorial Hall comprises most of the
public space inside the massive Corinthian
colonnade. Here are displays of paintings,
sculpture, and battle flags. NR, NHL.
Open M-F 9-5. ⛪

Women's City Club of Boston, 39-40
Beacon St., 1818. These twin houses with
bow fronts have been attributed to Alexander Parris. They contain what many
critics consider the most elegantly finished
and furnished rooms in the city. The fine
marble mantels, mahogany woodwork,
circular staircases, and interior shutters
display the best early 19th-century craftmanship. The ornamental plasterwork in
the vestibule of #39 and in the ceiling and

cornice of the front and back drawing
rooms of #40 is beautifully articulated.
NR, NHL. Open W 10-2 and 2-4. $2
adults, 50¢ children. (617) 227-3550.

CHARLESTOWN, founded in 1629, was
an independent town until its annexation
by Boston in 1874. Significantly it was
here that the first major battle of the
Revolution was fought—that of Bunker
Hill. A major port in the 18th century,
Charlestown was almost as valuable to the
British as Boston. When they burned down
most of the town following the battle, it is
said that $525,000 worth of proper-
ty—some 320 buildings—was lost. The
late Colonial and early Federal town
houses which took their place are now considered candidates for late-20th century
restoration.

Boston Naval Yard, east of Chelsea St., c.
1800. The most historic section of one of
the nation's oldest marine installations has
become part of the Boston National Historical Park. Originally called the Charlestown Navy Yard after the area on the north
side of the Charles River and inner harbor,
this is the home of the **U.S.S. Constitution**
("Old Ironsides") (1797), the oldest commissioned warship in the world, and the
U.S.S. Cassin Young (1943), a World War

II destroyer. The yard also contains a number of historic buildings, including the **Commandant's Quarters** (1805); the **Ropewalk** (1834-37), where the U.S. Navy's supply of cordage was long made; and other structures and facilities. Building 22, formerly a drydock pumphouse, houses the **U.S.S. Constitution Museum** where the story of the 44-gun frigate is told and illustrated. The museum is open daily 9-5. $1.75 adults, 50¢ children, and $1 tour groups and senior citizens. (617) 242-0543. *"Old Ironsides"* may be toured from 9:30-3:30 daily; there is no charge. The *U.S.S. Cassin Young* is still under restoration. NR, NHL.

Bunker Hill Monument, Monument Sq., 1825. Here is commemorated the first full-scale engagement between American militia and British troops in the Revolutionary War—the Battle of Bunker Hill. The 220-foot obelisk stands about at the center of the American redoubt on Breed's Hill on June 17, 1775. We lost—this first time around. The **Bunker Hill Museum** at 42 Monument Sq. presents lectures, films, and exhibits on the famous event and related local historical activity. It is open Tu-F 12-4 and Sa-Su 10-4. (617) 241-8220. A multimedia presentation entitled "Whites

of Their Eyes" is presented at the modern **Bunker Hill Pavilion** down on Water St. near the Naval Yard. Its hours are June-Aug, daily 9:30-6:30; Sept-May, daily 9:30-4:30. $1.50 adults, 75¢ children, special group rates. (617) 241-7575.

Phipps Street Burying Ground, Phipps St., 17th-19th centuries. The only remaining artifacts of pre-Revolutionary Charlestown are the brownstone and red sandstone markers of the cemetery. The British burned most of the village immediately after their victory at Bunker (Breed's) Hill in 1775. The markers date back to 1642; a majority of them are from the second half of the 18th century. Many have the highly imaginative folk art designs which so intrigue people today—winged death's heads, cherubs, and other spiritual beings. Later stones incorporate neo-classical designs such as urns, willow boughs, and lyres. Phipps Street is the burial ground of John Harvard, benefactor of the institution that bears his name. A 15-foot granite obelisk marks the site of his grave; the original marker was lost during the British occupation of the area. NR.

THE COMMON AND ENVIRONS. This central district in Boston is its most historic. Here are concentrated more im-

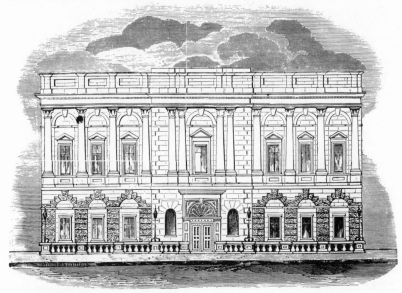

Boston Athenaeum

portant religious, political, and social institutions than can be found in most other American cities combined. Nothing about the area is regular or logically positioned. The streets run every which way; cemeteries pop up next to office buildings; swan boats ply the lake in the Public Garden across from The Ritz.

Boston Athenaeum, 10½ Beacon St., 1847-49. Philadelphia claims the earliest private or proprietary library society, but Boston's, founded in 1807, is the largest of these and has the distinction, among others, of playing part-time host to Gilbert Stuart's portraits of George and Martha Washington in an unusual sharing arrangement with the National Portrait Gallery in Washington, D.C. Large parts of the libraries of George Washington and John Quincy Adams are to be found here along with what is an almost endless collection of early pamphlets and tracts. Exhibits are mounted regularly. NR, NHL. Open June-Sept, M-F 9-5:30, Oct-May, M-F 9-5:30, Sa 9-4. Free. (617) 227-0270.

Boston Common and Public Garden, bordered by Beacon, Arlington, Boylston, Tremont, and Park Sts., 17th-19th centuries. The Common is America's oldest public park, founded in 1634; the Public Garden was laid out in the years 1839 to 1856. Charles St. separates the Common (50 acres) from the Garden (24 acres).

The Common is crossed by wide pedestrian walks and is the setting for a number of striking sculptural groups, the **Shaw Memorial** by Augustus St. Gaudens begin the most important work of art in the park. This was erected in 1897 as a tribute to Col. Robert Shaw of the 54th Massachusetts Infantry in the Civil War, the first regiment of free black men. The Memorial is located at the corner of Beacon and Park Sts. across from the State House. On the other side of the Common, on Boylston St., is the **Central Burial Ground.** This cemetery was laid out in 1756 and contains, among others, the remains of Revolutionary War soldiers. The Common was the scene of many military events and both the British troops and the patriots gathered here in the 1770s. To the present time, this common meeting ground has been a rallying point for protest and reform regardless of cause.

mont and School Sts., 1749-54. The first Anglican parish in Massachusetts and founded in 1688, King's Chapel is considered an excellent example of Georgian church architecture. Peter Harrison is credited with the original design, and his plans were followed for the later Ionic columned wood portico (1785-87), which is crowned with a Federal-style balustrade. The central core of the building is of cut Quincy granite. The interior architectural detailing and appointments are extremely handsome. There is a canopied pulpit and brilliant lighting fixtures; richly textured and colored fabrics are used in the box pews and elsewhere in the nave. The

The Public Garden is a quieter and more sedate place. The swan pedal boats serenely cross the surface of the figure-eight-shaped pond in the middle. A footbridge crosses the pond near its middle. Children especially enjoy a ride in one of these boats which are as celebrated in fact as they are in fiction, notably, Robert McCloskey's *Make Way for Ducklings*. The area was first laid out as a botanical garden, and the plantings still remain important in the scheme of things. NR.

Granary Burying Ground, 83-115 Tremont St., 1660-19th century. Located next to Park Street Church just across the northeast corner of the Common, this cemetery takes its name from the town granary which occupied the church site until 1809. More prominent Revolutionary War figures are buried here than in any other cemetery, including Peter Faneuil, Robert Treat Paine, Paul Revere, John Hancock, and the victims of the Boston Massacre. The Franklin family tomb with a 27-foot obelisk is the most prominent visual symbol, Benjamin Franklin's parents are buried here. There are approximately 1,700 graves and 200 tombs within the burial ground. Both simple markers and impressive monuments provide interesting reading and viewing. The large Egyptian Revival granite gates at the Tremont St. side entrance were designed by Solomon Willard in 1840. NR.

King's Chapel and Burying Ground, Tre-

overall effect is of an elegance not often found in New England's severe religious scene. Although the parish changed from Anglican to Unitarian, becoming the first such congregation in the United States in 1789, the rich aesthetic statement was left unchanged. In terms of liturgy, the church might be termed High Unitarian, as it continues to make use of a revised version of the Book of Common Prayer without, in this case, any Trinitarian references. NR, NHL. Open T-Sa 10-4 and for Sunday services.

The burying ground alongside the church dates from 1630, making it the oldest in the city. Among those buried here are John Winthrop, the colony's first governor, and John Cotton, a leader in the Boston church. When this cemetery became overcrowded in the mid-17th century, the Granary Burying Ground (see previous listing) was established.

Old City Hall, School and Province Sts., 1862-65. Many of the Boston's Second Empire buildings have been destroyed, but, fortunately, Old City Hall remains. Its elaborately layered facade was recently completely refurbished, and the building converted to commercial use. The building has often been compared to the Louvre in Paris, and it is true that the architects, Gridley J. F. Bryant and Arthur D. Gilman, were very familiar with the French mansard style. The style is one that was used with great effect in other areas of the city, notably along Commonwealth Ave. in Back Bay. NR, NHL.

Old Corner Bookstore, NW corner of Washington and School Sts., c. 1712. Few landmarks are as beloved as this ancient 3½-story brick building. For over 100 years it served as a residence; in 1828 it first housed a bookstore. In the mid-19th century the building became the home of the publishing firm of Ticknor and Fields. The store was a favorite meeting place of

the New England literary greats of the 19th century, men such as Emerson, Longfellow, Hawthorne, and Oliver Wendell Holmes. It is now maintained as a museum by the *Boston Globe.* NR. Open M-F 9-5. Free. (617) 929-2602.

Old South Meeting House, Washington and Milk Sts., 1729. This church is one of America's national shrines of liberty. It was here that the patriots of the 1770s most often met to protest and to organize. One of the most effective demonstrations planned at Old South was the Boston Tea Party. The British did their best to destroy the place by using it as a riding school in 1775. The interior, with a three-sided gallery and a high raised pulpit, was restored after the Revolution. Later the congregation which was moving to new quarters on Copley Square planned to tear down the old building, but this act of planned vandalism was stopped by a thoughtful citizenry. Old South was built as the Third Congregational Church, and is a two-story brick building with a side tower topped with a wood steeple. The building is owned and managed by the Old South As-

sociation in cooperation with the National Park Service. NR, NHL. Open daily Apr-Oct 10-6, Nov-Mar 10-4. 50¢ admission fee. (617) 482-6439. ♦♦

Old State House, 206 Washington St., 1713. Before it served as the capitol of the commonwealth (1776-98), this building was the official provincial seat of government for civic and military affairs. It occupies the site of a former provincial government building. The stepped gable of the handsome red brick landmark is an unusual feature in Boston. The State House was threatened with demolition several times, but since 1881 has rested safely as the headquarters of the eminent Bostonian Society. Exhibits illustrating the marine and local history of the Boston area are permanently ensconced. Outside the building on Washington St. a circle of cobblestones marks the site of the Boston Massacre of five patriots by the British on March 5, 1770. NR, NHL. Open summer, daily 9:30-5; winter, M-F 10-4, Sa 9:30-5, Su 11-5. 75¢ adults, 50¢ senior citizens, 25¢ children. (617) 242-5610.

Park Street Church, 119 Tremont St., 1809. This place of worship replaced the former town granary. It is a typical New England red brick meeting house, in this case with a towering Wren-type wooden steeple that rises 217 feet. The church's history is distinguished by an involvement with once unpopular social causes and organizations such as the American Temperance Society, abolitionist groups, and the Animal Rescue League. NR.

St. Paul's Church, 136 Tremont St., 1819-20. Refreshingly different from most other early Boston parishes, St. Paul's is a strikingly simple stone Greek temple with an Ionic-columned portico. It was designed by Alexander Parris and Solomon Willard and now serves as the cathedral of the Episcopal diocese of Boston. NR.

Washington St. Theater District, 511-599 Washington St., between Avery and West Sts., 1870-1935. The principal buildings of interest along what was Boston's Great White Way are the **Paramount** (1932); the **Savoy** (1928); and the **Mayflower** (1876, 1913). Of these, the Savoy is clearly the most sumptuous and visually interesting — inside and out. The French baroque interior is resplendent with marble columns, walnut paneling, and other luxurious touches. It is a 3,500-seat theater and has been renovated for use by the Opera Company of Boston. NR.

FANEUIL HALL-QUINCY MARKET-CUSTOM HOUSE AREA. The adaptation of Quincy Market for shops and restaurants has brought new life to this

Faneuil Hall

historic area. The renaissance in urban life has spilled over to the adjacent blocks. Only the elevated John F. Fitzgerald Expressway visually blocks a reuniting of the city with its historic waterfront, and in time, this modern incursion may be routed under or away from the area.

United States Custom House, McKinley Sq., 1834-37, 1913-15. The Custom House started out life as a much smaller building. Designed by Ammi B. Young in the Greek Revival style favored for public buildings in the early 1800s, it was positioned close to what was then the waterfront. The present shoreline is a product of later landfill. The building was drastically altered with the addition of an office tower. NR.

Faneuil Hall, Dock Sq., 1761, 1805-06. This is the first building the visitor comes to when entering the Quincy Market area. Next to Old South Church in importance as a Revolutionary War shrine, Faneuil Hall housed for years the **Ancient and Honorable Artillery Co.,** founded in 1638, and its museum of portraits, historical paintings and military relics. The first Faneuil Hall, a gift of merchant Peter Faneuil in 1742, burned completely to the ground in 1761 and was just as completely

rebuilt according to the original plans. Subsequent changes were the addition of a third floor and the doubling of the building's width by architect Charles Bulfinch in 1805-06. The first-floor level has always served as a market and continues in that role today. It is open seven days a week from 9-5 and, like the adjoining Quincy Market buildings, provides a place to shop and eat. The second floor—the historic Revolutionary period meeting room and the site of the debate of burning 19th-century issues such as slavery and states' rights—is open M-F 9-5, Sa 9-12, and Su 1-5. Free. (617) 242-5642. The Artillery Co. museum on the third floor is open M-F 10-4. It is closed for two weeks each Oct. Free. (617) 227-1638. NR, NHL. ♛

Long Wharf and Customhouse Block, foot of State St.; wharf, 1710-21; Customhouse Block, 1848. The wharf was once the city's busiest pier, and the Customhouse Block is typical of the massive granite buildings found there for housing shipments. Indian Wharf, once Boston's most historic, is gone and so, too, are many of the other wharf buildings. It is worth catching a glimpse of this enclave just above the Central Wharf and the Aquarium before the area changes further. NR, NHL.

Quincy Market, South Market St., 1825-26. The market was built in response to overcrowded conditions at the Faneuil Hall market and is one of Alexander Parris's best designs. The scene is crowded again, and the marketplace has become Boston's number-one tourist attraction. Try to avoid it on the weekends if at all possible, especially during the summer. The three main buildings—a two-story center-domed bulding of granite and two flanking structures (North and South markets)—offer a wide selection of merchandise. The whole complex once faced the harbor, but this is cut off by the Expressway and landfill. NR, NHL. Open M-Sa 9-5, Su 10-5. ⛪

Union Oyster House, 41 Union St., c. 1730. A "Ye" has been added to the name of the establishment, but, except for that, everything is about the same as it has been for the past 150 years. The brick building has always been a tavern and is a place that Daniel Webster is supposed to have frequented. NR. The restaurant and bar are open daily 11-9:30, and on F and Sa to 10. (617) 227-2750.

DORCHESTER. Annexed to the city of Boston in 1870, Dorchester still retains a quite separate identity—historical and otherwise. Situated SW of the downtown area, it is a vast residential district built up largely in the mid- to late-19th century. Few of the early farmhouses are still standing. The Dorchester Historical Society, however, has helped to save several important buildings of special interest to students of early Americana.

James Blake House, 735 Columbia Rd., Richardson Park, c. 1650, is the most interesting of the surviving Dorchester homes. It was moved in 1895 and restored at that time—a very early instance of historic preservation. Evidence suggests that this is one of the few buildings left in America that was built by a first-generation immigrant of the first wave of English settlement. The framing and joining are definitely within the medieval building tradition and the timbers used are

exceptionally heavy. NR. Open every second Sa 2-4 and by appointment. (617) 436-6251.

Clapp Houses, 195 and 199 Boston St., 1765, 1806. Two generations of the Clapp family made their livelihoods in the tannery business. Lemuel, the father, had a typical two-story clapboard home built in the mid-18th century; his son, William, is responsible for the adjoining brick and clapboard residence. His house now serves as the headquarters of the Dorchester Historical Society and is known for its period kitchen. The earlier building was once thought to have been the home of Roger Clap, a prominent Dorchester resident of the 17th century but this has been disproved. Both NR. Open every second Sa 2-4 and by appointment. (617) 436-6251.

Pierce House, 24 Oakton St., 1652. Eleven generations of the Pierce family resided here from the 17th century until the 1960s. Like the Blake House (see earlier listing), the 2½-story saltbox exhibits the traditional carpentry work of the first generation settlers. The house is now maintained by the SPNEA. There have been major changes since the 1600s; shingles were added to the clapboards in the 1930s and, earlier, a lean-to was tacked on. The interior appointments date from both the 18th and 19th centuries. NR. Open by appointment. (617) 227-3956.

DORCHESTER HEIGHTS-SOUTH BOSTON—THE HARBOR. Dorchester Heights is better known today by the name Telegraph Hill and is part of South Boston. This promontory affords a superb view of the harbor. During the mid-19th century the area was built up with handsome town houses. The neighborhood, however, never really caught on with Boston's trendsetters. An eminent Boston architectural historian could provide only this explanation: "the Lord in His wisdom saved for His poorer and less fashionable children the beautiful area which their wealthier cousins disdained." As for Boston harbor, it has never been developed except along military lines. Only recently has the Metropolitan District Commission sought to open up historic Fort Warren on Georges Island for tourism. Boston decided to turn her back on the harbor in the 19th century and is only beginning to reconsider the view.

Dorchester Heights National Historic Site, Thomas Park, Telegraph Hill, between Old Harbor and G St., South Boston, 1776. Situated on what is known historically as Dorchester Neck (annexed by the city in 1804) is one of the most important military sites in New England. George Washington and his army took to the summit of Dorchester Heights south of the city on the night of March 4, 1776, and within a few days succeeded—with the help of a violent storm at sea—in scaring off the British troops led by General Howe which were adrift in the harbor. Troops were again stationed here during the War of 1812, and a white marble tower commemorates the 1776 victory. NR, NHL. (617) 269-4275.

Fort Warren, Georges Island, Boston Harbor, 1834-63. A trip to Georges Island by boat is a pleasant and informative foray into the past. Fort Warren is a classic star-shaped 19th-century fortification and was especially important during the Civil War. At that time it was used for training purposes and as a prison for Confederate soldiers. Two of the South's Commissioners to France and England were held here; after the war it was an unhappy home for Alexander Hamilton Stephens and John Regan, vice-president and postmaster general, respectively, of the Confederacy. The fortifications were designed by Sylvanus Thayer, military engineer and superintendent of West Point from 1817-33. The fort is built largely of granite, and massive piers of this stone support the ramparts. The fort is owned and operated by the Metropolitan District Commission of Boston and is part of the Boston Harbor Islands Park. NR, NHL. The fort is open from Memorial Day-Oct 10th, daily 8-sunset. Free. Transportation is provided from either Long Wharf at the end of State St., or from Rowes Wharf on Atlantic Ave. Cost is approximately $3 per person. For further information, contact the MA Bay Lines. (617) 542-8000. ♙

JAMAICA PLAIN. This once independent community lies SW of downtown Boston and W of Dorchester. Its primary attraction is the Arnold Arboretum, a lovely green space which is, in part, a continuation of the bucolic park system designed by Frederick Law Olmstead.

Arnold Arboretum, 22 Divinity Ave., c. 1873. What was begun as a tree farm for Harvard University has become a major research institution. Along the paths visitors can enjoy more than 6,000 species of trees and shrubs. Olmstead helped to create a place that is as aesthetically pleasing as it is scientifically well-founded. Affiliated with Harvard University. Open May-June, daily 9-5; July-Apr, daily M-F 9-5. Free. (617) 524-1717. ♙

NORTH END. Boston's North End neighborhood is almost as historic as the downtown-Common area. Now that nearby Quincy Market has become so fashionable, the nearby North End is threatened with popularity. Since the 19th century it has been a largely Italian community. Tourists in the past would make their way to see such sacred sights as Old North (Christ Church) and the Paul Revere House, but would then retreat back down the crooked streets. Now visitors are likely to linger for awhile, perhaps along Salem St. to sample the food from outdoor markets, or to stop at one of the shops on Hanover St. The neighborhood is largely made up of three- or four-story brick attached dwellings once considered tenements. It is a flavorful, colorful neighborhood full of character and charm.

Pierce-Hichborn House, 29 North Sq., 1680-1710. Moses Pierce was the builder of his own three-story brick town house. Six rooms were allowed for in the narrow building; a service wing was added later. It is now open to the public as a typical Colonial-period town dwelling. NR, NHL. Nov-Apr 15, daily 10-4; Apr 15-Oct, daily 10-6. $1 adults, 50¢ senior citizens, 25¢ children (6-16). (617) 523-2338.

Old North (Christ) Church, 193 Salem St., 1723. Old North is Boston's earliest sur-

Paul Revere House, 19 North Sq., c. 1676. This is the only 17th-century house left in Boston's central-city area. Since it was the home of a Revolutionary patriot, it has always been considered worthy of preservation. The house was restored to its 17th-century form in 1908. The two-story frame dwelling is just one-room deep—as were most early houses—and the facade is distinguished by a second-story overhang. NR, NHL. Open Apr 15-Oct 31, daily 10-6; Nov-Apr 15, daily 10-4. 75¢ adults, 25¢ children. (617) 523-1676.

viving church, but it is not only age which had made this landmark famous. Poetry has helped. Longfellow penned the famous message, "One if by land, two if by sea" in his poem "The Midnight Ride of Paul Revere." The poet was referring to the signal which was to be given from the steeple of Old North to inform the patriots of the British troop movement on the night of April 18, 1775. The Redcoats chose the sea route and the church sexton Robert Newman hung two lanterns from the belfry to warn the residents of Charlestown that the enemy was crossing the harbor on its way to Concord. That steeple blew down in 1804 and was replaced by a similar model. It has been changed several times since. In most other respects, however, the church is as it was in the 18th century. It is still an active Episcopal parish. NR, NHL. Open daily 9-5; Su services at 9:30, 11, 4. Free.

Near Old North is the **Copp's Hill Burial Ground** bounded by Charter, Snowhill, and Hulls Sts., 1659-19th century. Four cemeteries laid out from the mid-17th century until 1832 are included. Consequently, there is an unusual variety of grave marker decoration and tomb art to be seen. Among the famous deceased are Cotton Mather, the 17th-century Puritan divine, and Edward Hartt, the builder of the *U.S.S. Constitution.* NR.

St. Stephen's Church, Hanover St. between Clark and Harris Sts., 1804. St. Stephen's is noted only for its beauty. The architect of this red brick Federal-style building was Charles Bulfinch. The three-story front pavilion with an open bell tower and a domed cupola is especially admired. The building has served Congregational, Unitarian, and Roman Catholic congregations. NR.

ROXBURY. Because its population has become largely black, Roxbury is scandalously overlooked in most historical guides and surveys. More is the pity. The community is one of Boston's oldest neighborhood enclaves and is rich in historical artifacts and associations. The historic center of Roxbury is John Eliot Sq.

John Eliot Square Historical District, c. 1750-1873. Included here is the frame

First Church in Roxbury (1804) and the Dillaway-Thomas House (c. 1750-54), which served as its parsonage. The church has also been known as the Church of John Eliot, apostle to the Indians in the 17th century and translator of the Bible into the "Massachusetts Indian language." Eliot was the first minister to serve the Roxbury church. The meeting house is in the Federal style, with a typical period interior that has a raised pulpit and a gallery. The Dillaway-Thomas House is a modest Georgian clapboard structure that has been very well preserved. The Roxbury Historical Society has its headquarters here, and it is open Su-F 9-5. Free. The society sponsors guided walking tours of Roxbury (part of the Black Heritage Trail) at a cost of $5 for adults and $2.50 for children. For further information, contact (617) 445-7400.

East Central Area

The east central cities, towns, and villages of Norfolk and Middlesex counties surrounding Boston proper are treated separately in the following listings.

Within a close distance of Boston are many small cities which could be mistaken for being part of the larger city. Cambridge, Quincy, Brookline, Watertown, and Somerville all adjoin Boston. Each has a proud historical tradition and a rich sampling of cultural institutions with deep roots in the local landscape. The towns and villages of Norfolk and Middlesex counties which encircle Boston—including Concord and Lexington, Medford, Arlington, Newton, Milton, and Braintree—are even more proud and independent in their ways. The amount of time and money invested in the maintenance of historic sites and buildings in these communities is undoubtedly unequaled elsewhere in the United States.

Acton

FAULKNER HOMESTEAD, 5 High St., 1707, 1774, c. 1840. This is one of two properties maintained by the local Iron Work Farm, the other being the **Jones Tavern** at 128 Main St. The two-story clapboard house has had a most versatile life as a meeting hall, a garrison house, a mill for dyeing and weaving cloth, and a courthouse as well as a residence. NR. Guided tours are offered on Patriots Day (third M in April) and the first Su of each month, May-Oct, from 2-5. The building is open by appointment at other times. 50¢ adults, 25¢ for children under 12. For further information, contact Iron Work Farm in Acton, Inc., Box 11, Acton MA 01720.

Arlington

JASON RUSSELL HOUSE, 7 Jason St., c. 1740. Evidence of how close to home the Revolutionary War was waged is amply displayed in this well preserved residence. Jason Russell, a prosperous farmer, was a member of the colonial militia and on April 19, 1775, lost his life when surprised by British troops returning from action at Concord and Lexington. Several of the Minutemen were more fortunate and took refuge in the basement of the house and kept the Redcoats at bay. Bullet holes are still visible in the woodwork. The Arlington Historical Society has carefully maintained the house since 1923 and displays a variety of 18th and 19th-century furnishings. The kitchen, with a black-and-white sponge-painted ceiling, is of special note. NR. Open Apr-Nov, Tu-Sa 2-5. 50¢ adults, 10¢ children under 12. (617) 648-4300.

OLD SCHWAMB MILL, 17 Mill Ln. and 20 Lowell St., 1860. Picture frames were made here in the 19th century with the aid of water and, later, steam power. Charles and Frederick Schwamb began their business in 1843 and rebuilt the wooden mill after a fire in 1860. Much of the old equipment remains in place and in use under the auspices of the Schwamb Mill Preservation Trust. NR. Open M-F 9-4. Free except for large tour groups for which $1 is charged. (617) 643-0554 or (617) 643-0640.

Braintree

THE GENERAL SYLVANUS THAYER BIRTHPLACE, 786 Washington St., 1720. One of the finest historic houses in New England open to the public, the Thayer birthplace honors the distinguished career of the man called the "Father of West Point." Thayer's home has been restored to the period of the 1780s, the decade of his birth. All of the furnishings date prior to 1785 and include such extraordinary antiques as a 1670 oak and ebonized press cupboard and a c. 1640 harmonium which belonged to Peregrine White who was born on the Mayflower *en route* to Plymouth. These pieces and many other fine examples of William and Mary, Queen Anne, and Chippendale craftsmanship are displayed in carefully composed period rooms. Owned and maintained by the Braintree Historical Society. Open Apr 19-Oct 12, Tu, Th, F and Su 1:30-4, Sa 10:30-4; Oct 13-Apr 18, Tu and Sa, 1:30-4. Nominal admission. (617) 848-1640.

Brookline

MARY BAKER EDDY MUSEUM, 120 Seaver St. The early history of the Christian Science religion is carefully exhibited here in paintings, letters, and memorabilia relating to the life of the founder. Affiliated with the Longyear Historical Society. Open Apr 1-Oct 30, Tu-Sa 10-5, Su 1-5; Nov 1-Mar 31, Tu-Sa 10-4, Su 1-4; closed Feb.

JOHN FITZGERALD KENNEDY NATIONAL HISTORIC SITE, 83 Beals St., 1909. Brookline was a perfect place to raise a family in the early 20th century. As long as there were only a few children, the house on Beals St. was perfect in almost every respect, and from 1915 to 1921 it served the Joseph Kennedy family very well. John F. Kennedy, America's 35th President, was born here on May 29, 1917, and the house has been restored to that year. In 1921 the family moved to another Brookline home on the NE corner of Abbotsford and Naples Rds., and lived there until 1927. The second house is still privately owned but can be viewed from the road. The Beals St. house is open daily 10-4:30. 50¢ adults, no charge for senior citizens and children. (617) 566-7937.

Cambridge

Cambridge is closer to Boston, both physically and temperamentally, than any other adjoining area, but still remains somewhat aloof. This may be because life has always been so well anchored in the institution of Harvard University. Cambridge is not as dependent culturally on the larger city as most of the suburban communities. Its own social and cultural institutions are every bit as venerable and valued. Just a brief visit to Harvard Sq., easily reached from Boston via the subway, will suffice to capture some of the ambience so distinctive to this major academic center.

CAMBRIDGE COMMON/HARVARD SQUARE. Centered around the V-shaped intersection of Massachusetts Ave. and Garden St. are some of the most important non-academic historic buildings in the area:

First Parish Church (Unitarian) (1833), Garden St., is a wooden Gothic Revival building and the home of the oldest parish (1633) in Cambridge. NR. It is situated next to the **Old Burying Ground** which contains over 80 17th-century headstones. Dexter Pratt, the "Village Blacksmith" of Longfellow's poem, is buried here—more famous in death than in life.

Christ Church (Episcopal) (1760), Garden St., was designed by the earliest known American-born architect, Peter Harrison. The interior is elegantly understated in the best Georgian Colonial manner. NR, NHL.

The Common, to the north of the churches, served as the main camp for Washington's Continental Army in 1775-76.

HARVARD UNIVERSITY CAMPUS. The best way to explore the campus is to take one of the student-guided tours available from mid-June through Aug. These leave from the Information Center at 1350 Massachusetts Ave. (617-495-1573). At other times of the year, the Center will provide maps and brochures to help you on your way. Among the landmark buildings to be visited are several in the old college Yard.

Massachusetts Hall (1718) is the oldest remaining building and was built as a dormitory to house 64 students. It was designed by Harvard president John Leverett and Benjamin Wadsworth. It now serves as administrative offices.

University Hall (1815) is one of Charles Bulfinch's Federal-style buildings and makes use of granite as well as red brick, a first for Harvard at the time. Positioned in front of the building is Daniel Chester French's sculptured likeness of John Harvard.

Other buildings in the Yard include **Hollis Hall** (1762), **Harvard Hall** (1764), and **Holden Chapel** (1744).

Henry Hobson Richardson, the master of an American style termed Richardsonian Romanesque, was responsible for several buildings at Harvard, one of which is located in Harvard Yard. This is **Sever Hall** (1878-80), a monumental classroom building in red brick. It is distinguished by the boldly arched front entrance and two cylindrical towers with conical caps. The windows are set in banded rows with decorative trim around them. Richardson also designed **Austin Hall** (1881-83), on the Law School campus slightly to the north. This is a less decorative stone building.

The remaining campus landmark which no Harvardian-for-a-day can afford to miss is **Memorial Hall** (1870-78), Cambridge and Quincy Sts. It took a long time to erect this sprawling late Gothic Revival hall in memory of Harvard's Civil War dead. Designed by William Robert Ware and Henry Van Brunt, the building has been called "an almost fanatic statement of the taste of its time." It is a flamboyant piece of work with multicolored tile roofing material and a facade which has fanciful stone trimming. Rose windows in this dining hall-memorial hall-theater are found on three sides. NR, NHL.

LONGFELLOW NATIONAL HISTORIC SITE, 105 Brattle St., 1759. For 45 years Henry Wadsworth Longfellow made this his home. It was originally known as the Vassall House and later as Craigie House. Georgian Colonial in style, the landmark dwelling served as headquarters for General Washington in 1775-76. The present furnishings and decoration date from the period of Longfellow's residence. The National Park Service staff has done a superb job of recreating the ambience of the years 1837-1882. It was in this house that Longfellow wrote such famous poems as "The Wreck of the Hesperus," "The Village Blacksmith," and "The Song of Hiawatha." NR, NHL. Open daily 10-4:30. 50¢ adults, no charge for children under 16 and senior citizens. (617) 876-4491.

On the way to see the Longfellow house you are likely to pass the **Dexter Pratt House** (1808), 54 Brattle St., the home of Longfellow's "Village Smithy"; and the **Oliver Hastings House** (1844-45), 101 Brattle St., a very sophisticated Greek Revival mansion built for a prosperous Boston merchant.

FRANCIS RUSSELL HART NAUTICAL MUSEUM, 77 Massachusetts Ave., brings one to the Massachusetts Institute of Technology campus which stretches out along the Charles River. The museum houses a remarkable collection of photos, plans, and ship models which never fail to impress anyone interested in marine history. Open 9-5 daily. Free. (617) 253-4444.

MOUNT AUBURN CEMETERY, 580 Mount Auburn St., 1831. America's first garden cemetery is certainly one of its most beautiful. There have been over 70,000 interments, with wooden, marble, and brownstone tombs, sarcophagi, obelisks, and headstones forming a veritable history of 19th-century funerary art. The most impressive sights are the Egyptian Revival entrance gate (1843); the Gothic Revival **Bigelow Chapel** (1843 and 1858); and a granite tower that rises 62 feet (1853). Among the notables who are resting along the picturesque lanes are Mary Baker Eddy, Julia Ward Howe, Charles Bulfinch, Winslow Homer, Edwin Booth, and Oliver Wendell Holmes. NR.

COOPER-FROST-AUSTIN HOUSE, 21 Linnaean St., c. 1680. This is thought to be Cambridge's oldest surviving house. The early Colonial clapboard was expanded in the 18th century. The building is now maintained by the SPNEA and is only open by appointment. NR. For further information, contact the SPNEA at Harrison Gray Otis House, 141 Cambridge St., Boston, MA 02114 (617-227-3956).

Chelsea

BELLINGHAM-CARY HOUSE, 34 Parker St., 17th-18th centuries. This amazing survivor from the mid-1600s first served as a hunting lodge for Richard Bellingham, one of the Massachusetts Bay Co. founders and later a governor of the colony. The lodge was expanded in the 1700s and once again altered in the Federal style toward the end of the century. NR. Maintained by the Gov. Bellingham Cary Association. Open mid-Apr-Oct 31, Th 2-5.

Concord and Lexington

Concord and Lexington have been inseparably linked by the events of April 19, 1775. **Minute Man National Historical Park** was created to commemorate the Battle of Lexington and the Battle of Concord and includes the North Bridge area in Concord and extends for four miles of Battle Rd. between Concord and Lexington.

Concord

CONCORD ANTIQUARIAN SOCIE-

TY, 200 Lexington Rd. This is one of America's leading historical museums. Founded in 1895, the society quickly took the lead in the acquisition and care of Revolutionary War period and early 19th-century memorabilia and furnishings. Part of the museum is located in the **Matthew Perkins House** (1895). The collections include what is thought to have been the lantern carried by Paul Revere on his famous ride and countless articles pertaining to the careers of Concord residents Henry David Thoreau and Ralph Waldo Emerson. NR. Open M-Sa 10-4:30, Su 2-4:30. $2 adults, $1 children; groups of 12 or more and senior citizens, $1.50. (617) 369-9609.

RALPH WALDO EMERSON HOUSE, Lexington Rd. and Cambridge Tpk., 1835. The famous Transcendental philosopher's personal belongings have been preserved in his Federal-style clapboard house. NR. Open mid-Apr-late Oct, Th-Sa 10-4:30, Su 2-4:30. $2 adults, $1 children 6-17. (617) 369-2236.

MINUTE MAN NATIONAL HISTORICAL PARK, The North Bridge Visitor Center, Liberty St. The focus of the Concord National Park facilities is on historic North Bridge and the "Minuteman" statue by Daniel Chester French. The center exhibits materials relating to the Battle of Concord. Open June 1-Aug 31, 8-6 daily; Sept 1-May 31, 8:30-5 daily. 🏛 (617) 369-6993.

OLD MANSE, Monument St., c. 1765. Adjoining North Bridge is this Georgian Colonial home which served as a sanctuary for Ralph Waldo Emerson and Nathaniel Hawthorne. It was built by Emerson's grandfather, the Rev. William Emerson, minister of the First Parish Church and first chaplain of the Continental Army. Hawthorne immortalized the house in his *Mosses From an Old Manse* (1846), written in the upstairs study. The building and eight acres are well maintained by the Trustees of Reservations. NR, NHL. Open mid-Apr-June 1, 10-4:30 Sa, 1-4:30 Su, and by appointment; June 1-Oct 31, 10-4:30 M-Sa, 1-4:30 Su and holidays. $2 adults, $1 children 11-16. (617) 369-3909.

ORCHARD HOUSE, 399 Lexington Rd., mid-19th century. Philosopher Bronson Alcott found a more stable resting place here than at Fruitlands (see Harvard, MA) or elsewhere in the Concord vicinity. It is here that Louisa May Alcott, one of his daughters, wrote part of *Little Women.* The house is open for tours and includes interesting memorabilia of the Alcott family as well as furnishings appropriate to the period. NR, NHL. Open mid-Apr-mid-Nov, M-Sa 10-4:30, Su 1-4:30. $2 adults, $1 students 6-12; special group rates. (617) 369-4118.

THOREAU-ALCOTT HOUSE, 255 Main St., c. 1820. The Greek Revival landmark was home for Henry David Thoreau from 1849 to 1862; here he wrote *Walden* (1854) and *Cape Cod* (published in 1865). Louisa May Alcott and her sister, Ann Pratt, bought the home in 1877 for their parents. Private, but may be viewed from the public way. NR.

THE THOREAU LYCEUM, 156 Belknap St., 19th century. The institution was founded in 1966 by thoughtful admirers of Thoreau's philosophy and writings. A small museum in the shingled dwelling next to the old Thoreau family lot contains exhibits on Thoreau's many activities and those of his Transcendental colleagues. A replica of his house at Walden Pond can be seen behind the Lyceum. Open M-Sa 10-5, Su 2-5. $1 adults, 50¢ students 8-18. (617) 369-5912.

WAYSIDE, Lexington Rd., MA 2A, 1775. This building should not be confused (as it often is) with the famous inn of the same name in Sudbury. The Alcotts lived here from 1845-48 and called the place "Hillside." Nathaniel Hawthorne renamed it upon purchasing the property in 1852 and lived here until his death in 1864. The strange tower which rises above the clapboard structure provided a secluded sanctuary for Hawthorne the writer. Wayside is part of the Minute Man National Historical Park. June-Oct 9-5:30; Sept-Oct and Apr-May, 8:30-5; Nov-Mar, W-Su 8:30-5. (617) 369-6993.

Concord vicinity

WALDEN POND, 1.5 miles S of Concord, 915 Walden St. Walden Pond State Reservation consists of 114 acres, including the lake, shoreline, and the site of the cabin where Henry David Thoreau attempted his noble experiment in simple living from 1845-47. There is a beach—and bathing facilities, too—so if the weather is warm, try to make your visit early in the day before the crowds arrive. NR, NHL.

Lexington

BUCKMAN TAVERN, 1 Bedford St., c. 1690. This is the oldest of the many inns that served Lexington's citizens and travelers to and from Boston. On the morning of April 19, 1775, when the battle took place, it was the meeting hall for Lexington's Minute Men; John Buckman, proprietor of the tavern, was a member of the company of soldiers. The interior of the two-story frame building has been restored to the Revolutionary period. It is one of three important properties maintained by the Lexington Historical Society. NR, NHL. Open Apr 19-Nov 1, M-Sa 10-5, S 1-5. $1 adults, 25¢ children under 16; special three-house combination rate for adults, $2.25 (see Hancock-Clarke House and Munroe Tavern). (617) 861-0928.

FOLLEN COMMUNITY CHURCH, 755 Massachusetts Ave., 1840-41. In a town of Revolutionary War sites and scenes, an octagonal church built in the mid-19th century may appear of little interest. It is, however, an attractive and unusual building with Greek Revival decorative elements. It was the first home of the Religious Society of East Lexington, the type of avant garde religious group established at this time in the sophisticated, intellectual circles of eastern Massachusetts. NR.

HANCOCK-CLARKE HOUSE, 35 Hancock St., 1698, 1734, 1962. Lexington's most historic house served as the parsonage of the First Church from the late 17th century through the Revolutionary War period. The 1½-story rear ell is the oldest part and was built by the Rev. John Hancock, the grandfather of the famous Revolutionary War statesman and signer of the Declaration of Independence. He and patriot Samuel Adams were visiting here on April 18, 1775, when Paul Revere arrived to warn them of the impending British invasion. Hancock and Adams were guests of the then-pastor of the church, the Rev. Jonas Clarke. The building is one of the three properties administered by the Lexington Historical Society and is furnished with an extraordinary collection of antiques. Many of the objects have historical associations with the Hancock or Clarke families. Open Apr 19-Nov 1, M-Sa 10-5, Su 1-5. $1 adults, 25¢ for children under 16; special three-house combination rate for adults, $2.25. (617) 861-0928.

LEXINGTON GREEN, bounded by Massachusetts Ave., Hancock St., and Harrington Rd., is the triangular piece of land where the Redcoats and Minutemen met for the first time and the first shot in the Revolution was fired. Among the notable monuments to the patriotic past are the **Hayes Memorial Fountain** and Lexington's Minuteman statue at the apex of the Green, and on the west side the granite **Revolutionary Monument.** The first monument to the War was raised in 1799; in 1835 the remains of those who had lost their lives on April 19, 1775 were placed in a tomb at the rear of the monument's foundation. A replica of **The Belfry,** the town's bell tower which used to stand on the Green, is now found on a hillside opposite it. The **First Parish Church,** positioned at the head of the Green, dates from 1847 and replaced the 18th-century meeting house. NR, NHL. 🚶

MINUTE MAN NATIONAL HISTORIC PARK, Battle Rd. Visitor Center, off MA 2A. Located between the battle sites in Concord and Lexington, this is an up-to-date facility for exhibits interpreting the Revolutionary War events and for the showing of *To Keep Our Liberty,* a film prepared by the National Park Service. Open Nov 1-March 31, W-Su 8:30-5; Apr 1-Oct 31, daily 8:30-5:30. Free. 🚶 (617) 862-7753.

MUNROE TAVERN, 1332 Massachusetts Ave., 1650-1700, and SANDERSON HOUSE, 1314 Massachusetts Ave., 1731-47. Both served as retreat locations for the British troops during the battles of Lexington and Concord. The tavern is now operated as a museum by the Lexington Historical Society. William Munroe was the proprietor of the tavern from 1770 to 1827 and in 1789 was host to

George Washington when the first president visited the Lexington battlefield. NR. Munroe Tavern is open Apr 18-Nov 1, M-Sa 10-5, Su 1-5. $1 adults, 25¢ children under 16; special three-house combination rate for adults, $2.25. (617) 861-0928.

MUSEUM OF OUR NATIONAL HERITAGE, 33 Marrett Rd. This is a superbly equipped modern facility sponsored by the Scottish Rite Masons fraternal order. The history of Freemasonry is the focus of research in the Van Gorden-Williams Library. Programs and exhibits, however, focus on much broader topics, including the Revolution and the American tradition in the decorative arts. Open Apr-Oct, M-Sa 10-5, Su 12-5:30; Nov-Mar, M-Sa 10-4, Su 12-5:30. Free. (617) 861-6559.
♈

For further information regarding historical sites in the Lexington area, contact or visit the **Visitors Center** at 1873 Massachusetts Ave., which is staffed by the Chamber of Commerce. Displayed here is a diorama of the Battle of Lexington.

Dedham

FAIRBANKS HOUSE, 511 East St., c. 1636. No frame building in the nation is more historic, because this is the oldest known surviving wooden building in America. Jonathan Fairbank and eight generations of the Fairbanks family have occupied the house. It has grown from a simple two-story, central chimney, one-room-deep dwelling to one with wings and a lean-to addition and is exceptionally well furnished with 17th- and 18th-century objects. NR, NHL. Open Tu-Su and holidays 9-5. $2 adults, $1 children under 12. (617) 326-1170.

While in Dedham you might want to visit the **Historical Society** at 612 High St. In addition to colonial-period furnishings, there is a fine collection of pottery wares produced in the 1890s. Open Sept-June, Tu-Sa 2-5; July-Aug, Tu-F 2-5. Free. (617) 326-1385.

Lincoln

THE GRANGE, Codman Rd., 18th-20th centuries. The mansion house on this sixteen-acre estate is a splendid Federal-style frame cube with clapboard walls, pedimented and shuttered windows, and a broad hip roof crowned with a balustraded deck. One architectural element builds upon another to great dramatic effect. The building started out much smaller and simpler in the early 1700s, but merchant John Codman decided in 1797-98 to find an architect who would create the at-

Fairbanks House

Some sense of the wealth and industrial ingenuity generated in Lowell during the 19th century can be gained by setting off on a self-guided walking tour in the National Historical Park area. Among the important sights, all of which can be visited, are: **City Hall** (1893), along Merrimack St., a great Richardsonian Romanesque palazzo; the **Merrimack Canal Gate House** (1848), corner of Dutton and Merrimack Sts., where the flow of water from three subteranean tunnels into the canal is controlled; and **St. Anne's Church and Rectory** (1825), corner of Kirk and Merrimack Sts., a Greek Revival stone building, the first church to be built in the then-new city of Lowell. It is said that attendance was obligatory for the mill "girls" in the early years.

mosphere of an English country seat. The design is attributed to Charles Bulfinch. There are four other buildings on the property as well as formal gardens. NR. The Grange, also known as Codman House, is owned and maintained by the SPNEA. Open June 1-Oct 15, Tu, Th, Sa, Su 12-5. $2 admission. (617) 259-8843.

Lowell

LOWELL NATIONAL HISTORICAL PARK and HERITAGE STATE PARK, downtown Lowell, including Merrimack, Kirk, Dutton, Market, and Shattuck Sts., 19th century. Lowell emerged in the 1820s as America's leading textile manufacturing center. This preeminence was maintained until the early 20th century. The industry was founded on a supply of cheap water power and a complex system of canals. Labor was abundant throughout the 1800s, and as Lucy Larcom, a mill hand, told the story in *New England Girlhood* (1889), employees were often exploited. It wasn't a particularly pretty scene, and since the early 1900s it has been a depressed one as the textile industry moved to the South. Lowell will never again be the great manufacturing center that it once was, but the city has been coming back economically and there is a new appreciation for the extraordinary industrial and transport facilities which remain.

Medford

ISAAC ROYALL HOUSE, 15 George St., 17th-18th centuries. In its time this was, as its name would seem to imply, a very rich house for America. Royall was a successful rum merchant of the early 18th century and took what was a simple early colonial house and transformed it into an elegant high-style Georgian mansion. This was the center of a 587-acre estate overlooking the Mystic River. The east facade is the most unusual, with vertical rows of windows extending in panels from sill to dentil cornice. The interior woodwork and other architectural detailing is similarly sophisticated. The house has been beautifully furnished by the Royall House Association. NR, NHL. It is open May-Oct 1, Tu-Th, Sa-Su 2-5. $1.50 adults, $1 senior citizens, 50¢ children. (617) 396-9032.

PETER TUFTS HOUSE, 350 Riverside Ave., 1675, is reputed to be the oldest surviving brick house in New England. It is one of only eleven known to have been built in New England in the 17th century. The windows were originally casement and there is evidence in the framing that medieval building practice was adhered to by the first owner. NR, NHL. The house is maintained by the SPNEA and is open only by appointment. $1 adults. Call (617) 227-3956 for information.

SALEM STREET BURYING GROUND, between Salem St. and Riverside Ave. on the edge of Medford Sq., 1660-1880. The 425 remaining stones of this family cemetery display the full range of symbolic carved designs popular in New England. There are "death's heads," cherubim, and other less fanciful or macabre touches. Almost all of the stones are slate and are in good condition. Members of all of Medford's early merchant and shipping families are buried here. NR.

Milton

MUSEUM OF THE AMERICAN CHINA TRADE, 215 Adams St., 1833. The historic trade between America and China commenced soon after the Revolution and grew in importance until the Civil War. Many of the merchants involved in the global maritime enterprise were headquartered in the coastal cities of Massachusetts, including Captain Robert Bennet Forbes who was the head of the trading firm of Russell and Co. in the 1840s. The prosperity which resulted from the exchange of goods is reflected in Forbes's house, a three-story Greek Revival design by Isaiah Rogers, and in the elegant furnishings. Chinese export porcelain made for the American market is beautifully displayed in the rooms of the Forbes House

which serves as the museum's headquarters. Other kinds of objects made in China—lacquerware, silver, textiles—are also on exhibit. The museum's archives contain thousands of documents and other printed matter, including photographs, which relate to the American trade with the Far East. NR. Forbes House is open Tu-Su 1-4; group tours are available from 1-4. $3 adults, $1.50 children. (617) 696-1815.

Close by the Forbes House is the **Dr. Amos Holbrook House** (1800), 203 Adams St., which is also maintained by the museum. Wings were added to this Federal residence in 1872 and 1907, but such original neo-classical details as the pedimented center entrance and porch with a balustraded deck still predominate.

Newton

JACKSON HOMESTEAD, 527 Washington St., 1809. The history of the many settlements which make up the sprawling town of Newton is the primary focus of attention in this historic house museum. How the early 19th-century residents might have lived is displayed in furnishings, clothing, and the toys provided children. The Jackson Homestead, however, has a history beginning long before 1809, its date of construction. At that time

Museum of American China Trade

Major Timothy Jackson took the deteriorating saltbox built by his ancestor Edward Jackson in 1679 and recycled parts of it for his new home. Six of the fireplaces have hand-carved 17th-century mantels; there are also many original doors from the earlier house. NR. Open July-Aug, Tu-F 10-4; Sept, M-F 10-4; Oct-June, M-F 10-4; 1st Sunday of month, 10-4. $1 adults, 50¢ senior citizens, 25¢ children 6-17. (617) 552-7238.

Quincy

Quincy is a relatively new town—as New England towns go. Not until the area had been recognized as the home ground of the Adams family and the center of a growing granite industry in the 1790s was the town incorporated separately from Braintree. From that time on it grew much more rapidly than the neighboring town and eventually became one of the major manufacturing cities of the state.

Despite its close proximity to Boston, Quincy—like Cambridge—has maintained a separate cultural identity. This independent historical viewpoint is based on the distinguished contributions of the Adams and Quincy families to the area and to the nation.

ADAMS ACADEMY, 8 Adams St., 1872.

This former private school houses the offices, library, and museum of the Quincy Historical Society. A Victorian Gothic building of rough-faced granite ashlar with brick trim, it served until 1908 as a boy's school and then was used for various civic purposes before being leased to the society. A fund started by President John Adams led to the establishment of the school, and Ware and Van Brunt, Boston's leading late 19th-century architectural firm, was responsible for the design. NR. Open M-F 9:30-3:30, Sa 12:30-3:30. Free. (617) 773-1144.

ADAMS NATIONAL HISTORIC SITE, 135 Adams St., 1731. Four generations of the eminent Adams family occupied this handsomely appointed house from 1788 to 1927—John Adams, John Quincy Adams, Charles Francis Adams, and Henry Adams. Henry's brother, Brooks, was the last family member to live at what became known as the "Old House." John Adams called it "but the farm of a patriot." It was, considered a mansion house, however, when purchsed by Adams in 1787, although not as large as Mrs. Adams would have liked. It was almost doubled in size in following years. Surrounding the house were some 40 acres. Approximately five acres remain.

The visitor to the historic site can tour

Adams National Historic Site

the house, a stone library building built by Charles Francis Adams in the 1860s, a stable, and well-tended gardens. The furnishings are, for the most part, Adams family pieces. NR, NHL. Open Apr 19-Nov 10, daily 9-5. 50¢ adults, chaperoned children under 16 free. 👫 (617) 773-1177.

The adjoining **Beale House** and property of 3½ acres is also included in the historic site. This building, however, is occupied and is not open to the public.

THOMAS CRANE PUBLIC LIBRARY, Coddington and Washington Sts., 1881. One of Henry Hobson Richardson's most successful buildings, the library is granite with red sandstone trim; the broadly arched entrance and pitched roof emphasize the Romanesque style. John La Farge was commissioned to produce opalescent panels for windows. NR. Open M-F 9-9, Sa 9-5; closed Sa, July and Aug.

QUINCY HOMESTEAD, 34 Butler Rd., 1706. The home of John Hancock's wife, Dorothy Quincy, this mansion house was partially built in the 1600s, 1706, and in the mid-18th century. The kitchen dates from the 1600s. It has now been opened as a museum by the Colonial Dames of Massachusetts. NR. Apr 19-Nov 1, Tu-Su 10-5. $1 adults, 50¢ for chaperoned children under 12.

COL. JOSIAH QUINCY HOUSE, 20 Muirhead St. (Wollaston), 1770. The Quincy family continued for several generations to provide leaders for the greater Boston community. Col. Quincy and his son, Josiah, Jr., were close allies of the Adamses; grandson Josiah III was president of Harvard and mayor of Boston. The handsome Georgian clapboard house was resided in by members of the family until the late 1800s. The property is now maintained by the SPNEA as a museum. The fireplaces, surrounded by English tiles, are especially noteworthy. The rooms are furnished with antique objects associated with the Quincy family. NR. Open June 1-Sept 30, T, Th, Sa 1-5. 50¢ admission. (617) 227-3956.

UNITED FIRST PARISH CHURCH (Unitarian), 1226 Hancock St., 1827-28. Considered the finest Greek Revival church in New England, it was designed by Alexander Parris along monumental lines with a projecting Doric portico made up of 25-foot-high columns. The granite edifice might well be called the St. Peter's of Unitarianism. Buried in a crypt within are four of the parish's leading members: John Adams and John Quincy Adams and their wives. NR, NHL. Open for tours Apr 19-Oct 12, M-F 9-5. Write or call in advance for tour reservations. (617) 773-1290.

Shirley

SHIRLEY SHAKER VILLAGE, S of Shirley on the Harvard Rd., 1793-1900. The Massachusetts Correctional Institution is located at the site of the former Shaker settlement founded in 1793. Most of the buildings have been greatly altered and some of them moved from their original sites. The Meeting House was taken down and transported to Hancock Shaker Village (see Pittsfield vicinity listing). There were once some 26 buildings arranged along Harvard Rd.; there are now 14. The village—made up of three Shaker "families"—dissolved in 1908, the remaining members moving on to nearby Harvard village. Applesauce making had been the main industry here on a tract that comprised over 2,000 acres. NR.

Sudbury

SUDBURY CENTER HISTORIC DISTRICT, Concord and Old Sudbury Rds. 17th-20th centuries. The principal historic buildings in the village are grouped around the triangular town green. The setting is customary, with the colonial **First Parish Church** (1797) at the west side; the **Greek Revival Town Hall** (1846, 1932) facing the church; and, the clapboard Greek Revival **Grange Hall** (1846) next to the Town Hall. Located at 427 Concord Rd., an avenue off the green, is architect Ralph Adams Cram's estate, **"Whitehall"** (1815 with a 1915 addition). The most interesting part of the estate, however, is the **St.**

Elizabeth's Chapel, a fieldstone Norman-style building. Cram, best known for his work on St. Thomas Church and the Cathedral of St. John the Divine in New York City, built the chapel for family use in the European tradition. It is now used as a regular church.

WAYSIDE INN HISTORIC DISTRICT, Old Boston Post Rd., 18th-20th centuries. Henry Ford began assembling his Colonial style village in the 1920s. The most important building is the inn (described also under the listings for Lodging and Dining) which was made famous by Henry Longfellow in his "Tales of a Wayside Inn." The building dates from c. 1700 and is said to be the oldest surviving inn in America. It was first known as Howe Tavern and was renamed the Red Horse Tavern after 1746.

Also on the grounds is the 1798 **Redstone School,** moved here in the 1920s; the **Martha-Mary Chapel** (1939); a reconstruction of an 18th-century **gristmill;** and other buildings. NR. The buildings are open daily 9-9. Admission, 50¢ adults; children free if accompanied by adults. (617) 443-8846. ♟

Waltham

GORE PLACE, 52 Gore St., 1805-06. This is a splendid place, a joy to visit. Christopher Gore decided that his summer home should be as handsome as possible. The site along the Charles River is as lovely as could be found, and the estate comprised some 400 acres. Gore turned to the French architect J. G. Legrand for the plans, and these were worked out in Paris. The red-brick house spreads over 170 feet along the ridge of a gently rolling hill.

Unlike many neo-classical homes of the period, the rooms are imaginatively varied in shape. The central spiral staircase is acknowledged as the most dramatic architectural element. The Adams-style woodwork throughout the elegantly furnished rooms is similarly accomplished. The grounds were landscaped by the English gardener Robert Murray in 1835-36. There is also a 1793 stable and an 1835 farmhouse on the grounds. Gore Place is maintained by the Gore Place Society. It is open Apr 15-Nov 15, Tu-Sa 10-5, Su 2-5. $2 adults, 50¢ children. (617) 894-2798.

THE VALE, 185 Lyman St., 1793-98. Also known as the Theodore Lyman House, The Vale is Waltham's best known country estate. It was one of the most ambitiously landscaped properties in early 19th-century New England. The main house was drastically remodeled and enlarged in 1882, but two rooms—the ballroom and parlor—have survived in their full Federal-period flavor. Of particular interest to the visitor are the greenhouses and gardens which are open year-round, Th-Su 10-4. The admission charge is $1.50 for adults, 75¢ for children. Plants are raised here and sold on a regular basis. The house is open only by appointment. It is available for weddings and other social functions. The Vale is maintained by the SPNEA. There are tours of the property from May 1-Oct 31 at 11, 12, 1, 2 and 3. (617) 893-7232.

Woburn

COUNT RUMFORD BIRTHPLACE, 90 Elm St., c. 1725. Count Rumford, né Benjamin Thompson (1753-1814), was a native-born scientific genius whose title and reputation were acquired in Europe. He is best known for his improvements in heating and cooking technology, including the drip coffee pot. Since his sympathies during the Revolution were decidedly Tory, he moved to England in 1775 and was a resident of Germany during the last years of his life. The Rumford Historical Association maintains the birthplace. Open year-round, W-Su 1-4:30. Free. (617) 933-0781.

The towns and villages of Essex county have long been recognized as among the most beautiful and historic in the state. Nearly all the localities are related in some way to the sea, and the maritime tradition has been reflected in the architecture, customs, and economy of the area for generations. Salem, Marblehead, Newburyport, and the Cape Ann region are visited by hundreds of thousands of tourists each year. Many come to enjoy the special blend of historical tradition and pleasant scenery which has made the area so popular.

Amesbury

JOHN GREENLEAF WHITTIER HOME, 86 Friend St., 1836. Whittier was one of the most popular 19th-century poets and an ardent crusader against slavery and militarism. A Quaker, he remained faithful to the simple verities of rural and small-town life. He lived in this ten-room frame house until his death in 1892. Most of the furnishings remain as he left them. Open Mar-Dec, Tu-Sa 10-4; Jan and Feb by appointment only. 50¢ adults, 25¢ children.

While in the Amesbury area, it is well worth making a trip to see the **Rocky Hill Meeting House and Parsonage** on the Portsmouth Rd. at Elm St., 1785. The church, open only by appointment, is considered the best example of a side-entrance building in the state. NR. Maintained by the SPNEA. For details regarding a tour of the interior, call (617) 227-3956. The white clapboard parsonage was moved here from a nearby site.

Andover (see also North Andover)

PHILLIPS ACADEMY, Main St., (MA 28), 18th-20th centuries. Now coeducational, Phillips Andover made its reputation as the oldest incorporated boys' school in the United States with a founding date of 1778. It has had as students, members of some of America's most distinguished families in the arts, sciences, politics, and business. The campus pleasantly mixes the new and the old. Among the landmark buildings are **Pearson Hall** (1818) and the **Phelps House,** of a similar age, both of which are said to have been designed by Charles Bulfinch. For the lover of American history and art, the **Addison Gallery** is a must. It is located on Chapel St. and houses a remarkable collection of paintings, ship models, sculpture, prints, and drawings. The museum is open Sept-July, Tu-Sa 10-5; Su 2:30-5; closed the month of Aug. and holidays. Free. ♿ (617) 475-7515.

DEACON AMOS BLANCHARD HOUSE AND BARN, 97 Main St., 1818-19. The Andover Historical Society maintains this property as a museum with antique furnishings, costumes, textiles, and early household implements on display. The museum is open W, Su 2-4 and other times by appointment. 50¢ adults, 25¢ children. (617) 475-2236.

America House at 147 Main St. is not noted for its good looks, but you may wish to pass by to salute the home of Samuel F. Smith. Here he wrote the words of "America."

Beverly

JOHN BALCH HOUSE, 448 Cabot St., 1636-18th century; CAPT. JOHN CABOT HOUSE, 117 Cabot St., 1781; JOHN HALE HOUSE, 39 Hale St., 1694.

John Balch House

All three homes are owned and maintained by the Beverly Historical Society. Headquarters is at the Cabot mansion. Antique furnishings, toys and dolls, and objects having to do with maritime history and transportation are exhibited at the various locations. NR. The Hale and Balch houses are open June 15-Oct 15, W-Sa 10-4, Su 1-4. Cabot House is open the same hours from June 15-Oct 15; and from Oct 16-June 14, W-Sa 10-4. $1 adults, 50¢ children. (617) 922-1186.

Boxford

BOXFORD VILLAGE HISTORIC DISTRICT, Main and Elm Sts., Middleton and Topsfield Rds., 17th-19th centuries. Boxford has been called by a well-known planning consultant, a "rare and near perfect example of the old New England village street style, with the broad, tree-shaded street, the common, church, old houses, and single country store." The **First Church** (Congregational) (1838) anchors one end of Elm St. and the **Holyoke-French House** (1760), the other. The half mile between the two buildings is the location for the **Town Hall-Grange** (1890), the **general store** (1840), and the **library** (1841). The Holyoke-French House was built by Samuel Holyoke, a Boston merchant, and is the most imposing residence in the village. A 2½-story Georgian Colonial, it was left to the Boxford Historical Society in 1940. NR. Open June-Oct 12, W, Sa, Su 2-4.

Danvers and Danversport

SALEM VILLAGE HISTORIC DISTRICT, Centre, Hobart, Ingersoll, Holten, and Forest Sts., 17th-19th centuries. Danvers was originally known as Salem Village, scene of the witchcraft hysteria of the 1690s. There are only a few 17th-century buildings left in the old village. The **Rebecca Nurse Homestead,** 149 Pine St., is, according to tradition, the 1678 house owned by Francis Nurse, whose wife Rebecca was hanged as a witch. The home is furnished with 17th and 18th-century antiques, and houses artifacts from the years 1650-1780. It is affiliated with the SPNEA and managed by the Danvers Alarm List Co. Open June 15-Oct 15, Tu-Sa 1-4:30, Su 2-4:30. $1 adults, 50¢ children under 16.

The Danvers Historical Society administers several historical properties, two of which are in close proximity. The **Derby Summerhouse** (1792-93) is located on the Endicott estate off Ingersoll St. It is a 2½-story neo-classical wooden building designed by Samuel McIntire, the gifted Salem carver and architect, for the use of merchant Elias Hasket Derby at his estate in Peabody. It served as a teahouse and garden observatory. Also found on the Endicott estate is **Glen Magna** mansion, a two-story Federal farmhouse that was transformed in the 1890s into a fashionable country retreat for Mrs. William Crowninshield Endicott. The grounds were laid out by the noted landscape architect Frederick Law Olmstead. NR. Both properties are open May 1-Oct 31, Tu and Th 10-4; other times by appointment. $1 adults, 50¢ children. (617) 777-2821.

Gloucester

A city that is the home of Henry Davis Sleeper, creator of Beauport, and John Hays Hammond, the builder of a castle, would appear to have an affinity for the extravagant and colorful. In truth, Gloucester is a more sober-minded place and is better known for its fishing and fish-products industry. Positioned at the head of Cape Ann, the area is beautifully situated to take advantage of both the economic and the aesthetic values of the sea.

BEAUPORT, 70 Eastern Point Blvd., 1907-34. This fabled house grew and grew and grew—from a shingled summer cottage to a 40-room mansion. The site, on a granite ledge overlooking the harbor, is perfect. Henry Davis Sleeper apparently could not control his enthusiasm for the house and antiques. A new room was always needed to house some imaginative find or finds—perhaps a Federal doorway, a collection of Revere silver, Lord Byron's bed, 18th-century paneling. All of this activity only came to an end with Sleeper's death in 1934. Since that time the SPNEA and private individuals who admired his work have made it possible to maintain the picturesque house and its extraordinary collection. NR. Open May 15-Sept 18, M-F 10-4; Sept 19-Oct, M-F 10-4, Sa-Su 1-4. $3 adults, $1.50 children. (617) 283-0800.

CAPT. ELIAS DAVIS HOUSE, 27 Pleas-ant St., c. 1800. This is the home of the Cape Ann Historical Association. In addition to the usual genealogical materials available for research, there is a fine collection of antique furniture, silver, china, and textiles. Of special interest are the paintings and drawings of Fitz Hugh Lane (1804-65), one of the early Gloucester artists known for his sea and shoreline scenes and ship portraits. Open June 1-Oct 1, daily 1-5; Oct-May, W, F-Su 1-5, Th 1-5 and 6-9. $2 adults, $1 children under 12, no charge if accompanied by an adult. (617) 283-0455.

HAMMOND CASTLE MUSEUM, 80 Hesperus Ave., 1926-29. Antiques of the Middle Ages and Renaissance are right at home in this stone castle by the sea. The most impressive object is the 8,600-pipe organ located in the Great Hall. The pipes rise eight stories high. The courtyard with an extravagant assembly of medieval architectural elements is a special delight in the summer months. The builder of this unusual building was John Jay Hammond, an electronics genius and inventor who held over 100 patents. NR. Open Apr-Nov, Tu-Su 10-4; Dec-Mar, 10-4. $3 adults, $1 children 12 and under. (617) 283-2080.

Haverhill

JOHN WARD HOUSE, 240 Water St., 1641. This is the headquarters of the Haverhill Historical Society. Ward was the

Beauport

town's first minister, and his home has been furnished with colonial-period antiques. There are also Indian artifacts, costumes, military paraphernalia, and portraits. Open summer, Tu-Sa 2-5; winter, Tu, Th, Sa 2-5. 50¢ adults, 25¢ students during school year; children no charge. (617) 374-4626.

JOHN GREENLEAF WHITTIER HOMESTEAD, 105 Whittier Rd., 1688. The boyhood home of Whittier is not nearly as well know as his later Amesbury residence, but it is a virtually-intact early Essex county farmstead. NR. It is open 10-5 Tu-Sa, 1-5 Su. (617) 373-3979.

Ipswich

Ipswich's historical resources are being uncovered and developed a bit more each year. Twenty-five years ago the town hardly rated more than a few lines in regional guides, but today — thanks to a very active historical society — Ipswich is regaining some of the luster it possessed in the dim past. It has the unusual distinction of being an early literary center of New England as the home of poet Anne Bradstreet and of Nathaniel Ward, author of *A Simple Cobbler of Agawam,* "Agawam" being an early place name for Ipswich.

THE JOHN WHIPPLE HOUSE, 40 S. Main St., 1795, and THE JOHN HEARD HOUSE, 53 S. Main St., 1640. Both are properties administered by the Ipswich Historical Society. The earlier building is the headquarters, and is a particularly fine example of a 17th-century house that was gradually enlarged — in this case in 1670 and the early 1700s — with the addition of a lean-to and a wing. John Whipple was a prominent colonial leader. A period herb garden has been planted on the grounds. NR, NHL. The John Heard House is representative of a more prosperous period in local history when the China trade was underway. The Heard family was involved in this enterprise, and family artifacts acquired in foreign trade are on display. Both houses are open Apr 15-Nov 1, Tu-Sa 10-5, Su 1-5. Admission to each house, $2 adults, children under 13 free; $3 adult combination ticket for both houses. (617) 356-2811.

Other buildings in the old village of Ipswich which are well worthy of the visitor's attention are the many private dwellings on High St. which date from the 17th and 18th centuries. Most of these were originally taverns, stores, or craftsman's shops as the street was the main thoroughfare between Boston and Newburyport.

On the north end of Main St. is **Meeting House Green,** the site of the **First Church of Ipswich,** (Congregational) since the early 17th century. The present clapboard building dates from 1832. During the 1600s the green was also the location of the jail, town pound and stocks, and a fort. The granite **Choate Bridge** (1764) carries S. Main St. across the Ipswich River. The span was widened from 20 feet to 35 in 1938. NR.

Lynn

HYDE-MILLS HOUSE, 125 Green St., 1836. Lynn's visible historical legacy is primarily industrial, and this is recognized in even such a gracious home as the Hyde-Mills. The residence is furnished with antique objects, but is also used to house a period shoe shop which is filled with the kind of items that relate to the early shoe industry. Open winter, M-F 1-4; summer, M-F 1-4, Sa 1-4. Free. (617) 592-2465.

Marblehead

Many a New Englander would be perfectly

happy to discover that heaven was like Marblehead on a sunny summer day. There would be a strong breeze, for Marblehead has been a yachting capital almost without rival on the New England coast for many years. The clubs are still there near the harbor. So, too, are numerous well-tended 18th- and 19th-century homes and public buildings, and the most important of these can be toured.

ROBERT "KING" HOOPER MANSION, 8 Hooper St., 1727-28.

Merchant prince Hooper was called "King" because of his regal manner and wealth. This was reflected as well in his residence with the front facade siding rusticated to imitate stone. The Georgian Colonial front section was added in the mid-1700s and illustrates the then-popular fashion for classical elegance. The building now serves as Marblehead's cultural center. NR. Open Tu-Su 1-4. $1 adults, 50¢ children. (617) 631-2608.

COL. JEREMIAH LEE MANSION, 161 Washington St., 1768. This is Marblehead's best residence and certainly one of the most impressive on the East Coast. The usual Georgian Colonial mansion has a row of five windows on each floor; the Lee mansion has seven. Most such houses are built of brick or are clapboard frame structures; the Lee mansion is built of wood, but the boards were cut and decorated to imitate stone in a manner similar to the facade of the Hooper mansion (previous listing). The wooden corner blocks were

similarly cut and finished to simulate stone. Col. Lee had the resources to effect such elegancies. It is said that he was the wealthiest New England sea merchant of his day. In 1804 the mansion was sold to the Marblehead Grand Bank and remained in its trusty hands until 1909 when the Marblehead Historical Society acquired the building for its headquarters. The bank made little major alteration in the interior which is now appropriately furnished with high-style antiques of the 18th century. The center hallway is an unusually spacious and noteworthy feature of the house. NR, NHL. Open May 15-Oct 14, 9:30-4; other times by appointment. $1.50 adults, 50¢ students and children. (617) 631-1069.

ST. MICHAEL'S CHURCH, 26 Pleasant St., 1714.

New England has many fine early Congregational and Unitarian churches, but those of the Episcopal persuasion are quite rare outside of Boston. St. Michael's, an 18th-century clapboard building, is fitted with early 19th-century Gothic Revival windows. It is possible that this is the oldest New England Episcopal church still in use. Beneath the edifice is a most unusual feature for an American religious building—a sepulchre where pew owners were once buried. NR.

OLD TOWN HOUSE, Town House Sq., 1728.

This was Marblehead's first government building and the main place where citizens gathered to argue the American cause in the late 1700s. A Georgian Colonial building, it was restored to its original form in 1966-68. NR.

Although not open to the public, there are other buildings which make a stroll or drive through Marblehead an especially pleasant experience. The **Elbridge Gerry House,** 44 Washington St. (1744-87), is the Georgian Colonial home of a signer of the Declaration of Independence and the fourth vice-president of the United States. NR. The **Gen. John Glover House,** 11 Glover St. (1762), is also a Georgian Colonial clapboard house. Glover was an important participant in the battles of Trenton and Princeton as well as in the famous crossing of the Delaware in which the Durham boats were manned by Marblehead men on Christmas Eve, 1776. NR, NHL.

Methuen

METHUEN MEMORIAL MUSIC HALL, 192 Broadway, 1907, was specially built to house a famous pipe organ that had been originally located in the Boston Music Hall. Philanthropist Edward F. Searles gave the building to the town and had it designed by English architect Henry Vaughan. The instrument is a thing of beauty to be viewed and to be listened to. NR. Open Apr-Dec daily and for concerts beginning first week of June, every W night, 8:30. Concerts: $4 adults, $1 children. (617) 475-1525.

Newbury-Newburyport

This area is extraordinarily rich in historic houses and public buildings dating from the 17th and 18th centuries. Many of these sites are associated with maritime history, for Newburyport was once one of the great shipping centers of the Northeast. It also became a center of superb craftsmanship — in silver, furniture, engraving, clockmaking. In the words of Newburyport's most famous novelist, John P. Marquand, "it is a vital, tolerant place, and still able to keep up with the times, if you get to know it." And the only way to become acquainted with Newburyport, is, in Marquand's words, to "walk for awhile; if you take your time you are bound to see a little of what Newburyport has meant, and still means, in this complicated nation."

Newbury is a separate village adjoining Newburyport to the south. It is an older settlement which gradually lost business to its sister city. Today the two municipalities blend into one, and street names continue from one place to the other.

COFFIN HOUSE, 14-16 High St., Newbury, c. 1654. The museum house of the Coffin family is noted for its fine furnishings and carefully preserved period rooms — an 18th-century kitchen and buttery, and an early 19th-century parlor with original wallpaper. Owned and maintained by the SPNEA. NR. Open June

1-Oct 15, Tu, Th, Sa-Su 12-5. $1.50 adults. (617) 227-3956.

CALEB CUSHING HOUSE, 98 High St., c. 1808. The Historical Society of Old Newbury is headquartered here in a Federal house built for a sea captain. It was later the home of the Cushing family, Caleb Cushing (1800-79) — a scholar, statesman, and diplomat — being the most famous member. The house is beautifully furnished with high-style 19th-century furniture and other decorative objects as well as a rich collection of paintings. The garden is celebrated for its specimen plants and 18th-century layout; particularly delightful is its early summerhouse. NR, NHL. Open May-Oct, Tu-Sa 10-4, Su -5; in other months by appointment. $1.50 adults, 50¢ for children under 16. (617) 462-2681.

FIRST RELIGIOUS SOCIETY CHURCH (Unitarian), 1801, and PARISH HALL, 1873, 26 Pleasant St. One of New England's most beautiful Federal-style churches, the Newburyport parish may have been designed by Samuel McIntire of Salem. The details of the perfectly proportioned facade are expertly realized. The interior has a U-shaped gallery and a raised pulpit. Serving as the first minister of the congregation was the Rev. John Lowell of the family later famous in Boston history. NR.

SUPERIOR COURTHOUSE and BARTLETT MALL, bounded by High, Pond, Auburn, and Greenleaf Sts., 1805. Charles Bulfinch was the architect of the old county courthouse which overlooks Bartlett Mall from High St. It is a 2½-story brick building with granite trim, and, like most other historic Newburyport buildings, it is basically neo-classical or Federal in style. NR. The Mall, the equivalent of a town common, is a handsome green area with a frog pond and terraced lawn.

U.S. CUSTOMHOUSE MARITIME MUSEUM, 25 Water St., 1835. A customhouse was a necessity of any major seaport city, and Newburyport's facility was in active operation until 1910. It has been cleaned up and recycled for use as a museum dedicated to telling the story of the area's maritime past. The federal government architect of the building was Robert Mills. The Greek Revival temple form was in great favor for such a public edifice in the 1830s. Newburyport's business district had suffered a devastating fire in 1811, and new buildings were largely of fireproof granite, as is the Custom House, or brick with massive fire walls.

Both floors are filled with exhibits. Located on the first floor is the **Office of the Collector of Customs** which has been furnished with 19th-century objects—a safe, strongbox, desk, chairs, rum barrels, tea chests, etc. Behind it is **Coast Guard Hall** with a mural of how the waterfront appeared in 1791. The first Coast Guard revenue cutter, the *Massachusetts,* was built in Newburyport, and the city claims the distinction of being the birthplace of the Coast Guard. Other areas of the museum display mementos of novelist John P. Marquand, ship's models, Far-Eastern souvenirs, and American and European antique furnishings. NR. Open Apr-Oct, M-Sa 10-4:30, Su 2-5; Oct-Apr, M-F 1-4. $1 adults, 50¢ children 5-16. ♔ (617) 462-8681.

High Rd. in Newbury is lined with an extraordinary group of early Colonial homes, all owned by the SPNEA, but open only by appointment. All, however, are close enough to the street to be enjoyed by the visitor in the area. The properties are

the **Dole-Little House,** #289, (c. 1700); the **Short House,** #39, (1732); and the **Swett-Isley House,** #4, (1670), formerly the Blue Anchor Inn. For further information regarding tours of these houses, call (617) 227-3956.

High St., the continuation of High Rd., in Newburyport also has a number of still-private homes that are well worth viewing. Among the most attractive of these elegant Federal mansions are the **Knapp-Healy House,** #47 (1805); the **Pettingill-Fowler House,** #164 (1792); the **Lord Timothy Dexter House,** #201 (1771); and the **Hale-Kinsman-Leary House,** #348 (1800).

North Andover

NORTH ANDOVER CENTER HISTORIC DISTRICT, roughly bounded by Osgood, Pleasant, Stevens, Johnson, and Andover Sts., 18th-early 19th centuries. North Andover developed a very separate identity from that of Andover proper as early as the late 1600s. The Andover meeting house was located here at that time, and in the succeeding years the area became the preferred neighborhood for well-to-do merchants and craftsmen. In the late 19th century a common was created in the center of the village. Most commercial activity then moved on to Andover, leaving North Andover a largely residential area. It has changed little since then.

Short House, Newbury

MERRIMACK VALLEY TEXTILE MU-SEUM, 800 Massachusetts Ave., 19th century. Nothing was more important to the industrial economy of 19th-century New England than the weaving industry, in particular the manufacture of woolens. The Merrimack Valley of northeastern Massachusetts was the center of this enterprise until the early 1900s. Here at this museum, the whole craft and business of weaving textiles is imaginatively brought to life. The implements and machinery used to make woolen cloth are in place and trained teachers are often on duty carding, spinning, and weaving. There are also displays of textiles, and documentary material such as photographs and prints which provide an historical context for the craft. The building itself was once the largest woolen mill in the world. Open Tu-F 10-5, Sa and Su 1-5. Guided tours are available T-F at 10:30, 1 and 3; Su 1:30 and 3. $2 adults, $1 children and senior citizens. 🏃 (617) 686-0191.

The North Andover Historical Society has carefully preserved some of the most historic buildings in town, and these may be visited. The 1715 **Parson Barnard House,** 179 Osgood St., is the best known of the buildings. It has been furnished and restored to display the tastes of four early owners of the home, including three early ministers of the 1833 North Parish Church. The **Johnson Cottage,** 153 Academy Rd., is also furnished with period antiques and objects. Both are open Su 1-5 and by appointment. 50¢ admission. The **Brick Store Building,** 3-5-7 Johnson St. (1829), is a general store and thrift shop run by the society. It is open M-Sa 7-1 and 2-6, Su 7:30-12:30.

STEVENS-COOLIDGE PLACE, 139 Andover St., c. 1800, is one of the handsome properties administered by the Trustees of Reservations. The main house was restored in the Colonial Revival style at some time and has been happily left just as is, without returning it to its earlier past. The Chinese export porcelain collection and other American decorative objects are noteworthy. Of even greater interest, however, are the landscaped grounds and gardens which include a serpentine wall, greenhouse, surrounding pasture land, and a small herd of Hereford cattle. The house ("Home Place") is open Apr 15-Oct 30, Su 1-5; by appointment, M-Sa. $1.50 adults, 50¢ children (6-16). Gardens: May 15-Oct 30, daily 8-sunset. Free. (617) 683-5308.

There are several privately-held mansions in North Andover which the visitor can easily view. Chief among these are the **Kittredge Mansion,** 56 Academy Rd. (1784), an imposing Federal-style clapboard residence suitable for a merchant prince; and the **Phillips Mansion,** 168 Osgood St. (1752), the elegant Georgian home of Samuel Phillips, a co-founder of Phillips Academy. The facade is dominated by a very handsome pilastered doorway.

Rockport

Do not attempt to enter the downtown area of this lovely Cape Ann village on a summer weekend unless you enjoy crowds. The artists who have made of Rockport a familiar scene across the country presumably executed their sketches of such landmarks as Bearskin Neck, the Congregational Church and "Motif No. 1," the old red sail loft, during the quieter hours of a weekday.

BEARSKIN NECK is mainly a commercial area of shops and restaurants. At one time this stretch of land, considerably enlarged over the years with fill, housed wharves, warehouses, and sheds which served the fishing trade. The **Pewter Shop** on South Rd. was built in 1775 as the Punch Bowl Tavern. At the end of Bradley Wharf is an exact reproduction of "Motif No. 1" which was destroyed in a 1978 blizzard.

The DOWNTOWN MAIN STREET HISTORIC DISTRICT includes Main, Cleaves, Jewett, and School Sts., 18th-mid-19th century. The Rockport Art Association, an important cultural center since 1921, is headquartered in the **1787 Tavern,** 12 Main St. This was the stop on the stagecoach line from Gloucester and, at one time, a rather boozy place. In 1856 early female proponents of Carrie Nation's hatchet-carrying habit tried to stop Rockport's menfolk from imbibing illegal spirits at this and other local watering spas. They used their trusty weapons on kegs, emptying the contents into the gutters. The ladies were tried for their actions and were acquitted.

The **Congregational Church,** on the south side of Main St., has been a quiet oasis since 1803 except for several exciting days during the War of 1812. The British shelled the edifice, leaving a hole in the bell tower. The cannon used in firing the offending ball was later captured and now rests on the church lawn.

Also located in Rockport is the **Sewall-Scripture House,** 40 King St. (1832). It is maintained by the Sandy Bay Historical Society as a museum. Featured are Indian artifacts, items relating to Rockport's early granite quarrying industry, decorative antique objects, dolls, toys, and other historical treasures. The house is open July 1-Labor Day, daily 2-5. Free. (617) 546-9533.

Rockport vicinity

THE OLD CASTLE (Jethro Wheeler House), N of Rockport on MA 127, Castle Lane, c. 1715. Sailors rounding the tip of Cape Ann at Pigeon Cove are said to have given this house its unusual name because of its appearance. The saltbox stands on a prominent point overlooking the water and has a very pronounced second-story overhang. The Pigeon Cove Improvement Society restored the house in the 1920s and continues to maintain it as a summer meeting place and museum. NR. Open July-Aug, daily 2-5.

Salem

Of all towns in New England, Salem breathes most deeply of history. Ever since a large part of its industrial quarter was destroyed in the early 1900s, hope for a more prosperous future has been invested in recapturing Salem's glorious past. With two well-established museums and research institutions—the Peabody Museum (founded 1799) and the Essex Institute

(founded 1848)—the task has been made somewhat easier. The town fathers have seized on every opportunity to make use of regional, state, and Federal funds to improve the facilities open to the public. Urban renewal funds have been intelligently invested in projects which have protected the historic character of Salem. The pedestrian mall created from Essex St. and the Old Town Hall Square has made that area more enjoyable to visit. The Salem Maritime National Historical Site, administered by the National Park Service has protected the old waterfront and made it attractive to the tourist. And Chestnut St., often called the most beautiful residential avenue in America, is just as handsome as it ever has been. The great Federal-style mansions of this and adjoining streets are national architectural treasures without equal elsewhere.

Exploration of Salem's rich history may take several days. One can delve, for instance, into such diverse subjects as 17th-century witchcraft, the China trade of the 1700s and early 1800s, or the Federal architectural tradition so expertly handled by such builders as Samuel McIntire. At almost every stop there are displays which interpret the past for you in an imaginative manner. Such an array of historical riches may, in fact, be too much to handle at first. Historic Salem is most easily broken into three divisions—the Chestnut Street area, the Essex Street Mall area, and the Derby Waterfront area. It is most appropriate to start one's tour along the waterfront.

DERBY WATERFRONT, bounded by Congress St. and Hawthorne Blvd. on the W, Essex St. on the N, Salem Harbor on the S, and Turner St. on the E, 18th-19th centuries. The place to begin is the nine-

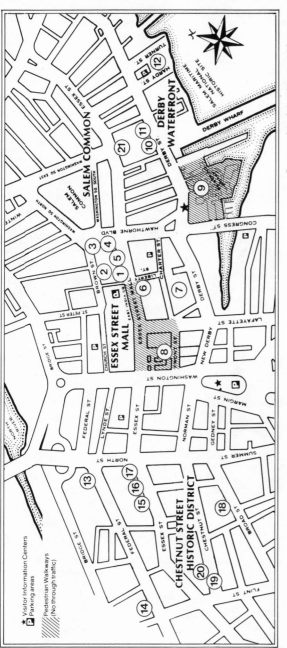

Courtesy of the Salem Chamber of Commerce

Salem

1. Essex Institute
2. John Ward House
3. Andrew-Safford House
4. Crowninshield-Bentley House
5. Gardner-Pingree House
6. Peabody Museum

7. The Burying Point
8. Old Town Hall
9. Voyage of the India Star, Salem Seaport Museum
10. Salem Maritime National Historic Site

11. Derby House
12. House of Seven Gables
13. Peirce-Nichols House
14. Assembly House
15. Ropes Mansion
16. First Church

17. Witch House
18. Pickering House
19. Chestnut Street
20. Stephen Phillips Memorial Trust
21. Narbonne House

acre **Salem Maritime National Historical Site** and the **Custom House.** The park is open daily from 8:30-5, and there is no charge to visit the nine historic houses and other buildings. The Federal brick Custom House, at the corner of Orange and Derby Sts. (1819), was made famous by Nathaniel Hawthorne who served as surveyor of the port from 1846-49. The building and its surrounding are described in the introduction to *The Scarlet Letter.* Behind the Custom House is the **Bonded Warehouse,** (1819), where cargoes were held in transit or for payment of duties. A little farther up Orange St. is the **Scale House** (1829), in which cargoes could be measured and weighed to determine value and duty. 👫

In the same block, fronting on Derby St. and the Derby Wharf, are three other important buildings. The first, next to the Custom House, is **Hawkes House,** named after Capt. Benjamin Hawkes who operated a shipyard across the way. Hawkes bought and completed a house that had been designed and built by Samuel McIntire in 1775 but left unfinished. The first owner, shipping merchant Elias Hasket Derby, had used it as a privateer prize warehouse.

Next to Hawkes House is the oldest brick residence in Salem, **Derby House** (1761-62). It is by far the most handsome of the maritime park buildings. The fine Georgian mansion is filled with high-style antiques and other appropriate furnishings. Captain Richard Derby built the home for his son, Elias Hasket Derby.

The last of the buildings facing the Derby wharf is the **West India Goods Store** (c. 1800), typical of the kind of store where imported goods were offered to the public.

Crossing Derby St. to **Derby Wharf** brings one to a section of the waterfront which was almost continually under expansion from the mid-18th century until the late 1800s. Of the fourteen warehouses that once filled the wharf, only one survives, and this had to be moved here from elsewhere in the city. Adjoining Derby Wharf is the much smaller **Central Wharf.**

Moving back across Derby St. and

toward Essex, one will come to the Narbonne-Hale House at #71. This ancient dwelling, dating from c. 1660, is also located in the Salem Maritime National Historic Site and has been the focus of much restoration work by the National Park Service. It is a two-story clapboard structure once owned by a family of fishermen and ship joiners. As a modest period dwelling, it is perhaps more typical of the middle-class residence of the early colonial period than many others.

While in the waterfront area, there are two other sections of historic interest outside of the park which can be explored — the Pickering Wharf and the House of Seven Gables complex of buildings.

The **House of Seven Gables,** 54 Turner St. (1668), is only one of eight dwellings in the area of Turner, Derby, and Hardy Sts. which date from the mid-17th century to the 19th century and which are now maintained by the House of Seven Gables Settlement Association. The main house, thought to be the locale for Nathaniel

Hawthorne's famous novel and thus named for it, began life as a four-room, four-gable residence. A tour of the building gives one an excellent feeling for 17th- and 18th-century building materials and forms. Other buildings in the House of Seven Gables complex which can be toured are the **Retire Beckett House** (1655); the 1682 **Hathaway House;** and the **Hawthorne Birthplace** (1740). NR. Open Labor Day-June, daily 10-4:30. $2 adults, $1 children 13-17, 50¢ children 12 and under. July-Labor Day, daily 9:30-6:30. $3 adults, $1 children 13-17, 50¢ children 12 and under. Admission covers all four houses. (617) 744-0991. **⑪**

On the **Pickering Wharf** is the **Salem Seaport Museum** and a commercial area of attractive shops and restaurants. The "Voyage of the India Star" is a theater-in-the-round multimedia show which relives Salem's maritime history. It is presented every half-hour at the museum. There are also exhibits devoted to the historic seaport. Open June 1-Labor Day, M-W 10:30-5:30, Th-Sa 10:30-8:30; Su 12-5; remainder of year, daily 10:30-5:30. $2 adults, $1.50 young adults 13-18, $1 children 6-12 and senior citizens. **⑪** (617) 745-9540.

ESSEX STREET MALL AREA, bounded by Church and Brown Sts. on the N, Washington St. on the W, New Derby and Derby Sts. on the S, and Hawthorne Blvd. and Salem Common on the E, 17th-19th cen-

turies. The principal buildings of interest in the historic town center are those associated with the Essex Institute and the Peabody Museum.

Essex Institute, 132-134 Essex St., **Plummer Hall** (1857) and the **John Tucker Daland House** (1851). The headquarters buildings of the Institute are joined together along Essex St. The Museum Galleries and administrative offices are housed in Plummer Hall and the J. D. Phillips Research Library in the Daland House. The Institute's collections of China trade objects, Massachusetts furniture, paintings, and portraits are practically without equal in the state. The library is a repository of over 500,000 printed items and 2 million manuscripts. It is, without question, one of the most important centers of scholarly and genealogical research in the United States. The Museum Galleries are open June 1-July 3, M-Sa 9-4:30, Su and holidays 1-5; July 4-Labor Day, M-Sa 9-6, Su and holidays 1-6; following Labor Day to May 31, Tu-Sa 9-4:30, Su and holidays 1-5. $1.50 adults, $1 senior citizens, 75¢ children 6-16. The Library is open M-F 9-4:30. $1.50 daily library use fee. (617) 744-3390.

The Essex Institute owns or administers nine other buildings, most of them the former homes of prominent Salem merchant families and exquisitely furnished with the best of their possessions. Seven of these buildings are found within the Essex Street Mall area adjoining the main institute buildings. The other two buildings—the Peirce-Nichols House and the Assembly House—are located in the Chestnut Street area and are discussed under that heading. Combination tickets for the museum and all the houses are available for $5 adults, $2.50 children, $3.50 senior citizens. Individual tickets are $1 adults, 75¢ senior citizens and 50¢ children.

The **Gardner-Pingree House** (1804-05) faces Essex St. and is next to Daland House. It is builder Samuel McIntire's masterpiece in the neo-classical Federal-style. The elegant red brick three-story brick building is topped with a wood balustrade and is entered through a raised, semi-circular columned porch. The original owner, John Gardner, was a prosperous importer, and the interior rooms display a richness of architectural detail rare in America at the time. McIntire's special talent as a carver is fully revealed in the beautifully worked mantelpieces found in the double parlor. The carved ornamental motifs are also repeated in door frames, the chair rail, and cornice. Of special note throughout the house are original early 19th-century wallpapers. The most unusual paper, found in the third-story hall, was painted by Michele Felice Corne, a noted Salem-area artist of the late 18th and early 19th centuries. The house is handsomely furnished with antiques appropriate to the Federal period. Gardner-Pingree House is open T-Sa 10-4. From June 1-Oct 15, the house is also open Su 1-4:30.

Around the corner is the **Crowninshield-Bentley House** (1727), mid-1700s, and remodeled after 1800. Moved to the Institute grounds from 106 Essex St. in 1960, this gambrel-roof house has been restored as a memorial to Louise du Pont Crowninshield who did so much to reinvest Salem with its former dignity and historical standing. Built for John Crowninshield, it was also the home of William Bentley, a minister and scholar, at the end of the 18th century until his death in 1819. The building has been restored basically to the mid-18th-century with allowances made for various changes and enlargement throughout that century. Open Tu-Sa 1-4. Also open June 1-Oct 15, Su 1-4:30.

Facing Washington Sq. is the **Andrews-Safford House** (1818-19). A very elegant Federal-style mansion, this building now serves as the Institute director's residence. It is, nevertheless, open for touring one day of the week—Th from 2-4. The two parlors—one furnished in the Empire style and the other a Renaissance Revival composition dating from the 1870s—provide a startling but welcome contrast. The original owner, Johnn Andrews, made a fortune in the Russian fur trade and decorated the house with expensive marble mantels, imported wallpapers, and hand-carved ornaments. The Safford family, who ac-

quired the house in 1871, added another layer of late-Victorian elegance.

The **John Ward House** (1684), just off Brown St., is the oldest of the buildings on the Institute grounds. It was moved here from nearby St. Peter St. in the early 1900s. It has been the subject of much restoration work since that time. The building was evidently constructed in three stages, the last being the addition of a lean-to. The second floor overhangs the first and two massive gables dominate the roof line. Two first-floor rooms are devoted to a period display of what the original restorer, George Francis Dow, felt were appropriate Pilgrim Century household items. The lean-to houses an apothecary's shop, a weaving room, and a small "cent" shop.

Located adjacent to the Ward House are the **Lye-Tapley Shoe Shop** (1830) and the **Vaughan Doll House**, each of which features special collections. The latter is housed in the 1688 Quaker Meeting House. Across the way from these small buildings are the **Gardner-Pingree Carriage House** (1804-05), with a summer gift boutique, and the summerhouse and garden of the Andrew-Safford House.

The **Peabody Museum** is the natural next stop after leaving the Essex Institute complex. The main building, **East India Marine Hall**, dates from 1824. A group of Salem ship captains organized the Salem East Indian Marine Society in 1799. The objective of displaying the artifacts of Salem's maritime history was greatly aided by the benefaction of philanthropist George Peabody. Today the museum stands as a major depository of materials on New England maritime history; the ethnology of the Pacific Ocean area explored by the New England traders, missionaries, and scientists; and the natural history of Essex County. Both permanent and temporary exhibits are very well presented and in particular bring to life the adventuresome and colorful aspects of the life at sea. NR, NHL. Open M-Sa 10-5, Su 1-5. $1.50 adults, 75¢ children. 🏃
(617) 745-1876 and 745-9500.

Just down the street (pedestrian mall) is **Old Town Hall**, 32 Derby Sq., 1816. This whole area has been very handsomely restored to its early 19th-century state. The brick Federal-style building once again serves as a public meeting hall and marketplace. A cultural arts center is also housed here. NR. (617) 745-4470.

Behind the Essex St. area is Charter St. Here is located **The Burying Point** (1637), the oldest cemetery in Salem. It includes the graves of Samuel McIntire, Gov. Simon Bradstreet, witchcraft court judge John Hawthorne, and Mayflower passenger Capt. Richard More. Nearby are the **Grimshawe House** and the **Goult-Pickman House.**

CHESTNUT STREET AREA, bounded by Flint St. on the W, Bridge St. on the N, North St. on the E, and Broad St. on the S, 17th-19th centuries. Chestnut St. was laid out in 1796, later than Essex and Federal Sts. where the bulk of the museum houses are located. It is Chestnut St., nevertheless, which has been singled out for its beauty. Perhaps because of the street's straight lines, the private Federal-style homes which line this thoroughfare stand out more majestically than those on adjoining crooked avenues. The whole area is one that must be toured on foot; cars are permitted, but the neighborhood was meant for leisurely strolling.

Assembly House, 138 Federal St., 1782, 1796. The building was remodeled by Samuel McIntire as a residence in 1796 after serving as a social hall; a mid-19th-century portico has been added. The customary neo-classical detailing is seen in the interior woodwork. The rooms are furnished in various 19th-century styles as befits a residence that served different generations of Salem families through the 19th century. The east front parlor is furnished with a carved Chinese export parlor set dating from the mid to late-1800s. Open Tu-F 2-4:30. Also open on Sa 2-4:30, June 1-Oct 15. Same rates as other Essex Institute houses.

Hamilton Hall, 9 Cambridge St., 1806-07. This was one of the buildings that took the place of Assembly House for social events after the latter building became a private home. Samuel McIntire designed the three-story brick structure for the Proprietors of the South Buildings. A large ballroom is located in the back half of the upper floors. NR. Private.

Peirce-Nichols House, 80 Federal St., 1782, 1801. The residence harmoniously mixes Georgian and Federal-style elements. The overall effect of the frame clapboard building is one of extreme elegance. This is heightened by the presence of boldly fluted Doric pilasters at each corner of the facade, a central Doric pedimented front porch, and the roof with a balustrade and belvedere above it. The mansion was built for Jerathmiel Peirce, an East Indian merchant, by Samuel McIntire. It was inherited by Peirce's son-in-law, Capt. George Nichols, in 1840. The handsomely appointed rooms contain some family furnishings, including furniture attributed to McIntire. Open Tu-Sa 2-4:30. Same admission rates as for other Essex Institute houses.

Stephen Phillips Memorial Trust House, 34 Chestnut St., c. 1800. Furnishings relating to the historic trade between China and the United States during the 19th century are handsomely displayed in this Federal home. Open May 29-Oct 17, M-Sa 10-4:30. $1 adults, 50¢ children under 12. (617) 744-0440.

Pickering House, 2 Broad St., 1651, 1841. Timothy Pickering, a fervent Federalist and former secretary of state (under John Adams), senator, and congressman, was born here. The house served ten generations of the Pickering family and is maintained by the Pickering Foundation. Open M 10-3 year-round; May 15-Oct 15, also Su 2-4:30 and by appointment. $1.50 adults, 50¢ children under 12. (617) 744-1647.

Ropes Mansion, 318 Essex St., 1727. Owned by the Trustees of the Ropes Memorial, a family foundation, the house is administered by the Essex Institute. It was restored several times in the 19th century. Chinese export porcelain and Irish table glass is featured among the furnishings. The formal gardens and greenhouse are unequalled in Salem. House open June 1-Oct 15, Tu-Sa 10-4, Su 1-4:30; Oct 16-May 31, Tu-F 2-4:30. $1 adults, 50¢ children. Gardens open M-Sa 8-4. No charge. (617) 744-0718.

Witch House, 310½ Essex St., c. 1764. Here is the place to go if you want to know more about the famed Salem witch trials. This is the restored home of Judge Jonathan Corwin, the Salem magistrate who held preliminary examinations of the "possessed" in 1692. These were held in this house. The building, owned by the city of Salem, is refreshingly free of cheap or sensational effects. Open Mar 1-Dec 1, 10-5 daily and by appointment; June 1-Labor Day, 10-6 daily. $1 adults, 25¢ for children under 12. (617) 744-0180. ♦♦

Saugus

SAUGUS IRONWORKS NATIONAL HISTORIC SITE, off US 1, c. 1648. The first ironworks established in the American colonies was reconstructed in the 1950s by the American Iron and Steel Institute and became a part of the National Park system in 1962. Only the **Iron Works House** (c. 1646) remains of the original buildings. It was the finest home in a community known as Hammersmith and was used for company business, family living quarters, and a schoolhouse for ironworkers. The Saugus works only survived until the 1670s, but the men trained there carried their skills to many other industrial outposts in the colonies.

A tour of the Saugus Iron Works starts at the Iron Works House and then moves on to the furnace, the forge, the ironhouse, and the slitting mill. At each of these locations the ironmaking process is displayed. In the mid-17th century there were only roughly a dozen mills in the world where wrought-iron bars could be slit into "flats" and "rod" for nails—as was the practice at Saugus. NR. Open Apr 2-Oct, daily 9-5; Nov-Apr 1, daily 9-4. Free. ♦♦ (617) 233-0050.

Located nearby on Howard St. in the town of Saugus is the **Boardman House** (c. 1680). It is a well-preserved example of a New England saltbox and is maintained by the SPNEA. NR, NHL. It is open by appointment only. $1 charge. (617) 227-3956 for further information.

Topsfield

TOPSFIELD TOWN COMMON HISTORIC DISTRICT, comprises the old town center surrounding the Common, 17th-20th centuries. Topsfield has grown considerably since World War II, but fortunately the scale and character of the Common area has not been disturbed. Of the ten buildings in the district, however, one is clearly superior to all the others. This is the 1683 **Parson Capen House** on Howlett St. Architectural historians consider it an outstanding example of Elizabethan design. It is constructed almost entirely of oak (even the clapboarding) and has a second-floor overhang with pendants at the front and gable ends. The interior central spiral staircase climbs along a massive stone chimney. The building was last restored in the early 1900s and is now the museum of the Topsfield Historical Society. Early American furniture is displayed therein. NR, NHL. Open June 17-Sept 9, W, F, Su 1-4:30. 50¢ adults, 25¢ children. (617) 887-8074.

Wenham

WENHAM HISTORIC DISTRICT, both sides of Main St. from Beverly city line to Hamilton town line, 17th-19th centuries. Wenham is one of the best preserved of New England villages; in the 19th century it became a favorite summer resort town and it has remained a fashionable enclave. The most prominent of the historical buildings is the **Claflin-Richard House,** 132 Main St., which is owned by the local historical society. It was built in 1662 and added to in 1673. The design incorporates such medieval features as second-floor and gable overhangs and windows with diamond-shaped panes. Two 1840 shoe shops are included on the grounds. The home is a center for the display of such collections as dolls, doll houses, miniatures, toys, costumes, fans, kitchen utensils, and other antique objects. NR. Open all year except Feb, M-F 1-4, Su 2-5; mornings by appointment. $1 adults, 25¢ children. (617) 468-2377.

Other notable buildings along the handsome Main St. are the **Richard Hutton House,** #185 (c. 1679); the **Hobbs House,** cor. of Monument Sq. (1688); and **Lummus Tavern,** #188 (1826).

Southeast, Cape Cod, and the Islands

The historical image of southeastern Massachusetts is much softer, more democratic than that sketched by harshly Puritan, bluenose Boston and its rocky northeastern neighbors. From Duxbury to the very tip of Cape Cod at Provincetown — where the Pilgrims first landed — tolerance for other beliefs and ways was more quickly established than in the Puritan colony to the north. Who else but the Pilgrims would have invited the Indians to a Thanksgiving dinner? Quaker settlers were more readily accepted and soon became important leaders in the shipping and whaling industries of such communities as New Bedford, Nantucket, Fall River, and Martha's Vineyard.

To an almost uncanny degree, the landscape of southeastern Massachusetts, in contrast to that of the northeast, mirrors the image shaped by history. The coastline is more gradual, sandier, sometimes billowing into graceful dunes. There is a peaceful quality about the tidal estuaries and the freshwater ponds where wild duck and the lowly cranberry are the only quarry pursued. Everywhere in southeastern Massachusetts there is history. You may hear about it from a Portuguese-American in Fall River or 12th-generation Anglo-American resident of Duxbury. Nearly every village has its historic house and museum. And the longer you stay in this pleasant corner of New England, the more important the past will be for you, too.

Barnstable

OLD CUSTOMS HOUSE, Main St., 1855. The **Donald G. Trayser Memorial Museum** is housed in this mid-Victorian brick building originally designed as a custom house by federal architect Ammi B. Young. As an important port, Barnstable required a special facility for overseeing the collection of custom duties. Marine articles, ship models, and Indian artifacts are the principal objects displayed. NR. Open July 1-Sept 15, Tu-Sa 1:30-4:30. 50¢ adults, 25¢ children 6 and older. (617) 362-2092.

OLD JAIL, Main St. and Old Jail Ln., late 17th century. The earliest known jail in the Plymouth colony, the wooden Barnstable facility is practically unique in New England. It is owned by the town, but is not open to the public. NR.

THE STURGIS LIBRARY, 3090 Main St., 1644. The library, founded in 1867, is said to be the oldest such building in the United States. It was originally the home of an early minister, the Rev. Lothrop. The library contains important genealogical and historical materials. Open M and F 2-5, Tu and Th 2-5 and 7-9, W and Sa 9-12 and 2-5. Free. (617) 362-6636.

Brewster

NEW ENGLAND FIRE AND HISTORY MUSEUM, Main St. Anyone with a love of fire-fighting lore will enjoy this display of antique equipment. While the primary emphasis is on the exciting work of firemen, there is also a Victorian apothecary shop on display, including a jar and bottle collection. The **Henry Hopkins Blacksmith Shop**, dating from 1867, has been reconstructed on the grounds. Open June-mid-Sept, M-F 10-5, Sa-Su 10-5; mid-Sept-Columbus Day, Sa-Su 10-3. $3 adults $2 children 6-12. Tours: $1.75 adults, 50¢ children, 75¢ student and children groups. (617) 896-5711. ⚭

Chatham

CHATHAM RAILROAD MUSEUM, 153 Depot Rd., 1887, and CHATHAM WINDMILL, Chase Park, Shattuck Pl., 1797. Chatham knows the value of interesting old buildings and has made them inviting to visitors. The Railroad Museum is housed in the only remaining station on Cape Cod still in its original condition. It retains the dispatching and ticket office. The building is a charming Queen Anne-Stick Style design. Directly behind the depot stands an ancient caboose. NR. The museum is open from the last M in June to the first F after Labor Day, M-F 1:30-4:30. Free. Donations accepted. ⚭ (617) 945-0783.

The windmill served as the principal gristmill in Chatham throughout the 19th century. A miller is still on hand to grind grain. NR. Open July-Labor Day, daily except Tu 9-12 and 1-4:30. Free. (617) 945-3163.

ATWOOD HOUSE, Stage Harbor Rd., 1752. Sandwich glass, sea shells, and Parian ware are among the many antiques and natural objects displayed at this local museum, maintained by the Chatham Historical Society. Open mid-June-mid-Sept, M, W, F 2-5. $1 adults, 50¢ children 12 and over, under 12 free. (617) 945-2493.

Cohasset

COHASSET MARITIME MUSEUM, Elm St., 1760. A former ship chandlery is the home of this seaport's marine museum. The story of Cohasset's seafaring folk begins as early as 1617 when Captain John Smith made a landing on the rocky shore. In the 1800s the town became an important center of the fishing industry. More recently, Cohasset has enjoyed a reputation as a summer resort. The museum features permanent and temporary exhibitions organized around local nautical traditions. Open mid-June-late-Sept, Tu-Sa 1:30-4:30. 75¢ adults, 50¢ children under 12. The museum can also be visited in tandem with two other Cohasset institutions which are affiliated with the historical society. A combination ticket is available for $1.50 per person. (617) 383-0773. ⚭

The other museums of interest to the visitor are **Cohasset Historic House**, an 1810 residence on Elm St., which is furnished with colonial antiques; and the **Independence Gown Museum**, S. Main St., which features costumes and accessories. Both these museums have the same hours as the Maritime Museum.

Dighton vicinity

DIGHTON ROCK, across the Taunton River from Dighton in Dighton Rock State Park. Imagine moving a 50-ton rock. The state of Massachusetts did so in 1964 to protect the boulder's cryptic symbols and inscriptions from being slowly washed away by the tidal waters of the Taunton River. The markings were first noted and recorded in 1680, and over 600 books and articles have been written about the inscribed message. It has been variously ascribed to Vikings, moon men, and ancient Indian tribes. See it and decide for yourself. NR. ⚭

Duxbury

JOHN ALDEN HOUSE, 105 Alden St., 1653. The home built by Alden and his third son, Jonathan, was where John and his wife Priscilla spent their later years. The Duxbury area was first explored by Alden, Miles Standish, and other Pilgrim fathers from Plymouth in the 1620s; it was made a township in 1637. Alden lived to the age of 89 and is buried in the Old Burying Ground on Chestnut St. The house is furnished with 17th-century antiques and artifacts. Owned and operated by the Alden Kindred of America, Inc. Open last Sa in June-Labor Day, Tu-Su, holidays

10-5. $1 adults, 25¢ children under 13. (617) 934-2788.

KING CAESAR HOUSE, King Caesar Rd., 1808, and CAPT. GERSHOM BRADFORD HOUSE, 931 Tremont St., 1808. Both buildings are representative of the Federal style and were built when Duxbury was a prosperous shipbuilding and fishing community. "King Caesar" was the nickname given Ezra Watson, a ship builder; Gershom Bradford was a sea captain. Both museum houses feature fine antiques and relics of maritime history and are maintained by the Duxbury Rural and Historical Society. The houses are open June 15-Labor Day, Tu-Su 1-4. $1 adults. (617) 934-5286.

STANDISH MONUMENT, Monument Rd., is set on the crest of Captain's Hill. It is 130 feet high and is topped by a statue of Miles Standish.

Fall River

Fall River is perhaps the most American of all New England cities by virtue of the fact that it became home to people from many different countries during the 19th and early 20th centuries. They came to work principally in the great granite cotton mills. By the early 1900s, a visitor was likely to find that either Portuguese or French was more commonly spoken than English. That situation has changed drastically since World War II, and today most of the mills are empty or used for other purposes. Fall River, after a period of acute depression, has reemerged as a vital commercial center. The historical institutions in town are being strengthened and a consciousness regarding preservation has been roused.

BATTLESHIP COVE, State Pier, is where the battleship **USS Massachusetts,** the submarine **USS Lionfish,** the destroyer **USS Joseph P. Kennedy, Jr.,** and **PT Boat 796** are moored in Mt. Hope Bay. Guided tours of these World War II vessels are given, and films and lectures are scheduled from time to time. On display are equipment and memorabilia associated with these ships. NR. Open daily 9-5. $3.50 adults, $1.75 children; special group rates. Combination tickets which include the Marine Museum (see following listing) are also available. (617) 678-1100. ♟

MARINE MUSEUM, 70 Water St. Fall River was the eastern terminus of the famed Fall River Line of steamships to New York. A rail link with Boston from Fall River had been established early in the 19th century. Service by rail and sea continued between Boston and New York via Fall River until the late 1930s. The side-wheelers of the 1800s were palatial vessels, and businessmen or vacationing families found themselves fortunate to be able to travel Long Island Sound on the Fall River Line. Mementos celebrating this important transportation facility are featured at the Maritime Museum, including lithographs, posters, oil paintings, and ship models. Open June 29-Labor Day, daily 9-8; day after Labor Day-June 28, M-F 9-5, Sa-Su, holidays 10-5. $1.25 adults; 75¢ children under 12. Combination tickets for use also at Battleship Cove are $4 adults, $2 children. (617) 674-3533.

GRANITE HOUSE (Elizabeth Hitchcock Brayton House), 451 Rock St., 1843. Now the home of the Fall River Historical Society, this is one of the finest early Victorian mansions in the state and representative of the great homes built by Fall River's mill owners. The mansion was located on Lower Columbia St. until 1870 and was then moved to its present location. Originally it was a Greek Revival building; a Second Empire reshaping with a mansard roof, elaborate dormer windows, and a bold columned portico came after the move. The interior was also remodeled at this time. The double parlor ceilings are stenciled and painted in a colorful manner; beautiful woods are used for paneling and doors, and in the fireplace mantels. NR. Open Mar-Dec, Tu-F 9-4:30, Sa-Su 2-4. Free. (617) 679-1071.

There are two other addresses in Fall River of special note. These belonged at one time to Lizzie Borden, accused of the axe murder of her socially prominent parents on August 4, 1892. The house at **230 Second**

St. was the scene of the crime; later, after Miss Borden was acquitted, she moved on to **306 French St.** She could never escape her notoriety. Both houses remain private residences today.

Falmouth

FALMOUTH HISTORICAL SOCIETY MUSEUMS: **Katharine Lee Bates House,** 16 Main, 1810; **Conant House,** Village Green, c. 1794; and **Dr. Francis Wicks House (Wood House),** Village Green, c. 1790. The society's two buildings on the green feature 18th- and 19th-century antique furnishings and objects relating to Falmouth's historic whaling and maritime past. The Bates House is the birthplace of the author of the poem "America the Beautiful." A parlor furnished in the Victorian style is the chief attraction at this historic site. All three houses are open June 15-Sept 15, M-F 2-5. $1 adults, 50¢ children for both houses on the green, and the same charge for the Bates House. (617) 548-1455.

Hingham

THE OLD ORDINARY, 21 Lincoln St., 1680. This house museum is sponsored by the Hingham Historical Society and features furnishings of the 17th and 18th centuries, a tool collection, and a colonial period tap room. Open June-Sept 15, Tu-Sa 1-4. $2 adults, 50¢ children under 12. (617) 749-0013.

OLD SHIP MEETING HOUSE, Main

St., 1681. The oldest surviving church in New England is also the oldest English colonial house of worship still standing in the United States. The frame building's unusual form has probably been responsible for saving it from destruction. The

builders were ship's carpenters and the roof, supported by curved timbers, resembles an inverted ship's hull. It is still the home of the First Parish in Hingham, Unitarian. NR, NHL. Open for tours July-Sept 1, T-Su, 12-5. $1 suggested donation. (617) 749-1679.

Marshfield

DANIEL WEBSTER LAW OFFICE AND LIBRARY, early 19th century, and WINSLOW HOUSE, 1699, Webster and Careswell Sts. The last remaining building of the famed politician's property was moved to the grounds of Winslow House in 1966. The office and library have been restored to the period preceding Webster's death in 1852, the same year he was denied the Whig presidential nomination. Webster is buried in the nearby **Winslow Burying Ground.**

Winslow House was built by Isaac Winslow and is furnished with fine antiques. It is a central-chimney frame house and was remodeled in the mid-1700s. Both buildings are open July-Labor Day, daily except Tu 10-5. NR, NHL. (617) 834-7329.

Martha's Vineyard

There is little on Martha's Vineyard that isn't historic, and the residents—summer and otherwise—like it that way. Because the island is somewhat isolated, it has been able to fend off attempts at wide-scale commercialization and "improvement" which have adulterated the scene elsewhere in coastal New England. The villages of Edgartown, Oak Bluffs, and Vineyard Haven on the eastern part of the island are known as "down island" places; those in the west— West Tisbury, Chilmark, Menemsha, and Gay Head—are considered "up island." All are fun to explore, but the visitor will find that the historic places open to the public are concentrated in the east; so, too, are most of the public restaurants and accommodations. For further information regarding these facilities as well as tours, excursions, and car ferries, contact Martha's Vineyard Chamber of Commerce, P.O. Box 1698, Vineyard Haven, MA 02568, (617) 693-0085.

THOMAS COOKE HOUSE, Cooke and Schools Sts., 1765. This is the headquarters of the Dukes County Historical Society and a good place to begin any historical tour of the island. Exhibits in the Cooke House include dolls and toys, china, glassware, whaling gear, ship models, scrimshaw, and other maritime artifacts. The new **Francis Foster Museum** on the grounds features exhibitions on the Vineyard's nautical past. Also to be seen in this museum complex are a reconstructed lighthouse, an herb garden, and a shed where carriages and boats are displayed. A research library is open year-round. The museum facilities are open June 15-Sept 15, Tu-Sa 10-4:30. $1 adults. Information on the society's activities may be had by calling (617) 627-4441.

DR. DANIEL FISHER HOUSE, 1840; VINCENT HOUSE, 1672; and WHALING CHURCH, 1843, all at Main and Church Sts. These buildings are maintained by the Historical Preservation Society of Martha's Vineyard, formed in 1975 to prevent demolition of some of the island's oldest buildings. The first property is used for professional offices; the others are open to the public. The Cape Cod **Vincent House** is believed to be the oldest surviving home on the island. In 1978 it was moved twelve miles from its original Great Pond location to the center of Edgartown. The restoration work has been very carefully executed, and the building is a living museum of architectural history. It retains its original hardware, brickwork, and woodwork. Open during the summer months, M-F 11-1 and 2-4. $1 adults. Admission also covers the **Whaling Church,** a Greek Revival building which serves as the town's cultural center. It has 160 box pews and a working organ dating from 1857. (617) 627-8017.

MARTHA'S VINEYARD CAMPGROUND, off Circuit Ave., mid-1800s. This facility in the village of Oak Bluffs to the north of Edgartown, formerly known as the Wesleyan Grove Camp Meeting, is now used for outdoor concerts and for religious purposes. Here are many tiny neo-Gothic summer cottages surrounding an open-air Methodist tabernacle. The buildings are owned by the Methodist Church and private individuals. NR.

FLYING HORSES CAROUSEL, 33 Oak Bluffs Ave. Oak Bluffs, 1876. When you feel you've had enough religion, you might wish to visit the nearby carousel. It was moved to this location from Coney Island in 1884. It is said to be the oldest operating platform carousel in the United States. NR. 🛉

RITTER HOUSE, Beach St., Vineyard Haven, is another property which has been saved by the Historical Preservation Society. The clapboard frame house is a Federal-period dwelling built in 1796. Miraculously, it survived the great town fire of 1883. The building is now used as the headquarters of the superintendent of schools.

SEAMAN'S BETHEL, next to the ferry dock, Vineyard Haven. The shingled building houses exhibits of artifacts from the Vineyard's halcyon days of steam and sail. It is open during the summer months from W-Su, 10-3:30. 50¢ admission.

Middleborough

MIDDLEBOROUGH HISTORICAL MUSEUM, Jackson St., administers a 1690 **law office**, the **Outhouse-Sproat Tavern** (1700), and two houses dating from 1820. Special attractions at the museum are a weaving room, blacksmith shop, and carriage shed with early vehicles. Unique to Middleborough is the collection of Gen. Tom Thumb memorabilia. Tom Thumb, P.T. Barnum's star midget whose real name was Charles Sherwood Stratton, married a diminutive Middleborough native, Mercy Lavinia Warren Bump. He died in his wife's hometown in 1883. The museum is open during July-Aug, W, F, Su 1-5. (617) 947-1969.

Nantucket

Nantucket, town and island, is nothing but sun, sand, and history. "Look at it," Herman Melville wrote in *Moby Dick*, "a mere hillock, an elbow of sand; all beach, without a background." One hundred years later, the background is more appreciated. It is made up of an extraordinary collection of 18th- and 19th-century sea captains' and merchants' homes, neoclassical public buildings, the churches of the Quakers and the descendants of the Puritan settlers, and in handsome maritime sites and facilities.

Nantucket was the first location in Massachusetts to secure zoning to protect its historic sites. Now the whole town has been granted recognition as a National Historic Landmark. Exploring its historic treasures would take many summer seasons. The following sampler is offered only as an inducement to further exploration.

A seasonal pass costing $4 will admit the visitor to a number of historic buildings administered by the Nantucket Historical Association. These are indicated in listings that follow by the initials NHA. Summer operating hours are the same for all these sites: daily 10-5. For information regarding other hours during the year, consult the Nantucket Historical Association, Box 1016, Union St., Nantucket, MA 02554. (617) 228-1894. Headquarters is the Old Town and County Bldg.

MUSEUMS AND LIBRARIES: **Nantucket Atheneum**, Main St., c. 1848; **Friends Meeting House**, Fair St., 1838; **Peter Foulger Museum**, Broad St.; and the **Whaling Museum**, Broad St., 1847.

The **Atheneum**, a handsome Greek Revival temple, is the second building to stand on this site and to serve as a town library. The first was destroyed with many other buildings then lining Main St. in an 1846 fire. It is open afternoons M-Sa.

Quakers once made up the majority of Nantucket's population, but the wealth and worldliness that were a product of the whaling trade led many residents to adopt fancier forms of worship. Today the **Friends Meeting House** serves as a museum devoted to the Quaker past. NHA. $1 admission.

The **Peter Foulger Museum**, named for Benjamin Franklin's maternal grandfather, is a major new center for exhibits of ship models, artifacts of the China trade, clocks, paintings, and other antique objects. NHA. $1 admission.

Next to the Foulger Museum is the **Whaling Museum**. For almost a century, beginning in the mid-18th century, Nantucket was the uncontested whaling capital of the world. A completely rigged whale boat is found at the museum along with thousands of other articles—scrimshaw, ship models, a candle press, sea chests—which define the whaler's world. NHA. $1.25 admission.

HOMES: **Jethro Coffin House (Oldest House)**, Sunset Hill, 1686; **1800 House**, Mill St.; **Hadwen House-Satler Memorial**, Main and Pleasant Sts., 1844; **Nathaniel Macy House**, 12 Liberty St., 1729; and **Maria Mitchell Association**, 1 Vestal St., 1790.

The **Jethro Coffin and Nathaniel Macy houses** reflect the simple taste of the early settlers. The form—a box with a lean-to attached—changed little from the 17th century through the first half of the 18th. The Coffin House, the earlier of the two, however, is covered with soft, silvery-gray

cedar shingles, whereas the Macy home is clapboarded. This latter type of finishing became more and more common for new dwellings of the prosperous whaling families. Both houses are operated by the NHA. 50¢ admission, Coffin House; $1 admission, Macy House.

The **Mitchell House** is better known as the birthplace of astronomer Maria Mitchell than as an architectural landmark. She was Vassar College's first professor of astronomy and a prominent Quaker educator. The association which maintains the house is just as devoted to educational programs in the natural sciences as it is to history. The house is open June 15-Sept 12, M-F 10-12 and 2-5, Sa 10-12. $1 adults, 25¢ children under 12. Library hours are June 16-Sept 13, M-F 10-12 and 2-5; mid-Sept-mid-June, M-Th 2-5. Free. (617) 228-9198.

The **1800 House,** built just ten years after the Mitchell residence, is a typical central-chimney dwelling. It belonged to a former high sheriff and is furnished with period antiques, including Chinese export porcelain, English china, and an unusual collection of Windsor chairs. Administered by the NHA. $1 admission.

Hadwen House is Nantucket's finest Greek Revival mansion and symbolizes the degree of wealth and sophistication attained by the whale-oil entrepreneurs in the early 1800s. It is built of brick and covered with clapboard. The interior spaces are fitted with elegant chandeliers, fireplace mantels, and architectural woodwork. A NHA property. $1 admission.

CHURCHES: **Unitarian Church** (Second

Congregational Meeting House), Orange St., 1809, 1830; **First Congregational Church,** 62 Centre St., 1852.

The earlier church follows the straightforward lines of the Federal style. The tower served as a watchtower for many years and still contains the town clock. The later Congregational building was designed in the Gothic Revival style, and the facade with pointed-arch windows and entrance makes a strongly "high church" aesthetic statement.

MARINE SITES: **Great Point Lighthouse,** Great Point, 1820; the **Lightship "Nantucket,"** moored at Straight Wharf.

Formerly maintained by the U.S. Coast Guard, the 75-foot stone **Great Point Lighthouse** is now administered by the National Park Service. The keeper's house is attached. NR. Open June-Sept, daily 9-6. The light and radio beam of the **"Nantucket"** guided boats leaving and entering the South Shoals. The ship is now open for touring and is a NHA property. $1 admission.

GOVERNMENT BUILDINGS: **Old Fire Hose Cart House,** Gardner St., 1875; **Old Gaol,** Vestal St., 1805; **Old Town Office,** 5 Washington St., 1830.

Antique fire equipment is the attraction at the **Hose Cart House,** and the admission is free. Also without charge is a visit to the **Old Town Office,** where a local government office of the 1850s has been recreated. The **Old Gaol** still has its stocks for punishing the wayward. It is a two-story building of oak logs and served the area until 1933. 30¢ admission. All these properties are administered by the NHA.

New Bedford

Nantucket's only serious rival in the whaling trade was New Bedford. And by the 1840s, New Bedford—better situated for railroad service and with a deeper harbor —was winning the contest. By the 1860s, of course, whale oil was being replaced by kerosene, and the industry slowly faded away. While whaling ships continued to sail from New Bedford (the last voyage was made in 1925), the city's trade shifted to textile making, as in nearby Fall River. The handsome old center of the city's commerce, built up during the height of the whaling era from 1800-50, grew grimier and less desirable. Not until the 1960s did the preservation fever catch on in New Bedford. Fortunately, there was much that could still be saved. The old center of town is now a delight to visit. It is best enjoyed on foot.

NEW BEDFORD HISTORIC DISTRICT, bounded by the waterfront on the E, Elm St. on the N, Acushnet on the W, and Commercial St. on the S, 18th-19th centuries. Among the most interesting buildings are:

Mechanics Bank and **Merchants Bank** Bldg. (Double Bank Building), 56-62 N. Water St., 1831. This superb Greek Revival temple was designed by Russell Warren, an architect responsible for many of New Bedford's public buildings. The facade is of polished granite, and the portico is supported by eight Ionic columns of wood. It is now the home of The Fisherman's Pension Trust.

Samuel Rodman House (New Bedford Glass Museum), 50 N. Second St., 1831. The building, a great stone mansion, has been restored and features exhibits of Pairpoint and Mt. Washington glass as well as other decorative objects made in the New Bedford area. The **Pairpoint Glassworks,** established in the city in 1880, is still open and information regarding tours is available at the museum. Open June-Sept, M-Sa 10-4, Su 1-5; Oct-May, Tu-Sa 10-4, Su 1-4. $1 adults, 50¢ children. (617) 994-0115.

New Bedford Institution for Savings (Third District Courthouse), Second and Williams Sts., 1853. For this building Russell Warren chose a Renaissance Revival design. After 1896 it was used to house the district court. It is again serving as a bank.

New Bedford Whaling Museum, 18 Johnny Cake Hill, is one of the finest marine museums in the country. The building is also the home of the Old Dartmouth Historical Society. Most of the exhibits deal with New Bedford's central position as a whaling center. There is an 1840s whaleship reproduced in half-scale, ship carvings, scrimshaw, and other nautical artifacts. Also of interest are the society's Gilbert Stuart portraits and some very well-executed examples of antique pewter, glass, and dolls. Open all year, M-Sa 9-5, Su 1-5. $1.50 adults, 75¢ children. 🏛 (617) 997-0046.

Seamen's Bethel, 15 Johnny Cake Hill, 1832, rebuilt 1867. A church for the seafaring, the bethel is the setting for Father Mapple's sermon in Melville's *Moby Dick.* The pulpit is prow-shaped. Since publication of the novel (1851) and after the 1867 fire, the front facade was redesigned, a tower added, and the original interior seating plan reversed.

U.S. Customhouse, Second and Williams Sts., 1834-36. Federal government architect Robert Mills designed this granite building with a monumental Doric portico. As a major American port, New Bedford required such a facility. It is still in use today, the oldest such American customhouse in operation.

North Easton

NORTH EASTON HISTORIC DIS-

TRICT, both sides of Lincoln, Maine, and Elm Sts., S side of Canton St., and W side of MA 138, 19th century. North Easton was a company town where the Ames family directed the manufacture of such products as shovels and tools. Frederick L. Ames (1835-93) was also a railroading financier (the Union Pacific) and a friend and patron of architect Henry Hobson Richardson. Ames, along with other members of the family, wanted the best for North Easton and its residents, and got it. Frederick Law Olmsted was brought in to landscape the grounds of many of the town's buildings. Among the most notable is the **North Easton Railroad Station,** off Oliver St., designed by Richardson in 1881. It is a one-story building with a great overarching roof and carved animal figures on the monumental granite walls. **Oakes Ames Memorial Hall,** named after Frederick Ames's uncle, dates from the same period. So, too, does the **Oliver Ames Free Library,** named for Ames's father. All are in the style designated Richardsonian Romanesque.

Orleans

FRENCH CABLE STATION, corner of Cove Rd. and MA 28, 1891. The first transatlantic cable was laid from Brest, France, to Eastham for a distance of 3,173 nautical miles in 1879. The line was the work of a French company, and the terminal was extended and moved to Orleans in 1891; the cable was finally carried as far as New York in 1898. It is hard to imagine that so important an operation was carried out in this simple clapboard building. The cable system was shut down in 1959, and the facility has become a museum. Much of the original telegraphic equipment is still intact. NR. Open July 1-Sept 5, Tu-Su 2-4. $1 adults, 50¢ children 7-18. (617) 255-1725.

Plymouth

Plymouth is the natural center of the tourism industry in southeastern Massachusetts and New England's most historic city. Sometimes the mixture of tourism and history can become wearying and confusing.

Pilgrim-this and Pilgrim-that can only be tolerated for a short period of time. As in the case of Plymouth Rock, it can become difficult to separate hype from history, legend from fact. Yet it can be said with absolute certainty that Plymouth has retained a healthy degree of her historic character. Whether the Pilgrims did use the Rock as a stepping stone will remain a controversy for years, but no merchant has been able to franchise its chips.

A good deal of hard work and devoted scholarship have gone into the preservation of Plymouth as an imaginative and valuable historical center. Such organizations as the General Society of Mayflower Descendants, The Pilgrim Society, the Plymouth Antiquarian Society, the Pilgrim John Howland Society, and Plimoth Plantation, Inc. operate museum houses and facilities which bring the past alive in a legitimate and compelling fashion.

THE WATERFRONT. What better place to begin one's journey through town than at **Plymouth Rock,** Water St., on the harbor? The sacred object is well protected from the elements and graffiti artists by a classical granite canopy raised in 1880 and designed by McKim, Mead, and White. The Rock lies at the foot of **Cole's Hill,** thought to have been the burial place of those who perished in the first winter of 1620-21. There is a memorial to these Pilgrims and, beneath that, a crypt containing bones exumed from unmarked graves in the 18th and 19th centuries. A large **statue of Massasoit,** the Wampanoag chief who befriended the settlers, crowns the hill. **Leyden St.,** off Water St. to the west, is where the Pilgrims first set down roots. The locations are marked by historical tablets.

Plimoth Plantation, a 17th-century recreation which is described more fully in later listings, has two buildings in the Water St. area. These are the **First House** and **1627 House,** which together provide an introduction to 17th-century architecture and life. They are open Apr-Nov, daily 9-5. 10¢ admission. **Mayflower II,** a replica owned by Plimoth Plantation, is moored at State Pier on Water St. It was built in England and brought across the

Atlantic in 1957. It was built as a place to learn about the ocean-going experience of the Pilgrims and may be toured. The times of admission are the same as the Water St. houses. $1.75 adults, $1.25 children 5-13. See details regarding combination tickets covering all exhibits and facilities of Plimoth Plantation under listing for Pilgrim Village.

THE PLYMOUTH ANTIQUARIAN SOCIETY was founded in 1919 and has safeguarded three of the town's most important historic houses, all of which are open to visitors. These are **Antiquarian House,** 126 Water St. (1809); **Harlow Old Fort House,** 119 Sandwich St. (1677); and **Spooner House,** 27 North St. (1747). Antiquarian House is typical of those built in the Federal style by wealthy Plymouth merchants in the early 19th century. The Harlow Old Fort House gets its unusual name because the early landmark was built from oak timbers of a 1622 fort. These heavy beams can still be seen in the walls and ceilings of the first-floor rooms. The cottage was first the home of William Harlow, and members of the family bearing this name continued to own it for 224 years. Much of the interior detailing is original, and the Great Hall, with exposed posts, framing, and huge fireplace, is especially noteworthy. NR. Spooner House serves as the headquarters for the Antiquarian Society. Like Antiquarian House, it is furnished with period antiques from the 18th and 19th centuries. All three houses are open May 27-Sept 15, Th-Sa 10-5, Su 12-5. Admission to each is $1.25 adults, 50¢ children. (617) 746-9697.

JABEZ HOWLAND HOUSE, 33 Sandwich St., 1667, 1750. The Howland family arrived on the *Mayflower,* Jabez being the son of a founding father, John. This was the first of Plymouth's old houses to be saved from destruction in the 20th century. Although it had been enlarged in the mid-18th century, it has since been restored in part to its earlier profile. The textile collection of this house museum is exceptional. NR. Open May 25-July 1, Sa-Su 10-5; July 2-Sept 14, daily 10-5; Sept 16-Oct 12, Sa-Su 10-5; Oct 12-Thanksgiving, Su 12-5. $1.25 adults, 50¢ children.

MAYFLOWER SOCIETY HOUSE, 4 Winslow St., 1754. The General Society of Mayflower Descendants has every reason to be proud of having saved this mansion from destruction in 1941. What would have replaced it would have been a parking lot overlooking Plymouth Rock. Because of his own sad story, such an ignominious end might not have surprised Edward Winslow, the first inhabitant of the house, and a great-grandson of the third governor of the colony. Winslow was forced to flee Plymouth during the Revolution because of his outspoken Loyalist sympathies, and never returned from Nova Scotia. Ownership of the mansion passed through several hands during the 1800s before ending up in those of Charles L. Willoughby, a Chicago lawyer, who wished to use it as a summer house. It was then considerably enlarged in the Colonial Revival style by Joseph Everett Chandler. The later heavier style, however, quite nicely complements the lighter and earlier. Willoughby saw to it that the roof balustrade was decorated at one place with a British coat-of-arms honoring the most un-American activities of the first owner. The Mayflower Society House is quite magnificently furnished with 18th-century antiques. It is open May 30-Oct 15, daily 10-5. $1.25 adults, 25¢ children. (617) 746-2590.

PILGRIM HALL, 75 Court St., 1824. This building houses the first public museum in America. Architect Alexander Parris built the Greek Revival building for the Pilgrim Society. The present granite Tuscan portico is a replacement for a wooden Doric one. The society is the principal depository of materials and artifacts relating to the Pilgrims. The library, in a wing added in 1904, is an important center for genealogical research. Open year-around, daily 9:30-4:30. NR. $2 adults, $1.50 senior citizens and groups, 25¢ children 6-15. (617) 746-1620.

THE NATIONAL MONUMENT TO THE FOREFATHERS, or the Pilgrim Monument, off Allerton St., 1859. At 81 feet, this is the tallest solid-granite monument in America. Scenes from Pilgrim history are depicted on marble slabs at the base. The monument is administered by the Pilgrim Society.

RICHARD SPARROW HOUSE, Inc., 42 Summer St., 1640. This is Plymouth's oldest house and, as such, has many stories to tell. It was substantially enlarged in 1750, and the earlier section was restored in the 1930s. Such elements as the first-floor fireplace, floorboards, and exposed gunstock corner posts are original. Richard Sparrow and his wife arrived in Plymouth in 1632 and in 1651 passed the house on to their son, Jonathan. NR. Open May-Oct 15,

M-Sa 9-5. $1.25 adults, 25¢ children. (617) 747-1240.

1627 PILGRIM VILLAGE and the WAMPANOAG SUMMER SETTLEMENT, PLIMOTH PLANTATION, Warren Rd., three miles S of downtown Plymouth. Founded in 1947, Plimoth Plantation is one of the most ambitious and well-grounded of the historical villages created for educational purposes. It is the only one of these centers devoted entirely to 17th century culture and to both aspects of it— that of the English immigrant and of the native American Indian.

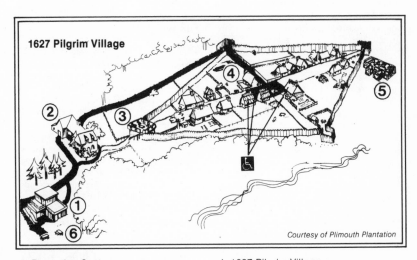

Courtesy of Plimouth Plantation

1. Reception Center
2. Orientation Center
3. Fort
4. 1627 Pilgrim Village
5. 17th Century Barn
6. Picnic Area

Dark colored path and designated houses are handicapped accessible.

The life of the average resident of early 17th-century Plymouth is recreated in **Pilgrim Village.** The emphasis is, naturally, on rural life—its skills and needs. A visitor's tour begins at the Orientation Center with a multi-image slide show which introduces one to the village and its very live participants. Upon leaving the center, one quickly learns that each one of these individuals is reliving the past and has assumed a 17th-century identity. They are using antique methods and materials in performing their daily tasks. The village's animals are varieties common long ago. A reception center contains the modern facilities—cafeteria, gift shop, book store, and exhibits.

Wampanoag Summer Settlement is a new program introduced in 1981. It is directed and staffed by native Wampanoag Indians. From May through October the various activities carried out in a 17th-century Indian village are pursued. Adult men and boys fish, hunt, and tend tobacco fields. Among the women's activities are the weaving of baskets and bags, preserving food, and preparing meals.

1627 Pilgrim Village and the Wampanoag Summer Settlement are open from May 1-Oct 31, 9-5. Admission to these areas is $4.50 adults, $2.25 children 5-13. A combination ticket honored at the Plimoth Plantation buildings at Water St. and on *Mayflower II* is $5.75 adults, $3. children. (617) 746-1622. 🏃

Provincetown

This popular summer resort town has never paid too much attention to history or to the traditional. Perhaps the Pilgrims knew something when they stopped here and then moved on to Plymouth in 1620. Not that there is anything wrong with the town. Commercial St. is fine for a stroll, and you just might meet your long-lost nephew Bruce there for a weekend with a few friends. If you do want to get away from the hubbub along the wharf, make a visit to the **Pilgrim Memorial Monument and Museum,** Town Hill. An obelisk rises over the complex and commemorates the Pilgrim landing. It also affords excellent views of the town. The museum is devoted primarily to local and natural history exhibits. Both are open mid-June-mid-Sept, daily 9-9; mid-Sept-mid-June, daily 9-5. There is a nominal fee. (617) 487-1310. Another stop you can make in town is the **Provincetown Heritage Museum,** Center and Commercial Sts., founded in the bicentennial year. It is housed in the 1860 Methodist Church and features a turn-of-the-century kitchen, antique fire equipment, and exhibits on Provincetown's past, particularly its fishing industry. Open June 12-Columbus Day, daily 10-6. $1 adults. (617) 487-0666. 🏮

Sandwich

TOWN HALL SQUARE HISTORIC DISTRICT, the Town Hall Sq. and adjoining streets, 17th-19th centuries. Sandwich grew rich in the 1800s on the manufacture of glass. Great homes were built, and the center of town was blessed with handsome public buildings such as the Greek Revival **Town Hall** (1834) and the **First Church of Christ** (1847). After the 1880s, when the glassworks was closed down, lack of money prevented the demolition or remodeling of the old. Old Sandwich survived quite nicely as a consequence, and the great glassmaking tradition is today celebrated in the modern **Sandwich Glass Museum,** 129 Main St., on the square. It has one of the best colored and lacy Sandwich glass collections in the United States. Open Apr 1-Nov 1, daily 9:30-4:30. $1.50 adults, 25¢ children under 12.
(617) 888-0251.

Located farther away from the square,

but still in the historic district on Water St. is **The Old Hoxie House** (1637). It may be the oldest home left standing on the Cape. The furnishings are antiques of the 17th century. Open June 18-Sept 30, M-Sa 10-5, Su 1-5. 50¢ adults, 35¢ children. (617) 888-1173. Also located on Water St. is the **Thornton Burgess Museum,** housed in a 1756 structure. Readers of the classic books of this charming children's fiction writer will enjoy seeing the original Harrison Cady illustrations and other memorabilia. The 56-acre **Briarpatch Nature Trail** is nearby. Open June 17-mid-Nov, M-Sa 10-4, Su 1-4. (617) 888-3083.

Also of interest is the **Yesteryears Museum,** Maine and River Sts., devoted to antique dolls, doll houses, and miniatures. Open May-Nov, M-Sa 10-5, Su 1-5. $2 adults, $1 children 2-12, $1.50 senior citizens. (617) 888-1711.

HERITAGE PLANTATION OF SANDWICH, Grove St., has grown larger and larger since its founding in 1969. The 76-acre site now includes the Lilly collection of miniature soldiers and antique firearms; an American folk art collection which includes scrimshaw, weather vanes, trade signs, and paintings; a 1912 carousel; an 1800 operating windmill; and an extensive collection of antique automobiles. The museum buildings are open May-Oct, 10-5 daily. $3 adults, $1 children. (617) 888-3300.

Wareham

TREMONT NAIL FACTORY HISTORIC DISTRICT, 21 Elm St., 19th century. This is the oldest cut nail factory in the state and one of the oldest in America. Factory complexes that have survived the vicissitudes of the economy for over 100 years are rarely encountered. The historic district consists of a main factory building (1848), six other manufacturing buildings, and two workers' houses. All of these buildings are shingled and in good condition. The main building is topped with a wooden cupola containing a cast-iron bell, dated 1851, which was once used to call the employees to work.

Nineteenth-century methods and some machinery are still used to produce cut nails at the factory. The history of the enterprise dates back to 1819; the present company has run the factory since the 1880s. NR. There is a store, the **Old Cooper Shop,** on the grounds where cut nails are sold along with other hardware products. An eight-minute film on the nail-making process is also shown here. (617) 295-0038.

Yarmouthport

THACHER HOUSE, King's Highway (MA 6A) and Thacher Ln., 1680s, and WINSLOW-CROCKER HOUSE, King's Highway (MA 6A), 1780. Both of these houses are maintained by the SPNEA. Only the Crocker House, however, is open on a regular basis (June-Oct 15, Tu-Th, Su 12-5); Thacher House is open by appointment. (Call the SPNEA for information [617] 227-3956.) Both are beautifully furnished with 17th- and 18th-century antiques. Crocker House was moved to this site from West Barnstable in 1935.

If you are in the Yarmouthport area during the summer, a stop at the **Capt. Bangs Hallet House,** 2 Strawberry Ln. (1840), would be worthwhile. It is a house museum maintained by the Historical Society of Old Yarmouth. Scrimshaw and ship paintings are featured along with fine antique furniture. Open summer months, M-Sa 1-4. 50¢ adults, 25¢ children. (617) 362-3021.

Lodging and Dining

IF Virginia is for lovers, then the Lord must have intended Massachusetts for connoisseurs. In no other state of the Union has so much attention been given to education, to the cultural foundations of everyday life. And in Massachusetts these foundations extend deeply into the past. The oldest house in town is venerated and is likely to have been built at least 300 years ago; the most popular tourist attraction in Boston is not Fenway Park, home of the Red Sox, but rather the 157-year-old Quincy Market complex. Many of the hotels, inns, and restaurants which play host to visitors from all parts of the world are recognized historic sites. Boston, unlike cities twice its size, has held on to at least a half dozen major hotels built from the 1890s through the '20s. And in the countryside, some of the oldest American inns have been carefully preserved for use today. With major tourist areas as the Berkshires, Cape Cod, Nantucket, Martha's Vineyard, Plymouth, Boston, Concord, Lexington, and the North Shore, it is perhaps not surprising that so much from the past has been saved and used in a thoughtful manner. Vermont has more beautiful Fall foliage; Connecticut and Rhode Island have more extensive beaches; Maine and New Hampshire boast higher mountains. But Massachusetts is the center, the place where it all started, and still the best place to begin today. The visitor will find that it is particularly economical to travel during the off-season. A surprising number of Massachusetts' inns are open all year, and, except in the Berkshire ski areas, rates fall drastically when the summer is over.

Amherst

LORD JEFFERY INN, 30 Boltwood Ave., on the Common, 01002. (413) 253-2576. David A. Nichols / Amherst Inn Co. This 20th-century colonial hotel has acquired charm and status because of its Little Ivy League setting. MAP, EP, moderate. AE, D, CB, M, V, PC. Pets welcome. Open all year. [¶]

PLUMBLEY'S OFF THE COMMON, 30 Boltwood Walk, 01002. (413) 253-9586. Ed Stewart. A pleasant mid-Victorian home is the site of a tasteful eatery offering everything from hamburgers to roast duck and prime ribs. Moderate. AE, M, V. Open all year.

Boston

AVERY HOTEL, 24 Avery St. (between Tremont and Washington), 02112. (617) 482-8000. An eleven-story brick building put up in 1923. 140 rooms. Moderate. AE, CB, DC, M, V. [¶]

COPLEY PLAZA HOTEL, 138 St. James Ave., 02116. (617) 267-5300. An impeccable Beaux-Arts palace on Copley Square across from Trinity Church. 450 rooms. Expensive. AE, D, CB, M, V. Small pets welcome. [¶]

COPLEY SQUARE HOTEL, 47 Huntington Ave., 02116. (617) 536-9000. An 1890s hotel that has been in a state of renovation since the 1970s and is now better than ever. 116 rooms. Moderate. AE, CB, D, M, V. [¶]

LENOX HOTEL, 710 Boylston St. at Pru' Center, 02116. (617) 536-5300. Another early 20th-century hotel blessedly spared the wrecker's ball. 225 rooms. Expensive. AE, CB, DC, M, V. ⟨¶⟩

THE PARKER HOUSE, 60 School St., 02108. (617) 227-8600. Where the famous dinner roll was born in the late 1800s; smack in the center of the principal historic district. 541 rooms. Expensive. AE, CB, D, M, V. ⟨¶⟩

RITZ-CARLTON, Arlington and Newbury Sts., 02117. (617) 536-5700. Where the Cabots can still safely meet people other than the Lowells. 257 rooms. Expensive. AE, M, V. ⟨¶⟩

Cambridge

SHERATON-COMMANDER HOTEL, 16 Garden St., 02138. (617) 547-4800 or (800) 325-3535. A pleasant corner of Cambridge; six floors of well-maintained Colonial Revival decor. 175 rooms. Expensive. AE, CB, D, M, V. ⟨¶⟩

Chatham

TOWN HOUSE INN AND LODGE, 11 Library Lane, 02633. (617) 945-2180. Russell and Svea Peterson. Just off Main St. lies the old Sears home, the best house in town and built in 1881. The Victorian mansion is the inn, and next to it is the non-housekeeping lodge. 19 rooms. EP, expensive. AE, D, CB, M, V, PC. Open all year.

Concord

COLONIAL INN, 48 Monument Sq., 01742. (617) 369-9200. Paul M. Barry. An inn since 1947, the Colonial dates back in part to 1716 and has housed a general store as well as boarders. For some time it was called the Thoreau House after Henry Thoreau's grandfather, a one-time resident. 60 rooms. EP, expensive. AE, D, CB, M, V, PC. Pets welcome. Open all year. ⟨¶⟩

Deerfield

DEERFIELD INN, The Street, 01342. (413) 774-5587. Paul J. Burns. Lodging and dining of the same quality and graceful charm as that to be enjoyed elsewhere on The Street. The furnishings are an instructive lesson in 20th-century colonial adaptation. 23 rooms. Expensive. AE, D, CB, M, V. Pets welcome. Open all year. ⟨¶⟩

Edgartown, Martha's Vineyard

CHARLOTTE INN, S. Summer St., 02539. (617) 627-4751. Gery D. Conover. An 1861 sea captain's house is a suitably elegant setting for this island inn. 18 rooms. Expensive. M, V, PC. Open all year. ⟨¶⟩

THE DAGGETT HOUSE, 59 N. Water St. (Box 1333), 02539. (617) 627-4600. Marguerite L. Miller. One building dates from 1750 and the second, across the street, from the early 1800s; both are comfortable, reasonably priced homes away from home. 25 rooms. Bed and breakfast, moderate. M, V, PC. Open all year.

Gloucester

WHITE RAINBOW, 65 Main St., 01930. (617) 281-0017. Jeanne M. Dyson. A restaurant located in the "Front Street Block" of Federal-style buildings. NR. Moderate. Open all year for brunch and dinner; hours vary from season to season.

Great Barrington

WINDFLOWER INN, Egremont Star Rte., Box 25, MA 23, 01230. (413) 528-2720. Barbara & Gerald Liebert and Claudia & John Ryan. Formerly the Fairfield Inn, the building is a mid-19th century farmhouse. 12 rooms. MAP, expensive. PC.

Harwich Port

COUNTRY INN, 86 Sisson Rd., 02646. (617) 432-2769. David & Kathleen Van Gelder. The Van Gelders call their simple establishment "a restful old inn." What better kind is there? 9 rooms. EP, expensive. M, V, PC. Pets welcome. Open all year. ⑪

Lenox

WHEATLEIGH, P.O. Box 824, 01240. (413) 637-0610. Susan & L. Linfield Simon. The 1890s summer estate of the Countess de Heredia, a veritable palace of a place more likely to be found on Lago di Como than in the Berkshires; sybaritic. 17 rooms. EP, expensive. PC. Open all year. ⑪

Nantucket

JARED COFFIN HOUSE, 29 Broad St., 02554. (617) 228-2400. Margaret & Philip Read. Five buildings make up the Coffin complex; each has been tastefully restored for public and private enjoyment. 46 rooms. EP, moderate. AE, D, CB, M, V, PC. Pets welcome. Open all year. ⑪

CLIFF LODGE, 9 Cliff Rd., 02554. (617) 228-0893. Katherine Lynch. A 1771 sea captain's home, widow's walk and all. 6 rooms. Inexpensive. PC. Open May 1-Nov 1.

THE CARRIAGE HOUSE, 4 Ray's Ct., 02554. (617) 228-0326. Jeanne & Bill McHugh. A pleasantly renovated and furnished carriage house dating from the 1860s. 7 rooms. EP, expensive. PC. Open all year.

THE WOODBOX, 29 Fair St., 02554. (617) 228-0587. The Tuteins. Nantucket's oldest inn was built in 1709. 9 rooms. Moderate. PC. Open May to mid-Oct. ⑪

Newburyport

THE WINDSOR HOUSE, 38 Federal St., 01950. (617) 462-3778. Fritz & Judith Crumb. Federal period building with rooms furnished in that style. 6 rooms. Expensive. M, V, PC. Open all year.

MORRILL PLACE, 209 High St., 01950. (617) 462-2808. Rose Ann Hunter. For lovers of neo-classical architecture, this inn provides a splendid setting. 9 rooms. Bed and breakfast, moderate. PC. Pets welcome. Open all year.

BENJAMIN CHOATE HOUSE, 25 Tyng St., 01950. (617) 462-4786. Herbert A. Fox. Three-story Federal mansion with attractive period touches. 5 rooms. Bed and breakfast, moderate. PC. Pets welcome. Open all year.

Provincetown

BRADFORD GARDENS INN, 178 Bradford St., 02657. (617) 487-1616. Jim Logan. A very quiet corner of P'town; a main building dating from 1820 and auxilliary accommodations. 8 rooms, 4 suites. Expensive. AE, M, V, PC. Open Apr 1-Nov 1.

Richmond

PEIRSON PLACE, MA 41, 01254. (413) 698-2750. Margaret & Lou Kingman. A home that has remained in one family since 1788; cottage and apartments also available. 10 rooms. Moderate. M, V, PC. Open Memorial Day-Veterans Day.

Salem

COACH HOUSE INN, 284 Lafayette St., 01970. (617) 744-4092. Patricia Kessler. A mid-Victorian sea captain's mansion. 15 rooms. Moderate. AE, D, M, V. Open all year.

Sturbridge

PUBLICK HOUSE, Main St., on the Common, 01566. (617) 347-3313. Buddy Adler. The quintessence of the modern New England historical experience—comfy and cute. 34 rooms. EP, expensive. Open all year. 🍴

Sudbury

LONGFELLOW'S WAYSIDE INN, 72 Wayside Inn Rd., 01776. (617) 443-8846. Francis Koppeis. America's oldest operating inn which forms the center of a museum complex started by Henry Ford in 1923. 10 rooms. MAP, EP, moderate. AE, D, CB, M, V. Open all year. 🍴

Ware

THE WILDWOOD INN, 121 Church St., 01082. (413) 967-7798. Margaret Lobenstine. A very homey, inviting Victorian inn furnished with antiques. 5 rooms. Inexpensive. M, V, PC. Open all year.

West Harwich

CAPE HALF HOUSE RESTAURANT, 21 Main St., MA 28, 02671. (617) 432-1964. Robert E. Howes. A 1767 authentic Cape half-house is the setting for this traditional restaurant. Closed Jan. Moderate. M, V.

4. VERMONT

VERMONT is one of the friendliest and, many say, the handsomest of the New England states. Although it has become prime vacationland for "flatlanders" from the south, it is a place where the past is still valued and the natural environment safeguarded. Vermont is Calvin Coolidge territory, a center of stout conservatism, yet it has also made room over the years for the renegade—from atheist Ethan Allen to the alternative life-style seekers of today.

Vermont was a bit reluctant about joining the Union. It did not become a state—the 14th—until 1791. When the first constitution for the republic of Vermont was drafted at the Old Constitution House in 1777, universal manhood suffrage and a statewide public educational system were established for the first time on the North American continent. The Vermont republic was not a major battlefield of the Revolution, although the British were defeated at Hubbardton Battlefield and again not far from the Bennington Battle Monument.

Historical sites such as these are popular with nearly everyone seeking ties to the past, but of equal interest are many of the old towns and villages which remind one of a quieter, less restless age. With its stately village green and clapboard church and homes, the achetypal Vermont community offers an amazing variety of attractions to the visitor. There is likely to be at least one fashionable old house which has been well furnished in 18th- or 19th-century antiques and opened to the public as a museum.

In winter, of course, there is the joy of skiing and the enjoyment of miles of powdery trails. Stowe has been the ski capital of the eastern United States since the early 1900s. Fall in Vermont is almost as celebrated. Thousands of "leaf peepers," as they are called by the natives, swarm across the hills in pursuit of crimson and gold and orange. The Green Mountains rarely disappoint.

The cities of Vermont—Burlington, Barre, Montpelier, St. Johnsbury, Bennington, Rutland, Brattleboro, St. Albans—are small by American standards, but they are packed with cultural and historical institutions of importance. It is in these centers or in the surrounding countryside that the major museums are located, among them the Bennington Museum, the Fairbanks Museum, and the Shelburne Museum. The industrial sites and attractions in the urban areas of the state will also attract the seeker of the old and picturesque. Vermont's historic industries—marble and granite quarrying, textiles, milling, maple sugaring—most usually offer displays and exhibitions to the public that remind us that the romance of history goes well beyond the veneration of parchment documents and powdered wigs.

In the pages that follow, and for the convenience of the traveler, Vermont has been divided into four geographic areas. The southern portion of the state includes the counties adjoining Massachusetts—Bennington and Windham—and Rutland county to the north of Bennington along US 7, the main north-south route. The Lake Champlain area includes the four counties which adjoin the lake—Addison Chittenden, Addison, Franklin, and Grand Isle. The third area—East Central Vermont—is made up of the counties along the Connecticut River to the east—Windsor and Orange—and the two adjoining interior counties of Washington and Lamoille. The fourth area has been called traditionally "the Northeast Kingdom" and includes the counties of Caledonia, Orleans, and Essex.

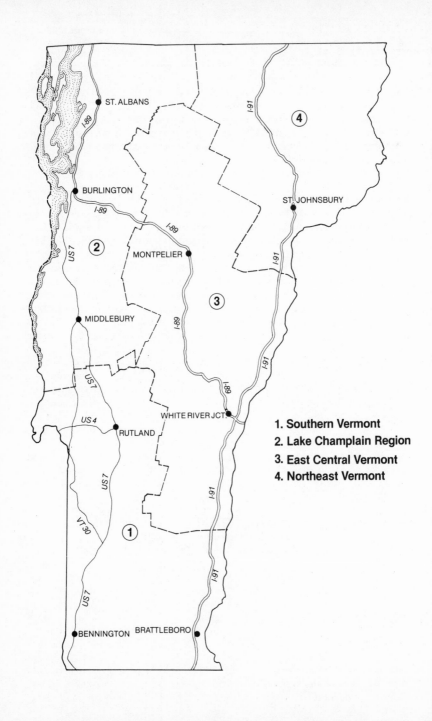

1. Southern Vermont
2. Lake Champlain Region
3. East Central Vermont
4. Northeast Vermont

Bellows Falls

ADAMS OLD STONE GRIST MILL MUSEUM, Mill St., 1831. One of the few surviving mills with its *original* machinery still intact. The museum also houses other 19th-century items, including farming implements and railroad memorabilia. A cooperative venture of the Bellows Falls Historical Society and the Chamber of Commerce. Open June-Aug, Sun 2-4; also by appointment. Donations accepted. 463-3706.

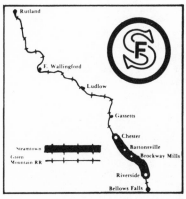

STEAMTOWN FOUNDATION FOR PRESERVATION OF STEAM AND RAILROAD AMERICANA, INC., (PO Box 71), US 5, 2 miles N of Bellows Falls. Steamtown, U.S.A. will delight every railroad buff—young or old. If possible, the visitor will want to take the 22-mile excursion trip between the museum and Chester Depot. There is no better way to enjoy the summer or fall landscape. The largest steam locomotive ever made—the Union Pacific "Big Boy"—is housed on the grounds. Special excursions are also organized by Steamtown. Open Memorial Day-mid Oct; daily 9:30-5:30. Combination train and museum ticket: $6.75 adults, $3.75 children, children under 2 no charge; group rates available as well as separate train and museum tickets. 463-3937. 👫

Bennington

BENNINGTON BATTLE MONUMENT, Monument Circle, 1891. The August 16, 1777 military engagement was fought two miles away (in New York State) but, no matter, you can spot the actual site from the observation platform of the 306-foot stone tower. Next to the Washington Monument, it is the most impressive memorial shaft in America. It is in the same neighborhood as the Bennington Museum and the First Congregational Church. Operated by the state Division for Historic Preservation. NR. Open Apr 1-Nov 1, 9-5. Admission, 50¢ adults, 25¢ children; special group rates. 828-3226. 👫

FIRST CONGREGATIONAL CHURCH, Monument Ave., 1804-1805. One of the most photogenic and well-preserved of Federal-style churches in New England. The interior, a cool, neo-classical space, is handsomely appointed. A walk around the graveyard—surrounded by a gracefully arching wooden fence—affords wonderful views of the church and its three-stage tower. Robert Frost is buried here. The building was designed by Lavius Fillmore. NR. Donations accepted.

BENNINGTON MUSEUM, W. Main St., 1855, 1937, 1960, and 1974. Founded at the time of the Centennial, the museum is an extremely pleasant place to visit. The library wing originally housed the first Roman Catholic parish in Vermont. The pottery collection, built around the well-known regional wares, is world famous. The pressed glass, furniture, and Grandma Moses collections are also worthy of attention. The Grandma Moses Schoolhouse (1838), moved from the nearby Eagle Bridge, NY, area, is attached to the museum building. Anyone searching for Vermont ancestors will find the library a gold mine of information. Guided tours. Open Mar-Nov, 9-5. $2 adults, $1 children 12-17, no charge for children under 12 if accompanied, 25¢ if not. 447-1571.

Brandon

BRANDON VILLAGE HISTORIC DISTRICT, along Franklin St. (US 7) and surrounding the two greens—Crescent Park & Central Sq., 19th century. There are no great monuments in Brandon but the village has over 245 buildings which testify to the wealth produced there in the 1880s. Two products, the Conant Stove and the Howe Scale, and marble cutting mills created the prosperity. **Central Sq.** contains a late 19th-c. bandstand, marble fountain, and 1886 granite memorial to Civil War veterans. One of the most flamboyant Victorian houses, the **Bird Cage**, faces Crescent Park. NR.

FORESTDALE IRON FURNACE, VT 73 and Furnace Rd., Forestdale area. The state has preserved the ruins of this historic site. The remains are impressive—a 60' high stone stack and arched openings at ground level, a brick bosh, stone-lined wheel pit, and stone retaining walls. The furnace produced much iron from 1810-55. Operated by the Division for Historic Preservation. NR. 828-3226.

Brattleboro

BRATTLEBORO MUSEUM AND ART CENTER, Old Railroad Station, 1915. Imaginatively housed in the former Union Station, the municipal museum features historical and art exhibits. Among the displays are examples of the Estey organ, manufactured in Brattleboro in what was the world's largest organ factory. Open May-mid-Dec, Tu-Su, 12-4. Donations accepted. 257-0124. Eleven **Estey Organ Co. Factory** buildings still remain on Birge St. Seven of these are covered with slate shingles, a most unusual architectural form. The company, which began making melodeons in 1853, finally closed its doors in 1961. NR.

Castleton

CASTLETON VILLAGE HISTORIC DISTRICT, along Main St. (VT 4A), South St., and Seminary St., 19th-early 20th century. A striking collection of residential and public buildings in the Federal and Greek Revival styles. Most of these are found lining the broad Main St., an important link between Fair Haven and Rutland. Of special interest are two frame Federal-style homes built by the town's master carpenter builder, Thomas Reynolds Dake: The **Meecham-Ainsworth House,** Main and Mechanic Sts., 1810; and the **Langdon-Cole House,** Main and North Sts., 1823.

CASTLETON MEDICAL COLLEGE BUILDING, South St., 1821. Located just outside the historic district is the two-story frame and clapboard building which housed the first proprietary degree granting medical college in the country. The school closed in 1861. The building was moved to this site on the Castleton State College campus. NR.

Dorset

KENT NEIGHBORHOOD HISTORIC DISTRICT, centered primarily around Dorset West Rd., Lane Rd., and Nichols Hill Rd. intersections, late 18th-mid-19th century. Dorset was important as the location for political conventions in 1775-76 which laid the groundwork for the "Free and Independent State of Vermont." Meetings were held at the inn of Cephas Kent. The building is gone but a marble monument was raised there in 1912. Almost all the homes in this area are traditional clapboard frame houses little changed from the early 1800s. Dorset is a superb place to get the feel of early Vermont settlement as time has largely passed it by. Most of the towns below it on US 7 have been extensively changed in recent years.

Dummerston

NAULAKHA, off U.S. 5, 1892-93. Rudyard Kipling lived here from 1892-96, and had the house designed by Henry Rutgers Marshall. It is a shingled affair somewhat resembling an Indian bungalow. Kipling wrote his two *Jungle Books* along with three other works while in residence. A family feud and scandal forced the return to England of Kipling and his Vermont-born wife in 1896. The home is still a private residence but may be viewed from the road. NR.

East Hubbardton

HUBBARDTON BATTLEFIELD AND MUSEUM, junction of Castleton-Hubbardton Rd. and Old Military Rd. to Mt. Independence. The only battle of the Revolution to be fought in Vermont occurred here on July 7, 1777. Col. Seth Warner and his Green Mountain Boys, aided by troops from New Hampshire and Massachusetts, forced the retreat of the British, under Gen. Burgoyne, back to Fort Ticonderoga. There is a visitors reception center with exhibit material and audiovisual equipment. NR. Operated by Division for Historic Preservation. Open Memorial Day-mid-Oct, daily 9-6. No charge. 828-3226.

Fair Haven

FAIR HAVEN GREEN HISTORIC DISTRICT, Park Pl., Adams, and Main Sts., mid-late 19th century. While many other Vermont towns were on a decline— industrially—in the late 1800s, Fair Haven was booming. Much of the prosperity created from the slate and marble industries can be seen today bordering the handsome town green. Among the most striking of the buildings are two Second

Empire and Italianate villas built of marble, the **Allen-Castle House** on West Park Pl. and the **Adams-Stannard House** on the corner of S. Park Pl. and Adams St. Across the street from the latter mansion is the Romanesque **Baptist Church.** Continuing around the green, on E. Park Pl., one will discover the stolid but colorful **First National Bank** of marble and brick which dates from 1870.

Fair Haven is one of those small industrial towns which the tourist is tempted to skirt while driving on major highways. When one discovers, however, such an excellent concentration of historic and imaginative buildings as that surrounding the green, the alternative of driving the secondary and back roads seems much more attractive.

Manchester

EQUINOX HOUSE HISTORIC DISTRICT, Main and Union Sts., 19th century. The center of Manchester Village, divided by Main St. (US 7), is dominated by a complex of resort buildings which has attracted tourists since the early 1800s. Among the regular guests at the **Equinox House** were Mrs. Abraham Lincoln and her son Robert who lived in nearby **Hildene,** Mrs. U. S. Grant, Theodore Roosevelt, and William Howard Taft. Manchester continues to this day to attract "flatlanders" from the South who may just wish to relax in the pastoral setting, take the Equinox Mountain Skyline Drive, or visit such historic attractions as Hildene and the **Museum of American Fly Fishing.** Both sides of Main St., however, may be just as interesting to explore. Marble sidewalks line each side of the street and lead to such buildings as the Greek Revival **Bennington County Courthouse** (1822, enlarged 1849), the **1st Congregational Church** (1871), the **Johnny Appleseed Bookshop** (1832 or 1833) which housed Manchester's first bank, the highly ornamented **Music Hall** (1868), and the hotel complex.

THE MUSEUM OF AMERICAN FLY FISHING, US 7, 1968. The Orvis Co., makers of fly-fishing equipment and other sporting supplies, began life in Manchester in 1856. Members of the family have contributed greatly to the architectural/historical character of the village. The fine art of angling is celebrated by the acknowledged masters of the trade. The exhibits include memorabilia associated with many important American figures. Open daily except major holidays, 9-5. No charge. 362-3300.

HILDENE, US 7, 1904. The summer home of Robert Todd Lincoln and his family is a splendid Georgian Colonial Revival manor house designed by the firm of Shepley, Rutan and Coolidge. The Lincoln estate comprised 412 acres, and visitors today can enjoy the formal gardens, a recently restored gazebo, and nature trails through fields and woods. Rarely can one combine the pleasures of nature with those of architecture and the decorative arts. Many of the original furnishings of the 24-room mansion are on view. Included is a 1908 Aeolian pipe organ in the main entrance hall which peals forth as grandly today as it did years ago. Operated by Friends of Hildene, Inc. NR. Open May 23-Oct 25, daily 10-4. $3 adults, $1 students 6-14, $2 tours; no charge children under 6. 362-1788.

North Bennington

NORTH BENNINGTON HISTORIC DISTRICT, principally along VT 67 and VT 67A, 19th century. Except for its "Old" district, nearby Bennington has lost much of its historic character; North Bennington, the center of which lies approximately 4 miles northwest of Bennington proper, is historically alive and thriving on its past. The **Park-McCullough House,** described below, is the prize possession, but there are other pleasing prospects. The **Welling Mill** at the foot of Main St. on the beautiful Paran Creek has been imaginatively converted into private housing. The striking stone building with stepped gable ends and lintels made from millstones, may be viewed from the public way. Near the other end of Main St. is the **North Bennington Depot,** now owned by the town which has overseen its handsome

restoration. The elaborate brick Second Empire style station served as the general offices of the Bennington and Rutland Railroad in the late 1800s and marked the junction of two major lines to Massachusetts and New York.

THE PARK-McCULLOUGH HOUSE, cor. West and Park Sts., 1864-65. Unquestionably one of the most attractive and authentically restored Victorian mansions in the Northeast, it also serves as a community center. Trenor W. Park built the Second Empire house as a showplace in which to entertain his associates in railroading and other businesses; later it became the home of his son-in-law, John G. McCullough, Governor of Vermont (1902-04). The mansion contains 35 rooms and is superbly furnished with period pieces. On the grounds are found a stable with antique carriages, a miniature playhouse, and a formal garden. Operated by the Park-McCullough House Assoc. NR. Open May-Oct, Su-Th 12-4. $2.50 adults, $1.50 students 12-18, $1 children 6-12. Tours. 442-2747.

Pittsford

COVERED BRIDGES: **Cooley Covered Bridge,** 1.2 miles S of Pittsford across Furnace Brook, 1849; **Depot Covered Bridge,** 0.8 mile W of Pittsford across Otter Creek, c. 1840; **Hammond Covered Bridge,** NW of Pittsford across Otter Creek, 1842.

NEW ENGLAND MAPLE MUSEUM, US 7, 1977. A visit to Vermont is never complete without at least one stop along the way to partake of the lore of maple sugaring. The history since the time of the Indians is explained simply and graphically. The Danforth Collection of sugaring artifacts is considered the world's largest. Open Mar 16-Dec, daily 8:30-5:30. $1 adults, 50¢ children 12 and under, 50¢ tours. 483-9414. ♦♦

Proctor

MARBLE EXHIBIT, Main St. Marble collection and sculpture gallery; film on quarrying. Open end of May-end of Oct, daily 9-5:30. Operated by the Vermont Marble Co. $1.50 adults, 50¢ children. 459-3311.

WILSON CASTLE, 1867. Just what a 32-room castle is doing in Vermont is anyone's guess but we're glad it's there. The Wilson Family Foundation has filled it with fine oriental and European furniture and other decorative objects. The estate comprises some 115 acres. Open mid-May-June and Sept-mid-Oct, daily 8-6; July-Aug, daily 8-8. $2.95 + tax adults, $2.45 + tax seniors, $1 + tax students, 35¢ + tax children, $2.25 + tax tours. 773-3284.

Rockingham

ROCKINGHAM MEETING HOUSE, off VT 103, 1787-88, 1801. Located on a hillside overlooking the Williams River valley, this public building meant for worship and town affairs can be seen and enjoyed for miles. It is not as beautiful as those designed by Lavius Fillmore for Bennington and Middlebury, but Rockingham somehow seems closer to God in its simplicity. The exterior is a clapboarded rectangle with the entrance on the long side rather than the gable end. Inside there is a main floor and a gallery, each with box pews. The pulpit is raised above the floor nine feet, being reached by a set of stairs. Above it is the original sounding board. The walls are suitably white with the only relief being provided by a pale gray-blue decorating the window sash, surrounds and gallery face.

The cemetery is older than the meeting house and has a number of slate stones

with naive spirit designs. These have been attributed to four or five stone cutters. The building was first restored in 1906 and has been painstakingly cared for since that time. Maintained by the town of Rockingham. Open during summer months.

VERMONT COUNTRY STORES AND MUSEUM, VT 103, 1945. This museum is as much a product of our times as the Rockingham meeting house was of the 18th century. The Vermont Country Stores, however, have done a fine job in interpreting the more recent past. The collection of Rogers sculpture groups, trade posters and broadsides, and the Eisenhower collection is outstanding. Also to be seen is the 1889 Tufts antique marble and silver soda fountain and the reconstructed 1820 grist mill. Open all year except major holidays, M-F 9-5. No charge. 463-3855.

Rutland

RUTLAND COURTHOUSE HISTORIC DISTRICT, US 7 (S. Main St.), Center and Washington Sts., early 1850s-1900. The Italianate style **Post Office** which now serves as the Rutland Free Library, is found at the corner of Center and Court Sts. Designed by Ammi B. Young and built in 1856-58, it set the monumental tone for the neighborhood. The Italianate county **Courthouse** was built in 1869. Most of Rutland's wealth came from the marble industry and the **George Chaffee House,** at 16 S. Main St., is typical of the elaborate Queen Anne residences built by the first families in the 1880s-90s. The 1892 residence now houses the Chaffee Art Center operated by the Rutland Area Art Assoc. NR. Open June-Oct, M-F 10-5. Donations accepted. 775-0356.

RUTLAND HISTORICAL SOCIETY MUSEUM, 101 Center St., 1825. A refurbished bank building serves as the headquarters of this thriving organization which also serves the towns of Proctor and West Rutland. Exhibits and collections interpret and display aspects of 19th and early 20th-century domestic life. Open Memorial Day-Labor Day, daily except M 1-5.

Shaftsbury, Center Shaftsbury, and South Shaftsbury

The Shaftsbury area should not be overlooked. A bypass, US 7, between Bennington and Arlington contains nothing of interest whereas old US 7, now numbered 7A, leads past a procession of historic properties.

ROBERT FROST HOUSE, US 7A, 1769. Considered the oldest house in town, it was purchased by Frost in 1920 and remained his home for nine years. The building is also called the "halfstone house" and has 22-inch thick stone walls. Private but visible from road.

ROBERT FROST FARM (THE GULLY), ¼ mile east of US 7A on Buck Hill Rd., 1790. The farm was a quieter place than the roadside stone house. Frost spent his summers here from 1929 until the death of his wife nine years later. The 1½-story Cape Cod is privately owned. NHL.

MUNRO (MONROE)-HAWKINS HOUSE, ½ mile S of Center Shaftsbury on US 7A, 1807. One of several farmhouses designed by master architect Lavius Fillmore in the Federal style. The second-story center Palladian window is especially handsome. Private but visible from road. NR.

CENTER SHAFTSBURY BAPTIST CHURCH, US 7A, 1846. The cemetery is much older than the church and contains the graves of 18th century settlers who founded the oldest Baptist society in Vermont in 1768. The building is maintained by the Shaftsbury Historical Society and serves as a museum and auditorium. Open June-Oct, Sa, Su, holidays 2-4. Donations accepted. 442-4580.

GOVERNOR JONAS GALUSHA HOMESTEAD, US 7A, 1783, 1805. The most interesting part of this distinguished farmhouse is the front section in the Federal style. This is said to have been designed by Lavius Fillmore, and the center second-story Palladian window with the arched heads in the side lights is a characteristic Fillmore touch. Galusha,

governor from 1809-12 and 1815-19, was quite an extraordinary craftsman and contributed much of the hardware, as well as fireplace panelling, and the lunette windows at the gable ends. The interior has been sensitively restored in recent years and contains some original family pieces. Although a private residence, it is possible to arrange a tour. The house is visible from the road and sits on a 174-acre farm property. NR. Owned by Mr. and Mrs. A. Ranney Galusha, RR 1, Box 101, Shaftsbury, VT 05262.

PETER MATTESON TAVERN MUSEUM, East Rd., 1780. Operated by the Bennington Museum, the homestead lies off US 7A. Earlier known as the Topping Tavern, the building has been carefully restored and furnished. The emphasis is given to presenting as lively a demonstration of rural life in the late 18th century as possible. A working blacksmith shop is included on the grounds, and live animals are part of the farm scene. Open May 22-Oct 31, F-Su 12-4. $2 adults, $1 children over 12. 442-5225. ⛹

Sudbury vicinity

HYDE'S HOTEL, VT 30, 1 mile S of Sudbury, 1865. The hotel is no more, although spring water—which helped to create its reputation—is still bottled on the grounds. Hyde's is typical of the kind of grand resort hotel which once dotted Vermont. In the gay '90s there were such features as a bowling alley and billiard hall, casino and cabaret dance hall, card game building (Round House)—all elements still visible today. Harry Truman, Calvin Coolidge, Horace Greeley, and Henry Ford stopped here. The buildings are wonderfully whimsical flights of fancy in the best tradition of summer resort architecture. The hotel closed in 1973.

Wilmington

WILMINGTON VILLAGE HISTORIC DISTRICT, VT 9 (E. and W. Main), and VT 100 (N. and S. Main), 19th century. Located midway between Brattleboro and

Bennington on the Molly Stark Trail (VT 9), Wilmington has entertained visitors for more than 150 years. The historic district of 59 buildings contains many which provide services for the traveler. Most of the attractive buildings are Greek Revival or vernacular Victorian with the gable ends fronting on the street. Wilmington is a very compact, cohesive group of fine buildings representative of the early to mid-19th century.

Windham County

COVERED BRIDGES: **West Dummerston Covered Bridge,** Dummerston Center Rd. and VT 30, 1872; **Green River Covered Bridge,** across the Green River, early 1870s; **Scott Covered Bridge,** VT 30, Townshend, 1870. Two of these scenic spans are along the main road between Brattleboro and the Manchester area. The Townshend bridge is longest single span in the state — over 165 feet; the total length of its three spans over the West River is 276 feet. This last bridge is maintained by the state Division for Historic Preservation.

Lake Champlain Region

Addison

JOHN STRONG D.A.R. MANSION, VT 17, near Chimney Point, 1975. The handsome late Georgian Colonial house has been administered by the Vermont State Society of the D.A.R. since the 1930s and it adjoins farm property which comprises the D.A.R. State Park. Chimney Point is an old French settlement (Hoquart) dating from the 1740s; it was abandoned after the French and Indian War and all that remains to see are cellar foundations in the park. John Strong built his Flemish bond brick house on one such foundation. The exterior brickwork closely resembles that found on earlier houses in south Jersey. The glazed headers are arranged in diamond-shaped patterns. The Strong family came to the area from Connecticut, but there were settlers as well from New Jersey and perhaps an experienced mason or two among them. The mansion overlooks Lake Champlain and is as handsome inside as out. The D.A.R. has furnished it with fine period antiques. NR. Open May 15-Oct 15, F-M, 10-5. $1 adults; children under 12 free. 759-2309.

CHIMNEY POINT TAVERN, VT 17 and 125 at Lake Champlain bridge, 1784. The state Division for Historic Preservation is in the process of restoring the brick and frame building. Part is open to the public. It was built by Benjamin Paine who operated a ferry across the lake to Crown

Point. The taproom somehow survived major change over the years. NR. For information, telephone 828-3226. Open mid-May-mid-Oct, Tu-Su 9-5. Donations accepted.

Burlington

Burlington is best known as the home of the University of Vermont, founded by Ira Allen (brother of hero Ethan) in 1791. It is one of those gritty industrial cities which has made an interesting comeback in recent years. Now, it appears to have chosen restoration over urban renewal or removal as was often the case. There is still little that is quaint about Burlington but there is much that is impressive, even elegant. Few small cities are as beautifully positioned —

on a gradual rise above Lake Champlain with the Adirondacks to the west and the Green Mountains to the east.

HEAD OF CHURCH STREET HISTORIC DISTRICT, Pearl and Church Sts., 19th century. Three public buildings form the district in downtown Burlington. The **Unitarian Church**, 1816, lies at the "head" of Church on Pearl, and is perhaps the most impressive religious building in the state. It is constructed of brick in the Federal style and is the work of Peter Banner, an architect who may have been assisted by Charles Bulfinch. The church has a square steeple tower topped by a two-tier octagonal spire. The entrance pavilions and tower combine to form a most impressive main facade through which one enters the church. The interior has been remodeled several times but still contains a three-sided gallery supported by Doric columns.

The second of the three buildings is the five-story **Masonic Temple**, 1898, on the southwest corner of Church St. It is a Richardsonion Romanesque brick affair designed for the Grand Masonic Lodge of Vermont by John McArthur Harris of the Philadelphia firm of Wilson Brothers & Co. On the opposite corner of Church is the **Richardson Building** (Abernathy's Department Store), 1895. the style has been variously described as "Chateauesque" or Norman because of a high hip roof and use of dormers, chimneys, and what appear to be towers. Only the first floor was used commercially; the remaining space in the four-and-a-half story building was devoted to apartments.

FOLLETT HOUSE, 63 College St., 1840. Not included in the Head of Church Street is this last important lakefront mansion. Designed in the Greek Revival style by Ammi B. Young with a wooden Ionic colonnade, it is now used as a clubhouse by the Veterans of Foreign Wars. NR.

WINTERBOTHAM ESTATE, 163 S. Willard St., c. 1820. A fascinating group of buildings—main house with flanking galleries and wings, connecting barn and stable; and law office. Both Greek Revival and Italianate elements appear in the many details. Now owned by the city of Burlington. NR.

UNIVERSITY GREEN HISTORIC DISTRICT, University of Vermont campus, 1825-1926. The central green, donated by Ira Allen, has remained intact over the years and is the primary visual organizing principle for the campus. At the outskirts of the campus are also several fine private residences which have been converted to university or fraternity use.

The "college row" on the east side of the green contains many of the historic buildings of interest. The tallest of these is the **Ira Allen Chapel** with a bell tower rising 170 feet; at night a beacon flashes from the tower making it visible for many miles. The chapel is a rather typical late Georgian Revival design from the firm of McKim, Mead and White.

Billings, next to the chapel to the south, was designed by H.H. Richardson between 1883-85 and is interesting inside and out. It was intended as a library (it is now the student center) with each of the rooms rising a full two stories. Interior balconies surround the sides, and these are lit through clerestory windows.

Williams Science Hall is next in the row, and is cruciform in plan. Wilson Brothers & Co. of Philadelphia provided the design in 1894 (four years before the downtown Masonic Temple) and based it on Ruskin's plan for the Oxford Museum in London.

Among the most interesting of the once private homes is the **Moore-Woodbury House,** 416 Pearl St., 1815. There have been two late 19th-century additions made to the basic Federal-style brick rectangle. The house was the site of many important social affairs in the late 1800s and early 1900s. It was then the home of Urban Woodbury, mayor of Burlington and governor of Vermont. Among the visitors were William McKinley, Theodore Roosevelt, and William H. Taft. Democrats were presumably persona non grata. The home is now an apartment house.

Grassmount (Thaddeus Tuttle House), 411 Main St. (U.S. 2), 1804. This elaborate mansion now serves as a girls' dormitory and let's hope that they enjoy it. It is a very handsome Federal brick house with a five-bay main facade, the windows of which are surrounded by semicircular blind arches; Ionic pilasters separate the second-story bays and extend to the cornice. An oblong center cupola was added in the mid-century and there is also a wooden balustrade around the roof. This was also the home of Cornelius P. Van Ness, governor of Vermont from 1823-26.

Edward Wells House (Delta Psi House), 61 Summit St., 1891-92. A Boston architect, E.A.P. Newcomb, was brought in to design this picturesque mansion in the Queen Anne style. Edward Wells, a patent medicine merchant and dye manufacturer, ordered the finest in craftmanship and materials. The brick and stone exterior incorporates exceptionally well carved wooden ornament. The carver has been identified as Albert M. Whittekind (1859-1943). Few cities in the country—including San Francisco—can boast of a better designed Queen Anne residence.

Fairfield

PRESIDENT CHESTER A. ARTHUR BIRTHPLACE AND CHURCH, off VT 36, 1953. Yes, '53, because the birthplace is a replica put up by the state. There is something very refreshing about the Arthur site. It is modest in scope and tasteful in execution—quite different from the usual imperial modern presidential production. Included in the 35-acre park is an

1830s brick church where the President's father preached. Operated by the Division for Historic Preservation. Open June-mid-Oct, W-Su 9:30-5:30. Free. 828-3226.

Ferrisburg

ROKEBY MUSEUM, US 7, c. 1790. Rowland Evans Robinson was a great connoisseur of Vermontiana and an accomplished illustrator. His house served as a station on the underground railroad and Robinson's father headed the Vermont Anti-Slavery Society, the papers of which are preserved at Rokeby. NR. Affiliated with the Rowland Evans Robinson Memorial Assoc. Other buildings on the site are an icehouse, schoolhouse, and barn. Open May 15-Oct 15, M, W-Sa 9:30-5. Su 1-5. $1 adults, 75¢ children. 877-3406.

Grand Isle

HYDE LOG CABIN, US 2, 1783. Probably the oldest surviving log cabin in the United States in near original condition. Parts have been rebuilt and a new roof was required when the state of Vermont acquired the building in 1952. The repair work required on the 1½-story cabin was carefully done using local materials whenever possible. During the summer months the cabin is leased to the Grand Isle County Historical Society, which has also furnished it. NR. Open July-Labor Day.

Jericho

MARTIN CHITTENDEN HOUSE, W of

Jericho on VT 117, 1790-97. It is said that Thomas Chittenden, the first governor of Vermont, built this Federal-style house as a wedding gift for his son. It dates from the same period as the John Strong House (see Addison) at Chimney Point, and features the same sort of patterned brickwork. Martin, too, became governor of Vermont (from 1813-15), and the house—inside and out—is an elegant reflection of a family's fine taste in architecture and furnishings. It is privately owned but is visible from the road. NR.

OLD RED MILL(CHITTENDEN ROLLER MILLS), W of Jericho, VT 15, 1856, 1885. The Jericho Historical Society has devoted itself to the restoration of this gristmill. The late 19th-century roller equipment for grinding grain is still in place and can be demonstrated. The handsome space in the five-story building is also used for art exhibitions, offices, a craft shop, stores, and a community room. Open Apr-Dec 25, M-F 10-5, Su 1-5; Jan-Mar, W and Sa 10-5, Su 1-5. Museum tours, June 15-Oct 14, F-Su 1-5. $2 adults, $1 children. 899-3225.

Middlebury

Few towns in the Northeast have been more carefully maintained over the years than Middlebury. The best of town and gown seems to have come together here; one moves from the famous college campus to Main St. without suffering the sort of aesthetic dislocation common in many other centers of learning. Main St., in fact, is more interesting than academia.

MIDDLEBURY VILLAGE HISTORIC DISTRICT, The Village Green and Court Sq., Main St. (US 7) and other streets radiating from the green and square. Approximately 275 buildings are included within the district, of which 57 are deemed to have "outstanding historical or architectural significance." Included among them is the **Middlebury Inn**, North Pleasant St., which is described under lodgings; not included is the Middlebury College campus which lies southwest of the district. Middlebury is a town that one should explore leisurely by foot if possible. Walking tours are sponsored by the Chamber of Commerce, 35 Court St., 388-7579.

Congregational Church, Main St., 1806-9, dominates Middlebury because of its beauty and postion at the top of a hill. Lavius Fillmore was brought to town to design the church and as at Bennington, he based his plan on plates in Asher Benjamin's *Country Builder's Assistant* (1797). The church is considered Fillmore's best work; there are other examples in town as well. The steeple—consisting of five increasingly detailed and textured tiers—is a confectioner's delight.

Charter House, 27 N. Pleasant St., 1790s, is of more historic interest than architectural. Middlebury College was founded here in 1798 in a meeting between the trustees of the predecessor institution, Addison County Grammar School, and Yale President Timothy Dwight.

Horatio Seymour House/Community House, 3 Main St., 1816. A very elegant brick residence in the Federal style. It once was the home of J. W. Stewart, governor and U.S. senator.

David Nichols House, 28 Weybridge St., late 1830s. Recognized as the finest Greek Revival house in Middlebury, a considerable distinction in a place where the style was mastered. The palmette motif which appears on the facade pilasters is especially noteworthy. The architect may have been James Lamb who was also responsible for the Wilcox-Cutts House in Orwell (which see).

The President's House, 3 South St., 1854. The frame clapboarded residence of Middlebury College presidents since 1918 combines Greek Revival and Carpenter Gothic elements. The one-story porch enlivens the rather severe neo-classical form.

Hagar Phelps House, 89 Main St., 1813-15. Lavius Fillmore is responsible for the woodwork—the interlace frieze and fretwork, the Palladian window and arched and keystone doorway.

Federation Building, 88 Main St., c. 1805. Another handsome Federal style building, this of brick and at the gable ends, of Flemish cross bond or pattern brickwork, as in the Martin Chittenden House, Jericho and the John Strong Mansion, Addison.

Sheldon Art Museum, Archaeological and Historical Society, 1 Park St., 1829. The marble industry began in Middlebury, and its founder, Eben Judd, built a suitably impressive Federal/Greek Revival brick mansion with marble Ionic columns and fancy marble sills and lintels. Henry Sheldon bought the house in 1875 and seven years later opened his own museum. It is considered the earliest incorporated village museum in the United States. The collections center on 19th-century household furnishings—pianos, clocks, portraits, china, etc. The museum is also an important research center. Open June 15-Oct 15, daily except Su and holidays, 10-5; winter, by appointment. $2 adults, $1 senior citizens, 50¢ children. 388-2117.

St. Stephens Episcopal Church, Main St., 1827. An early Gothic Revival stone building on the Village Green. Lavius Fillmore, a parishioner, was responsible for the exterior woodwork.

Clinton-Smith House, 18-20 S. Pleasant St., 1884. Architect Smith did for Middlebury in the late 1800s what Fillmore accomplished earlier. Smith's Queen Anne buildings, including his own residence, are all imaginatively designed and make use of first-rate materials. The residence employs granite and brick in various combinations as well as wood detailing on the porch and peak of the main roof. A carriage house at the rear is also dramatically designed and constructed.

Painter-Wainwright House, head of Merchants Row at S. Pleasant St., 1802, 1830s. Gamaliel Painter was responsible for bringing Lavius Fillmore to Middlebury and that accomplished gentleman almost certainly executed the elaborate wood frieze, cornice, balustrade, and stringcourse of the two-story frame residence.

Springside, 39 Seminary St., 1836, sits on a hilltop surveying Seminary St. It is a brick Greek Revival home to which wings were added in 1853 along with a fine cast-iron fence and colored Bohemian glass to the doorway.

MIDDLEBURY COLLEGE CAMPUS, W of business district, contains **Painter Hall**, 1816, given by Gamaliel Painter, and the **Emma Willard House**, 1809. Classes in the Middlebury Female Seminary were first held here; in 1821 Mrs. Willard opened the more famous school in Troy, NY. NR, NHL.

Middlebury vicinity

COVERED BRIDGES: **Halpin Covered Bridge**, NE of town, mid-19th century. The highest covered bridge—41 feet above the stream—in the state. **Pulp Mill Covered Bridge**, NW of town, off VT 23, c. 1820. Vermont's oldest surviving covered bridge and one of two remaining that are "double barreled," i.e. two-lane. NR.

Montgomery and Montgomery Center vicinity

COVERED BRIDGES: **Comstock Covered Bridge**, off VT 118 over Trout River, 1883; **Fuller Covered Bridge**, Town Rd. over Black Falls Brook in village, 1890; **Hectorville Covered Bridge**, 1.8 mile S of Montgomery Center over south branch of Trout River, 19th century; **Hutchins Covered Bridge**, S of Montgomery Center over south branch of Trout River, 1883; **Longley Covered Bridge**, NW of Montgomery over Trout River, 1863; **West Hill Covered Bridge**, 3.2 miles S of Montgomery over West Hill Brook, mid to late 19th century. The Jewett brothers—Sheldon and Savannah—were the local builders of most of these bridges. They plied their unique trade for over thirty years. NR.

Orwell vicinity

MOUNT INDEPENDENCE HISTORIC SITE, 3 miles NW of Orwell off VT 22A, 1776. Directly across Lake Champlain from Fort Ticonderoga, Mount Independence was an important American garrison. Remaining today is evidence of a star fort, a hospital area, and numerous gun emplacements. The state of Vermont is developing the site as an historic park. After Ethan Allen captured Fort Ticonderoga, a floating bridge was thrown up between the two installations; this was destroyed when the British recaptured Fort Ticonderoga. NR, NHL. Open mid-May-mid-Oct, W-Su 9-5. Free. 828-3226.

WILCOX-CUTTS HOUSE, 2 miles S of Orwell on VT 22A, 1843. Pure Greek Revival temple form and designed by James Lamb who is also known for the David Nichols House in Middlebury. The house was built for Linus Wilcox, an early breeder of Merino sheep, and it was later owned by Henry T. Cutts, who specialized in Morgan horses. Private but visible from the public way. NR.

Richmond

ROUND CHURCH, Bridge St. and Cochran Rd., 1812-13. The Round Church is actually sixteen-sided, with entrances on three of the cardinal sides and the pulpit positioned at the fourth. The interior gallery extends around thirteen sides, and there are box pews and a raised pulpit. Used since 1880 for town meetings, the edifice was intended for Vermont's first "union" congregation, but the united denominations soon split from one another. NR.

Ripton vicinity

ROBERT FROST FARM, 1 mile N of VT 125, 3 miles E of Ripton, 1940-63. This was Frost's last home, a cabin in the Green Mountains for the summer and fall months of the year. The farm is privately held. NR, NHL.

St. Albans

FRANKLIN COUNTY MUSEUM, Church St., 1861, is housed in the nine-room Franklin County Grammar School. It contains items of local historical interest—early medical instruments, tools, household furnishings, and, in keeping with special St. Albans activities, railroad equipment and Civil War memorabilia. Open July-Aug, Tu-Sa, 2-5; other times by appointment. No charge. 527-7933.

CENTRAL VERMONT RAILROAD HEADQUARTERS, a complex bounded by Federal, Catherine, Allen, Lower Welden, Houghton, and Pine Sts., 19th-20th centuries. For railroad buffs, an important and still working facility serving the state's major rail carrier. NR.

HOUGHTON HOUSE, 86 S. Main St., 1800. A Federal-style frame house which is the match of any mansion in Middlebury or Old Bennington. The exterior features a handsome Palladian window and the interior hall and parlors are extremely fine in their woodwork. The house still contains many original furnishings. NR. Private but visible from the street.

Shelburne

SHELBURNE FARMS, off US 7, 1887-early 1900s. The manorial estate of the Webb family was established in 1885 with 4,000 acres along the shore of Lake Champlain. Today, some 1,685 acres with two miles of lake frontage remain. Dr. and Mrs. William Seward Webb could not have chosen a more perfect setting. Mrs. Webb, William Henry Vanderbilt's daughter, probably felt some sense of competition with her brothers who created such baronial homes as Biltmore in North Carolina and the Breakers in Newport. Robert Henderson Robertson was responsible for the design of many of the buildings, and Frederick Law Olmstead and Gifford Pinchot advised on the landscaping of the grounds. **Shelburne House,** the 1899 principal dwelling, has 110 rooms and is built in the Elizabethan Tudor Revival style of brick with stucco and timbering. Other interesting buildings are the c. 1890 **Gate House** in the Swiss style, the **"Tree House,"** a c. 1890 playhouse, and the huge **Farm Barn,** built on five levels in 1887 with a central court.
   Set up originally as a model stock farm,

Shelburne Farms now contains a modern dairy and is used for tree farming. Family residences are scattered on the grounds. Shelburne House is open for concerts, workshops, and seminars from time to time. The 1902 **Coach Barn** has been turned into an environmental studies center. NR. For further information, contact: 985-3222.

THE SHELBURNE MUSEUM, US 7, 1947. The late Mr. and Mrs. J. Watson Webb created this unique village just below Burlington to display their incomparable collection of Americana to the public. Williamsburg may have been a model, but Shelburne has developed its own character. Although the theme is "Early American," most of the buildings and the objects on display in them are from the early to late 19th century. Shelburne has a great deal more to say about the early republic and developing nation than, say, Old Sturbridge Village or Plimoth Plantation. It is fitting, then, that its one official

national historic landmark be the side-wheeler "Ticonderoga." It dates from 1906 and in its own way is as important a vessel as more illustrious military ships. The 220-foot long "Ticonderoga" was active on Lake Champlain until 1953 and is great fun to visit today. But this is only a beginning at Shelburne. Of some 48 facilities, 25 are historic structures which have been moved to the museum grounds and filled with treasures. Among the most interesting are:

Prentis House, Hadley, Mass., 1733, features displays of 17th and 18th-century needlework and Delft.

General Store, from Shelburne village, c. 1840, offers displays of every type of general merchandise as well as a post office, tap room and barber shop, apothecary shop, compounding room, doctor's and dentist's offices.

Vermont House, from Shelburne village, 1790, is furnished with fine American antique furniture and displays a French scenic wallpaper.

Hat and Fragrance Unit, from Shelburne village, c. 1800, houses the Shelburne collection of quilts and coverlets and is worth a special visit. Also to be seen are shell dolls, doll houses, rugs, samplers, commemorative toiles, and laces.

Stagecoach Inn, Charlotte, VT, c. 1783. Shelburne's collection of American folk art is as noted as its quilts and coverlets. Here are gathered weather vanes, figureheads, trade signs, circus figures, cigar store Indians, etc.

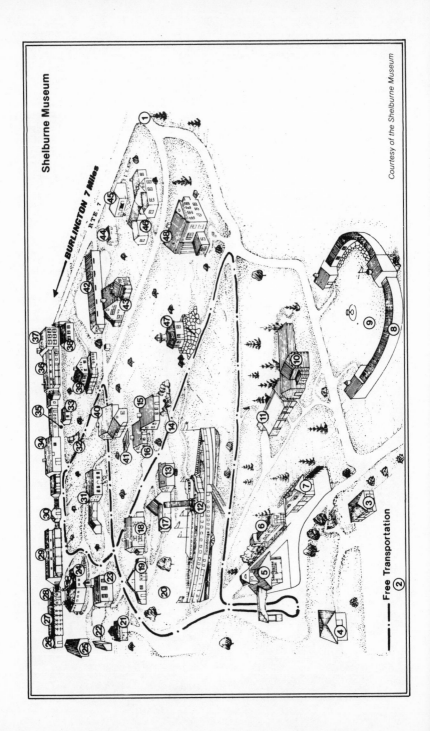

Shelburne Museum

BURLINGTON 7 Miles

R.T.E. 7

Free Transportation

Courtesy of the Shelburne Museum

1. Entrance
2. Parking Area
3. Toll Booth and Information Center
4. Public Restrooms
5. Shelburne Railroad Station
6. Railroad Train Shed
7. Railroad Freight Building and Steam Locomotive
8. Circus Parade Building
9. Rock Garden
10. Beach Gallery
11. Beach Hunting Lodge
12. Sidewheeler "Ticonderoga"
13. Diamond Barn
14. Rose Garden
15. Prentis House
16. Stencil House
17. Museum Shop
18. General Store
19. Tuckaway Barn
20. Picnic area
21. Blacksmith and Wheelwright Shop
22. Meeting House Shed
23. Charlotte Meeting House
24. Horseshoe Barn
25. Horseshoe Barn Annex
26. Live Bee Exhibit
27. Red Shed
28. Weaving Display
29. Shaker Horsestand Shed
30. Castleton Slate Jail
31. Vermont House
32. Smoke House
33. Little Stone Cottage
34. Hat and Fragrance Unit
35. Herb Garden
36. Toy Shop
37. Variety Unit
38. Vergennes School
39. Stagecoach Inn
40. Dutton House
41. Colonial Vegetable and Herb Garden
42. Covered Bridge
43. Dorset House
44. Sawyer's Cabin
45. Up-and-Down Sawmill
46. Webb Gallery
47. Colchester Reef Lighthouse Gallery
48. Electra Havemeyer Webb Memorial Building

Colchester Reef Lighthouse Gallery, Colchester Reef, Lake Champlain, 1871, is a handsome Victorian building in which maritime prints and paintings and ship figureheads are displayed.

The newly constructed buildings also contain exhibits of considerable interest to history buffs and devotees of American antiques. Both the **Webb Gallery** (1960) and the **Electra Havemeyer Webb Memorial Bldg** (1967) are rich in paintings and furnishings which deepen one's sense of cultural identity and tradition.

Free transportation is provided throughout the 45 acres. There is a steam train to be enjoyed; demonstrations of various crafts are presented at various points in the attractively landscaped grounds. A cafeteria is housed in an 1835 Vermont barn.

Open May 15-Oct 17, daily 9-5; mid-Oct-mid-May, Su 11-4. $6.75 adults, $2.75 children 6-15; under 6 free; groups $4.75 per person, minimum 15, tour leader and driver free. 985-3346. ⍟

Shoreham vicinity

HAND'S COVE on Lake Champlain, c. 1775 or 1783, 1841-42. Ethan Allen chose a beautiful setting for the muster of his Green Mountain Boys in May, 1775 before the assault on Fort Ticonderoga. Little is left from the Revolutionary era but there is **Herrick House,** a log frame dwelling which probably originated as a blockhouse either during or just after the War of Independence. There is also a Greek Revival farmhouse, the home of the Handy family—Augustus (1803-78), congressman and senator from New York, and a long line of distinguished lawyers. NR. Private but visible from lake.

LARRABEE'S POINT COMPLEX, VT 74, SW of Shoreham, 1799, 1823, c. 1835. A ferry has run from this point to the New York shore and back since 1799; in 1890 a chain was drawn across the lake for steering. A stone store and warehouse and wharf dating from the 1820s can be seen along with the 2½-story **Larrabee House,** c. 1835, a brick Greek Revival building. Larrabee was the ferry owner and ran a tavern here. Larrabee Point is also the site of the former U.S. Hotel (1847-1915). NR.

South Hero

SOUTH HERO INN, South St. and US 2, 1829. A dressed stone main building, 2½ stories, with a two-story frame ell added in 1860. Early 1900s guest cottages are found to one side. NR. Private; visible from road.

Vergennes

VERGENNES HISTORIC DISTRICT, along Main St., Otter Creek Falls, Mc-Donough Dr., Maple and N. Maple Sts., North St., Green and Park Sts., late 18th-early 20th centuries. Vergennes' history as an industrial and military site recommends it to the historically-minded tourist. Among some 80 buildings in the district, several are of special interest.

Stevens House, Main St., overlooking City Park, c. 1815, enlarged in 1843, and re-modeled in the 1870s. The build-ing—which grew like Topsy—served at various times as a hotel, tavern, and stage-coach stop.

St. Paul's Episcopal Church, Main St., 1834. A Gothic Revival style brick building with a center tower. The entire second-story tower height is spanned by a quadruple hung window with gothic sash and 192 panes.

Gen. Samuel Strong House, 64 W. Main St., 1796. Two-story frame house with two elaborate facades on the south and east sides. Private, but visible from street.

Weybridge

UVM MORGAN HORSE FARM, Morgan Horse Farm Rd., off US 7, 1907. Col. Joseph Batell was founder of the American Morgan Register and led the way in developing this American horse breed. The main barn had a handsome mansard roof. Also on the grounds is the Battell House, a brick Greek Revival residence. Operated by the University of Vermont. Guided tours of the stables and audio-visual presentation on the Morgan horse and farm. Sixty registered stallions, mares, foals, and geldings. NR. Open May 1-Nov 1, daily 9-4. $1.75 adults, 50¢ teens, free under 12. 388-2011. 🚹

Williston

WILLISTON VILLAGE HISTORIC DISTRICT, both side of US 2, (Main St.), 19th century. Williston is lucky; it was by-passed by Interstate 89. Route 2 traffic slowed down considerably, and Main St. became less threatened by "progress." The village—only one house deep on each side of the main street—owed its prosperity in

Main Barn, UVM Morgan Horse Farm

the past to agriculture and the patronage of the politically astute Chittenden family. At least two Chittenden houses—**Aseltine House,** second from the corner of N. Williston Rd. and Main and **Wortheim House,** next to it—are handsome early 1800s Federal frame and clapboard resi-dences. Across the road on the SW corner is the brick Greek Revival **Bradish House,** c. 1840, with a hip roof and cupola. Near the western end of the central village is the **Congregational Church,** a 1-story brick Gothic Revival building with a three-tier steeple.

East Central Vermont

Barre

BARRE HISTORIC DISTRICT, Depot Sq., North and South Main St., Washington St., east side of Montpelier & Barre RR right-of-way, 1870s-early 1900s. Not until the marble industry was firmly established (with a direct rail link to the South) did Barre blossom forth as a major center of manufacturing. The downtown buildings date from this period—the 1880s and '90s—and make lavish use of the handsome material which has gone into so many major American buildings. At one time there were 119 companies in town and the prosperity they created can be seen in such buildings as the brick and marble **City Hall and Opera House,** 12 N. Main Street, from 1899, and the **Soldier and Sailors Memorial,** 1924, which anchors the northern end of City Park. There were once also 70 marble quarries in town. One of the major firms, **Rock of Ages,** Main St., Graniteville, is still very much in operation and offers free guided tours of the world's largest granite quarry. Train rides are also possible around and about the quarry. Tours daily, 8:30-5; plant observation platform open, M-F, 8:30-3:30; quarry train ride, M-F, June 1-Sept. 30. $1.50 adults, 50¢ children. 476-3115.

Brookfield and Brookfield Center

BROOKFIELD VILLAGE HISTORIC DISTRICT, VT 1, along Sunset Lake, 18th-19th centuries. The **Floating Bridge** (1936) across the lake has become a major tourist attraction; fortunately, the village has not become overrun with camera-laden voyeurs. One enters the west end of town on a dirt road which, for those used to interstates, can be a put-off; interstate 89 zips by without an exit here. When crossing Sunset Lake—by foot or car—you are actually moving over two ramps (one at each end), a stable center section, and 380 50-gallon barrels. The framework is of timbers and the decking of planks. Such a timber pontoon bridge was not unusual in 19th-century America; today, it is an anomaly.

The town itself is a pretty affair with a generous sprinkling of Greek Revival style buildings which look right at home and line the main street, Ridge Road. There is the **Town Hall,** (mid-1800s), **Public Library** (early 1800s), and a complex of buildings which form the **Green Trails Inn** (see Lodging). With both a lakeside view and pleasant tree-lined streetscape, it is hard to imagine a more pleasant place in which to linger away at least a few Fall or Summer days.

The **Marvin Newton House,** 1835, lies further down Ridge Road in Brookfield Center. It is the frame home of the Historical Society of Brookfield, and is open during July-Aug on Sundays from 2 to 5. Free. Donations accepted. NR.

Calais

KENT'S CORNER HISTORIC DISTRICT, 1 mile E of Maple Corner, 19th century. A crossroads village that offers more of interest than many towns, Calais's principal historic attraction is the **Kent Tavern Museum,** 1837. Known as "A. Kent's Hotel," the handsome brick house was a restful stop on the Montpelier-Canada stage road. The Kent family (including radio tycoon Atwater Kent) has lived here for generations, and has helped to keep the tiny village and its surrounding countryside unspoiled by modern development. The tavern museum, owned and operated now by the Vermont Historical Society, is a center hall, two-room deep building; a large ballroom is to be found on the 2nd floor. The rooms are well furnished with period antiques. Open July-Aug, Tu-Su 12-5. $1.50 adults, 75¢ children. 223-5660.

Nearby is the **Kent's Corner Saw Mill** and pond. The machinery is still in place as if awaiting the day when water power is again deemed feasible. Just down the road (south) from the tavern is the frame **Old West Church,** 1823-25. It, too, is unspoiled by "remodeling." The original unpainted pine bow pews are found on the first floor and overhanging galleries define the second level.

Cavendish

GLIMMERSTONE, VT 131 between Proctorsville and Cavendish, 1844-47. Ornate Gothic Revival cottages have not weathered well in modern-day America. Perhaps because Glimmerstone is made of stone, taking its name from the shiny mica schist, it has held up over the years. The fancy bargeboards which decorate the many gables and the unusual type of stonework, known as "snecked ashlar" from the alternating bonding system, are delightful visual touches. Although a private residence, it is visible from the public way.

Less interesting but certainly worth a look-see is the **Cavendish Universalist Church,** 1844, also situated on VT 131. It, too, is built of alternating courses of large ashlar blocks and flat schist slabs. The church is now the home of the Cavendish Historical Society. Open June-Oct, Su 2-5. NR.

Chester

STONE VILLAGE HISTORIC DISTRICT, both sides of VT 103, Chester Depot, 19th century. Cavendish provides just a hint of what is to be found in Chester Depot. There are seventeen principal buildings in the unusual stonework and these are positioned on each side of VT 103. Included is the **Unitarian Church,** a **schoolhouse,** and **tavern,** as well as **homes.** It appears that the masons who built most of the buildings were Scotsmen from the Aberdeen area who were familiar with the technique of "snecking" or securing large slabs of gneiss with pieces of mica schist. The village might well be the enchanted one, Brigadoon. It lies in the lovely Williams River valley and has a composure that is both charming and comforting.

Lamoille County

COVERED BRIDGES: **Mill Covered Bridge,** and **Morgan Covered Bridge,** 1887, both Belvidere, off VT 109 over North Branch of Lamoille River; **Gates Farm Covered Bridge,** off VT 15, over Seymour River, Cambridge, 1897; **Grist Mill Covered Bridge,** E of Cambridge, over Brewster River, 19th century; **Poland Covered Bridge,** off VT 15, over Lamoille River, Cambridge Junction, 1887; **Power House Covered Bridge,** off VT 100, over Gihon River, Johnson, 1870; **Scribner Covered Bridge,** E of Johnson, over Gihon River, 19th century; **Waterman Covered Bridge,** S of Johnson, over Waterman Brook, 1868; **Village Covered Bridge,** over North Branch of Lamoille River, Waterville, c. 1877; **Jaynes Covered Bridge,** and **Montgomery Covered Bridge,** both NE of Waterville, over North Branch of Lamoille River, c. 1877.

If you're looking for covered bridges, you'll know by now that Lamoille County is Mecca. Most of the bridges have been reinforced in some way to carry today's heavier traffic, but they *are* still in use. The most famous of the county's bridges, the **Fisher Covered Railroad Bridge,** is described under the heading of Wolcott.

Ludlow

BLACK RIVER ACADEMY, High St., 1888, and LUDLOW GRADED SCHOOL, High St., 1871-72. Thanks to the patronage of Calvin Coolidge, these adjacent town school buildings have survived into the 1980s. Architecturally, they are not very interesting but anyone interested in education will find the recreated 1890s schoolroom of the Academy worth a visit. Both buildings are operated as a town museum by the Black River Historical Society. NR. Open May 26-Oct 16, daily except W & Th 9:30-5:30. Free. 228-5050.

Montpelier

Montpelier is one of the most pleasant and least bureaucratic in appearance of state capitals. There is little about the city which suggests the monolithic and inhuman. The state government has made effective use of a wide variety of period buildings in the area of the state house—Second Empire, Richardsonian Romanesque, Italianate, Queen Anne—to house various governmental offices. Adaptation seems to be the golden rule. The historical hero of the town is Admiral George Dewey whose father, Dr. Julius Dewey, founded the town's second most important institution, the National Life Insurance Co.

MONTPELIER HISTORIC DISTRICT, State St. (US 2) and Main St. (VT 12), 19th century. The gold-leaf dome of the State House can be seen for miles and defines much of Montpelier's activity and *raison d'être*. There is nothing French about the city, although, as in neighboring New Hampshire, French Canadians have settled here in the 20th century. The setting is superb. There is no way to duplicate the usual boring American grid arrangement of blocks in the narrow valleys formed by the Winooski and the North Branch rivers. Most of the downtown area has burned to the ground several times and there is little in it that dates from earlier than the 1870s —save the State House.

Vermont State House, State St., 1833-38, 1859. Vermont's principal seat of government could only have been built of granite and decorated with marble. Since the 1830s, when architect Ammi B. Young finished his work, drastic changes have been

required in the building. A high dome on a circular drum, for instance, replaced a low, saucer dome after a fire in 1857. The Representatives' Hall and the Senate Chamber are extremely graceful spaces which make effective use of various kinds of marble, fine plasterwork, and bronze lighting fixtures.

Pavilion Hotel, 109 State St., 1970s, houses the **Vermont Museum** of the Vermont Historical Society. This is the third Pavilion to rise on this spot; the first in 1807-8, became the center of social life for out-of-town legislators as well as the permanent residents of town. The second building, dating from 1876, was demolished and an exterior copy put in its place. It's a

cosmetic approach to preservation, but it works in this case as the scale and character of the neighboring period buildings are not violated. The museum is housed on the first floor and features displays of fine and decorative arts as well as farm and industrial equipment relating to Vermont. Open M-F 8-4:30. 828-2291.

Wood Art Gallery, Main St., housed in the Kellogg-Hubbard Library, 1895. Thomas Waterman Wood (1823-1903), a Montpelier native, established his own museum and with every passing year there is more appreciation of his romantic genre scenes and those of his contemporaries T.G. Brown, A.B. Durand, and others which are on display. His home, **Athenwood,** (see following listing) is also worthy of attention. Open winter months, Tu-Sa 12-4; summer months, Tu-Sa 9-1. Free. 229-0036.

Outside of the historic district is ATHENWOOD and the THOMAS WATERMAN WOOD STUDIO, 41 and 49 Northfield St., 1850 (house), 1880s (studio). Although privately owned, the property can be viewed from the street. Its picturesque Gothic Revival elements—diamond-paned windows, fancy bargeboards defining the eaves, board-and-batten siding—owe their design to artist Wood. The location is similarly romantic, perched high above the Winooski River. NR.

COLLEGE HALL, Vermont College campus, Ridge St., 1872. This Mansard-roofed Second Empire concoction, with elaborate exterior and interior architectural detailing, contains a c. 1884 double manual pipe organ. NR.

Northfield

CENTRAL VERMONT RAILWAY DEPOT, W end of Depot Sq., 1852. Vermont's oldest station was altered around the turn of the century with Eastlake ornamentation. The building is also the last element left of the former Vermont Central Railway headquarters. *See* St. Albans. NR.

NORWICH UNIVERSITY MUSEUM, Main St., (VT 12), ¼-mile N of Jct. VT 12

and VT 12A, 19th century. The historical collections of America's oldest military college are housed in the basement of **White Chapel.** The memorabilia and military paraphenalia date back to the founding of the school in 1819 in Norwich. The move to Northfield came in 1867. Among the famous alumni are Admiral George Dewey, General Alonzo Jackman, and General Grenville Dodge. Open when the college is in session, M-F 2-4; other times by appointment. Free. 485-5011, ext. 235.

COVERED BRIDGES: **Northfield Falls Covered Bridge** and **Slaughterhouse Covered Bridge,** both N of Northfield off VT 12, over Dog River, late 19th century; **Stony Brook Covered Bridge,** SW of Northfield, off Vt 12A, over Stony Brook, 1899; **Upper Cox Brook Covered Bridge,** N of Northfield, off VT 12, over Cox Brook, 19th century; **Lower Cox Brook Covered Bridge,** off VT 12, 1872.

Plymouth Notch

PLYMOUTH HISTORIC DISTRICT (Calvin Coolidge Historic Site), VT 100, 19th century. Coolidges have lived in this Green Mountains valley for generations and still reside amidst the pleasant hills. Few United States presidents have enjoyed home more than Calvin Coolidge. Coolidge, of course, was in Plymouth Notch when called to the presidency by the death of Warren G. Harding the night of Aug. 3, 1923. He returned to the hamlet, his birthplace, as often as he could and is buried there. Of the fifteen buildings found in the town, the most important have been given to the state of Vermont. They are not architectural masterpieces but unpretentious, solid symbols of a much simpler age—even for Vermont. Coolidge reminisced about his home town: "It was a fine atmosphere in which to raise a boy . . . . There was little that was artificial. It was all close to nature and in accordance with the ways of nature. The streams ran clear. The roads, the woods, the fields, the people—all were clean." They still are, although it requires a maintenance crew and stiff littering fines to keep the present as pristine.

The state Division for Historic Preservation maintains five buildings, and the stone **Visitor's Center and Museum,** 1972, is a good place to start. You may then want to visit the following:

The Coolidge Homestead was "home" from the time the President was four years old until his death in 1933. The "Oath Room," the place where Col. John Coolidge swore in his son, is the most important space and is furnished as it was in 1923. The other rooms are similarly turned out in late Victorian finery.

The Coolidge Birthplace, c. 1840, is across the street from the Homestead and is a bare-bones dwelling. The village's general store was once attached, but this appendage was replaced with a separate, new store around the corner by the President's son before the state purchased the birthplace in 1968.

The Wilder Barn contains three floors of farm tools, antiques, and machinery original to the Plymouth area. The barn was once owned by the President's aunt and uncle and is outstanding for its size and construction.

The Wilder House, next door to the Coolidge Homestead, is a hospitality center and the village's only restaurant.

The Calvin Coolidge Historic Site buildings are open mid-May-mid-Oct, daily 9-5. Admission for the Homestead and Birthplace is $1 for adults 14 years and over. 828-3226.

Other sites in the historic district that you may wish to visit or view are the 1840 **Plymouth Union (Congregational) Church and cemetery,** where the President is buried; the 1868 **Brown House,** the family home of Carrie Brown Coolidge, Col. John Coolidge's second wife; and the one-room **Plymouth schoolhouse.**

South Royalton

SOUTH ROYALTON HISTORIC DISTRICT, principally Chelsea St., North and South Windsor Sts., and Railroad St., mid-late 19th century. South Royalton, the largest of the towns bearing the name Royalton, is living proof that Vermont is as much Victorian as it is Colonial in spirit. Although taste for the Federal in design survived well into the mid-1800s throughout the state, a preference for a more romantic and eclectic building style gradually took hold. South Royalton was founded in 1848 as a railroad town—the Vermont Central. As a local historian explains, the town enjoys "exceptional architectural unity that comes from having all its houses, stores, church, and school built at the same time in the same style—a very restrained Greek Revival—and all new at once." The original residential section is primarily made up of homes in this first of the Victorian revival styles. The commercial district along Chelsea St. reflects the later Queen Anne and Italianate Revival. The 1887 Queen Anne **Railroad Station and Baggage House** occupies one side of the **Village Park;** the 1887 commercial **"Block,"** borders another side. The rest of the park is surrounded by Greek Revival style buildings. The park is a fascinating complex with elaborate bandstand;

granite Civil War statue; a memorial, also in granite, honoring WWI, WWII, Korean, and Vietnam veterans; a fountain; cannon; and the 1915 Handy Memorial, a Revolutionary War commemorative piece. Paths which bisect the park come together at the center fountain. NR.

Springfield

EUREKA SCHOOLHOUSE, VT 11 E of Springfield at Gould's Mill, c. 1790. The square, one-room building is considered the oldest surviving school in the state. It is operated by the Division for Historic Preservation and has been furnished as a typical 19th-century school. A picnic area and a Town lattice truss covered bridge adjoin. NR. Open mid-May-mid-Oct., daily 9-5. Free. 828-3226.

HARTNESS HOUSE INN, 30 Orchard St., 1904. Now an inn and restaurant (see Lodging), this was the residence of James Hartness, governor of Vermont in 1921-22 and a wealthy machine and toolmaker. A Shingle Style house is an unusual sight in Vermont, Colonial Revival being a much more popular mode for the homes of the rich in the early 1900s. But even more unusual is the strange apparatus positioned on the front lawn. This is a telescope or, more accurately, what its inventor, Mr. Hartness, called a "Turret Equatorial Telescope." As explained by the present-day owners of Hartness House, "It is nothing more than a giant clock with a ten-inch, 600-power eye." NR.

SPRINGFIELD ART AND HISTORICAL SOCIETY, Elm Hill, 9 Elm St., 1865. Springfield has long been famed as a center of skilled toolmaking and machining. Less known is the fine collection of pewter, pottery, dolls and carriages, costumes and other decorative objects which are brought together in the 1865 Edward W. Miller house. Open May-Dec, M-F 12-4:30. Free. 885-2415.

Stowe

STOWE VILLAGE HISTORIC DISTRICT, along VT 100 and 108, Main, Maple, Park, Pond, Depot, Railroad and School Sts., Sunset Ave., and Mountain Rd., 19th century. The "Ski Capital of the East" has somehow managed to escape some of the worst effects of tourism, in particular, the proliferation of inappropriate fast-food emporiums. Main St., (VT 100) contains most of the commercial buildings of interest, including the **Green Mountain Inn** (see Lodging), the main block of which dates back to the first half of the last century. The neo-classical **Community Church,** on the south side of Main, is noted for its graceful steeple visible up and down the valley. Stowe became an important tourist center in the mid-1800s because of its unusually beautiful location between Mount Mansfield to the west and Hogback Mountain to the east. It was once also a major logging region but this industry, along with farming, has been largely swallowed up by the sport of the slopes.

The **Stowe Historical Society Museum** is located in the library section of the neo-Colonial **Akeley Memorial Building** on Main St. It features exhibits of local photographs and memorabilia along with displays of costumes, household antiques, etc. Open M-F 2-5.

Strafford

STRAFFORD VILLAGE HISTORIC DISTRICT, along Morrill Highway and Sharon Brook Rd., 1770s-mid-1800s. Strafford is your classic rural Vermont village. Nestled between two ridges in the Ompompanoosuc River valley, it has not been a very busy place since the 1830s—thus its composure. The predominant style of the approximately 30 buildings is the Greek Revival and the building medium is wood. Standing at the head of a traditional green is the 1779 **Meeting House.** It was the first building in the settlement. The most notable building in the area, however, is the **Justin Smith Morrill Homestead,** an 1848-51 Gothic Revival residence of extremely imaginative design. Morrill, the father of the Land-Grant College acts, which established and then furthered the principle of federally assisted higher education, first served in the U.S.

House of Representatives (1854-66) and then the Senate (1866-98). The home is a charming "cottage" of seventeen rooms and is furnished with family antiques. Also included on the property are seven agricultural outbuildings. NR, NHL. Operated as a house museum by the Division for Historic Preservation. Open mid-May–mid-Oct, Tu-Su 9-5. Free. Donations accepted. 828-3226.

Tunbridge vicinity

COVERED BRIDGES: **Mill Covered Bridge,** W of VT 110, over First Branch of White River, 1883; **Cilley Covered Bridge,** SW of Tunbridge, over First Branch of White River, 1883; **Flint Covered Bridge,** NE of Tunbridge, off VT 110, over First Branch of White River, 1845; **Howe Covered Bridge,** S. of Tunbridge, off VT 110, over First Branch of White River, 1879. All are frame with vertical siding and all, except the Flint Covered Bridge, are multiple king post truss bridges. Flint is a queen post truss bridge. With the exception of the Howe bridge, each is still in use.

Weathersfield Center

WEATHERSFIELD CENTER HISTORIC DISTRICT, Center Rd., late 18th-early 19th centuries. Only two buildings comprise the district but both are worthy of admiration. The **Meeting House,** 1821, is a very sophisticated brick building which served the town and the Congregational assembly. The facade is strikingly neo-classical with three entrances, each with a round-arch fanlight. A Palladian window is set above the center entrance. The bell tower rises in three stages and is ornately decorated.

The first minister in the village built the house which now carries his name—the **Reverend Dan Foster House.** Originally, in 1785, it was just a 1½-story building of fairly functional Colonial design. This portion is now an ell to a larger, 1825, 2½-story main section with a fancy center doorway and molded cornices. The ten rooms are now furnished with 18th and 19th-century objects by the Weathersfield Historical Society. The society has also restored the adjacent **Old Forge,** a working forge and bellows. NR. Open last week in June-first week in Oct, W-M 2-5; also by appointment. 263-5230.

Weston

THE FARRAR-MANSUR HOUSE, on the Green, 1797. Captain Oliver Farrar's house has served as an inn and a private residence over the years. Since 1932 it has been an historic house museum, among the earliest in America. Weston, one of Vermont's most photogenic communities of clapboard houses and shady lanes, has long treasured the past and made it inviting for outsiders. The house contains an extraordinary collection of decorative objects and antiques which tell the story of Weston and its early families. The ballroom on the second floor (Farrar Room) is a 16 x 40

foot space that served such various community functions as a courtroom and social center. The kitchen contains a fascinating collection of early utensils, household devices, pewter and Staffordshire. And just off the kitchen is the Playroom with a small piano, doll house, child's tea set, and a collection of dolls. Several hours could easily be spent in this historic house. NR. Operated by the Weston Historical Society. Open Memorial Day weekend-June, Sa 1-5, Su 2-5; July-Labor Day, W-Sa 1-5, Su 2-5; Labor Day-Columbus Day, Sa 1-5, Su 2-5. $1 adults, no charge for children under 12. 824-6630.

The **Weston Playhouse** also looks out upon the Green. One of Vermont's oldest professional summer theater companies is housed there. The original theatrical home was a rebuilt Greek Revival Congregational Church but this has since burned to the ground. It has been replaced with a similarly dignified building which fits the proper Weston scene. The village has probably never looked better in all of its history. The Green was—before the Civil War—a frog pond, and until the 20th century, Weston was hardly noticed by outsiders. It owes much of its present prosperity to the enterprise of Vrest Orton, founder of the now-famous Vermont Country Store, located here and in Rockingham.

Windsor

WINDSOR VILLAGE HISTORIC DISTRICT, along Main St., Depot Ave., State St., and around Court Sq., late 18th-late

19th centuries. Vermont has no more historic town than its original capital city. There is an interesting mixture of residential and commercial architecture, of very fancy and merely functional design. Windsor also became an important center of industrial activity in the early 1800s.

The **Old Constitution House,** 16 N. Main St., (US 5), 1777, is the most important historic site in town. It was here that Vermont's first constitution was adopted; in which room this historic event occurred is still an arguable matter but the date was July 8, 1777. The two-story frame building, which once served as a tavern, has been moved here from its original site. "The Birthplace of Vermont" museum is operated by the Division of Historic Preservation. NR. Open mid-May-mid-Oct, daily 9-5. Free, donations accepted. 828-3226.

Windsor House, cor. N. Main and State

Sts., 1836, has fought for its life a number of times. A well-known hotel in the old days, the columned Greek Revival building has recently been adapted for use as a restaurant, a crafts center, and for other community purposes. It is the headquarters for Historic Windsor, Inc., the organization which has spearheaded the area's preservation program.

Three gifted architects were responsible for some of Windsor's most beautiful early buildings—Alexander Parris, Ammi B. Young, and Asher Benjamin. The Parris commission, **St. Paul's Episcopal Church**, 1822, is a brick monument to neo-classical good taste. The tiered bell tower rises majestically over the downtown area. **Old South Congregational Church**, 1798, is credited to Asher Benjamin, at the time a resident of the town. Author of the most influential early American builders' manuals, Benjamin is also responsible for a number of Federal-style residences. A monumental portico was added to the church in 1879; the interior was restored in 1922 to what was considered its original state. Young, the official architect of federal government buildings in the mid-1800s and architect of the State House in Montpelier, provided the design for the **U.S. Post Office**, 1852. As with many other buildings designed by Young, cast iron was widely employed for architectural detailing.

Yet another type of building which has survived in Windsor is the Gothic Revival-style **McIndoe House**, 1849. The exterior is ornately finished with scroll sawn pendant drops, finials, and verge boards. It is a house worthy of Andrew Jackson Downing, the mid-19th century popularizer of the style.

The **American Precision Museum**, 196 Main St., occupies the 1846 armory and machine shop business founded by the Robbins and Lawrence Co. and carried on by successor firms. Yankee genius is well chronicled in the history of the various firearms and toolmaking firms that have labored here. Robbins and Lawrence is recognized as having been a pioneer in the development of mass production and the use of interchangeable parts. NR, NHL. Open Memorial Day-Nov 1, M-F 9-5; Sa-Su, holidays, 10:30-4:30. $2 adults, 75¢ children. 674-5781.

CORNISH-WINDSOR COVERED BRIDGE, *see* Cornish, NH.

Wolcott

FISHER COVERED BRIDGE, SE of Wolcott, over Lamoille River, 1908. The Fisher Bridge has been protected by the state as it is the last remaining covered span used by a railroad, in this case the St. Johnsbury & Lamoille County. It also sports a full-length cupola (to allow smoke to escape). The state strengthened the bridge with the addition of steel beams. A picnic and rest area is found adjacent. NR.
♦♦♦

Woodstock

WOODSTOCK VILLAGE HISTORIC

Fisher Covered Bridge

DISTRICT, practically the entire village, late 1700s-late 1800s. Dozens of historically and architecturally significant buildings define what is probably Vermont's most handsome village. The outstanding examples are many times more distinguished than the majority of the best buildings to be found in other towns. Woodstock has been blessed by wealth and private philanthropy. It has been and continues to be the home of important people who value the traditional and well-wrought. The Woodstock Inn is a major resort complex; unfortunately, the building is only historic in spirit, the original having been replaced. Among the finest of the surviving buildings are:

The Dana House, 26 Elm St., 1807. Woodstock's Historical Society is housed here and the focus is on the decorative arts from the period 1800-60 — furniture, ceramics, glass, silver, textiles. A barn houses a display of farm, household, and craft tools. The house is a handsomely turned out frame and brick Federal mansion with grounds that reach down to the lovely Ottauquechee River. The most famous of the Danas, John Cotton Dana (1856-1929), a librarian and museum director, is remembered in the library of manuscripts bearing his name. NR. Open May 30-Oct 30, M-Sa, 10-5; Su 2-5:30, Dec-Apr by appointment. $1.50 adults, $1 senior citizens, 50¢ children, 25¢ pre-schoolers. 457-1822

Also to be found along Elm St. are the **Job Lyman House** (1809) and the **First Congregational Church,** 1807, altered 1859 and 1890. The next historically interesting building is:

The George Perkins Marsh Boyhood Home, 54 Elm St., 1805-1807, 1885, including extensively landscaped grounds. This is most appropriate because Marsh, a distinguished lawyer and diplomat of the mid-19th century, is the man who laid the philosophical foundations for the American conservation movement. The home was later redesigned by famed Victorian architect Henry Hudson Holly and became the residence of Frederick Billings, a railroad magnate and benefactor of many Vermont institutions. The home is private but visible. NR, NHL.

The Ottauquechee D.A.R. House, on the Green, 1807, is the second of Woodstock's house museums. The exhibits in the seven-room museum range from Revolutionary War materials to furniture and other household furnishings. Owned and operated by the Ottauquechee Chapter of the D.A.R. Open June-Aug, M-F 2-4.

There are many other buildings around the Green which will delight the visitor. **The Windsor County Courthouse, 1855,** dom-

inates the scene and is distinguished by an octagonal tower which is topped by a dome. North of the Green is the main business district, a collection of well-maintained two-story Victorian buildings of brick and stone.

The covered bridge in the village is, like the Woodstock Inn, only historic in design. It was built in 1969 and is faithful to traditional materials and construction techniques. A true antique covered bridge, the **Lincoln Covered Bridge,** is found SW of town off US 4. It was built in 1877 and uses a Pratt truss of a 136-foot single span.

Northeast Vermont

Brownington

BROWNINGTON VILLAGE HISTORIC DISTRICT, Hinman and Brownington Center Rds., 18th-19th centuries. A remarkable story of achievement despite great odds lies at the heart of historic Brownington. It is Alexander Lucius Twilight's story, the first black graduate of a college in America (from Middlebury in 1823), minister of the church and director and builder of the county grammar school, and state legislator (1836-37). Brownington, a buccolic neo-Colonial Northeast Kingdom hamlet, does seem an unlikely place for such an early lesson in civil liberties. In fact, the author of a recent article on the village completely ignored the fact that its most prominent citizen was a black

man. His great monument is the **Old Stone House** or, as he termed it, "Athenian Hall," 1836. This four-story granite building served as the county grammar school until nearly 1860. It has been the museum of the Orleans County Historical Society since the early 1900s. The society also includes on its three-acre tract such other properties as **Alexander Twilight's house,** c. 1820 and 1830s, and the **Cyrus Eaton House,** 1834. Other important buildings in the village are the Greek Revival **Congregational Church,** 1841, but with a drastically remodeled interior from late in the century; and the community's first school and church, the **Academy,** now the Brownington Grange Hall and a community center.

The society's buildings are open May 15-Oct 15 from 9-5. $1 adults, 50¢ children. 754-2022.

Caledonia County

COVERED BRIDGES: **Greenbanks Hollow Covered Bridge,** S of Danville over Joes Brook, 19th century; **Chamberlin Mill Covered Bridge,** W of VT 114, over South Wheelock Branch of Passumpsic River, 19th century; **Bradley Covered Bridge,** N of Lyndon on Vt 122, over Miller Run, 1878. These three bridges— still in use today—are typical of a design found throughout the county. The vertical siding extends only one-third the way down, thus exposing the side structural members. The effect is rather crude, if not rude. As one historian has put it, this method makes "them look unfinished or like ladies hiking up their skirts."

Old Schoolhouse Bridge, S Wheelock Rd., over Cold Hill Brook, Lyndon, c. 1871, is a more conventional form. It is the state's last bridge with side covered walkways for pedestrians. All are NR.

Derby Line

HASKELL FREE LIBRARY AND

OPERA HOUSE, Caswell Ave., 1901-1904. One-half this landmark building is in Canada, and the other in the United States. It was all planned that way, and on this most peaceful of international borders the arrangement causes no problem. The Classical Revival building was given to Derby Line and its adjoining sister city, Rock Island, Quebec, by Martha Stewart Haskell. The opera house interior was finely executed and is widely used in the summer; the library functions all year round. Open Tu, W, Th, Sa 11:45-4:45; Th 7-9 pm as well. Free (819) 876-2471.

Canaan

JACOB'S STAND (Alice M. Ward Memorial Library), W. Park St., 1846. The building took its name from its function as the northernmost American stop or "stand" on the Franklin, New Hampshire, to Montreal stage route during the 19th century. It is as well known, however, for its identification with the anti-slavery movement. The first owner, Fernando C. Jacobs, was very much involved in helping slaves to escape into Canada, and the "stand" was used as a stop on the Underground Railroad until 1860. The building's unusual neo-Palladian temple style is unique on this northern frontier. NR.

East Burke

BURKLYN HALL, Bemis Hill Rd., 1904-1908. An extraordinary mansion house worthy of Newport or West Palm Beach, Burklyn Hall was built by New York hotel executive Elmer Darling and designed by the firm of Jardine, Kent & Jardine. After a period of time as a state-owned property, it has reverted to private ownership. It remains, however, on the National Register, and for good reason. The building is a three-story frame Georgian Colonial with a two-story portico front, a gabled pediment, and a wealth of other classical details such as Palladian windows. The interior is even more lavish, with such extravagances as a billiard room, drawing or music room in the style

of Louis XVI, and a mahogany-paneled dining room. Other features of the estate are an illuminating gas producing machine (once commonly found in isolated country estates), a wine cellar, and a central vacuum system.

Guildhall

GUILDHALL VILLAGE HISTORIC DISTRICT, around the Essex County Common and W and N of the Common on VT 102, 19th century. Little has changed since the mid-19th century in what is the county seat of Essex and the oldest village in the Northeast Kingdom. The Common is the center of activity and of interest to the visitor. Here at the head of the greensward is found the 1831 Greek Revival Court House and, on the SW corner, the Guild Hall which combines the 1795 Judd Store and the former Hartshorn Law Office. The Guild Hall serves as the town hall. The village occupies a prominent position above the Connecticut River, and the Common leads down from Court House Hill to the river.

Island Pond

ISLAND POND HISTORIC DISTRICT, Main, Railroad, Depot, Cross, Paquette, and South Sts., 1853-early 20th century. Situated approximately halfway between Montreal and Portland, ME, Island Pond owes its existence to the Canadian Grand Trunk Railway, now part of the CNR system. Since 1853, when the first trains came through, the station has served as both a customhouse and terminal. The present brick and granite depot was built in 1903-1904 by the Grand Trunk and was part of a large rail complex, most of which has now disappeared. On Main and Cross Sts. are a number of commercial buildings which served the community of railroading families. Except for the station, the rest of the international town is built of wood from nearby forests. This is hardly your quaint sort of Vermont country town. Rather, it is an important economic and technological link in the Northeast Kingdom.

McIndoes

McINDOES ACADEMY, US 5, 1853. Education was a very important concern in every New England village and the buildings erected in pursuit of learning rival only the churches in distinction. **McIndoes Academy,** a public secondary school, was open until 1969 and now serves as a museum, library, and community center. It is a handsome neo-classical two-story building with an Ionic portico and a two-tiered cupola. The village, naturally, also includes a traditional white frame Congregational Church, 1850. The hill just south of the tiny village provides an excellent view of the upper Connecticut River valley. NR.

Newport City

OLD COLONY MAPLE SUGAR FACTORY, Bluff Rd., 2.8 miles from the Newport exit on I-91 and ½ mile from US 5. A restored 1905 railroad coach is used for the showing of a film on sugaring. There is also a tour of the factory. Free. Open daily, M-F 8-11:30 and 12:30-4. 334-6516 🏃

Ryegate vicinity

WHITEHILL HOUSE, N of Ryegate on Groton-Peacham Rd., 1808. Scotsmen from Inchinin Parish, near Glasgow, were the first settlers of the Ryegate area. John Witherspoon, an early president of Princeton, owned the entire township and gradually sold the land off to settlers such as James Whitehill, builder of this two-story house. It is unusual in making use of granite fieldstone and not wood. The style is Federal—restrained and tasteful. Frame additions were made later, including a 1½-story connected barn. The oldest house in the Ryegate area, it is now maintained by the Whitehill Home and Library Association. NR.

St. Johnsbury

MAIN STREET HISTORIC DISTRICT, Main St. and intersecting streets, 19th-early 20th centuries. St. Johnsbury is a most remarkable small city. If Middlebury is the most pleasing of the larger Vermont villages of the early 19th century, then St. Johnsbury is the most striking of the late 1800s, although the first impression may be one of grime and neglect. Architecturally and historically, it has treasures unknown in cities many times its size. Why these extraordinary riches? The Fairbanks family of the scale industry must be thanked for its inspiration and benefactions. On the other hand, St. Johnsbury may have escaped some of the horrors of the 20th century by the fact of its relative geographic isolation and very real economic decline. A boom town is never a very culturally interesting place, although the kind of money needed to invest in art and architecture is made in such places. And a great deal of money was obviously made in St. Johnsbury one hundred years ago. It was, most fortunately, invested in the future and, to some significant degree, for the pleasure and edification of the public.

Of St. Johnsbury's two nationally recorded historic districts—Main Street and the Railroad Street—Main Street is far more important. Eighty significant buildings—including the **Athenaeum, Fairbanks Block, Brantview,** the Estabrooks **House, North Congregational Church,** and **The Fairbanks Museum**—are to be found along or just off Main St. They are all located on what is known as the Plain, above the rest of the town.

The buildings which are privately held and are not accessible to the public are for the most part residences built from the period of the 1820s to the 1890s. Starting at the top of Main Street and centered around Arnold Park is the **Esterbrooks House,** 123 Main, and across from it, the **Ruiter-Laperle House,** 120 Main. Both are Queen Anne extravaganzas and were designed by Lambert Packard, a local gifted architect who may have apprenticed with H. H. Richardson. Packard was the official Fairbanks family architect. Sixteen of his buildings are included in the district.

Down Main just a bit are two earlier homes—the **John Huxham Paddock House,** 116 Main, with a full temple-form Greek Revival portico, and the **Ephraim**

Paddock House, 115 Main, 1820, a late Federal-style mansion. Other impressive houses are the **Jewett-Ide House,** 111 Main, with a mansarded tower and the **C. H. Stevens House,** 110 Main, an 1888 Packard design. The residential north section of Main comes to an end at Summer Street Common, and the public sector of the street begins.

St. John's Church, Winter and Main Sts., 1897, and the **North Congregational Church,** 72 Main, 1881, were both designed by Lambert Packard and are massive brick structures with stone trim. Each is also supplied with an impressive bell tower.

The Fairbanks Museum and Planetarium, Main and Prospect Sts., 1891, was a gift of the Fairbanks family. The 1½-story sandstone building is deceptively simple from the outside — as was probably Packard's aim. The interior presents a remarkable display of wood, cast iron, and glass. The barrel-vaulted ceiling of the 40-foot wide and 135-foot long exhibition hall is completely covered with oak wainscoating. The museum features exhibits in the fields of natural history, astronomy, and energy technology. Open Sept 1-June 30, M-Sa 10-4, Su 1-5; July-Aug, M-F 9-9, Sa 9-5, Su 1-5. $2 adults, $1.50 senior citizens and students, $1 children, $5 family. The Planetarium hours are different. For further information: 748-2372. 🏛

Further down Main, around the "Bend," is the **Fairbanks Block,** 38 Main, 1892. Another Packard design, it is one that has been somewhat obliterated at ground level, but fancy brickwork — round panels, a corbelled cornice and stepped gable — is visible. A more important survivor is the extraordinary library, the Athenaeum, two buildings down the street.

St. Johnsbury Athenaeum, 30 Main St., designed by John Davis Hatch, assisted by Lambert Packard, 1872. A pure French Second Empire design was expertly carried out in red brick. The Athenaeum, which serves as the town's public library, is also a Fairbanks family charity. It has the distinction of being the first endowed free public library in the state and the oldest unaltered museum in the United States. The interior will fascinate anyone with its floor to ceiling carved ash bookcases, cast-iron spiral stairways, alternating oak and black walnut floors, and ornate lighting fixtures. The Athenaeum's collection of Hudson Valley School paintings and the works of other late-Victorian artists is exceptional. Alfred Bierstadt's "Domes of the Yosemite" occupies a special niche in the west wall designed for it in 1873 when the art gallery addition was made. Open M, F 9:30-8; Tu-Th, Sa 9:30-5. Free. 748-8291.

Continuing on down Main to the intersection of Eastern Ave., one arrives at the **Caledonia County Courthouse,** 27 Main St., a small park with a Civil War monument, and the **South Congregational Church,** 11 Main, 1852. The church is one of the few neo-classical religious buidings in town. Beyond the church are the Gothic brick academic buildings of **St. Johnsbury Academy,** a private school which also serves by special arrangement as the public high school. Positioned at the south end of the district is the most important of the Fairbanks family homes, **Brantview,** foot

of Main St., 1883. This great Queen Anne brick home was designed by Packard for William P. Fairbanks. It is approached along a 500-foot "avenue" formed by firs.

There are, of course, many other Fairbank homes in town as well as the **Fairbanks-Morse Scale Works,** red brick buildings on Western Ave. St. Johnsbury's other important industry has been maple sugar. Cary Maple Sugar Co. has been responsible for establishing the town as the "Maple Center of the World."

MAPLE GROVE MAPLE MUSEUM, US 2, eastern edge of town. Found here is old and new sugaring equipment that has been used in what is the world's largest factory devoted to the product. Guided tours are available M-F. The museum itself is open M-F 8-5 and Sa-Su and holidays 9-5. 50¢ adults, free for children under 12. 748-5141.

Lodging and Dining

VERMONT is the place to go for quiet living on a modest, tasteful scale. The countryside is not dotted with large, splashy resort complexes but, rather, features quite intimate inns and guesthouses. These, however, must be tracked down on the back roads. Most are not to be found along the major highways, routes which, like others in the United States, feature *Psycho*-like motels with knotty pine paneling and vibrating beds from the 1950s. These places, too, will be historic in time, but while the rock maple ages, there are more interesting pleasures to enjoy every season of the year. Vermont's inns are renowned during the foliage and ski seasons, but may be enjoyed at less cost during the summer months when hiking, canoeing, and bicycling are possible. While most visitors will travel by car, there are other kinds of tours—hiking, canoeing, cross-country skiing—tours which include historical sights that can be arranged to suit your special outdoor interests. Further information regarding these trips can be secured from most of the following recommended inns. The traveler should also gather more information on meal plans, which differ from place to place and season to season.

Arlington

SYCAMORE INN, US 7, 05250. (802) 362-2284. Tom & April Erwinski. Here is a pleasant historic oasis on busy US 7; once the home of Ethan Allen's brother, Ira, and a stagecoach stop between New York and Montreal. 11 rooms. MAP, EP, inexpensive. AE, M, V, PC. Open all year.

Bethel

GREENHURST INN, 05032. (802) 234-9474. Lyle & Barbara Wolf. A handsome 1890s summer home provides a relaxing resting place in any season; library of 3,000 books. 9 rooms. EP, moderate. PC. Dogs welcome by prior arrangement. Open year-round.

Brandon

CHURCHILL HOUSE INN, VT 73, RD 3, 05733. (802) 247-3700. Michael & Marion Shonstrom. The Churchill family home, built in the 1870s, must have been bustling then. It is now—with hikers, skiers, canoeing enthusiasts. The Forestdale Furnace is ¼ mile away. 8 rooms. MAP, expensive. M, V, PC. Open year-round.

Brookfield

GREEN TRAILS COUNTRY INN, Box 402, 05036. (802) 276-3412. Joyce Butler, manager. Located across from the Floating Bridge, Green Trails can't be missed. It started out as a home and has grown into an inn since 1932—with care. 15 rooms. EP, moderate. PC. Open all year with exception of Apr. and Nov.

Brownsville

THE INN AT MT. ASCUTNEY, Box 283, 05037. (802) 484-7725. Eric & Margaret Rothchild. A typical rural complex of farmhouse, barn, and stables dating from the post-Revolutionary period; inn and lounge added in mid-1880s. 8 rooms. Moderate. M, V, PC. Closed "mud season and after the leaves 'til snow." 🍴

Grafton

THE HAYES HOUSE, Bear Hill Rd., 05146. (802) 843-2461. Margery Hayes Heindel. This *is* Mrs. Heindel's house — built around 1803 and lovingly cared for since. 4 rooms. Bed and breakfast, inexpensive. PC. Open all year. Dogs welcome. Special rates: stay 7 days, pay for 6.

THE OLD TAVERN, Main St., 05146. (802) 843-2231. Lois M. Copping. An establishment dating back to 1788 and restored by The Windham Foundation in 1965 *without* telephone or television sets in the rooms. Hurrah! Accommodations for 100 in tavern, annex, and guesthouses. EP, expensive. PC. Closed Christmas Day and Apr. 🍴

Jamaica

THREE MOUNTAIN INN, Main St., 053343. (802) 874-4140. Charles & Elaine Murray. Center chimney 1780 colonial with 5 welcoming fireplaces; thoughtful attention is given to every detail of the decor and service. 8 rooms. MAP, expensive. PC. Open May-Apr. 🍴

Lower Waterford

RABBIT HILL INN, 05848. (802) 748-5168. Eric & Beryl Charlton. The original tavern dates from 1795; main inn, 1830; carriage wing, 1855. Cross-country ski center and nature walks. 21 rooms, EP, moderate. M, V, PC. Closed Apr. and Nov. 🍴

Ludlow

THE GOVERNOR'S INN, 86 Main St., 05419. (802) 228-8830. Byron & Melissa Schmidt. The 1890s Victorian home of Gov. Stickney; as colorful and comfortable as an eminent Victorian's home should be. 10 rooms. MAP, EP, expensive. Pets welcome by reservation. M, V, PC. Open all year.

Middlebury

THE MIDDLEBURY INN, Court Sq. (Box 631), 05753. (802) 388-4961. Frank & Jane Emanuel. Carefully restored post-1817 brick inn located in the center of the Middlebury historic district. 75 rooms. MAP, EP, moderate. M, V, PC. Open year-round. 🍴

North Hero

NORTH HERO HOUSE, Champlain Islands, 05474. (802) 372-8237. Roger &

Caroline Sorg. Off season mailing address: Roger & Caroline Sorg, 71 Broad St., Flemington, NJ 08822. A family-style summer resort complex dating to the 1890s; also included are earlier 19th-century buildings. 23 rooms. Moderate. PC. Special meal plan. Open late June until Labor Day. ⑪

North Thetford

STONE HOUSE INN, Box 47, 05054. (802) 333-9124. Art & Dianne Sharkey. After serving as a home for members of the same family from 1835 to 1957, the Stone House has been comfortably adapted for guests. 4 rooms. Inexpensive. M, V, PC. Inn open all year; restaurant open Apr.-Oct. ⑪

Plymouth

SALT ASH INN, Jct. VT 100 and 100A, 05056. (802) 672-3748. Ginny & Don Kroitzsh. Located in the heart of the Coolidge countryside, the Salt Ash has served as an inn since 1852 as well as a general store, post office, and stagecoach stop. 11 rooms. MAP, EP, moderate. M, V, PC. Open during winter, fall foliage months, and summer weekends. ⑪

Proctorsville

GOLDEN STAGE INN, P.O. Box 218, 05153. (802) 226-7744. Tom & Wende Schaaff. For nearly 200 years the Golden Stage has provided accommodations for travelers; at one time it was known as the "Skinner Place," being the home of Cornelia Otis Skinner. 10 rooms. MAP, EP, moderate, winter months; inexpensive, summer. M, V, PC. Open year-round. ⑪

Randolph

WINDOVER HOUSE, RFD #2, 05060. (802) 728-3802. George & Shirley Carlisle. Since 1800 the Windover has been known variously as Burt Place, the Steadman Inn, and Mid State Villa. Renovated in the 1960s. 8 rooms. MAP, EP, inexpensive. PC. Open all year.

Rutland

1787 GOVERNOR'S TABLE, 49 N. Main St., 05701. (802) 775-7277. Cecilia & David Zumwinkle. The Georgian Colonial 1787 home of Governor Williams (1850-51) now houses a most attractive restaurant with 6 dining rooms. Moderate. AE, D, CB, M, V, PC. Open M-Sa 11:30-5 for lunch, 5:30-10 for dinner; Su 12-9 for brunch, dinner.

St. Albans

THE CHARLIE VERMONT RESTAURANT AND PUB, One Federal St., 05478. (802) 527-7977. Dine in the midst of St. Albans' historic railroad district, across from the Central Vermont Railroad headquarters. The restaurant is located in an 1850s foundry building. Inexpensive. PC.

St. Johnsbury

ECHO LEDGE FARM INN, US 2 (P.O. Box 77), East St. Johnsbury, 05838. (802) 748-4750. Rosina, Larry & Philip Greenwood. A *real* farm, perhaps not unlike that occupied by most inn/farmhouses in the past. 6 rooms. Inexpensive.

Shoreham

SHOREHAM INN AND COUNTRY STORE, Main St. (VT 74 W.), 05770. (802) 897-5081. Cleo & Fred Alter. A handsome, historic setting along the eastern shore of Lake Champlain; an inn since 1799. Inexpensive. PC. Open all year.

Springfield

HARTNESS HOUSE INN, 30 Orchard St., 05156. (802) 885-2115. George & Cherrill Staudter. Expensive. AE, M, V, PC. Pets welcome. Open all year. NR.

Stowe

GREEN MOUNTAIN INN, Main St. (Box 220), 05672. (802) 253-7201. Pat & Becca Tursi. Stowe's most historic hostelry has been greeting visitors since the 1830s. Since it is so sturdily built, this tradition will undoubtedly last for many more years. 61 rooms. MAP, EP, moderate, AE, M, V. Open all year. 🍴

Weston

THE DARLING FAMILY INN, VT 100, 05161. (802) 824-3223. Chapin & Joan Darling. A very tastefully restored and furnished 150-year-old farmhouse; housekeeping cottages also available. 5 rooms. MAP, moderate. AE, M, V, PC. Open all year.

Wilmington

NUTMEG INN, VT 9 (P.O. Box 818), 05363. (802) 464-3351. Joan & Rich Combes. An 180-year-old farmhouse and carriage house form the nucleus of this cozy inn. 9 rooms. MAP, EP, expensive. PC. Open Dec. 26-mid-Apr., Memorial Day-Oct.

Windsor

WINDSOR STATION RESTAURANT, Depot Ave., 05089. Rudy Aldighieri. Located in the Windsor historic district renovated railroad station (1900). AE, M, V. Inexpensive. Open 11:30-2:30, lunch; 5:30-10, dinner.

Woodstock

NEW ENGLAND INN, 41 Pleasant St., 05091. (802) 457-9804. Robert & Sally Reilly. Once a part of a 40-acre Ottauquechee River estate dating from 1899; confortably 100 years "behind the times." 9 rooms. M, V, PC. EP, moderate. Pets welcome. Open year-round.

5. NEW HAMPSHIRE

WINTER scenes from New Hampshire fill the television screen every four years at the beginning of a new national presidential campaign. Candidates are seen greeting visitors along a quaint Main Street, leading to the overall image of the state as an old-fashioned outpost of neat white clapboard homes and shops nestled in the hills. This view is not far from the reality discovered by visitors to such picturesque villages as Canaan and Orford.

Missing from the pastoral scene captured by the media are the brick and stone mills and other industrial sites which made 19th-century New Hampshire an important part of America's economic base. The shell of the largest cotton textile factory in the world, Amoskeag Mills, survives in part today in Manchester; Harrisville was a village entirely devoted to the manufacture of woolens. Today, the buildings form Historic Harrisville, and modern design firms are making use of some of the buildings. Technology, once discreetly hidden from the traveler seeking an understanding of America's past, is now frequently displayed with pride as proof that history is written not only by pointed quills, but by nuts and bolts and gears.

New Hampshire was settled much earlier than its neighbor Vermont. As early as the 1630s such areas as Portsmouth and Exeter along the Atlantic coast were the objects of English emigration. Portsmouth began life as Strawbery Banke, a name that is continued in use today to designate the city's most historic neighborhood. By the late 1700s Portsmouth was a very fashionable and sophisticated seaport, and its handsome Georgian Colonial homes, many now open to the public, testify to both the prosperity and the fine craftsmanship of the time.

Interior New Hampshire, broken up by higher and higher mountain ridges as one proceeds northward, was more slowly settled and has little of the elegance of the coastal south. It is here that one discovers the small towns and crossroad settlements full of white clapboard buildings that vary in style from the formal Greek Revival to the Queen Anne summerhouse. The state's rugged hills have always provided a sanctuary for artists, musicians, writers, or just summer vacationers seeking a rest. The MacDowell Colony near Peterborough was established in 1907 as an artists' colony and has nobly served that purpose. In Cornish, sculptor Augustus Saint-Gaudens' summer home is magnificently maintained and offers a sculptor-in-residence summer program. Further north in the White Mountains are such famous hostelries as the Mount Washington Hotel at Bretton Woods, where both the international set and the common man have found rest and relaxation.

For the convenience of the visitor to New Hampshire in any season, this guide has been divided into three areas. The Southern region includes the three counties adjoining Massachusetts—Chesire, Hillsborough, and Rockingham—which tourists are most likely to explore first. The Central region includes the counties of Sullivan, Merrimack, Belknap, and Strafford which stretch across the middle of the state from the Connecticut River to the Maine state line. The Northern section covers the vast White Mountain National Forest and includes the counties of Grafton, Coos, and Carroll.

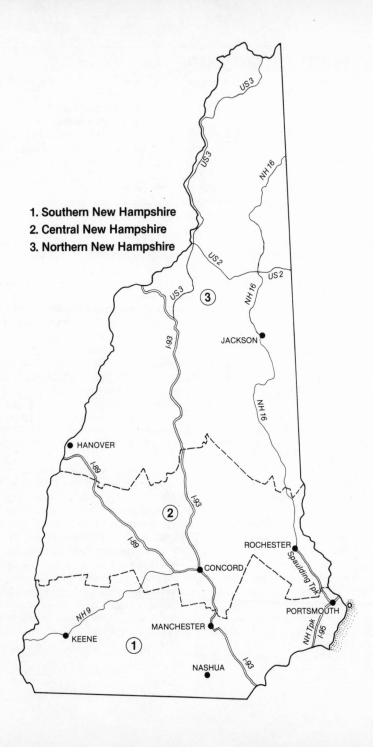

1. Southern New Hampshire
2. Central New Hampshire
3. Northern New Hampshire

Derry vicinity

ROBERT FROST HOMESTEAD, NH 28, 1900-1909. Until 1906 Frost farmed the rocky soil for a living. It is then that he developed his mature poetic style and composed many of the poems to be included in his first two volumes (1913-14). In addition, many of his famous later works drew from experiences on the Derry farm. NR, NHL. Operated by the State Division of Parks. Memorial Day-June 15, Sa-Su 9-5; June 16-Labor Day, W-Su 9-6. 50¢ over 18.

Exeter

FRONT STREET HISTORIC DISTRICT, 1-100 Front St., 18th-19th centuries. The buildings in the district display a harmonious blend of architectural styles. Most notable are several fine three-story Federal residences which reveal how fully this style was refined in southeastern New Hampshire.

The Sleeper House, built by George Sullivan in 1809, is the earliest and most altered of these Federal homes, featuring a Victorian porch added before 1885; the **Gardner House** (1826) also exhibits a portico and fanlight which are Colonial Revival additions of the late 19th century. The **Dudley House** at 14 Front St., is another Federal house, but with a later Doric portico addition. It served as the home of two prominent local physicians.

The district, however, is not limited to these domestic examples. The **Congregational Church** (1798) at 21 Front St. is the fifth meeting house to have been built in town and the third on this particular site. The building was host to numerous religious and secular gatherings throughout its history.

Of course, no discussion of Exeter would be complete without some mention of the **Phillips Exeter Academy,** the famous boarding school for boys which dates to 1783 and is bisected by Front St. Though several of the original buildings have been replaced, many of the dormitories dating from the academy's rapid expansion in the late 19th century remain, as well as fine Georgian and Colonial-style buildings from the 1920s and '30s by Ralph Adams Cram. Exeter's central attraction, the academy's brick buildings, possess a charm well-suited to an old institution nestled under the elms in a village which once served as New Hampshire's revolutionary capital. A map is available to guide visitors on a walking tour through the splendid campus. NR. 🏃

The Ladd-Gilman House, Governor's Lane and Water St., 1721, was once the home of Nicholas Gilman, a New Hampshire delegate to the Constitutional Convention in 1787. The original brick structure was later expanded into the present rambling residence, the interior of which is finished with deep window seats, paneled wainscoting, and huge fireplaces. It was also owned for a time by the eccentric Ladd family, one of whom was known to keep a coffin in the house in case of emergency. Operated as a museum by the Society of the Cincinnati. NR, NHL. May-Oct, Tu and Th 2-4. Group tours available. Free. 778-1308.

GILMAN GARRISON HOUSE, 12 Water St., c. 1690, is not located in the district but nearby to it. This unusual building was originally constructed as a fortified garrison to thwart Indian attacks with walls of massive hewn logs. The front wing was added by Gen. Peter Gilman in 1772 to provide a proper place of entertainment for Gov. Wentworth and his staff. The rooms of this wing are distinguished by their paneling and elaborately carved woodwork. Later, Daniel Webster boarded at the house while a student at the nearby academy. Operated as a SPNEA museum. NR. June 1-Oct 15, Tu, Th, Sa, Su 12-5. $1.50 adults, 50¢ children.

Fitzwilliam

THIRD FITZWILLIAM MEETING HOUSE (TOWN HALL), Village Green, 1817. This photogenic Federal-style church is another in a long line of classic New England structures patterned after an Elias Carter design. Notable are its lavish display of great oak and pine, and its majestic spire built around a mast which was hoisted by a crew of ship riggers brought up from Boston especially for the task. NR.

Francestown vicinity

OLD COUNTY ROAD HISTORIC DISTRICT, S of Francestown off NH 186. The dirt roads traversing the district are lined with continuous rows of stone walls, corridors of overhanging maples, orchards, and weatherbeaten barns which form the typically New Englandish back-

drop for numerous fine examples of Georgian and Federal residences. Notable is the "saltbox" form of the 1774 **Asa Lewis House** in the south end of the district, the Federal detailing of the c. 1800 **Stephen Rolfe House** in the northern end, and the majestic Federal residence of **William Starrett** (1806), distinguished by its four tall corner chimneys, in the eastern section of the district. NR.

HARRISVILLE HISTORIC DISTRICT, N of NH 101, 19th century. A unique example of a 19th-century rural manufacturing village — certainly more picturesque and visitable than the state's more urban mill centers. This self-contained village tumbles through the little valley, dotted by the restored remnants of the old wooden mills and their outbuildings. Notable among the brick remnants are the 1832 **Harris Mill** and the **Cheshire Mill,** which consists of three buildings. While none are open to the public, a stroll past the simple, yet dignified residences and boarding houses of the workers offers the visitor a tangible sense of life in a small rural industrial town a century ago. The local residents must be commended for their timely formation of Historic Harrisville, Inc., an organization largely responsible for the preservation of the village's unspoiled character. During the summer Harrisville Designs, a modern firm which occupies several of the mill buildings, offers week-long courses in various aspects of the spinning and weaving craft. Its address is Box 51, Harrisville, NH 03540.

Hillsboro

FRANKLIN PIERCE HOMESTEAD, NH 9 and 31, 1804. The compact, white clapboard home of our 14th president and the state's most illustrious former resident, is a fine example of the simple Federal houses typically found in this part of New England. The interior is neat but sparse, containing some exquisite French wallpaper and a second-floor ballroom. Operated by the State Recreation Division. NR, NHL. Late June-Labor Day, daily except M, 9-5. 50¢ adults, under 18 free. 478-3165.

Franklin Pierce Homestead

Keene

COLONY HOUSE MUSEUM, 104 West St., c. 1817. Housed in the 155-year-old home of Keene's first mayor, Horatio Colony, the museum contains fine collections of early 19th-century glass, Hampshire Pottery, Staffordshire historical ware, and cast-iron toys. May-Oct 15, Tu-Su 10-4:30. $1 adults, children free. 357-0889.

THE WYMAN TAVERN, 339 Main St., 1762. The large 2½-story frame dwelling with large chimneys and a columned entrance was built by Capt. Isaac Wyman, who led his small band of Minutemen on their march to Lexington early on the morning of April 21, 1775. The first meeting of the trustees of Dartmouth College was also held here in 1770. Currently a museum housing books, portraits, and antique furnishings. NR. May-Oct, Tu and Th 1-4. Donations accepted. 357-3855.

Manchester

AMOSKEAG MILLS, E bank of the Merrimack River, 1838-1915. This mile-long chain of 19th-century manufacturing buildings literally rises out of the east bank as an extraordinary example of industrial efficiency and urban community planning. Once the largest manufacturer of cotton textiles in the world, turning out 50 miles of cloth an hour, the Amoskeag complex was one of the few 19th-century millyards which featured decent housing and accommodations for its workers. For information regarding tours of the millyards, contact the Manchester Historic Association. 622-7531.

MANCHESTER HISTORIC ASSOCIATION, 129 Amherst St. Don't go here just to find out about Amoskeag. This local history museum features a 3,500-volume library of books, and a plethora of collections from the decorative arts to guns, toys, and fire-fighting equipment. Tu-F 11-4, Sa 10-4. Free. 622-7531.

ZIMMERMAN HOUSE, 223 Heather St., 1951. Though not "historical" by some standards, this Frank Lloyd Wright house is one of the few examples of his mature "Prairie Style" architecture in the Northeast, exhibiting the floating concrete slab design and the attention to detail (right down to the mailbox) which were characteristic of the work of this 20th-century master builder. NR.

Nashua

ABBOT HOUSE, 1 Nashville St., 1804. This exceptional late Georgian House has a white wooden front and ends of red brick. The handsome entrance consists of a wide front door with fanlight and brass knocker; the interior is enhanced by antique furnishings. Once the home of a prestigious local lawyer, Daniel Abbot who, on the occasion of President Andrew Jackson's visit to Nashua, was introduced to the President as "the father of Nashua." NR. Restoration plans are underway. Contact the Nashua Historical Society, 5 Abbot St., 03060.

New Castle

FORT CONSTITUTION, Walbach St., 18th-19th centuries. Originally a British stronghold called Fort William and Mary, it was the scene of one of the first overt acts against the Crown when seacoast colonists briefly captured the fort on Dec. 14, 1774. One hundred barrels of gunpowder were carried away and secreted under the meeting house pulpit in Durham. From there they were later carted by oxen to Bunker Hill just in time to be issued to the soldiers on the eve of the battle of Bunker Hill. Only the base of the walls of the 17th-century fort remain, but the stone and brick remains of the later 1808 Fort Constitution are gradually being restored. Operated by the state Division of Parks. NR. Open all year. Free. 🏃

New Ipswich

BARRETT HOUSE, (FOREST HALL), Main St., 1800. The exceptional three-story Federal residence has extensive grounds which include a Gothic Revival summer house on a terraced hill behind the main house. The twelve museum rooms of the main house contain many fine examples of 18th- and 19th-century furniture and antique musical instruments, all descended through the Barrett family. SPNEA. June 1-Oct 15; Tu, Th, Sa, Su 12-5. $2 adults, $1 children. (617) 227-3956.

Peterborough

ALL SAINT'S CHURCH, 51 Concord St., 1923. A superb Norman Revival church by Ralph Adams Cram set back from the street amid flat lawns, its setting evokes the atmosphere of an English country churchyard. Locally-quarried granite was used for the characteristic central tower, while the interior—from woodwork to stained glass—is a craftsmen's delight. NR. While in town, visit the **Peterborough Unitarian Church** at Main and Summer Sts. An earlier brick church dating to 1825, its dominant exterior feature is a frame clock tower topped by a gold-leafed dome. NR.

MACDOWELL COLONY, W of US 202, 1907. This 400-acre plot with its 27 buildings was established as an artist's colony in 1907 in memory of Edward MacDowell, the first American composer to gain an international reputation for serious music. Many of the studios are located in secluded surroundings. Among the notable buildings are the **Log Cabin** where MacDowell worked; **Hillcrest,** the home of MacDowell and his wife when they spent their summers here; and the **Eugene Coleman Savidge Memorial Library.** Aaron Copland, among others, has spent time at the colony. A sign at the entrance reads, "Visitors Most Welcome, Save on Sunday." NR, NHL. M-Sa 2-5.

PETERBOROUGH HISTORICAL SOCIETY MUSEUM OF AMERICANA, Grove St., 1917. Features an extensive collection of early Americana, including ceramics, early toys, dolls, china, and pewter. Open year-round. M, Tu, W 12-4 in winter; July-Aug, M-F 2-4. 924-3235.

Portsmouth

Located at the mouth of the Piscataqua River, Portsmouth was established as a township in 1631 by the Council of Plymouth. It was soon renamed Strawbery Banke by the first settlers of the area who couldn't help but notice the abundance of wild strawberries which flourished along the shore. In 1653 the area was finally incorporated as a town under its present name.

Prior to the Revolution Portsmouth was

the seat of the British provincial government, with the local Wentworth family producing three royal governors. During the War for Independence, however, the town was the scene of numerous bitter clashes between patriots and Tories. Blessed with an abundance of local timber, the town of Portsmouth subsequently rose to prominence in the 19th century as a major shipbuilding and commercial center. Today, the ghosts of Portsmouth's merchant princes and sea captains can still be felt to linger along the decayed wharves, and an old-world atmosphere persists along the narrow thoroughfares.

The stately mansions lining Middle Street, erected from the profits of the West Indian trade, serve as visible reminders of Portsmouth's past glory. The builders brought with them from England a sense of style; even the early saltbox and gambrel-roofed houses are well-proportioned and often feature tidy gardens in the rear. But it is the tall, square mansions along Middle Street which typify Portsmouth in its heyday. With ship's carpenters and craftsmen milling around the streets in the 19th century, it's no wonder that so many would be commissioned to adorn the homes of the merchant princes. The artisans were ever attentive to the molding of chimney caps, to the sweep of granite steps and coping, and to the careful working of hand-wrought designs in cornices and railings.

It is a credit to today's community that many of these well-wrought mansions have been restored to their original splendor. A number of them have been open to the public for some fifty years, allowing visitors the opportunity to share the rich interiors and period furnishings housed within. In addition, the formation of Strawbery Banke, Inc., during the 1960s resulted in the undertaking of one of the major restoration projects in this country, enabling a unique sampling of early American structures a chance to be saved from the devastation of so-called urban renewal.

RICHARD JACKSON HOUSE, Northwest St., 1664. Believed to be the oldest in the city, this medieval-looking saltbox has weather-stained clapboards which cover

the timber and masonry skeleton. The windows are replicas of the original leaded glass sash. The interior is sparse with ceilings of exposed beams and wide-board floors. Operated by the SPNEA. NR. $1, by appointment only. 227-3956.

JOHN PAUL JONES HOUSE, 43 Middle St., 1758. The two-story frame house with a gambrel roof is set at right angles to the street. Erected in 1758 by Capt. Purcell, the house was kept as a boarding house by his widow after his death. Here John Paul Jones stayed while overseeing the construction of the *Ranger* on Badger's Island in 1777. Housed within are items of early Americana, and a fine display of Sandwich glass. Operated by the Portsmouth Historical Society. NR, NHL. June-mid Oct, M-Sa 10-5. $1.50 adults, 50¢ children. 436-8420.

GOVERNOR JOHN LANGDON HOUSE, 143 Pleasant St., 1784. Surrounded by handsome landscaped grounds,

this stately 18th-century house was the home of a prosperous merchant. Langdon was active during the Revolution and served as president of the U.S. Senate during its first session in 1789. He administered the oath of office to both Washington and Adams. The exterior proportions of the house are monumental; the interior is lavishly embellished with carvings and furnished with family antiques. It's not surprising that Washington spoke warmly of the house when entertained there in 1789. Operated by the SPNEA. NR, NHL. June 1-Oct 15, Tu-Su 12-5. $2 adults, $1 children. Special group rates. 431-1800.

MacPHEADRIS-WARNER HOUSE, 150 Daniel St., 1718-23. The oldest brick house in the city, this magnificent edifice, with its gambrel roof topped by a balustrade, exemplifies the large, early Georgian residences that were once popular in the New England colonies. The central hallway contains murals by unknown artists, and the rooms are filled with furniture and early books. Operated by the Warner House Association. NR, NHL. June 15-Oct 15, M-Sa 10-4; Su 2-4:30. $2 adults, 75¢ students. Group rates. 436-5909.

MOFFATT-LADD HOUSE, 154 Market St., c. 1764. Capt. John Moffatt, a wealthy merchant, had ship's carpenters build this house as a wedding gift for his son Samuel. The ungrateful son skipped off to the West Indies in 1768 to escape his debts, leaving the Captain to occupy the house with his daughter-in-law and daughter. One can still imagine a lonely Lady Moffatt pacing the balustraded captain's walk, hoping for her husband's return. She eventually joined her husband, and the old Captain lived to a ripe old ninety-four. The house overlooks the old wharves and is elaborately decorated and furnished. Operated by the Society of Colonial Dames. NR, NHL. June 15-Oct 15, M-Sa 10-4, Su 2-5. $2 adults, 75¢ children. Group rates. 436-8221.

PORTSMOUTH ATHENAEUM, 9 Market Sq., 1804. Considered one of the best-preserved Federal period public structures in New England, this tall brick building features the familiar four tall chimneys and widow's walk. It contains a 30,000-volume library of general history and rare books, models of clipper ships built in Portsmouth between 1825 and 1873, and historical pamphlets, including the first issue of the *New Hampshire Gazette*. NR. Open all year. Th 1-4 for general visiting, Tu by appointment. Free. 431-2538.

RUNDLET-MAY HOUSE, 364 Middle St., 1807. Perched on a terrace with its original courtyard and garden layout still intact, this superb three-story Federal mansion is furnished entirely with family furniture and accessories, including many items fashioned by famed local craftsmen. Operated by the SPNEA. June 1-Oct 15, Sa-Su 12-5. $1.50 adults, 75¢ children. Group rates.

ST. JOHN'S CHURCH, 105 Chapel St., 1807, is the first brick church built in New Hampshire. Upon its completion it was considered one of the state's finest religious edifices. The church also represents one of the earliest designs of the noted American architect Alexander Parris, who later designed several granite buildings in Boston, including the Faneuil Hall (Quincy) Market. A "Vinegar Bible," printed in 1717 and one of four in this country, is preserved in a carved rosewood case. Through the glass cover the word "vinegar," a misprint of "vineyard" in the Biblical parable, can be seen. The church also features one of the oldest organs in the country, built in England in 1710, and used for a time at Boston's King's Chapel. The names of Benjamin Franklin and Daniel Webster appear in the records as proprietors of the stately white pews. NR.

STRAWBERY BANKE, Court and Marcy Sts., and both sides of Hancock and Washington Sts., 18th-19th centuries. Named for the profusion of wild berries found on the shores by the first settlers of this coastal town (1630), Strawbery Banke is an historic waterfront neighborhood and living museum which retains an unparalleled richness of early buildings spanning several architectural periods. Saved from urban renewal in the 1960s, the 35 buildings are largely original to the area—making a stroll down the narrow streets akin to turning back the clock to a bygone era of sea captains, craftsmen, and wealthy merchants.

The uniqueness of Strawbery Banke relates to its 350-year survival and the changes in the area which are documented nearly everywhere one looks. When the area was renamed Portsmouth in 1653, its history was only beginning. The **Capt. John Sherburne House** (c. 1695) is the oldest house on the Banke and dates from this early period. For most of the 17th century the area was used for farming, fishing, and the exploitation of local lumber. This early dependence on the land is reflected today by several gardens which are planted and tended by staff and neighbors—gardens containing only plant materials indigenous to the area prior to the 19th century. The area's age of prosperity as an active maritime center during the 19th century is reflected today by the importance given to crafts. Many of the buildings at Strawbery Banke were once the homes and shops of craftsmen, and today the association operates one of the oldest boat shops in America, as well as one of two remaining copper clench nail machines. The emphasis at Strawbery Banke is on "living" history. With this in mind, eight of the buildings have been adapted to house exhibits and demonstrations on a variety of topics.

Finally, the concern with documenting the area's numerous changes over the years is reflected in the five homes which are fully restored and furnished to reflect the lifestyles between 1770 and 1860.

Thomas Bailey Aldrich Memorial, c. 1797. One of Portsmouth's most famous literary figures spent his youth here in the

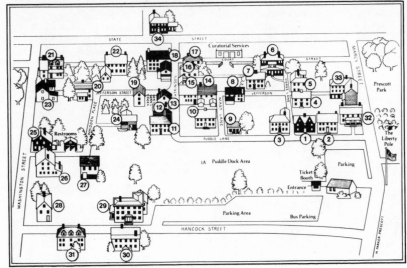

Courtesy of Strawbery Banke, Inc.

Strawbery Banke

1. Capt. John Sherburne House
2. Capt. James Drisco House
3. Peter Lowd House
4. Joshua Jackson House
5. Capt. Thomas Hough House
6. Shapley Town House
7. Capt. John Wheelwright House
8. James Marden House
9. Dinsmore Blacksmith Shop
10. Yeaton-Walsh House
11. Joshua Jones House
12. & 13. The Leonard Cotton Tenant Houses
14. The Winn-Yeaton Connected Houses
15. Peacock House
16. Reuben Shapley House
17. William Cotton House

18. William Pitt Tavern
19. Dr. John Jackson House and adjacent Herb Garden
20. Rider-Wood House
21. Stephen Chase House
22. Thomas Bailey Aldrich Memorial
23. Aaron Conant House
24. The Boat Shop
25. Deacon Penhallow House
26. Capt. Keyran Walsh House
27. Old State House
28. Daniel Webster House
29. Gov. Goodwin Mansion
30. Stoodley's Tavern
31. Joshua Wentworth House
32. Dunaway Store
33. Jefferson House
34. Kingsbury House

mid-1800s. Aldrich later immortalized the house in *The Story of a Bad Boy*. In 1908 the house was restored and furnished by the Aldrich family.

Stephen Chase House, c. 1762. The home of a wealthy merchant, this handsome Georgian house features a gambrel roof

and a beautifully carved entrance frontispiece. The interior is furnished with items descended through two Chase families.

Gov. Goodwin Mansion, c. 1811. One of the few houses in Strawbery Banke which was moved into the area, it's furnished as it would have been when the Goodwins lived

Stephen Chase House

Gov. Goodwin Mansion

here from 1832-82 and includes many family pieces and a miniature figurine exhibit.

Capt. Keyran Walsh House, c. 1796. Bought by a prosperous sea captain in 1796, later owner Walsh transformed it into one of the finest dwellings in the neighborhood, featuring unusual painted graining and marbling of the interior woodwork, and appropriate Chippendale and Federal furniture.

Captain John Wheelright House, c. 1780. Notable for its abundance of fine interior paneling, the house is furnished in the period of the American Revolution.

All of these homes and the remaining buildings and exhibits are operated by Strawbery Banke, Inc. The entire district is on the National Register of Historic Places. Apr 15-Nov 15, daily 9:30-5. $4.50 adults, $3.50 senior citizens, $2.50

students, $1.50 children. Group rates. 436-8010.

WENTWORTH-COOLIDGE MANSION, Little Harbor Rd. 2 miles S of Portsmouth; 1695, 1730, 1750. One-time home of Benning Wentworth, first royal governor of New Hampshire, the earliest saltbox portion was added to in the 18th century. The result is a rambling frame complex. It overlooks the harbor. NR, NHL. Operated by the state Division of Parks. May-Oct, Tu-Su 1-5.

WENTWORTH-GARDNER HOUSE, 140 Mechanic St., 1760. Built by ship's carpenters for the younger brother of the state's last royal governor, the plan is a standard four-room Georgian with wide clapboarding rusticated to imitate cut stone. Although the house was sold to the Metropolitan Museum of Art in 1918, the original plan to move it to New York was abandoned. The richness and delicacy of the interior woodwork is extraordinary and is believed to have required eighteen months to execute. The hand-painted paper in the dining room, and the four restored rooms on the first floor, each with a fireplace, are just some of the reasons why this house should not be missed. Operated by the Wentworth-Gardner and Tobias Lear House Association. NR, NHL. May-Oct, Tu-Su 1-5.

Walpole

MUSEUM OF THE WALPOLE HIS-

TORICAL SOCIETY, Main St., 1830. The Walpole Academy, a well-preserved Greek Revival temple, has served as a museum since 1950, housing collections of wedding gowns, portraits, and furniture of

the founding Bellows family. Also, a library of rare documents features the first novel said to have been printed in this country. NR.

Central New Hampshire

Acworth

ACWORTH CONGREGATIONAL CHURCH, N end of town common, 1821. The isolated village of Acworth (pop. 500) boasts a meeting house which is one of the most elaborate in New England. The projecting central bay and square tower relate well to the main block of the church, while the crisp lines of the towering steeple are executed with fine attention to detail and proportion. The lofty nave was framed over in 1886 to create two floors instead of one, and the upper worship room was given a "Gothic' look according to the fashion of the day. Originally attributed to Elias Carter, the church is said to have been constructed for $6,000 and several barrels of rum. Perched atop a small rise in pristine splendor, it is a sight not to be missed. NR. Open Su mornings, June-Sept; otherwise, apply at the post office.

Canterbury

CANTERBURY SHAKER VILLAGE, Shaker R. off NH 106, 1792-1800s. Twenty-two buildings serve as a tangible reminder of a thriving Shaker society which once boasted 300 members. Their

communal efforts and religious dedication here created a legacy in architecture, furniture making, crafts, and religious song and dance which has become a hallmark of the tradition. Due to the poor quality of the local soil, this particular community maintained its economic livelihood largely by selling textiles, farm implements, and household goods (including a patented early washing machine) to the "world people." The community's humble beginnings date to 1782 when Mother Ann Lee sent two of her followers to preach the word in the Canterbury hills. Though the village has experienced a steady decline since its heyday in the early 1800s, it has managed to survive. The non-profit foundation,

Shaker Village, Inc., was formed in 1973 to perpetuate the Shaker legacy. The two remaining sisters still greet and talk with visitors, whose daily attendance is limited to preserve the tranquility of the village. Guided tours are given through five furnished buildings, including the **Trustees Building** (1838), the only surviving brick structure at Canterbury. It is best to wear comfortable shoes, as the tour takes nearly two hours. NR. May 19-Oct 13, Tu-Sa; tours on the hour 10-4. $3 adults, $1 children. Group rates. 783-9977. ♦♦

Charlestown

OLD FORT NUMBER 4 ASSOCIATES, NH 11, 1745. The first settlement in town was made in 1740 by a group from Massachusetts who built the fort shortly thereafter. For may years the most advanced northern white settlement, its location was of strategic importance. In 1747 the fort, under the command of Captain Phineas Stevens, was beseiged by 400 French and Indians; their hasty retreat to Canada marked the beginning of English supremacy in northern New England. During the Revolution No. 4 was a rendezvous point for General Stark and his troops en route to the battle of Bennington. Today seven reconstructed fort buildings house Indian artifacts, colonial furnishings, tools, and weapons. A Revolutionary War battle reenactment is held in July; cooking demonstrations are given in an 18th-

century kitchen. June 22-Sept 1, daily 10-5; June 1-17 and Sept 7-22, Su 11-5; Sept 27-Oct 12, Sa-Su 11-5. $2.75 adults, $1.25 children, $2.25 seniors. 826-5094. ♦♦

Claremont

UNION EPISCOPAL CHURCH, NH 12A, 1771-73. Located in an easterly direction on Old Church Road, this wood frame structure is the oldest standing Episcopal church in the state, serving the second oldest parish. Said to have been built by master carpenter Ebenezer Rice, the building was probably based on the design of Queen's Chapel in Portsmouth. The heavy timber framing system which supports the roof is particularly noteworthy for those interested in such early engineering practices. The layperson will likely appreciate the clean lines of the exterior clapboarding or the delicate balustrades which surmount the box-type pews on the interior even more than the roof. Though the structure remains largely unchanged, there have been some alterations over the years.

MONADNOCK MILLS HISTORIC DISTRICT, both sides of the Sugar River, 1830s. In 1831 the Sugar River Manufacturing Company was granted a charter for manufacturing cotton and woolen goods; in 1846 the mill and company name was changed to Monadnock. The Monadnock Company continued producing textiles, including the famous Marseilles quilts, until 1932, during that time constructing sixteen buildings for a variety of purposes. Though production has long since ceased, only two structures have been lost and the remaining buildings comprise a rare example of a substantially complete early New England mill complex.

The Sullivan Machine Company began a similar operation in 1868 on a site further downstream. Today, a proposal to combine these mill complexes into a single Claremont Village Industrial District is being studied. Though mere shells of their former glory, these haunting millyards still provide a visual drama in their architecture and the spaces they define—as well as providing a stark example of America's manufacturing strength at the height of the Industrial Revolution. NR.

Concord

CONCORD HISTORIC DISTRICT, bounded roughly by N State St., the B&M railroad tracks, Horse Shoe Pond, and Church St.; 1730s-mid-20th century. Located just above the floodplain of the Merrimack River, this predominantly residential district of brick and frame houses was one of the earliest sections of town to be divided into lots for houses. The district exhibits well-preserved examples of various architectural styles.

Rev. Timothy Walker House, 276 N. Main St., c. 1733. The best example of the Georgian style to be found in the district, this gambrel-roofed building is closely related to houses of the same period in such coastal towns as Portsmouth and Newburyport. Classical detailing is expressed in the window pediments and the elaborate doorway.

Timothy Walker House, 217 N. Main St. Epitomizing the Federal style of the early 19th century, its plan is one room deep with two chimneys placed on the rear wall.

Joseph B. Walker Cottage, 278 N. Main St. This superb Gothic Revival cottage, based on a design by the romantic architect Andrew Jackson Downing, features board and batten walls and the characteristic medieval pendants and mouldings.

The district's most famous house, the **Pierce Manse,** at 14 Penacook St., was moved here from its original site at 18 Montgomery St. Regretfully, this museum and memorial to our 14th president was recently gutted by fire. NR.

NEW HAMPSHIRE HISTORICAL SOCIETY MUSEUM AND LIBRARY, 30 Park St., 1912. A long, one-story building of white granite, designed by Guy Lowell of Boston, it has two wings faced with Doric pediments. The main doorway is flanked by Ionic pillars; a heavy cornice surrounds the building. A massive sculpture carved from local Concord granite by Daniel Chester French depicts the progress of history. The building contains a rare collection of records and manuscripts dealing with New Hampshire history; pottery, china and glassware, paintings and antique furniture are also featured in four period rooms. Open all year, M-F 9-4:30, W til 8 pm. Free. 225-3381.

NEW HAMPSHIRE STATE CAPITOL, Main St., 1816-19. Built of Concord granite and Vermont marble, this severe neo-classical structure features a columnar porch which rises the full height of the facade; the entire structure is surmounted by an octagonal dome. The original front portion was occupied June 2, 1819. The State House is thus the nation's oldest state Capitol in which a legislature still meets in its original chambers. A Hall of Flags, statues, and portraits of state notables are housed within. Free.

Cornish

SAINT-GAUDENS NATIONAL HISTORIC SITE, off NH 12A, 1800. The home, studio, and gardens of one of America's most noted sculptors are preserved here amid the tranquil countryside. In 1885, while working on his *Standing Lincoln,* Saint-Gaudens was attracted to Cornish by a friend who assured him there were "plenty of Lincoln-shaped men up there." The artist's 2½-story brick Federal home, which he named "Aspet," was originally a tavern (c. 1880) known as "Hug-

gin's Folly" and had an unsavory reputation. Saint-Gaudens had it remodeled by the architect George Fletcher Babb. Noted for his statue of *Diana* atop the old Madison Square Garden, the masterful equestrian statue of *Gen. Sherman* (1900), and the *Shaw Memorial* on Boston Common, Saint-Gaudens gathered about him in New Hampshire the Cornish Colony of promising young artists and influenced their release from the shackles of academic conservatism. NR, NHL. May 15-Oct 31. Guided tours 8:30-4:30. 50¢ adults and children over 15. A sculptor-in-residence program is offered during the summer. 675-2175.

While in the vicinity, don't miss the **Cornish-Windsor Covered Bridge** (1866), W of Cornish. It is the longest wooden covered bridge in the U.S. (See also under Sullivan County.)

Dover

ANNIE E. WOODMAN INSTITUTE, 182 Central Ave. Founded in 1915 to serve the local community in areas related to local history, natural history, and art, the complex consists of three distinct structures joined by a colonnade. The Federal **John Parker Hale House,** (1813) is the former home of an active abolitionist, U.S. senator, and minister to Spain; it became the core of the insitute when acquired in 1915. Altered slightly to accommodate the museum's historical and decorative arts collections, the house retains its original woodwork, staircases, and paneled shut-

ters. The 1818 Federal-style **Woodman House** is a three-story brick affair with a hipped roof similar to the Hale House; it houses the institute's natural history collections. The **Damme Garrison** (c. 1675) is a one-story wooden structure originally erected on the Black River Road as protection against Indian attacks. The garrison was moved to its present location and a protective covering was constucted. It contains collections of household articles and clothing. NR. Open all year, Tu-Su 2-5. Free. 742-1038. While walking down Central Ave., stop to admire the **Religious Society of Friends Meeting House,** a two-story c. 1768 Quaker structure with characteristic twin doors. John Greenleaf Whittier, the famous poet, was a frequent visitor here.

WILLIAM HALE HOUSE, 5 Hale St., 1806. The finest Federal-style dwelling constructed in Dover, it is symbolic of the town's mercantile prosperity at its peak. The three-story frame clapboard structure is one of the few dwellings that can definitely be attributed to the noted New England architect, Bradbury Johnson. The interior has been altered somewhat, but retains its unusual stairway which curves along the central hallway. Currently owned by St. Thomas's Episcopal Church. NR.

Durham

DURHAM HISTORIC DISTRICT, vicinity of Main St. and Newmarket Rd., 17th-19th centuries. This district of tree-shaded streets contains approximately 35 significant buildings that are representative of the town's growth from its orgins in the early 17th century to the height of its prosperity as a shipbuilding and trading center in the 1830s. One notable building in the district is the **Frost House** on Newmarket Rd. (c. 1649, 1680). The elaborate frame house bears little resemblance to the original primitive garrison house built by Valentine Hill, the Boston merchant whose deeded land eventually became the town of Durham. The **Sullivan House** at 23 Newmarket Rd. (c. 1740), was the home of Gen. John Sullivan, who distinguished himself by taking part in the seizure of powder from the British at Fort William and Mary, thereby becoming one of the first Americans to actively rebel against British rule. A much later structure, the **Durham Town Hall** (c. 1825) on Old Landing Rd., dates from the town's days as a prosperous commercial center. The two-story structure currently houses the Durham Historical Association Museum. Though closed temporarily, the museum usually exhibits memorabilia related to the town's history. 868-5560.

Franklin

DANIEL WEBSTER BIRTHPLACE, off NH 127, 1780. The small, two-room frame farmhouse in which one of the nation's most distinguished statesmen and orators was born and spent his boyhood was restored in 1913. The building contains numerous antique furnishings of the period 1782-1852. Operated by the state Division of Parks, Memorial Day-June 15, Sa and Su 9-6; June 16-Labor Day, W-Su 9-6.

Henniker vicinity

OCEAN BORN MARY HOUSE, 1 mi S on US 202, 1776-86. The imposing quality and overall form and elevation of the house resemble the more sophisticated Portsmouth residences. Legend tells the story of a young immigrant couple on their way across the Atlantic from Ireland in 1720. When their ship was overcome by

pirates at sea, the young wife promised to name her young daughter "Mary" after the wife of one of the pirates—in return for their safety, of course. The pirate also asked that on the young girl's wedding day she wear a particular piece of brocaded silk. She did so, and Ocean Born Mary lived to be ninety-four and is buried locally in Henniker.

Merrimack County

COVERED BRIDGES: **Bement Covered Bridge,** Center Rd., Bradford, 1854; **Hopkinton Railroad Bridge,** E. of NH 103, Hopkinton, 1849. This double span over the Contoocock River remains the oldest covered railroad bridge in the U.S. **Dalton Covered Bridge,** Joppa Rd., Warner, 1853; **Waterloo Covered Bridge,** Newmarket Rd., Waterloo, 1859-60.

New London

NEW LONDON HISTORICAL SOCIETY, Little Sunapee Rd., This local historical society maintains an outdoor museum complex consisting of the 1820 Scytheville house; 1800 Griffin barn; 1820 blacksmith shop, 1830 country store, schoolhouse, carriage house, and corn crib. July-Aug, W and Su 2-4, and by appointment. Free.

Sullivan County

COVERED BRIDGES: **Cornish-Windsor Covered Bridge,** W of Cornish City, 1866. The 450-foot double span remains the longest wooden covered bridge in the U.S.

Cold River Bridge, (McDermott Bridge), off McDermott Rd., Langdon vicinity, 1869; **Corbin Covered Bridge,** off NH 10, Newport vicinity, 1845-65.

Northern New Hampshire

Bath

BATH COVERED BRIDGE, off US 302 and NH 10, 1832. The fifth covered bridge to span the Ammonoosuc River on this spot, it's a favorite among photographers and painters. Records indicate it to be the oldest such structure in a state with an abundance of these so-called "kissing bridges." NR.

Berlin

ST. ANNE'S CATHOLIC CHURCH, 58 Church St., 1900. Monumental in scale, this lovely brick edifice dominates the skyline of the French-Canadian mill town. Highlighting the interior are oak pews with fine Victorian detailing and a huge pipe organ built by Cassavantes, a famous maker of these musical wonders. NR. Two other churches should also be included in any stroll through Berlin:

CONGREGATIONAL CHURCH, 921 Main St., 1882. The first church built in Berlin, its elaborate stick work and decorative use of shingles make this a prime example of eclectic Victorian architecture. Despite its period flare, the use of stained glass remains simple, reflecting well the attitude of the simple Protestant but dignified church which is so typical in New England. NR.

HOLY RESURRECTION ORTHODOX CHURCH, Petrograd St., 1915. The onion domes and Eastern European decorations make this Russian Orthodox edifice an exciting and unique site in what is a traditional New England town. Russian icons and murals adorn the interior. NR.

Bretton Woods

MOUNT WASHINGTON HOTEL, 1902. Since its opening, this most luxurious of New Hampshire's mountain resorts has remained the largest wooden building in all of New England. It was designed in the Spanish Renaissance style with white stucco walls and red roof. Still operated as a resort with extensive grounds and recreational facilities. NR. See Lodging and Dining for details regarding accommodations.

Center Sandwich

ELISHA MARSTON HOUSE, Maple St., c. 1850. Home of the Sandwich Historical Society, the building houses a fine collection of furniture, paintings, and farm implements. Displays of such crafts as spinning and weaving are featured. July-Aug, M-Sa 11-5; June and Sept, M-Sa 2-5. Free. 284.6269.

Canaan

CANAAN STREET HISTORIC DISTRICT, along Canaan St., 18th-19th centuries. The outline of the district as it exists today took form after 1800 when the area became a trading and stagecoach center along the old Grafton Turnpike, which ran from Andover through Canaan to Hanover and Lyme. The **Canaan Town Hall** (1796) dates even earlier and is the oldest public building in the district, originally serving as a meeting house. Built in the Federal style, its white clapboard exterior is distinguished by a tower entrance and an eight-sided cupola. Diagonally across the street is the **Canaan Town Library and Museum**, (1839), a later Federal structure with double open porches across the facade. At the north end of the street, the pure Gothic Revival **Old North Church** (1828) is remarkably well preserved. Also in this area is the **Main Hall** (1831) of Canaan College. This Greek Revival building served earlier as a tavern stop on the old stagecoach route; later in the century it functioned as an inn when Canaan was popular as a summer resort. The historically-minded can be thankful that the railroads decided to pass by this small town; the result is a well-preserved 19th-century community with few modern intrusions. NR.

Enfield

ENFIELD SHAKER HISTORIC DISTRICT, NH 4A, 1793-1929. Thirteen Shaker buildings survive from this self-sufficient community which once included 350 members and 3,000 acres. Until the 1840s a devout band of believers produced large quantities of textiles. They also initiated the practice of packaging seeds which was later adopted by other Shaker communities. The village is distinguished as the home of architect Moses Johnson, who designed numerous Shaker meeting houses throughout New England. The huge granite **Church Family Dwelling House** (1837) is the largest Shaker structure in existence. The last seven believers sold the property to the LaSalette Fathers (who still maintain the thirteen remaining buildings), and moved to Canterbury in 1923. NR. Mem Day-Labor Day, daily 9-4:30; Sept-June, Sa & Su 9-4:30. Walking tour and slide series. Free. 632-4301.

In Enfield proper is the **Lockehaven Schoolhouse Museum**, on S. Main St., which preserves an 1864 schoolhouse and features interesting exhibits on New England education in the 19th century. June 14-Oct 4, Su 2-5. Free.

Franconia

ROBERT FROST PLACE, Ridge Rd., 1830-1840. One-time home of the quintessential New England poet, the unspoiled locale where Frost penned many of the poems in his Pulitzer Prize-winning fourth book. Unlike the Frost farm in Derry, which features an audio-visual display, this simple frame house and its quiet surroundings provide the visitor with a less commercial interpretation of the Frost mystique. Memorial Day-June and Sept-Oct, Sa-Su 1-5; July-Aug, Tu-Su 1-5. $1.50 adults, 75¢ children. 823-5510.

Hanover

DARTMOUTH COLLEGE, Main and Wheelock Sts., 1769. Established four years after the arrival of the first settlers, "for the instruction of the Youth of the Indian tribes . . . and others," this picturesque liberal arts college has dominated the sleepy town ever since. The college remained fairly small until the late 19th century, and the white brick buildings along Old Dartmouth Row stand as a reminder of the college's days as a struggling institution. The Georgian **Dartmouth Hall,** built in 1791, is surmounted by a square tower with an open belfry. The building was destroyed by fire in 1904; a fireproof replica now stands in its place. Also on the Row is the 1829 **Wentworth Hall.** A fine grouping of Georgian Colonial Revival structures which reflect the school's rapid expansion at the turn of the century borders the tree-shaded green to the west. To the north of the green is the conspicuous white spire of the **Baker Memorial Library,** a gift in 1926-28 of a New York banker as a memorial to his uncle (class of 1859). The building suggests Independence Hall in design, and the bells in its graceful tower still ring out the changing of classes. More than one million volumes and notable frescoes by the Mexican artist Jose Clemente Orozco are housed within this stately building which harmonizes well with Old Dartmouth Row. The library is open M-F 9-5; Sa 11-4; Su 2-5 during the academic year. Tours of the campus leave from the information booth beside the green during the summer. 646-2255.

Lancaster

WILDER-HOLTEN HOUSE, 226 Main St., 1780. This was the first two-story dwelling in Coos County; legend recalls its days as a stop on the underground railroad. Constructed foursquare and sturdy with planes and nails forged on the site, it is now operated as a museum by the Lancaster Historical Society and features pewter, lustreware, and other antiques and memorabilia related to the history of Lancaster. NR. House tours during July and Aug. 50¢ adults, 25¢ children.

North Conway

CONWAY SCENIC RAILROAD, NH 16 and US 302. The restored depot was once the terminus for ski trains from Boston. An excellent example of Victorian railroad architecture, the station serves as the focal point of the scenic railroad operation which includes a one-hour train ride in antique coaches. NR. Departures: 11 am, 1 pm, 2:30 pm, and 4 pm; Sunset Special leaves 7 pm on summer evenings. $3.50 adults, $1.75 children. 356-5251. 🚻

Orford

ORFORD STREET HISTORIC DISTRICT, NH 10, late 18th-early 19th centuries. Washington Irving, after a visit to Orford, wrote: "In all my travels in this country and Europe, I have seen no village more beautiful. It is a charming place. Nature has done her utmost here." Indeed, the district's natural splendor owes much to the famed mall, described in the *Boston Evening Traveller* as, ". . . level as a house floor, straight as a line, and skirted with trees on both sides." Set back from the road with its row of overhanging branches

Wheeler House, Orford St. Historic District

are seven houses built over a period of time from 1773 to 1839. These houses extend on both sides of Orford Street for a half mile, and while the district would be incomplete without even one of these architectural gems, two deserve special mention: The **Samuel Morey House** (1773), located in the middle of the row and begun by Orford's first minister, was the only house along the way for many years. The house was bought by Samuel Morey in 1799. With the money he obtained from the patent rights to the first internal combustion engine, Morey was able to construct a handsome addition. The **Wheeler House,** built between 1814 and 1816, is significant as the only Orford residence reputed to have been designed by a professional architect — probably Asher Benjamin, a student of the Boston-based Charles Bulfinch. This Federal-style landmark features a low-pitched roof topped by a handsome balustrade and is one of the most often photographed of the Orford houses. NR. While the houses along Orford St. are private and the interiors inaccessible, a drive or stroll through the tree-shaded mall is recommended.

Wolfeboro

LIBBY MUSEUM, NH 109 Indian relics, local history, maps, and country artifacts bring back the fascinating history and quaint charm of New England life during the 18th and 19th centuries. Late June-Aug, Tu-Su 10-5. $1 adults, 50¢ children. 569-1035.

While in Wolfeboro stop by the 1778 **Clark House** and the adjacent 1860 **Schoolhouse** on S. Main St. Handmade quilts are on display and special demonstrations are often featured on weekends during July and August in the refurnished interior of the Clark House. Operated by the Wolfeboro Historical Society. June 30-Labor Day. $1 adults, 50¢ children. 569-3900.

Lodging and Dining

WHILE New Hampshire is most often associated with its magnificent resort hotels in the White Mountains, the state is also dotted with small, secluded inns with fewer than ten rooms, each inn reminiscent of the traditional New England setting found in the sister state of Vermont.

The coming of the railroads in the late 1800s signaled a boom for tourism in the state, and many of the larger resorts and clubs thrived during this period. Families arrived by the trainload during the hot summer months, seeking the coolness of the mountains. Many of the large establishments, however, barely survived on their earnings from just one season of tourism in the pre-skiing past. Today, carloads of skiers flock to New Hampshire's slopes in winter, and once again country hotels and inns near the slopes are thriving. Here in both historic hotels and rustic farmhouses converted into inns, travelers can enjoy all the seasons and the many historical sites and scenes which border nearly every New Hampshire lane.

Bretton Woods

MOUNT WASHINGTON HOTEL 03575. (800) 258-0330 in the Northeast or (603) 278-1000. (See previous Bretton Woods listing for more detailed information.) 300 working rooms. MAP, expensive. Formal dining room seats 300. AE, D, CB, M, V. Open May 15-Oct. 31. Restaurant open year-round. ¶

Bridgewater

PASQUANEY INN, NH 3A, 03222. (603) 744-2712. Marge & Roy Zimmer. Built in 1840, this old New England inn located in the picturesque lake region also houses an extensive collection of antiques. Rooms: 28 summer, 18 winter. MAP, EP, moderate. M, V, PC. Open May-Oct. 15, Nov.-Mar. 31. ¶

Conway

THE DARBY FIELD INN, Bald Hill, 03818. (603) 447-2181. H. Marc & Marily Donaldson. Built as a farmhouse in the early 1800s; converted to a guest lodge in the 1940s. Borders the White Mountains where guests can hike, ski, or just relax and enjoy the view. 11 rooms. MAP, expensive. AE, M, V, PC. Open year-round. ¶

Eaton Center

PALMER HOUSE INN, NH 53 at Crystal Lake (P.O. Box 12), 03832. (603) 447-2120. Frank & Mary Gospodarek. Built securely into the side of a hill, the inn dates back to 1884 when summer guests arrived by train and stayed for the season. Today's guests still enjoy the antique furnishings, spacious rooms, and fine country cooking. 4 rooms. MAP, moderate. PC. Bed and breakfast. Open year-round. ¶

Fitzwilliam

FITZWILLIAM INN, NH 119, 03447. (603) 585-9000. Barbara & Charles Wallace. Since 1796 this old-fashioned inn has been serving guests in this forgotten corner of the state. Enjoy the Sunday evening concerts in winter or a summer stroll through local antique shops. 21 rooms. EP, inexpensive. AE, M, V, PC. Pets welcome. Open year-round.

Olive Metcalf

Francestown

THE INN AT CROTCHED MOUNTAIN, 03043. (603) 588-6840. John & Rose Perry. This 150-year-old colonial house offers a spectacular view of the valley, with great fishing and skiing nearby. EP, moderate. Pets allowed. Closed in early Nov. ¶

TORY PINES RESORT, NH 47, 03043. (603) 588-6352. Dick Tremblay & Jack Sullivan. Georgian colonial built in 1799. Dining rooms feature fireplaces; rooms are across the road in what was once an old barn. Golf course nearby. MAP, EP, moderate. AE, D, CB, M, V, PC. Open daily year-round.

Franconia

FRANCONIA INN, 03580. (603) 823-5542. Robert, Richard, & Alec Morris. The present inn was built following a disastrous fire in 1934 which destroyed the McKenzie farm, known for generations as a gracious "farm resort." 29 rooms. MAP, EP, expensive. AE, M, V. Open May-Oct. and Dec.-Mar. ¶

THE HORSE & HOUND INN, Wells Rd., 03580. (603) 823-5501. Sybil & Bob Carey. This pre-1830 farmhouse was converted and added to extensively in 1945. The inn features bright, airy rooms—with fresh fruit set out to welcome guests. Chamber music played at dinner. 7 rooms. EP, expensive. PC. Open year-round exc. mid-Apr.-mid-May.

Hancock

THE JOHN HANCOCK INN, 03449. (603) 525-3318. Glynn & Pat Wells. An inn since 1789, this beautifully weathered colonial hostelry is the epitome of bucolic hospitality. It is located in a town that has barely changed in two centuries. 10 rooms. EP, moderate. Open year-round.

Henniker

COLBY HILL INN, Western Ave., 03242. (603) 428-3281. The Glover Family. The original inn dates to 1821. Once a working farm; 5 acres with old barns and sheds remain to offer a glimpse of old-time farm life. 27 rooms. MAP, expensive. AE, D, CB, M, V, PC. Package plans available. Open year-round. 🍴

Jackson

CHRISTMAS FARM INN, NH 16B, 03846. (603) 383-4313. William H. Zeliff, Jr. The original saltbox section is believed to have been built in 1778; the main building in 1786. This versatile building has served as a jail, a church, and a farmhouse before settling as an inn. 27 rooms. MAP, expensive. AE, D, CB, M, V, PC. Open year-round. 🍴

THORN HILL LODGE, Thorn Hill Rd., 03846. (603) 383-4242. Donald & Gail Hechtle. Built in 1895. The spacious Victorian living room affords a magnificent view of Mt. Washington. Chalets available. 12 rooms. MAP, moderate. AE, V, M. Restaurant open for breakfast and dinner. 🍴

WHITNEY'S VILLAGE INN, NH 16B, 03846. (603) 383-6886. Darrell Trapp. Serving guests since 1840, the inn features the first ski lift and snowmaking apparatus in North America. Whitney's combines the complete services of the best resort hotels with the intimacy of a quiet country inn. 42 rooms. MAP, EP, expensive. AE, M, V, PC. 🍴

Kingston

KINGSTON 1686 HOUSE, Main St., 03848. (603) 642-3637. Peter Speliotis. Main house built in 1686 is the oldest in town. This is the place to dine if you're looking for the relaxed pleasures of a historic spot. The large linden tree outside was planted in 1776 by Josiah Barlett, signer of the Declaration of Independence. Moderate. AE, D, CB, M, V, PC. Daily 5:30-10. Closed M.

Laconia

HICKORY STICK FARM, RFD #2, 03246. (603) 524-3333. Scott & Mary Roeder. The original set of farm buildings dates back to colonial times. Don't forget to sample the roast duckling, famous throughout New England. Moderate. AE, M, V. Open Memorial Day-Columbus Day. Dinners 5-9, Su 12-9.

Lyme

THE LYME INN, on the Common, 03768. (603) 795-2222. Fred & Judy Siemons. Constructed in 1809. Operated as a hotel and a tavern until its conversion to an inn in 1938. Valuable antiques throughout make every room different from the other. The innkeepers should be blessed for banning TVs from the charming period rooms. 15 rooms. Bed and breakfast. Expensive. Open year-round.

New London

NEW LONDON INN, Main St., 03257. (603) 526-2791. George Adame. Built in 1793. The inn's decor retains the flavor of the colonial era. A favorite stopover for summer boaters, winter skiers, and fall foliage admirers. 20 rooms. EP, moderate. M, V, PC. Open year-round. Ⓨ

North Conway

THE HOMESTEAD RESTAURANT, S. Main St., 03860. (603) 356-9500. Conrad & Cynthia Briggs. Occupies a quaint red Cape dating to 1793. Traditional New England menu includes chowder and Indian pudding. Moderate/expensive. AE, M, V. Special half-portion rates. Daily 4:30-10.

STONEHURST MANOR, NH 16, 03860. (603) 356-3113. Peter Rattay. This turn-of-the-century mansion, set back among stately pines, features oak, wicker, and stained glass for those who prefer their New England in the Victorian mode rather than in the traditional Colonial. Accommodations and meals. EP, MAP, expensive. AE, M, V. Open year-round. Ⓨ

North Sutton

FOLLANSBEE INN, P.O. Box 92, 03260. (603) 927-4221. Larry & Joan Wadman. Once a farmhouse, this inn on Lake Kezar typifies the charm of the New Hampshire lake country. Good food, beautiful rooms, and a New England church next door. In a word—lovely. 23 rooms. MAP, moderate. M, V, PC. Open year-round. Ⓨ

Northwood

THE RESORT AT LAKE SHORE FARM, Jenness Pond Rd., 03261. (603) 942-5921. Ellis & Eloise Ring. 150 acres surround this old farm complex built in 1848. Scenic lake view. 28 rooms. AP, expensive. PC. Open all year. Ⓨ

Portsmouth

WENTWORTH-BY-THE-SEA, Box 597, 03801. (603) 436-3100. Popular resort hotel established in 1873. 3 stories with 245 rooms; cottages also available. MAP, expensive. AE, MC, V. Closed late Oct.-early May. ⊓

Shelburne

PHILBROOK FARM INN, North Rd., 03581. (603) 466-3831. Nancy Philbrook & Constance P. Leger. Original farmhouse dates to 1834; addition added in 1861 when the Philbrooks welcomed their first guests to the serenity of the White Mountains. 19 rooms. MAP, expensive. PC. Pets welcome in cottages. Open Dec. 26-Mar. 31, May 1-Oct. 31.

Snowville

SNOWVILLAGE INN, 03849. (603) 447-2818. Patrick & Ginger Blymyer. A huge porch surrounds this c. 1916 house and offers a magnificent view of the mountains. 14 rooms. MAP, EP (during week), expensive. AE, D, CB, M, V, PC. Closed Apr.-May.

Sunapee

DEXTER'S INN, Stagecoach Rd., (Box M), 03782. (603) 763-5571. Frank & Shirley Simpson. Main house dates to 1801. The Simpsons boast with good cause that their inn is like a comfortable home in which guests mingle with the family and their pets, including a 500-pound pig named Gracie. A wonderful, friendly, informal place. 17 rooms. MAP, expensive. PC. Open mid-May-foliage season.

Whitefield

PLAYHOUSE INN, US 3, 03598. (603) 837-2527. Noel & Lucienne Laean. 1890s home remodeled as an inn in 1940. Rousing cabaret entertainment and summerstock theater offered in remodeled barn. 12 rooms. MAP, EP, inexpensive. M, V, PC with I.D. Open mid-May-Oct. ⊓

SPALDING INN CLUB, Mountain View Rd., 03598. Ted Spalding. Originally a railroad hotel on the western slope of the White Mountains, this superb resort has managed to retain in spirit and in form the genteel family vacations that were enjoyed generations ago. The emphasis is on the outdoors and on graceful dining. A delightful change from almost anything you can find today. 70 rooms; cottages available. AP, expensive. AE, M, V, PC. Open daily late May-late Oct. ⊓

6. MAINE

LONG before Maine's rugged shores and inland waterways were explored by French and English traders in the 16th and 17th centuries, early Indian tribes had set a pattern of movement through the area which is, to some degree, followed by travelers to this day. The tribes spent their winters hunting in the rugged, mountainous interior and their summers along the Atlantic coast where they found the climate appealing and the fishing plentiful. Today's visitor is attracted to the populous shore areas during balmy weather, and hunting, fresh-water fishing, and skiing beckon as the seasons turn cold.

Maine's natural resources virtually determined its commercial development. The fishing industry is still a prime economic factor along the coast. The vast forests of the interior provided an abundance of lumber for a thriving shipbuilding industry and also made possible the prosperity evident in the graceful mansions of the State's logging and shipbuilding entrepreneurs.

Other industries were also heavily dependent on the state's natural resources, and today their influence on Maine's development comes down to us in the preservation of such oddities as the galamander in Vinalhaven, an enormous wagon once used to transport giant slabs of granite from the quarries.

The beauty of both coastal and inland Maine has been a stimulus for some of America's outstanding artists and writers. Henry Wadsworth Longfellow grew up in Portland; Sarah Orne Jewett in South Berwick. Harriet Beecher Stowe wrote her classic *Uncle Tom's Cabin* while residing in Brunswick. Painter Winslow Homer immortalized his state's rocky shores and sturdy fishermen, creating much of his most famous work in a studio at Prout's Neck.

Members of various religious groups have contributed enormously to the state's rich history and to its lasting architectural treasures. An early Shaker settlement in New Gloucester — a complex of exquisitely simple, beautiful buildings — still prospers. Then there are the bold Catholic landmarks of the Acadians of Madawaska, and, of course, the traditional white-steepled churches that immediately suggest "New England" to the popular imagination.

Maine's geography has profoundly affected the course of her political and international relations. The long coastline and many rivers invited attack by the French and British, while the northern border was the subject of interminable disputes. Evidence of the fortifications built for defense in both areas remains: Portland's Fort Gorges, Augusta's Fort Western, and the inland Fort Knox are only a few examples, each with a fascinating story to tell.

A different form of protection is afforded by the historic lighthouses which dot the coastline. Most of the earliest ones, such as Portland Head Light, still serve as navigational aids.

The guide to Maine which follows has been divided into four geographic regions, chosen both for the traveler's convenience and for the variety of historic diversions each offers. Southern, Central, and the Northeast Coast include a wealth of maritime attractions. The farther north one travels, the less populous and more rugged the country becomes. The Northern Interior, by far the largest area, includes Bangor — the state capital and still an active lumbering center — and the breathtaking scenery of Maine's north woods, where the historic settlements are far apart and half the joy of discovery is in the journey itself.

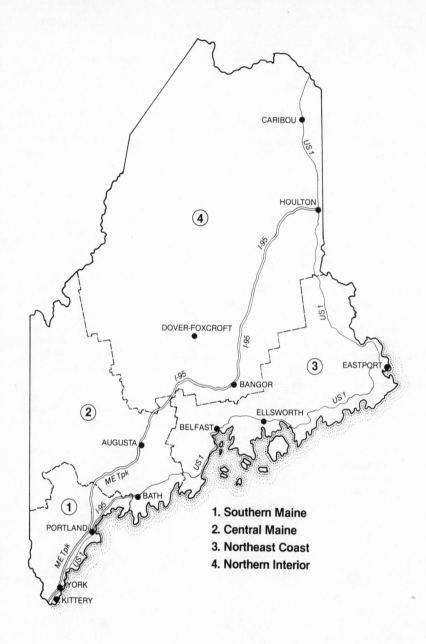

1. Southern Maine
2. Central Maine
3. Northeast Coast
4. Northern Interior

Southern Maine

Brunswick

BOWDOIN COLLEGE, 1802. Nathaniel Hawthorne, Henry Wadsworth Longfellow, and Franklin Pierce are among the famous alumni of Bowdoin, one of the oldest colleges in the nation, whose attractive campus dominates the town of Brunswick. In 1794 the Commonwealth of Massachusetts, of which Maine was then a part, granted a charter for the school's establishment, and it opened in 1802 upon comple-

tion of its first building **Massachusetts Hall.** The design of this simple three-story brick landmark is echoed in that of **Winthrop Hall,** built in 1822. Both buildings are austere, but handsomely proportioned. Another early campus building is **Maine Hall,** originally completed in 1808, which twice burned and was rebuilt, most recently in 1836. This four-story brick dormitory with a pedimented pavilion is the most lavish in design of the early campus buildings. Part of the Bowdoin campus is in the **Federal Street Historic District,** roughly bounded by Mason, Maine, College and Federal Streets, whose buildings date from the late 18th to early 20th centuries. As you walk along the tree-lined streets, you'll pass the work of many famous 19th-century architects, including Richard Upjohn, whose **Bowdoin College Chapel** was completed in 1855. This handsome, formidable granite building with twin square towers is designed in the Romanesque style. The lavish interior, with richly-frescoed walls and ceiling, is in surprising contrast to the simplicity of the

facade. Designs by John Calvin Stevens and the firm of McKim, Mead and White are also to be found within the district, with examples of many of the most popular styles of the period, including the Shingle-Style **Psi Upsilon Fraternity House,** the Italianate Bowdoin College **President's House,** and the Federal-style **Professor Parker Cleaveland House.** NR. Two museums are also located at Bowdoin:

Museum of Art, Walker Art Building, 1894. A broad collection of Colonial and Federal portraits and many works by Maine's own Winslow Homer are featured in this dignified, well proportioned red brick landmark by Charles McKim. Summer Tu-F 10-5 and 7-8:30, Sa 10-5, Su 2-4; winter Tu-F 10-4, Sa 10-5, Su 2-5. Free.

Peary-MacMillan Arctic Museum, Hubbard Hall. Here are displays of polar artifacts and equipment relating to the arctic explorations of Admiral Robert Peary and his chief assistant, Admiral Donald MacMillan, both Bowdoin alumni. (Hours and admission same as Museum of Art.) For more information about Bowdoin, call 725-8731.

PEJEPSCOT HISTORICAL MUSEUM, 11 Lincoln St., 1857. Housed in the two-story brick landmark once owned by Captain George McManus, a prominent Brunswick master mariner, the museum collection includes a fine display of regional memorabilia and Indian artifacts. The building itself is an excellent example of the Greek Revival-Italianate transitional style, and features a wide, two-story front balcony. NR. Open all year, M-F 1-5. Donations accepted. 729-4622.

HARRIET BEECHER STOWE HOUSE, 63 Federal St., 1804. In this two-story white frame building Mrs. Stowe wrote her indictment of slavery, *Uncle Tom's Cabin,* in 1851-52. It is said that her inspiration for the book came while at services in the **First Parish Church** on nearby

Maine St. (1846, NR), and a pew is so marked. The house, now an inn with public restaurant, is full of nautical memorabilia, and Mrs. Stowe's study remains intact. See listing under inns for information about accommodations. NR, NHL. Open all year. 725-5543.

Cape Elizabeth

PORTLAND HEADLIGHT, Portland Head (off Shore Rd.), 1790. One of only four lighthouses in existence whose construction was authorized by President Washington, the Portland light has never been rebuilt. Local masons constructed the 72-foot tower of random stone rubble. The present keepers' quarters, a frame structure finished in clapboards and shingles (1891), replaced the original 1816 building. Operated by the Federal Government. NR.

TWO LIGHTS, off ME 77, 1874. Located in the 40-acre Two Lights State Park, these twin cast-iron towers illustrate the use of a double-light system as an aid in determining distance from shore. Operated by the Federal Government. NR. Apr 15-Nov. Small fee.

Harpswell vicinity

EAGLE ISLAND, Casco Bay, 1904. Ex-

Two Lights

plorer Robert E. Peary purchased this small, rugged island in 1880, naming it for the whaling ship which first took him to the Arctic, and later built a Shingle-Style cottage here to serve as his summer home. Eagle Island was the base for planning the 1909 expedition during which he reached

Portland Headlight

the North Pole. Operated by the state. NR. June 20-Labor Day, daily 10-6. Free.

HARPSWELL MEETING HOUSE, ME 123, 1757. Used as both a church and town meeting hall until 1844, and since then as Harpswell's meeting place, this simple, clapboarded, two-story frame landmark is virtually unaltered, and a superb example of the New England Colonial church, with its three-sided second floor galleries, rounded arched windows, and box pews. Municipal. NR, NHL. July-Aug, daily 2-4. Free.

While in the area, you might also enjoy a look at **Merriconegan Farm,** probably the most extensive and impressive example of an extended building design extant today. In an excellent state of preservation, it comprises two complete houses with residential ells, sheds, and two large barns, one at either end. The entire complex is gradually assembled and connected between the early 1830s and 1897. Magnificently located on a rise overlooking Harpswell Bay, it is easily visible from ME 123. Privately owned. NR. Also on ME 123 is the **Elijah Kellogg Church,** a simple frame building of interest primarily because of its association with the noted clergyman and children's book author (1843). NR.

Kennebunk

BRICK STORE MUSEUM, 117 Main St., 1825. William Lord's modest two-story brick building served as a general store,

but there is little in the scale or exterior design which marks it as a commercial structure. Its Federal-style railing masks the gable roof beneath which, in the attic, a hoist wheel used to load merchandise remains in place. Permanent exhibits relate to Colonial times, including extensive marine displays, furniture, carriages and portraits. NR. Open all year, Tu-Sa 10-4:30. Donations accepted. 985-4802.

The museum operates the **Taylor-Barry House** at 24 Summer St., a Federal-style former sea captain's home dating from 1803, of interest for its period furnishings and stenciled hallway. Open June 15-Oct 15, Tu-Th 1-4. $1 adults, 50¢ children. 985-3129.

KENNEBUNK HISTORIC DISTRICT, both sides of ME 35 from the Kennebunk River to US 1, and adjacent streets, 18th-19th centuries. Stately trees line the streets of this predominantly residential area, with its churches and homes designed in a wide vareity of architectural styles, including Federal, Queen Anne, and Greek Revival. Perhaps the most unusual is the **Wedding Cake House** (on ME 35), a white frame building of the late-Federal style completed in 1826, then completely covered with elaborate Gothic scrollwork in 1855. The house and its adjacent barn are private, so may be viewed from the ex-

First Parish Church

terior only. A stroll through the district illustrates the way of life of the shipbuilders and craftsmen who settled in the area. **The First Parish Church** (1773) at Main St. and Portland Rd. is a simple, rectangular two-story frame building with an imposing tower at its front gable end which was added c. 1838. Its square belfry contains a bell cast by Paul Revere and Sons. Open Thursdays during the summer months. 985-3700.

Kennebunkport

KENNEBUNKPORT HISTORIC DISTRICT, bounded by South, Maine, North and Lock Sts. and the Kennebunkport River, c. 1745-20th century. This area reflects the development of the town as an important seaport and its metamorphosis into a thriving summer resort in the late 1800s. Predominantly of frame or brick construction, the buildings reflect the popularity of 19th-century neo-classical design. Notable buildings include the **Captain Lord Mansion** (described following) and the **South Congregational Church** (1824) whose tower is remarkably similar to that of the First Parish Church in Kennebunk, described previously. The facade of the South Congregational is much more elaborate, however, as evidenced by its pointed arches and Roman Doric pedimented portico added in 1912. A row of carriage sheds with arched openings still stands at the right of the church, a surviving example of an early form of parking facility which was a common adjunct to rural and village churches. NR.

KENNEBUNKPORT HISTORICAL SOCIETY MUSEUM, North St., c. 1900. Housed in the former **Town House School,** a restored rural building, the museum exhibits concentrate on local history and genealogy. The adjacent **Clark Building** houses marine artifacts and displays. Open July-Aug, Tu-Th 1-4, Sa 10-12; June and Sept, Tu 1-4; and by appointment. Free. 967-2028.

CAPTAIN LORD MANSION, Pleasant St., 1812. Built for Nathaniel Lord, shipbuilder and seafarer, this 15-room mansion, designed in the Federal style with an octagonal cupola and large rear ell (added in 1895), still retains much of its original furnishings and wall coverings. The landmark is now an inn (see listing under inns for information about accommodations), but it is open for public tours. NR. Memorial Day-Labor Day, W-Sa 3:00 sharp. $2.50 adults, $1 children. 967-3141.

SEASHORE TROLLEY MUSEUM, Log Cabin Rd. Said to have one of the most comprehensive collections of electric streetcars in the world, the museum features more than 100 different vehicles, including buses, mail cars, locomotives, and freight cars. Several are available for brief rides. New England Electric Railway Historical Society. NR. Summer, daily 10-6; June, Sept and Oct, Sa-Su 12-5. $3.25 adults, $1.75 children. 967-2712. 🚹

Kittery Point

FORT McCLARY, Kittery Point Rd. off ME 103, 1809. The original fortification on this site dates from the early 18th century and was variously called Pepperrell's Fort and Fort William (after Sir William Pepperrell). It was named for a Major McClary, who died at Bunker Hill, after the Revolutionary War. Remains of a rifleman's house, a barracks, and a powder magazine are visible inside the walls, but the fort's most notable feature is its six-sided blockhouse with a granite first story topped by an overhanging wooden second story. State park. NR. Open Memorial Day-Oct 15, daily 10-6.

On nearby Pepperrell Road (ME 103) are a number of noteworthy early homes with interesting historical connections. All are on the National Register, but unfortunately only one is currently open to the public. Visible from the road, however, and well worth viewing, are: **William Dean Howells House** (c. 1870), which served as the summer home of the popular author and *Atlantic* editor from 1902 until his death in 1920 (owned by Harvard University); **Lady Pepperrell House** (c. 1760), an imposing hip-roof mansion built by the widow of Sir William Pepperrell, commander of the Maine militia. Operated by SPNEA and open by appointment. (617)

227-3956. NHL. The **William Pepperrell House** (1682) is a 2½-story frame structure built by a successful English colonist and later owned by his son, a businessman and commandant, who was the only native-born American to be made an English baronet.

Naples

NAPLES HISTORICAL SOCIETY MUSEUM, Village Green, ME 302. The museum complex includes the main building, an early jail, and a bandstand. Its collection features local historical items and slide presentations on the Cumberland and Oxford Canal and Sebago-Long Lake steamboats, both of great importance to the development of commerce in the region. Open daily July-Aug, 10-5; May-June and Sept-Oct by appointment. Donations accepted. 693-6220. The nearby **Songo Lock** on the Cumberland and Oxford Canal, one mile off ME 114 south of Naples, was built in 1830 and restored in 1911. The canal connected Portland with Harrison at the head of Long Lake, allowing goods to be transported to and from remote sections of the state. It is still in use. NR. Open daily June 15-Labor Day.

New Gloucester

NEW GLOUCESTER HISTORIC DISTRICT, including both sides of ME 33 and 231, mid-18th-late-19th centuries. The boyhood home of William Pitt Fessenden, U.S. senator and Lincoln's Treasury secretary, is but one of a number of buildings which embellish a 19th-century farming community virtually unspoiled by modern intrusions. Most of the structures are frame, and a stroll will uncover a variety of delightful styles ranging from Colonial to Gothic Revival.

THE SHAKER MUSEUM, Sabbathday Lake, on ME 26, late 18th-19th centuries. The Shakers founded a community here in

Sabbathday Lake Meetinghouse

1783, and by 1850 their village contained more than 25 buildings, of which over half remain today. The majority are simple frame buildings of graceful proportion, and the complex as a whole is an outstanding example of early Shaker architecture. The three-story **Meeting House,** built in 1794 and virtually unaltered, was the heart of the community. The first floor was used solely for worship, the second partitioned for apartments and working space, and the third reserved for visitors from other Shaker societies. As the community grew, additional space was needed for living quarters, and in 1839 a **Ministry Shop** was erected next to the meeting house to provide privacy for the Ministry elders and eldresses. **The Trustees' Office and Dwelling** of 1816 has been remodeled several times, and a new **Dwelling** of brick, completed in 1884, dominates the land beside it, with five stories containing 48 bedrooms in the main house. An ell houses a kitchen and dining room, meeting room, and root cellar.

The Shaker custom dictated that the workshops, barns and other outbuildings be constructed in a row behind the dwelling and meeting house. Extant are the **Sisters' Shop,** actually a group of buildings completed between 1821 and 1910; the 1824 **Herb House,** the only one of its kind remaining in the United States, and the 1850 **Boys' Shop,** where boys who lived in the community slept, were schooled, and learned useful trades. Today it serves as the orientation and welcome center, and four of the second-floor rooms are open with displays of period furnishings. Several of the other buildings are open as well, with

collections including furniture, textiles, folk art, early American tools, farm implements — a wide variety of objects united in the simplicity, inventiveness and utility of their designs and in the unadorned beauty they convey to the viewer. Numerous exhibits demonstrate the simple and productive lifestyle of the Shaker community, whose modern-day members still live and work on the grounds. NR, NHL. Open May 30-Labor Day, Tu-Sa 10-4:30. $2.50 adults, $1. children. 926-4597.

Newfield

WILLOWBROOK AT NEWFIELD, Main St., 19th century. Plan to spend a leisurely visit at this museum village, whose restored buildings include an 1810 school house, the 1813 **William Durgin Homestead,** as well as reconstructions of shops of the period illustrating how business was conducted in the 1800s, from carpentry to printing, and banking to boat-building. More than 10,000 separate items are displayed. They range from carriages and sleighs to musical instruments, toys, and costumes. Privately owned. Open May 15-Sept 30, daily 10-5. $3.50 adults, $2 children. Group rates. 793-2784.

Portland

Years before Portland gained its present name in 1786, settlements variously called Machigonne, Casco and Falmouth were known to have existed here at separate times. The northerly isolation of the peninsula in those years made the town(s) vulnerable to attack, and several times an early community was leveled by Indians and/or the French, only to rise again through the perseverance of early residents. Portland's excellent harbor was an open invitation to enemy naval action, and during the Revolutionary War the community was severely damaged again — this time by British cannon. In spite of these setbacks, however, when Maine became a state in 1820, Portland was its largest and fastest growing town. This was due in large part to the town's flourishing mer-

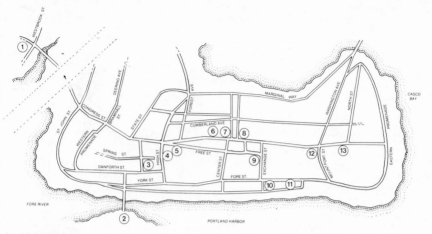

Portland   *Courtesy of the Greater Portland Chamber of Commerce*

1. Tate House, Stroudwater area
2. Portland Headlight
3. Victoria Mansion
4. McLellan-Sweat Mansion
5. Neal Dow Memorial
6. Longfellow House
7. Maine Historical Society

8. First Parish Church
9. Old Port Exchange
10. Mariner's Church
11. U. S. Customhouse
12. Eastern Cemetery
13. Portland Observatory

cantile and maritime trades. The development of railway transport later in the 19th century linked the city with the lumbering and farming industries inland, and one of the great commercial fleets of the time was available to ship goods to all parts of the world. Both by rail and by sea, Portland retained its links with other flourishing towns to the south, allowing an exchange of goods, services, and information which has contributed so much to the cultural richness found here today.

Because of this colorful history, Portland is undoubtedly the most eclectic and fascinating city in Maine, and its residents, with great pride in their heritage, have taken care to preserve or restore many of its finest buildings. The places of historic interest listed can only scratch the surface of the many to be found here, and it is recommended that the traveler plan to spend several days in the area in order to enjoy Portland to its

fullest. **Greater Portland Landmarks,** 165 State St., 774-5561, and the **Greater Portland Chamber of Commerce,** 142 Free St., 772-2811, offer brochures describing many of the buildings, and have maps with suggested walking tours of various areas. Greater Portland Landmarks offers both guided walking tours and bus tours which emphasize the city's past. Advance reservation is required.

An imposing structure visible across the harbor from the waterfront, but not accessible except by private boat, is **Fort**

Gorges. It was built as part of the defense of the city during the Civil War, but never garrisoned, as the development of superior naval vessels soon made it obsolete. Its irregular granite hexagonal form dominates Hog Island. NR.

CONGRESS STREET: The greatest concentration of historic sites and museums in Portland is found along this one, long street, which roughly bisects the downtown area. Following are some highlights:

Neal Dow Memorial, #714, 1829. A substantial late-Federal brick home owned by General Dow, the leading 19th-century proponent of the prohibition of alcohol. The house served as the center of the temperance movement during Dow's lifetime. Its owner was responsible for drafting the "Maine Law," making his state the first to prohibit alcohol, which became the model for similar legislation elsewhere. Operated by the Maine WCTU. NR, NHL. Open all year, M-Sa 11-4. Free. 773-7773.

Eastern Cemetery, Congress at Mountford St., 1668. Eastern was the first burial location in Portland. Called "Field of Ancient Graves" by early settlers, its more than 4,000 graves include those of prominent local religious, political, and business leaders, such as F.O.J. Smith, newspaper editor and U.S. representative, who was one of the state's most controversial 19th-century public figures. NR. Open all year.

First Parish Church, #425, 1826. Founded in 1674, and rebuilt twice during the 18th century on its original site, the present stone building is the oldest of its type in Maine. It was here that the state constitution was drafted. Artifacts on view trace Portland's history from the 17th century to the present. NR. Open June-Aug, Tu 12-3. Free.

Longfellow House (Wadsworth-Longfellow House), #487, 1786. The boyhood home of Henry Wadsworth Longfellow contains furnishings, records, and personal possessions of the family. Built by Longfellow's maternal grandfather (with a third story added in 1815), this was the first brick house constructed in Portland, with material brought from Philadelphia.

First Parish Church

Operated by the Maine Historical Society. NR, NHL. Open June-Sept, M-F 9:30-4:30. $2 adults, $1 children. Group rates. 772-1807. The **Maine Historical Society**'s collection is housed next door, at #485, in a simple Georgian Revival building (1907). Paintings, prints, photographs, glass, pottery and furnishings relating to both the local area and the state are on view. NR. Open all year, M-F 9-5. Free. 774-1822.

Portland Observatory, #138, 1807. Built as a signal tower and used as a watch tower during the War of 1812, the 82-foot tall frame, shingled structure commands an excellent view of Portland Harbor. The wives and sweethearts of Portland's sailors found it an unequaled vantage point from which to await the return of the ships. Municipal. NR. Open June-Labor Day, daily 10-8. 50¢ adults, 25¢ children. 773-5779 or 774-0637.

PORTLAND WATERFRONT, roughly bounded by Federal St. and Portland Harbor, and by Pearl and Cross Sts., 18th-20th centuries. The waterfront historic district includes a wide variety of buildings illustrating the commercial evolution of the city. A number of the historic structures are open to the public.

Mariner's Church, 368-74 Fore St., 1828. Built as a place of worship and education for Portland's seamen, the church now houses several shops and the Old Port Tavern. It is part of the Old Port Exchange, a recently restored group of 19th-century buildings between Exchange and Pearl Sts., which houses many interesting shops and restaurants.

U. S. Customhouse, 312 Fore St., 1872. An elaborate French Renaissance building, designed by Supervising Architect of the U.S. Treasury Alfred B. Mullett, it boasts

magnificent chandeliers, painted and gilded ceilings, carved woodwork and marble floors. Federal. NR. Open all year, M-F 8:30-5. Free. 780-3326.

SPRING STREET HISTORIC DISTRICT, bounded roughly by Pine and Congress Sts. on the NW, and Danforth St. on the SE, 19th century. Portland's booming maritime trade and the prosperity it fostered are nowhere better illustrated than by the comfortable homes which fill this district. The oldest of these is the **Daniel How House** (1799) at 23 Danforth St., a 2½-story brick landmark which combines elements of the Colonial and Federal periods, displays a low roof line and paired, large windows. Also noteworthy is the **Charles Q. Clapp House** at 97

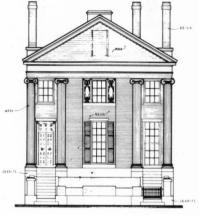

Spring St., designed in the Greek Revival style, a two-story brick home with pedimented front gable and tall Ionic columns on its side entrances. Clapp was an early real estate developer. **Park Street Row**, 88-114 Park St., completed in 1835, is the largest row house complex ever built in Maine, with fourteen attached single family units, each of brick with brownstone door frames, window sills, and lintels. An iron balcony railing runs the length of the row on the second of its four stories. None of the homes mentioned above is open to the public, but there are several intriguing buildings within the district which may be visited:

McLellan-Sweat Mansion, 111 High St., 1800. The Portland Museum of Art, Maine's oldest public museum, is housed in this three-story brick landmark and in an adjacent, later wing. Basically Federal style, the house is highlighted by a semicircular entrance portico with fluted Doric pillars, and by an unusual flying staircase within. The museum collection includes American painting and decorative arts, early glass, and the mansion's period furnishings. NR, NHL. Open all year, Tu-Sa 10-5, Su 2-5. Mansion: $1 adults, 50¢ children. Museum: free. 775-6148.

Victoria Mansion, (Morse-Libby Mansion), 109 Danforth St., 1859. R. S. Morse, a New Orleans hotel owner who hailed from Maine, built this elaborate, two-story Italianate brownstone as a summer home, and eventually returned to live here permanently. Period furnishings, including many original to the house, may be seen along with elegant marble fireplaces, French carpets, and mahogany, rosewood and chestnut paneling. Operated by the Victorian Society of Maine Women. NR, NHL. Open mid-June-Labor Day, Tu-Sa 10-4. $1.50 adults. 772-4841.

STROUDWATER HISTORIC DISTRICT, western bank of the Fore River, 1727-1860s. This primarily 19th-century village district includes the local burial ground and sites of the former landing, mills, tanneries, and shipyards which supported the economy of the region. A section of the Cumberland and Oxford Canal is in the district. Of special note is the **Tate House,** 1270 Westbrook St., 1755. George Tate, a senior agent to the British

Royal Navy, built this three-story Georgian home with feathered clapboarding and indented gambrel roof, and occupied it until 1794. Much of the original exterior material remains, and the interior is enhanced by fine woodwork and hardware. Period furnishings and artifacts are on display. Operated by the Society of Colonial Dames. NR, NHL. Open July 1-Sept 15, Tu-Sa 11-5, Su 1:30-5, and by appointment in June and from Sept 15-Oct 15. $1.50 adults, 50¢ children. 772-2023.

Saco

DYER-YORK INSTITUTE MUSEUM, 375 Main St. Several rooms in this building have been decorated and furnished to reflect living quarters of the past, including a Colonial kitchen and bedrooms of the Empire and Federal periods. Changing displays periodically complement the permanent exhibits of china, paintings, and other furnishings. Open May-Oct, Tu-Sa 1-4. Free. 282-3031.

Scarborough

WINSLOW HOMER STUDIO, Winslow Homer Rd., Prout's Neck, c. 1870. Homer, particularly noted for his seascapes, landscapes, and Civil War illustrations, converted an empty stable near his brother's cottage into his home and studio. NR, NHL. Private, accessible to the public only by appointment. 883-2249.

RICHARD HUNNIWELL HOUSE, ME 207, Black Point Rd., 1684. One of the earliest extant buildings in Cumberland County, this 1½-story frame, shingled home was built for an Indian War military officer and township leader. The restored building now houses a gift shop featuring local crafts. NR. Municipally owned. Open July-Dec, F-Su 12-4.

SCARBOROUGH HISTORICAL MUSEUM, US 1. The former generator house of the Portland-Saco Electric Railway now contains a collection of farm and household implements, photographs, books, and maps of local interest. Operated by the Scarborough Historical Society. Open July-Aug, Tu, Th 2-4 and by appointment.

South Berwick

HAMILTON HOUSE, Vaughan's Lane, c. 1785. Colonel Jonathan Hamilton, a Portsmouth, NH merchant, built and occupied this dwelling until his death in 1802, locating the foursquare Georgian mansion on a hill above his wharves and warehouses on the Piscataqua River. In later years the house was the setting for Sarah Orne Jewett's historical novel, *The*

Tory Lover, and a friend of Miss Jewett purchased it in 1898 as a summer home, refurbishing it in the Colonial Revival style it bears today. Operated by the SPNEA. NR, NHL. Open June 1-Oct 15, Tu, Th, Sa, Su 12-5. $2 adults, $1 children. 384-5269.

JEWETT MEMORIAL, 101 Portland St., 1774. This imposing Georgian mansion was owned in the 19th century by the Jewett family, whose most prominent member was author Sara Orne Jewett, born here in 1849. Most of her works were written at home, including *A Country Doctor* and *The Country of the Pointed Firs,* and her bedroom-study is as she had arranged it. Other rooms contain fine paneling and original 18th- and 19th-century wallpapers. Operated by the SPNEA. Open June 1-Oct 15, Tu, Th, Sa, Su 12-5. $1.50 adults. 227-3956.

South Windham

PARSON SMITH HOUSE, 89 River Rd., 1764. Built by the Reverend Thatcher Smith, minister of the community from 1762 to 1826, on the site of Old Province Fort, an early stockade against Indian attack, the 2½-story frame Georgian home is unusually sophisticated for its date and location. An 18th-century kitchen and many Smith family pieces are on exhibit. Operated by the SPNEA. NR. Open June 1-Sept 15, Tu, Th, Sa, Su 12-5. $1.50 adults. 892-5315.

Yarmouth

YARMOUTH HISTORICAL SOCIETY MUSEUM, Merrill Memorial Library, Main St. The society maintains a large collection of local artifacts and memorabilia relating to the area and to maritime life, including costumes and civil war mementos. A restored one-room schoolhouse, the 1736 **Old Ledge School** on nearby West Main St., is open to visitors in July and Aug, W, F 2-4. 846-5654. The museum itself is open in May, June, Sept and Oct, W, Sa 3-5; in summer W, F 3-5 and by appointment. 846-5004.

On nearby Hillside St., the **North Yarmouth and Freeport Baptist Church,** believed to be the oldest of its denomination extant in the state (1796), is located. Extensive alterations to the exterior in 1825 and 1837 have resulted in an unusual combination of Colonial, Federal, Gothic, and Greek Revival features. The building still serves Yarmouth in many ways — as the site of annual high school commencement exercises and the occasional location for concerts, meetings, and plays. NR. Owned by the town of Yarmouth, it is open to visitors weekly during the summer months. If you find time to stroll the campus of **North Yarmouth Academy,** on ME 115, you'll see several classic examples of the Greek Revival style prevalent in 19th century academic architecture, among them **Russell Hall** (1841) and **Academy Hall** (1847). NR.

York

YORK HISTORIC DISTRICT, including the villages of York Corner, York Harbor, and York Village, 17th-20th centuries. A tour of this enormous district along the banks of the York River, which, taken as a whole, forms the municipality of York, gives a clear picture of the area's historic and commercial development—from early settlement in the 1600s to major involvement with shipbuilding in the 18th century, and the subsequent emergence of the community as a popular resort area in the latter part of the 1800s. Among the many and varied buildings to welcome visitors are:

Emerson-Wilcox House, Lindsay Rd. and York St., 1742. The house has had a varied history as general store, tavern, tailor shop, post office, and private residence. It now serves as a museum of local history and American decorative arts. Operated by the Old York Historical Society. Open mid-June-Sept 30, M-Sa 10:30-5, Su 1:30-5. $1.50 adults, 50¢ children, or a combination ticket admitting visitors to the Old Gaol Museum (see listing) may be purchased). 363-3872.

John Hancock Warehouse, Lindsay Rd. at York River, 1790. Hancock's greatest fame lies in his service as a Revolutionary statesman and signer of the Declaration of Independence. His active involvement in commerce, as represented by this building, is less known. At the age of 27 he fell heir to the vast mercantile holdings of his uncle, Thomas Hancock, one of the foremost businessmen of colonial America. One of the properties he inherited was this shingled frame warehouse which served as a wharf, store, and storehouse. Old tools and antique ship models are among the objects currently on display. NR. Operated by the Society for the Preservation of Historic Landmarks in York County. Open May 29-Sept 12, M-Sa 10:30-5, Su 1:30-5. Free. 363-4974.

Jefferds Tavern, Lindsay Rd., 1760. This mid-18th-century saltbox inn has been relocated from its original home in Wells. Its chimney and much of the old paneling remain along with many period furnishings. The tavern was built by Captain Samuel Jefferds to serve as a stagecoach stop for travelers en route between York and Kennebunk. Operated by the Society

for the Preservation of Historic Landmarks in York County. Open Memorial Day-mid-Sept, M-Sa 10:30-5, Su 1:30-5. $1 admission. 363-4974.

George A. Marshall Store, Lindsay Rd., 1867. The 19th-century store still operates as such, featuring the work of local artisans along with displays of historic merchandise and artifacts. Operated by the Society for the Preservation of Historic Landmarks in York County. Open mid-June-mid-Sept, M-Sa 10-5, Su 1-5. Free. 363-4974.

Old Gaol Museum, Lindsay Rd. and York St., 1653. Built as a King's prison for the then province of Maine, the York jail is said to be the oldest English public building in the United States. Its original one-room stone section is flanked by frame extensions with clapboarded ends. The first early stone cell was expanded throughout the 18th and early 19th centuries as need arose, and it served as a jail until 1879. Dungeons, cells, and jailer's quarters may be viewed, along with extensive historic displays. NR, NHL. Operated by the Old York Historical Society. Open mid-June-Sept 30, M-Sa 10:30-5, Su 1:30-5. $1.50

adults, 50¢ children under 16 (or combination ticket available with Emerson-Wilcox House, described earlier). 363-3872.

Old Schoolhouse, Lindsay Rd., c. 1755. This single-story, one-room frame building is one of the earliest 18th-century schoolhouses extant in New England. Current exhibits include early furniture, period clothing, and school materials. NR. Operated by the Society for the Preservation of Historic Landmarks in York County. Open Memorial Day-mid-Sept, M-Sa 10:30-5, Su 1:30-5. Free. 363-4974.

Elizabeth Perkins House, South Side Rd., 1731. The central small cottage was built in 1686 with extensive additions made in the 18th century. Many of the Perkinses' family furnishings, including fine antiques, are on display. Appropriately, the last descendant, Elizabeth Perkins, founded the York Preservation Society. Operated by the society. Open mid-June-Labor Day, M-Sa 10:30-5, Su 1:30-5. $1 admission. 363-4974.

Jonathan Sayward House, 79 Barrell Lane, c. 1720. This frame Georgian Colonial was the residence of Sayward and his son-in-law, Nathaniel Barrell, an eccentric merchant whose business failed when he refused to oppose the Stamp Act. As a delegate to Boston's ratifying convention in 1787, he voted in favor of the Constitution, thus directly opposing the wishes of the townspeople. The simple exterior of this sizeable home belies the magnificent furnishings which still are displayed in its spacious rooms. Queen Anne and Chippendale chairs, fine French china, Chinese porcelain, and many family portraits are but a few of the items which have been preserved virtually intact by Sayward's descendants. Operated by the SPNEA. NR. Open June 1-Oct 15, Tu, Th, Sa, Su 12-5. $2 adults, $1 children. 227-3956.

York Institute Museum, 375 Main St. A colonial kitchen, 18th- and early 19th-century bedrooms, numerous family artifacts, and furnishings are among the exhibits to be found here. The nearby **Dyer-York Library** has an extensive collection of historical items. The museum is open from May-Oct, Tu-Sa 1-4. Free.

York vicinity

McINTIRE GARRISON HOUSE, on ME 91, 5 miles W of York, c. 1645. One of the oldest log buildings still remaining in America, it is representative of the sturdy architecture that was widely used in New England during the 17th century as a defense against Indians. Fortified houses such as this one, with thick, protective walls, were built in almost all New England towns, and they were particularly common in the frontier settlements of Maine and New Hampshire. Much like ordinary houses in plan and appearance, garrison houses were used in time of peace as one-family dwellings. NR, NHL. Private — may be viewed only from the exterior.

Central Maine

Alna

OLD ALNA MEETING HOUSE, ME 218, 1789. This 2½-story clapboarded frame meeting house still retains its original box pews; hand-hewn pillars support a balcony extending around three sides of the sanctuary. Its hour glass pulpit is an unusual feature. NR. Open July and Aug, W and Sa 2-4 and by appointment. Donations accepted. Just down the road you'll find the **Alna Center School,** one of the oldest one-room schools in the state (1795). This simple frame building with its hexagonal open cupola was in use until 1962. It is furnished with early pieces, and is open during the same hours as the meeting house. NR. Donations accepted. 586-5536.

Auburn

ANDROSCOGGIN HISTORICAL SOCIETY, 2 Turner St. (County Building). The society's museum presents a good general introduction to local history and genealogy, with early furniture, dishes, linens, tools and Civil War memorabilia on display. Open M-F all year (except holidays) from 1:30-4:30. Free. 784-9586. While you're in the area, you might also like to drop in at the **Auburn Fire Department Museum,** 550 Minot Avenue, which has artifacts and early photographs relating to fire fighing in the vicinity. The museum's 1933 Ahren Fox Pumper will be of special interest to children. Open daily 8-5 all year. Free. **Knight House,** Great Falls Plaza (1796) is a 1½-story Cape Cod which is the oldest frame house in Auburn. It has been completely restored and furnished with period pieces, and an adjacent shoe shop demonstrates early tools and methods of shoe manufacturing. An herb garden on the property may provide inspiration for gardeners. Open July-Aug, Tu and Th 1:30-4. Donations accepted.

Augusta

It might almost be said that Augusta developed as the result of a war. It had been the site of a trading post in the early 1600s, but the settlement had been abandoned for many years before Captain James Howard, commander of Fort Western was relieved of his post at the end of the French and Indian War and decided to remain in the area, thus becoming Augusta's first permanent settler in 1759. The fort which became his home was considered at that time to be within the town limits of Hollowell, and did not receive its current name and separate status until late in 1797. Thereafter, with the growth of shipbuilding and trading on the Kennebec River, Augusta mushroomed. Rivalry with Hallowell continued until 1829, when Augusta was chosen over its neighbor as the brand new state capital.

BLAINE HOUSE, 162 State St., c. 1830. This two-story frame residence with hipped roof and twin cupolas has been the official governor's mansion since 1919, thus continuing a political tradition that had its beginnings in 1863, when James G. Blaine, the house's original owner, was first elected to the House of Representatives. Known as the "Plumed Knight," Blaine went on to be Speaker of the House, was later elected to the Senate, and served two terms as Secretary of State before meeting defeat for the first time as a presidential candidate in 1884. His library has been restored to its original appearance, and many of the original Blaine family furnishings are on display, along with such curiosities as a silver service from the battleship *Maine*, which was recovered fully ten years after the ship was sunk. Operated by the state. NR, NHL. All year, M-F 2-4 and by appointment. Tours are conducted on the half hour. Free. 289-2121.

FORT WESTERN, Bowman St., 1754. Built during the French and Indian War as part of the defense of the Kennebec River, Fort Western is one of two extant pre-Revolutionary forts in the state. The 2½-story log building which served as the commandant's residence and later his permanent home has been lovingly restored to reflect its original appearance. The two block houses and the stockade are careful reconstructions, completed in the early 1920s by descendants of the commandant. Operated by the city of Augusta. NR, NHL. Mid-May-Labor Day, M-Sa 9-4:30, Su 2-4. Guided tours available beginning June 23. $1 adults, 50¢ children. Group rates. 622-1234.

MAINE STATE HOUSE, State and Capitol Sts., 1832. This imposing four-story

an important river port because of its location on the Kennebec, and became a prominent center for printing and publishing. Among the most interesting buildings in the district is the curious **"Birdcage"** on Second St. (1838), with double twelve-sided spherical parlors. This unassuming small cottage boasts impressive Ionic columns across its front. Also on Second St. is **Row House**, the only known example of a wooden attached building in the state, whose five units with their off-centered doors and pedimented dormers were built c. 1840 as rental properties. Near the river on Water St. is the **Crossroads Coffee House**, known when built in 1813 as "At the Sign of the Bible," the first bookstore east of Portland. A surviving reminder of the booming granite era of the 19th century can be seen at the **Hallowell granite sheds,** opposite Franklin St. (between Winthrop and Central Sts.), where skilled Italian and Portuguese stone cutters created monuments and statuary now gracing such notable buildings as the Albany (New York) State House, Chicago's Marshall Field and New York City's Hall of Records. A trip to the **Hubbard Free Library** on Second St. will uncover a fine collection of early newspapers, housed in an 1880 landmark of local Maine granite.

granite capitol with its soaring central dome and stately colonnaded front is considered one of the most notable achievements of architect Charles Bulfinch, even though considerable alterations, including the addition of the dome and large side and rear wings, were made from 1891-1910. Its echoing rotunda displays portraits of former Maine governors and an extensive collection of the state's battle flags. Operated by the state. NR. Open all year, M-F 8-5. Free. 289-3771.

The nearby **Maine State Museum** in the capitol complex features many displays and artifacts covering various aspects of Maine history. Special exhibits review fishing, agriculture, shipbuilding, quarrying and lumbering—the most important and diverse of Maine's industries. Open all year, M-F 8-5, Sa 10-4, Su 1-4. Free. 289-2301.

Immediately adjacent to the city of Augusta is the **Hallowell Historic District**, composed of most of the town of Hallowell, which serves today as an important suburb of the capital. The town was settled in 1754, and 85 percent of the buildings within the district were constructed during the 18th and 19th centuries. Hallowell was

Bath

You'll want to spend at least a day or two here, for perhaps nowhere else in Maine is the seagoing heritage of the state so clearly defined as in this scenic river town. The deep waters and shallow, sloping banks of the Kennebec have provided ideal conditions for shipbuilding since the first private vessel was built here in 1743 (near the site of the current U.S. Customhouse on Front St.) And for more than two hundred years Bath has been famed for its ships and its sailors. The tradition continues today, and if you're lucky you may be on hand to watch the launching of a new vessel. But if not, you will still find an inexhaustible variety of things to do and see.

Maine Maritime Museum, the largest public museum in the state, has extensive collections housed in five locations through-

out Bath, including an historic wooden tugboat. The **Sewall House** at 963 Washington St. displays both fine and folk art in an 1844 pillared mansion. Many of the museum's 15,000 artifacts are included in interpretive displays, and a "please touch" room, with its ship's wheel and bell, is most popular with children. Along at 880 Washington is the **Winter Street Center,** in the former Winter Street Church (1843). This wooden, Gothic Revival structure with its three-stage 100-foot tower was once the spiritual center for Bath's captains and shipbuilders and is now used as a working site for the museum and for numerous community programs. Half the space is reserved for thematic exhibits containing ship models, half-models, historic photos and regional maritime history. The **Apprenticeshop** at 375 Front St. affords an experience in "living history." Students in an eighteen-month "labor for learning" program learn to build classic Maine coast boats, including dories, pinkies, skiffs and sloops. Onlookers are welcome here and at the **Percy and Small Shipyard** at 263 Washington, where a similar program offers trainees the opportunity to replicate traditional craft from those on display. The shipyard is notable for being the only surviving one of its type in America where large wooden sailing ships were built. Here you will find the *Seguin,* the oldest U.S. registered wooden steam tug (1884). It has

no equal. Her trainee restoration program and shiphouse can be visited by the public. Museum entrance fees include (in season) round trip passage aboard the M/V *Sasanoa,* a 50-foot Coast Guard certified vessel which operates between the shipyard and other museum sites. This voyage affords a river view of the city's historic waterfront and of modern cargo and naval vessels under construction at the thriving Bath Iron Works. The Maine Maritime Museum is operated by the Marine Research Society of Bath. NR. Open all year (May-Oct, daily 10-5), though seasonal conditions may limit access. 443-6311.⚓

You'll want to save some time—and shoe leather—to stroll through the city itself. The **Bath Historic District** encompasses a large portion of the downtown area, and many of the fine homes and churches built in the 19th century during Bath's most active shipbuilding period still stand today. All of the Marine Museum's sites are located within the district; along with the **U.S. Customhouse and Post Office** (1858) at 25 Front St., whose restrained, classical masonry design evolved from the architect's concern that the structure be totally fireproof; and the Greek Revival **Swedenborgian Church** (1843), to name only two other buildings of note. As a pleasant outing, you may wish to cross the river on ME 128 to view the **Days Ferry Historic District,** where you'll find more than a dozen private brick and frame homes, all fronting the route, which date from the 1750s to the mid-19th century, and present a variety of pleasing architectural styles.

Bethel

MOSES MASON HOUSE MUSEUM, 15 Broad St., 1813. This 2½-story frame landmark, with two end chimneys and a graceful fanlight over the center door, is a fine example of the New England Federal style. Although the interior of the house has been modernized, outstanding wall murals in the front hall and stairway, the work of artist Rufus Porter, remain. Porter's lovely rural and harbor scenes seem to contrast sharply with his other talents: he was the founder of *Scientific American* and was also an avid inventor. His art is complemented by period furnishings of the early and mid-19th century. Privately maintained. NR. July-Aug, Tu-Su, holidays, 1-4; June and Sept by appointment. $1 adults, 50¢ children. 824-2908.

The Mason House stands within the **Broad Street Historic District**, notable for its Shingle Style houses and its summer resort air. The **Gehring Clinic**, off ME 5 (1896), a well-proportioned Georgian Revival home, was the residence and clinic of John G. Gehring, an early psychotherapist who prescribed gardening and landscaping of the spacious grounds as part of the therapy for his patients.

STEAM ERA RAILROADIANA EXHIBIT AND MUSEUM, Bog Rd. exit off US 2. A retired railroad conductor operates this collection of artifacts, papers, photographs and models of the steam era of the railroad, with knowledgeable and enthusiastic commentary for the railway buff. Take the children. Late June-mid-Oct, Th-Su 9:30-4:30 and by appointment. $1 adults, 50¢ children. 836-2673. ♦♦

Boothbay

BOOTHBAY RAILWAY VILLAGE, ME 27. Two restored railroad stations house displays pertaining to the steam era, as well as a collection of antique automobiles. Admission includes a ride on an old-fashioned steam train which runs on a narrow gauge track through a village of restored and reconstructed buildings. Mid-June-mid-Sept, daily 9-5. $3 adults, $1.50 children. 633-4727.

THE BOOTHBAY THEATRE MUSEUM, Corey Lane. Theatre memorabilia from the 18th century to the present is housed partially in the 1784 Nicholas Knight-Corey House, which stands on the site of an historic tavern. Stage furniture and props, costumes, autographs, posters, souvenirs and other curiosities are on view. Mid-June-mid-Oct, M-Sa; guided tours at 10 and 3 by reservation only. Admission $3. 633-4536.

GRAND BANKS SCHOONER MUSEUM, 100 Commercial St. Celebrating the cod fishing industry which has been particularly important to this area of Maine, the museum includes the *Sherman Zwicker,* one of the last remaining dory fishing boats (1942). A documentary explains the fishing industry of the region, and displays of maritime gear are included. Mid-June-mid-Oct, daily 9-5. $1.50 adults, 75¢ children, tours of the boat $1. 633-4727.

China Village

CHINA VILLAGE HISTORIC DISTRICT, on Main and Water Sts., and Neck Rd., with several buildings on Canton and Peking Sts., 19th century. This small community on the shores of China Lake retains much of the flavor it must have had nearly two centuries ago when first settled by farmers attracted by its beautiful natural setting. Most of the homes remain private residences, but the visitor can get an idea of their charm by dropping in at the **Albert Church Brown Memorial Library** on Main St., housed in the two-story frame **Fletcher-Main House,** whose graceful Federal design dates from c. 1827. (Open all year, Tu and Th 2-5, Sa 10-12; free). Even 20th century buildings have been constructed with an eye towards preserving the charm of an earlier era: note the Post Office on Main St. (1960) whose Colonial Revival style blends in unobtrusively with its surroundings.

Damariscotta

CHAPMAN-HALL HOUSE, Main and Vine Sts., 1754. Believed to be the oldest building remaining in the community (an 1845 fire destroyed most of its neighbors), the Chapman-Hall House is a 1½-story frame Colonial Cape with a central chimney and five-bay front. Its charm is typical of the farmhouses of the period, including wainscoting, paneling, and an adjacent herb and rose garden. Operated by the Chapman-Hall House Preservation Society. NR. Mid-June-Labor Day, Tu-Su and holidays, 1-5. Admission 50¢.

The nearby **Main Street Historic District**

presents an interesting contrast to the old farmhouse: most of its buildings are commercial in purpose, and several interesting office blocks, dating from the mid-19th century, attest to the popularity of the Greek Revival style.

Dresden

POWNALBOROUGH COURTHOUSE, ME 128, 1761. This Georgian-style three-story frame building was constructed only a year after Lincoln County was established. Initially living quarters were located on the first and third floors, while court was held on the second. From the late 18th century until just a few years ago, the building was a private residence. Now a museum with a large collection of spinning and weaving equipment and early farm implements, the only extant pre-Revolutionary courthouse in Maine has largely been restored to its original condition. Operated by the Lincoln County Cultural and Historical Association. NR. July and Aug, W-Sa 11-4, Su 10-4 and by appointment. $1 adults, 25¢ children. 737-2504.

If you're in Dresden on a weekend or holiday, drop by the Brick School House and Museum, also on ME 128, where from 1-5 (and by appointment) you may have a look at a restored one-room schoolhouse of the early 19th century, with period furnishings on display. 737-8892.

Farmington

NORDICA HOMESTEAD MUSEUM, Holley Rd. off ME 4, c. 1840. Opera buffs will be enchanted by a visit to the birthplace of Madame Lillian Nordica, née Norton, internationally-acclaimed soprano (1857-1914). Her father built this small frame house with gable roof and rear ell long before Madame Nordica's birth, and it serves today as a memorial to her talent. Many of the concert gowns, stage jewelry, programs, music and other mementos of the diva's career are displayed by the Nordica Memorial Association. NR. June-Labor Day, Tu-Su 10-12,

1-5 and by appointment in Sept and Oct. $1 adults, 50¢ children. 778-2042.

In nearby West Farmington one can imagine how Madame Nordica might have spent her early school days: the Little Red Schoolhouse on Wilton Rd. (1852) served as the only center of learning in the area until 1957. The Farmington-Wilton Historical Society has restored the tiny building, and furnished it with early desks, books, lunchboxes and other curiosities of early education. The schoolhouse also functions as a local information center. NR. July 1-early Sept, daily 10-5 and by appointment. 778-2234.

Hallowell (see Augusta)

Livermore

NORLANDS LIVING HISTORY CENTER, Norlands Rd. off ME 4, 19th century. You may stroll the grounds of this 430-acre working farm and watch daily and seasonal rural activities such as maple sugaring and ice cutting; watch participatory programs in the 1823 one-room school and 1828 church; and visit the large, Italianate-style Washburn Mansion (1867). The property was purchased by Israel and Martha Washburn in 1809; they raised three daughters and seven sons, four of whom became Congressmen, one a banker, one a naval officer and one the U.S. commissioner to Paraguay. Visitors who elect to steep themselves in the farming activities of old may sign up for three days of intensive, live-in activity. First assume the guise of an early member of the community by visiting the local cemetery; then learn how that member performed his or her daily chores—laundering, cooking, harvesting—more than one hundred years ago. Live in one of the residences on the property, and take your meals in an old-time kitchen. NR. July and Aug, W-Su 10-4; Sept-June schooldays. Adults $2, $1 children, group and special rates. 897-2236.

Monhegan Island

THE MONHEGAN MUSEUM, Lighthouse Hill, 1824. A pleasant ferry ride to the island, noted for its beauty and the wide range of plants and animals to be found there, should include a visit to this granite lighthouse and adjacent white frame keeper's house. The beacon still flashes its warning to ships at sea, but for the past thirty years or so modern technology has enabled the light to be maintained by remote control. The Monhegan Associates, a group dedicated to preserving the beauty of the island, now run a museum in the keeper's house, where island history and industry (primarily fishing and lobstering), Indian artifacts and exhibits of natural history are displayed. NR. July-Labor Day, daily 11:30-3:30 and by appointment. Free.

Monmouth

MONMOUTH MUSEUM, Main and Maple Sts., 19th century. This complex of restored and reconstructed buildings illustrates various aspects of 19th-century rural Maine life. The buildings include a carriage house, country store, blacksmith shop, livery stable, stencil shop, and pottery shop—each filled with artifacts and mementos of the time. July-Aug, Tu-Su 1-4 and by appointment. Donations accepted. 933-4444.

Nearby **Cumston Hall** on Main St. is an impressive Richardson Romanesque design adapted in frame and clapboarding. Now used primarily for summer theatre presentations, it is a fine example of turn-of-the-century multi-purpose community architecture. You may enjoy a play there in season, or inquire at the town offices within to look at the domed and vaulted hall with its original interior woodwork intact. NR.

Newcastle

Two fine 19th century churches grace this pretty tree-lined village on the banks of the Damariscotta River. **St. Patrick's Catholic Church** on Academy Rd. is a lovely small brick building crowned with a spire added nearly 60 years after its completion in 1807. One of the last bells cast by Paul Revere is located here. Both Colonial and Federal styles are evident in its design, and a round stained-glass window tops the main entrance. The church is notable for being the oldest of its denomination in Maine, and possibly New England; Newcastle was the first Catholic parish in the state, having been established in the late 18th century by a French priest whose mission was the conversion of the local coastal Indians. The nearby **St. Andrew's Church** on Glidden St. was the first church built in the Cottage Gothic Style in the U.S. Its one-story frame building design with gabled entrance porch and diamond-paned rectangular windows was the work of English Gothic architect Henry Vaughan, and the first church he designed in this country (1883).

North Edgecomb

FORT EDGECOMB, Old Fort Rd., Davis Island, 1808. A commanding presence overlooking the Sheepscot River, Fort Edgecomb was built to protect nearby Wiscasset, for a time the most important shipping center north of Boston. Its large, octagonal two-story blockhouse features sturdy log construction and a shingled roof. NR. Memorial Day-Labor Day, daily 9-6. 25¢ adults.

Paris Hill

PARIS HILL HISTORIC DISTRICT, 19th century. As the county seat from 1805-1895, Paris Hill came to prominence as the residence of governors, U.S. congressmen and senators, and Hannibal Hamlin, Abraham Lincoln's first vice president. The village remains essentially untouched by time, primarily because the railroad bypassed the area, and the county seat moved on. Buildings to note particularly include the **Baptist Church,** with its three-stage clock tower and fluted columns, the two-story frame **Paris Hill Academy** with its pedimented front facade and commanding belfry, and the **Oxford County Jail** (now Hamlin Memorial Hall), which is open today as a public library and museum displaying items of local historical interest, along with many Hamlin family belongings. Adjacent is the Hamlin family home, now privately owned. The hall is open all year; summer Tu-Sa 10-4, winter Tu-F 3-5, Sa 9-2. Donations accepted.

Pemaquid and vicinity

COLONIAL PEMAQUID, off ME 130, Pemaquid Beach, 16th and 17th centuries. Recorded history dates the first settlement at Pemaquid from 1625, when an Indian chief named Samoset sold the peninsula to John Brown for the magnificent price of 50 beaver skins. Pemaquid's strategic importance, however, was as the last English outpost in the area between the St. Croix and Kennebec rivers, and a total of four forts were erected here as defense against Indians and pirates between 1630 and 1729. The third of them, **Fort William Henry**, has been reconstructed as it would have appeared in 1692. Recent archaeological excavations have revealed the foundations of more than a dozen early buildings—several homes, a tavern, a meeting house and a jail among them—along with many artifacts which are housed in an adjacent museum. Operated by the state. NR. May 30-Labor Day, daily 10-6. 50¢ adults, 25¢ children. 677-2423.

THE FISHERMAN'S MUSEUM, ME 130 at Lighthouse Park, 1827. A former lighthouse keeper's home adjacent to the Pemaquid Point Light now houses photographs, charts, and ship models connected with Maine's important fishing industry. Memorial Day-Sept, M-Sa 10-5, Su and holidays 11-5 and by appointment. Donations accepted. 677-2494.

HARRINGTON MEETING HOUSE AND MUSEUM OF OLD BRISTOL, Harrington Rd, c. 1775. The main doorway of this Georgian frame building is reached by way of its early cemetery. This unusual juxtaposition is due to the meeting house having been moved in the 1840s from its original position across the grounds. At that time the interior was remodeled, but recent restoration has re-

turned it to its 18th-century appearance. A balcony overlooking the simple box pews below displays the books, photos and memorabilia of the Old Bristol Museum. Operated by the Pemaquid Historical Association. NR. July-Aug, M, W, Sa 2-4:30 and by appointment. Donations accepted. 677-2587 or 677-2400.

Phillips

PHILLIPS HISTORICAL SOCIETY, Pleasant St., c. 1830. Once the private home of a succession of railroad families, this simple 19th-century building now houses an extensive collection of artifacts relating to the narrow gauge Sandy River and Rangeley Lakes Railroad, along with many period furnishings and tools. Open by appointment from June-Aug. Donations accepted. 639-4001.

The Phillips Historical Society also maintains **Sandy River Railroad Park** nearby, with its collection of original steam locomotives and reproductions. You may ride a restored narrow gauge train along a half mile of roadbed which follows the original path of the railroad. Open May-Nov, 1st and 3rd Sundays of each month and major holidays 10-6; also by appointment. $1 adults. 639-4001.

Popham Beach

FORT POPHAM, ME 209, Hunnewell Point, 1861. This imposing granite fortification was built during the Civil War to prevent a Confederate invasion from the Kennebec River. Its 30-foot walls enclose a parade ground, and a moat surrounds the whole. The area has been an important one in the history of Maine's defense since the Revolutionary War, when George Washington ordered Colonel Benedict Arnold to lead an expedition northward through Maine to attack Quebec City. What we now call the **Arnold Trail**, from which Arnold and some 1100 troops began their arduous journey, had its beginnings here. Interpretive panels describe the 154-mile march through the Maine wilderness, which barely half of Arnold's men survived. More recently, adjacent **Fort**

Baldwin was built to defend the coastline during World War I. NR. Both it and Fort Popham are state parks, and open from April 15-Oct 15 daily, 9-sunset. Free. 389-1335.

Rangeley

RANGELEY LAKES REGION HISTORICAL SOCIETY, Main and Richardson Sts. Rangeley has the good fortune to be situated in what is considered by many residents and visitors to be the most beautiful part of Maine. This interior region boasts more than 40 lakes and ponds within ten miles of the town, nestled among scenic mountains that offer a wide range of outdoor activities for every taste. The society's displays concentrate on local history of the region, and will help to give the visitor a better picture of its development. July-Sept, Tu, Th, Sa 10-2. Donations welcome. On Dodge Pond Rd. (off ME 4) you can stop by the **Wilhelm Reich Museum**, which displays the library, scientific equipment, paintings and other memorabilia of this pioneering natural scientist. July and Aug, Tu and F 10-4 and by appointment. Adults $2.50. 864-3443.

Richmond

RICHMOND HISTORIC DISTRICT, bounded by South, High and Kimball Sts. and the Kennebec River, 19th century. Fashionable homes, churches, and industrial and commercial structures in a variety of styles reflect the wealth of residents of this river town who prospered from their extensive shipbuilding activities as well as later millwork and other business enterprises. A visitor to the **Richmond Rural Museum** at 23 Kimball St. will discover a working blacksmith shop, wheel shop, grist mill, and displays of 19th-century life in the area. NR. The museum is open from May 1-Oct 1, daily 9-4:30. Donations accepted.

Topsham

TOPSHAM HISTORIC DISTRICT, east of the town center, 19th century. Just across the Androscoggin River from Brunswick, Topsham grew to prominence during the early 19th century because of its expensive lumbering industry, which made it, for a time, the most active commercial center west of Bath. The present historic district developed as a residential area to which prominent business leaders of the time were attracted because of close proximity to the town center as well as magnificent river views and gently sloping hills. Village laborers, too, needed to be close to their livelihood, and therefore you can see today, in many cases next to each other, both the elegant homes of wealthy merchants and the modest dwellings of the poor much as they must have appeared more than 150 years ago. All of the more than 50 buildings within the district are frame, and white is the predominant color. The simple styles harmonize well with each other, and the area retains many of its fine shade trees. The **Whitten Library and Memorial Building** at 8 Pleasant St. (1838) houses a museum room containing local historical items. The building itself is notable for its curving interior staircase and original wall coverings. July-Aug, W 2-5. Free.

Waldoboro

OLD GERMAN CHURCH, Bremen Rd., 1772. Samuel Waldo, founder of Waldoboro, was responsible for bringing German settlers to the area in 1752. They built and worshipped in this simple frame church which was moved to its present location in 1794. Its box-like pews, galleries, and the hanging wine-glass-shaped pulpit date from the 19th century. NR. The grounds, including an early cemetery, are open all year. The building itself is open July-Aug, daily 1-4 by appointment. Donations accepted. 832-5100.

Nearby on ME 220, near its junction with ME 1, stands the **Waldoboro Historical Society Museum,** a complex of early buildings including a restored country school and town cattle pound (1819). Museum displays include an early 20th century farm kitchen, shipbuilding memorabilia, tools, documents and photographs. July-Aug, daily 1-5. Donations accepted.

Walpole

OLD WALPOLE MEETING HOUSE, S. Bristol Rd., 1772. One of the state's oldest churches, it is still used as a place of worship. The simple frame building retains its original box pews and hand-carved and paneled pulpit. For the first 24 years of its existence it was a Presbyterian church, turning Congregational in the late 18th century. June 15-Labor Day, daily 9-5 (services Su at 3 during July and Aug.). Donations accepted. 563-3983.

Waterford

WATERFORD HISTORIC DISTRICT, ME 35, 18th-20th centuries. Located on the western shore of Keoka Lake, the Waterford Historic District comprises about a quarter of the township of the same name. As it contains the town hall and municipal offices, it is considered the most important village of the four comprising the township, and features near its mid-point an open common. As in most rural Maine villages, the houses and other buildings are, for the most part, generously spaced, and they are little changed from their 19th-century appearance. Most of the 27 buildings in the district are residential, but a library, church, school, lodge hall and general store are included, as well as a hotel and annex—all in good condition, and a majority in the Greek Revival and Federal styles. The general atmosphere reflects Waterford's history as a relaxed, comfortable summer resort.

Waterville

REDINGTON MUSEUM, 64 Silver St., 1814. This 19th-century home was built by local resident Asa Redington as a wedding gift for his son, and remained in the family for more than 100 years. It now houses the collection of the Waterville Historical Society, which has reconstructed five period rooms, along with two museum rooms displaying Civil War items, Indian artifacts, and other memorabilia. A 19th-century apothecary has also been reconstructed on the premises. May 15-Sept 29, Tu-Sa 2-6 and by appointment. Admission $1. 672-9439.

Perhaps one of the oddest landmarks in New England is the **Two-Cent Bridge,** spanning the Kennebec River at Temple St. Built as a toll footbridge for millworkers commuting between Waterville and neighboring Winslow, this 700-foot-long steel suspension bridge is considered to be the only private toll footbridge in the country. The toll no longer applies, but you can still see the tollkeeper's house on the Waterville side. NR.

Waterville's claim to fame lies in its success as an industrial center, but it is also, and no less importantly, the home of the prestigious **Colby College,** which was founded here in 1813. Located on Mayflower Hill, the campus contains an art museum boasting an excellent collection of American works, and takes special pride in its collection of John Marins, Winslow Homers and indigenous folk art. M-Sa 10-12, 1-4:30, Su 2-4:30. Free. 873-1131. After you visit the museum, you might also enjoy seeing the magnificent organ designed by Albert Schweitzer, located at **Lorimer Chapel.** The campus's **Miller Library** maintains a collection of books, manuscripts, and letters of famous Maine authors such as Edward Arlington Robinson. Admission is free.

Winslow

FORT HALIFAX, ME 201, 1754. Just across the river from Waterville, this simple blockhouse belies its appearance as the oldest extant fortification of its type in the eastern U.S. Benedict Arnold rested here during his expedition to Quebec along the trail which now bears his name. Interpretive displays are maintained by the state. NR, NHL. May 30-Labor Day, daily 10-6. Free.

Wiscasset

WISCASSET HISTORIC DISTRICT, seaport area, 18th-19th centuries. Cherished

Lincoln County Court House, Wiscasset Historic District

today as a tranquil summer haven for artists and writers, the port town of Wiscasset (the name means "Meeting of Three Tides") is little altered from a century ago. Its tree-lined streets connect the stately homes of sea captains and shipping masters, some of whose descendants still live here today. Colonial, Federal and Victorian styles are all represented, and, whether of brick or frame, designed for public use or personal solitude, the buildings together present a most picturesque and pleasant appearance to the visitor to this sleepy river town. Among the historic landmarks open for inspection are:

Castle Tucker, Lee and High Sts., 1807. This imposing mansion was built by Judge Silas Lee and remodeled in 1858, when its portico was added. The lavish Victorian wallpaper and furnishings remain. July-Aug, M-Sa 11-4 and by appointment. $1 adults, 50¢ children. 882-7364.

Lincoln County Museum and Old Jail, Federal St., 1811, 1837. Until the state prison was built in 1824, this thick-walled granite building was the principal incarceration place for Maine criminals. Six cells remain on each of its two lower floors; the upper floor housed debtors, women, and the ill. Exhibits of local historic interest,

changed periodically, are located within. NR. July-Aug, Tu-Sa 10-5 and by appointment. $1 adults, 50¢ children. 882-6817.

Maine Art Gallery, Warren St., 1807. The Red Brick School (also known as the Old Academy Building) is now the home for a collection of paintings by local artists. The building's walls are of handmade mud brick, varying in size and thickness, and it is somewhat surprisingly crowned by a white frame hexagonal cupola containing an open bell tower. Maintained by the Lincoln County Cultural and Historical Association. Open all year, M-Sa 10-4, Su 1-4. Donations accepted. 882-7511.

Musical Wonder House, 18 High St., 1852. This early sea captain's home displays a private collection of more than 1,000 music boxes, player pianos and organs, singing mechanical birds and dolls, and related memorabilia arranged within several rooms furnished with 19th-century pieces. June 1-Labor Day, M-Sa 10-5, Su 1-5. $5 adults, $2.50 children. 882-7163. 🚻

Nickels-Sortwell House, Main and Federal Sts., 1807. Celebrated for its elaborate facade whose entrance door is flanked by mullioned sidelights and crowned by a wide, elliptical fanlight, this graceful Federal-style mansion was constructed for local sea captain William Nickels of Cambridge, Massachusetts. It became home for the mayor, Alvin Sortwell. Many Sortwell family furnishings are included among its period pieces. Operated by the SPNEA. NR, NHL. June 1-Sept 30, Tu-Su 12-5. Admission $2.

Northeast Coast

Acadia National Park

The rugged beauty of the park's more than 33,000 acres is found among a number of islands and the Schoodic Peninsula, with its principal area being contained on the largest of the islands, Mount Desert, (also the home of historic Bar Harbor, described below). Acadia was established to preserve the natural beauty of this part of Maine's rocky coastline with its stark mountains and numerous offshore islands. Along with the breathtaking natural vistas and myriad flora and fauna, the Acadian experience should include some knowledge of the peoples who settled here long ago.

Mount Desert Island was inhabited when Champlain named it in 1604. The story of those inhabitants is told in the **Abbe Museum** at Sieur de Monts Spring through exhibits and Indian artifacts, including dioramas of seasonal Indian occupations, stone and bone tools, basketry, and birch bark items. Open May 30-Oct 15 daily 10-4 (July and Aug 9-5). Donations accepted. 288-3519.

Other collections which interpret the period of the French and Indian colonization of the park area with displays of early tools and crafts, may be found at the **Islesford Museum** on Little Cranberry Island (accessible by ferry). Ship models and photographs depicting island life in the 19th and early 20th centuries are also included in this 1928 landmark and its adjacent Blue Duck Ships Store. NR. Open mid June-mid-Dec, daily 9-4. Free. 288-3338.

Above the coast are the forests and mountains of the park, made accessible by a 40-mile system of carriage paths, bridges and gatehouses, whose handsome stonework was made possible through the generosity of John D. Rockefeller, Jr., who also gave more than 11,000 acres to the park. The broad, smooth graveled pathways encircle Jordan Pond and Eagle Lake, and wind around the flanks of Sargent and Penobscot Mountains, affording stunning views of Somes Sound and Frenchman Bay. NR.

Bar Harbor

WEST STREET HISTORIC DISTRICT, West St., 19th-20th centuries. Bar Harbor's scenic beauty was first immortalized by artists in the 1840s, most notably Thomas Cole, founder of the Hudson River School. By 1855 a number of local residents had begun to open their homes to summer boarders, or "rusticators" as they were frequently called. Clinging to the shoreline in one of the few areas to be spared the holocaust of a major 1947 forest fire which destroyed many landmark homes, the West Street district presents in a close-knit, easily seen group, a superb collection of Maine's famous Shingle-Style summer "cottages." Most are still privately owned, but the **Manor House** (once called Boscobel), built in 1887 by a wealthy summer resident, is now an inn. (See Lodging.)

Belfast

CHURCH STREET HISTORIC DISTRICT, Church St. from High to Franklin Sts., 19th century. The tidy, well-planned appearance of this charming coastal town is a tribute to its first settlers, predominantly Irish as the name implies, who chose to build a community here in 1770, and made sure that it was carefully planned along democratic principles so that all would receive their just share. Almost all of the buildings within the district span three successive styles — Federal, Greek Revival, and Italianate — which contribute to the feeling of comfortable security they impart. The most noteworthy landmark, by far, is the **First Church of Belfast,** a beautiful Federal structure located at the north end of Church St., whose graceful proportions and lacy, openwork clock tower have made it a familiar landmark for decades (*see* cover photo). As you stroll along the street, another home worthy of

First Church

special notice is the large, two-story Greek Revival home at #1, which in 1840 was built for James Patterson White, mayor of Belfast and state senator. Its elaborate balustraded cupola is a special feature (private).

If you have time, have a look at the **Primrose Hill Historic District**, situated, as its name implies, on a beautiful rise above the downtown area. The area of High and Anderson Sts. displays a number of large, four-square 19th-century homes, with an excellent representation of styles from Federal to Gothic Revival. Developed as a residential area by prominant Belfast citizens, the area still reflects the taste and wealth of these leading families.

Blue Hill

BLUE HILL HISTORIC DISTRICT, Main St., and adjoining streets, 19th-20th centuries. This quintessential coastal Maine village was aptly named, for it sits atop a lovely rise overlooking the Atlantic and Mount Desert Island. As is the case with so many of Maine's seaports, Blue Hill's early growth was spurred by the fishing and shipbuilding industries; today it is noteworthy as a summer resort, and one of its major attractions is the number of artists and craftsmen who congregate here, and whose works are on display

throughout the town. A stroll through the district will be surprising and pleasant because of the variety of buildings, both private and commercial, which exist harmoniously together. The landmarks include, among others, a newspaper office, the Town Hall, "The Old Red Store," a Victorian-era drug store, and a number of graceful private homes. One of the residences on Water Street, **Holt House,** an 1815 Federal two-story frame dwelling, is now the home of the Blue Hill Historical Society. The interior has been restored with period furnishings, artifacts, records and other memorabilia relating to the history of Blue Hill and environs. July-Aug, Tu, F 2-5. Donations accepted.

Just on the outskirts of town on Outer Main St. (ME 15), stands the **Jonathan Fisher Memorial.** This 18th century barn and adjacent later frame homestead (1814) with Doric pilasters and low hipped roof were originally the property of Blue Hill's first settled minister for the Congregational Church. Fisher was a linguist, printer, inventor, artist, architect, teacher, poet and botanist. With all of these talents, he served the church and community loyally for more than 40 years. A number of his paintings and furnishings are on view. NR. July 1-mid Sept, Tu and F 2-5, Sa 10-12. Admission 50¢. 374-2780 or 374-2459.

Bucksport

BUCKSPORT HISTORICAL SOCIETY MUSEUM, Main St., 1874. This small, Italianate frame structure was built as part of the Northwest American and European Railway Company's short-lived plan to shorten European sea voyages by extending rail facilities to Nova Scotia. The Historical Society's exhibits focus on local history and memorabilia, with period clothing and furnishings, along with special displays relating to Maine's native son, Admiral Robert E. Peary. NR. July-Aug, W-F 1-4 and by appointment. Admission 50¢. 469-2591.

Camden

CONWAY HOUSE AND MARY MEEK-

ER CRAMER MUSEUM, Conway Rd., 1770s. The sturdy Cape Cod house is a significant example of 18th-century rural frame construction. The original portion has been enlarged, and the last addition was made in the early 1800s. Laths in the walls and ceilings are of hand-split hemlock, and other features include wide floor boards, a double brick hearth and unusual hinges. Near the house are an old heavy-timbered barn and a blacksmith shop, both in good condition. The barn contains a collection of early carriages, sleighs, farm implements and tools, while the house contains the Camden-Rockport Historical Society's collection of period furnishings and memorabilia. NR. July-Aug, M-F 1-5. Admission $1.

Castine

CASTINE HISTORIC DISTRICT, 18th-19th centuries. A small, fortified trading post called Pentagoet was established in what is now Castine as early as 1630. The area was selected because the coastline was quite easily defensible. The small peninsula is almost entirely surrounded by water. Because of this attraction, it was often the site of combat, as the British, French, and for a time even the Dutch sought to control it. The strife continued until well into the 19th century. In 1779 the British established a fort on the peninsula which resulted in one of America's most ignominious defeats during the Revolutionary War. And the British controlled Fort George again during the War of 1812, a decade after Castine was incor-

porated as a village in its own right. During the period following the War, Castine became one of the wealthiest towns of its size in New England, and it was then that many of the fine buildings remaining today were constructed. A cross section of late 18th and 19th-century architecture can be found here, including early Capes, several magnificent Federal period houses, an abundance of Greek Revival architecture, and several elaborate summer homes of the late 19th century.

The only extant pre-Revolutionary home in Castine is now part of the **Wilson Museum** on Perkins Street. **John Perkins House** (1765), with handhewn timbers and pedimented center door, is a good example of vernacular Georgian architecture. The house survived Castine's turbulent times and was moved to its present site and restored about a decade ago. It is furnished in period style with family and local pieces, and a working blacksmith shop is adjacent, along with two late 19th-century hearses, which add a somewhat discordant, though interesting note. The Wilson Museum prides itself on its collection of prehistoric artifacts and its maritime displays. Museum: May 27-Sept 30, Tu-Su 2-5, free. House and outbuildings: July-Aug, W-Su 2-5, admission $1. 326-8753.

Castine today is the home of the Maine maritime Academy, and its training ship, **"State of Maine,"** is available for inspection at the end of Sea Street every day from 9-4 when she's in port. Free.

FORT GEORGE, 1779-1815. Earthworks, two restored powder magazines, and a restored bastion are what remain of this significant British fort, built to protect English interests and settlements in lower Canada. (See preceding discussion under Castine Historic District) which they then destroyed when peace was declared after the War of 1812. Operated by the state. NR. May 30-Labor Day, daily 10-6. Free.

Columbia Falls

RUGGLES HOUSE, Main St., 1818. The most unusual feature of this graceful, Federal-style frame residence is its flying

staircase, which divides at the landing into two reverse stairs without lateral supports. Thomas Ruggles, prominent local timber merchant, hired an English woodcarver to decorate the interior, and outstanding examples of his work are the mantels, the fluted window sills, and the carved cornices. The Ruggles House Society maintains this landmark's period furnishings and historical records. NR. June 1-Oct 15, M-Sa 9;30-4:30, Su 11-4:30. Donations accepted. 288-4939.

Ellsworth

COLONEL BLACK MANSION, West Main St., 1826. The imposing three-story brick landmark with its wide Ionic columned porch was constructed as both residence and office by a young Englishman, John Black. Richly furnished with authentic period pieces and accessories, the house and its adjacent garden and carriage house are well worth a visit. Operated by the Hancock County Trustees of Public Reservations. NR. June 1-Oct 15, M-Sa 10-5. $2 adults, $1 children. 667-8671.

ELLSWORTH PUBLIC LIBRARY, 46 State St., 1817. The former Colonel Meltiah Jordon House, a frame, two-story building with a central octagonal cupola, has served as the town library since 1897. Open all year, Tu-Th 10-5, F 2-8, Sa 2-5. Free. 667-2307. The nearby Ellsworth Congregational Church (1846), with

fluted Doric columns and three-sectioned central tower, is a fine example of the traditional New England meeting house clothed in Greek Revival garb.

STANWOOD HOMESTEAD MUSE-UM, Bar Harbor Rd., (ME 31), 1850. Birdwatchers will be especially interested in this 1½-story neo-classical home on its 50 acres of wildlife preserve, which served as the outdoor workshop of Cordelia Stanwood, pioneer ornithologist. She spent 50 years of her life in the study of local wildlife and chronicled the life cycles of many of the state's birds. The house is maintained as a memorial to Miss Stanwood and contains many of the original family furnishings and ornithological artifacts. June 15-Oct 15, daily 10-4 and by appointment. Donations accepted. 667-8683.

Isleboro

This small island (also called Long Island) in Penobscot Bay is about a half-hour ferry ride from Lincolnville—just far enough from the mainland so that to reach it gives one a feeling of peace and seclusion. An 1850 lighthouse is now the home of the **Sailors' Memorial Museum** (at Grindle Point, near the ferry dock), displaying maritime and orther historic coastal artifacts primarily concerned with local heritage. Municipally-operated. June-Sept, Tu-Su 10-4. Donations accepted. 734-6445. Not far away is the **Islesboro**

Historical Society, whose displays of island memorabilia—boat models, textiles, a 100-year-old weaving loom—are appropriately housed in the 1803 **Old Town Meeting House.** The Society offers changing slide programs, art and photographic shows as well. Mid May-mid Sept, daily 10-4 or by appointment. Donations accepted. 734-6439.

Lubec vicinity

ROOSEVELT CAMPOBELLO PARK, ME 774, Campobello Island, 1897. Jointly run by the governments of the U.S. and Canada because of its 2,600-acre sprawl across the border, the island, accessible by bridge, was Franklin D. Roosevelt's summer home until he contracted polio in 1921. The family's Dutch colonial "cottage" of 34 rooms is maintained with most of its original furnishings intact. Late May-mid Oct, daily 9-5. Free. 752-2922.

The easternmost point in the United States is crowned by the **West Quoddy Light Station** in Quoddy Head State Park. (1808, rebuilt 1858). Picturesquely sited, with a magnificent view across Quoddy Roads to the palisades of Grand Manan Island, the brick light, with its red and white stripes, is an internationally known landmark. Operated by the Federal government.

In nearby Lubec, on County Road, you can visit the **Old Sardine Village Museum,** a complex of fifteen shops and displays which, as the name implies, depicts the growth of the local sardine industry from 1879 to the early 1900s. May-Oct, daily 9-7. Admission charge.

Machias

BURNHAM TAVERN, Main and Free Sts., 1770. This two-story indented gambrel-roofed clapboard building dates from seven years after the arrival of the first settlers in the Machias area. It is also the only building in eastern Maine connected with the American Revolution: the townsmen met in the tavern and made plans to erect a liberty pole on the village green and to capture the British vessel *Margaretta*. Their plan succeeeded, and

the first naval battle of the revolution resulted. Exhibits of local history and period furnishings are housed within. Maintained in part by the DAR. NR. Open mid-June-Labor Day, M-F 10-5, Sa 10-3 and by appointment. $1 adults, 25¢ children. 255-4432.

STEAM LOCOMOTIVE "LION," University of Maine at Machias, 1846. One of two locomotives built for the Whitneyville and Machiasport Railroad, the second steam railroad in Maine, which was organized specifically to transport lumber from Middle Falls to Machiasport, the "Lion" saw service for half a century. It is housed, with a bicentennial Conestoga wagon, in a special building on O'Brien Ave. near the UMaine campus. Open year round, daily 9-5. Free.

While you're in Machias, there are two other landmark buildings you might enjoy seeing: the **Centre Street Congregational Church** (1837), a superb example of the Gothic Revival style, with pointed-arched side openings and a three-story crenelated clock tower; and the **Washington County Courthouse,** an imposing brick late-19th century building, where Clara H. Nash, the first woman admitted to the bar in New England, began her law practice in 1872.

Both are included on the National Register of Historic Places.

Machiasport

GATES HOUSE, ME 92, 1807. This 2-story frame residence with its L-shaped, low hipped roof and graceful fanlight is an unusually refined Federal style building for its early date and location. The Machiasport Historical Society has furnished several of its rooms in period style, and a maritime room has ship models and other exhibits pertaining to the sea. NR. June 15-Sept 15, M-F 9-5 and by appointment. Donations accepted. 255-8860.

Machiasport vicinity

FORT O'BRIEN, south of town on a secondary road, 1775. Fort O'Brien (also known as Fort Machias) was hastily thrown up by the townspeople as protection against a force of British who arrived by ship. The opposition was prompted by a British attempt to procure lumber from the area for barracks. Named for the leader of the force which captured the British ship *Margaretta* (see Burnham Tavern in Machias), the fort was later captured by the British during the War of 1812, and the barracks were set afire. The earthworks and powder magazine, however, still remain. Maintained by the state. NR. May 30-Labor Day, daily 10-6.

Owl's Head

OWL'S HEAD TRANSPORTATION MUSEUM, ME 73 at Knox County Airport. This is a participatory museum of early airplanes and automobiles, with an early 100-ton steam engine, restoration workshop and library. May 27-Oct 7, daily 10-5. $3 adults, $1.50 students, $1 children. Special rates.

In Lighthouse State Park on Penobscot Bay stands the **Owl's Head Light** (1826), still in use, and operated by the Coast Guard. A white-painted brick tower with an adjacent keeper's house and storage buildings, the Owl's Head Light is one of the most picturesque in the state. NR. Daily 10-4 (Park: 10-dusk). Free.

Prospect

FORT KNOX STATE PARK, ME 174 (off ME 1), 1844. Maine's largest fort was constructed soon after settlement of the dispute between Great Britain and the U.S. over the location of the northeastern border, and was garrisoned during the Civil and Spanish-American wars. Surrounded by a 20-foot-high granite wall, the fort measures 350 by 280 feet. Magazines, barracks, storehouse, gun emplacements, a dry moat, and rifle galleries can still be seen, but the blacksmith shop, implement house, and hospital which supported the impressive fortification no longer exist. NR, NHL. May 1-Nov 1, daily 9-sunset. $1.50 per car. 469-7719.

Rockland

WILLIAM A. FARNSWORTH LIBRARY AND MUSEUM, 19-21 Elm St., c. 1854. A collection of 18th-20th century American painting, including many works by N.C., Andrew and Jamie Wyeth, is next door to the classical town house of wealthy Rockland businessman William A. Farnsworth. The residence is preserved in its original state, with all of the lavish furnishings and equipment, including china and glassware, which were chosen by the family. NR. June 1-Sept 30, M-Sa 10-5, Su 1-5. Museum free, house $1. 596-6457.

On nearby Limerock St. stands the **Shore Village Museum,** operated by the city of Rockland, with exhibits of lighthouse equipment and marine gear, and historical artifacts relating primarily to the Civil War. June-Oct, M-Sa 10-5, Su 1-5; otherwise M-F 1-4 and by appointment. Free. 236-3206, 594-4950.

Searsport

PENOBSCOT MARINE MUSEUM, Church St., 19th century. Four brick and frame landmarks house an extensive collection of marine paintings, ship models and memorabilia, antiques and furnishings which commemorate the age of sail and steam, and Maine's period of seagoing prosperity. In the mid-19th century Searsport had as many as eight shipyards in operation at once, and it still ranks second only to Portland in the state. The buildings themselves have stories to tell: the **Searsport Town Hall**, a 1½-story Greek Revival brick structure; the **Captain Merithew House**, a two-story Federal with its collections of navigational instruments and pressed glass (c. 1816); the **Nickels-Colcord-Duncan House** of 1860, and the **Fowler-True-Ross House** of 1825, both gable-roofed, 2½-story frame buildings redolent of marine lore. You'll want to save plenty of time to tour the complex. NR. May 24-Oct 15, M-Sa 9:30-5, Su 1-5. $2 adults, $1 teens, 50¢ children. Group rates. 548-6634. ⚔

The **Searsport Historical Society** also maintains a small museum on Main St. which, although overshadowed by the Penobscot, is well worth a visit. Their exhibits concentrate on local mementos, town records, early photos, and clothing. July-Sept, W-Su 1-5 and by appointment. Donations accepted. 548-2915.

Thomaston

THOMASTON HISTORIC DISTRICT, between Wadsworth St., and ME 131 on Blue Star Memorial Hwy, 17th-20th centuries. A comfortable, unpretentious community along the banks of the St. George River, with an eclectic mix of architectural styles and both public and private buildings. Your main interest in the district will surely be in visiting the famous **Knox Mansion** (Montpelier), on High St. just off ME 1. This majestic two-story building, a reconstruction from the original architect's drawings, has eighteen carefully-appoint-

ed rooms, many of them furnished with the Knox family's possessions. Henry Knox was the youngest major general of the Revolutionary War (at 31), credited with planning all of the battles won by George Washington, under whom he then served as Secretary of War. Memorial Day-Labor Day, daily 9-5. $1 adults, 25¢ children. Operated by the Maine State Department of Conservation.

The Thomaston Historical Society is presently restoring the **Knox Building** on lower Knox St., which was used to house servants from the Knox estate, and later was refurbished as a railroad station. The building dates from c. 1790. Have a look while you're in the area, and see how they're coming along.

Vinalhaven

VINALHAVEN HISTORICAL SOCIETY MUSEUM, High St., 1838. Accessible by ferry from the mainland, Vinalhaven Island is very much a workingman's community, and the collection of the local historical society reflects that with displays of fishing and seafaring instruments, farming tools, and granite industry artifacts. The museum building is an early church (1838), built in Rockland and moved to the island in 1875.

Perhaps the most unusual landmark in Maine is the **Vinalhaven Galamander**, which stands in Bandstand Park. This massive iron and oak wagon (a restoration from the original materials) was one of many used to transport huge blocks of quarried grainite, which for a time was the island's main industry. A derrick or lever attached to a rope tackle was used to lift the granite from the ground, and an eight-horse team was required to pull the galamander to its destination. Municipally-operated. NR.

Northern Interior

Ashland

ASHLAND LOGGING MUSEUM, Gar-

field Rd. The lumbering industry has been of vital importance to Maine's economy for many years and is centered in the beautiful north country. A central museum building and adjacent blacksmith shop and machine shed house artifacts and exhibits explaining the industry, including massive log haulers and sleds used to transport the raw wood. Open Memorial Day-Labor Day, exhibit area daily, buildings Sa-Su 3-5 and by appointment. Free. 764-4279.

Bangor

The city of Bangor, located on the west bank of the Penobscot River, grew to prominence during the 19th century as a thriving lumber port. Massive logs cut from the great northern Maine forests were floated downriver to Bangor, where many mills flourished to cut and finish them. By the 1870s the greater Bangor area, including its sister city, Brewer, just across the river, had become known as the largest lumber port in the world. Each season some 200 million board feet of wood were processed in its mills and exported to cities around the globe. It was in Bangor that the legendary Paul Bunyan is supposed to have been born in 1834, and a mammoth 1½ ton kitsch statue of the invincible woodsman is found adjacent to the Bangor Auditorium on Main St. Today the mills are gone, replaced by more modern factories at the edges of the forest where lumber, having been processed, is now shipped by truck and rail to market. The fortunes made during Bangor's heyday, however, can still be seen in a number of graceful mansions, lovingly preserved, many of which stand along wide, tree-lined boulevards in the Broadway Historic District (see following).

BANGOR HISTORICAL SOCIETY, 159 Union St., 1836. This two-story brick Greek Revival-style mansion with its columned front porch and ornate dormers was built for Thomas A. Hill, a prominent local businessman, and later occupied by Allen Gilman, first mayor of Bangor. The Bangor Historical Society's collection of local artifacts, early paintings, and Civil War memorabilia has been displayed here since 1952. NR. Apr-Dec, Tu-F 10-2. $1 adults, 25¢ children. Group rates. 942-5766.

BROADWAY HISTORIC DISTRICT, on Broadway, bounded by Park, Center, Garland, Essex, and State Sts., is highly recommended for its beautiful 19th-century mansions built primarily by the lumber magnates of the era. In style the buildings imitate those of Brahmin Boston. Predominantly Greek Revival in style, these landmarks are generally brick or frame and are set well back from the wide, shaded streets. The **Jonas Cutting-Edward Kent House,** at 48-50 Penobscot St., is a particularly impressive example of the Greek Revival style (1837). This two-story frame double house boasts five Doric pilasters dividing its front facade into four recessed bays, and twin ground-floor entrances each flanked by Doric columns. The house was built for law partners Jonas Cutting and Edward Kent, influential Bangor residents. Kent later went on to become governor of Maine. (Private, but easily seen from the street). As you stroll throughout the district, you can visit one of the most imposing of the mansions, **Isaac Farrar House** (also called Symphony House), at 166 Union St. Designed in the Greek Revival style in 1833 as the first major commission of famous architect Richard Upjohn, this 2½-story brick landmark now houses the Northern Conservatory of Music. Farrar, a wealthy lumberman, commissioned marble fireplaces, intricately carved woodwork, mahogany paneling, and stained glass windows as part of the mansion's appointments. NR. Open all year, M-F 9-5 and by appointment. Free. 942-6746.

THOMAS HILL STANDPIPE (BANGOR STANDPIPE), Jackson St., 1898. This massive steel-plated tower, 75 feet in diameter and 50 feet high, was built as a water tower and still serves as a major storage facility for the Bangor Water District. The circular tower has a winding interior staircase which leads to its conically-roofed observation deck, from which is afforded a superb view of the entire city. NR. Open daily. Free.

MORSE COVERED BRIDGE, Valley Ave. in Coe Park, 1882. Spanning the picturesque, tree-shaded Kenduskeag stream,

this rustic frame bridge with peaked roof is the oldest in Bangor and the longest remaining covered bridge in the state at 212 feet. Now used as a pedestrian crossing, the bridge crosses an area of the stream over which slaves were ferried during the Civil War as part of the underground railway system which led from the South to freedom in Canada. The nearby **Samuel Farrar House** at 123 Court Street (1836) was a stopover and hiding place for many of the fleeing blacks. Its three underground cellars connected to an underground tunnel which extended down to the water's edge. In addition to its important role in history, the Farrar House, now a Pentecostal church, is a first-rate example of the Greek Revival style. NR.

Nearby on the Penobscot River, at the mouth of the Kenduskeag, is the site of the **Penobscot Expedition,** where in 1779 an American naval force under the command of Dudley Saltonstall burned or scuttled nine of its war vessels and several transports as it fled from the advance of a much smaller British force. As recently as 1955, several cannon were discovered here during dredging operations. NR.

MOUNT HOPE CEMETERY DISTRICT, US 2, 1834-36. One of the earliest examples of a park-like Victorian cemetery, containing sections designed for burials and separate areas for horticultural enhancement, sprawls on 300 acres surrounding Mount Hope. Important as one of the first steps toward a more formal city parks movement, the cemetery contains very good sculptural monuments. NR.

Brownville Junction vicinity

KATAHDIN IRONWORKS, 5 miles N on ME 11, then 6 miles on gravel road, 1843-90. An enterprising man named Moses Greenleaf discovered iron ore on Ore Mountain in 1843, and two years later the ironworks was incorporated. It operated, except for the years of the Civil War, until the late 19th century, smelting surface ore into large ingots or pigs. At its busiest, the works employed 200 workers, and the complex included two large boarding houses, a town hall, a school, post office, company store, and two farms. Only one of the fourteen original charcoal kilns ("beehives") and the tower of the blast furnace remain. Operated by the state as a park. NR. May 30-Labor Day, daylight hours. Free.

Dexter

DEXTER HISTORICAL SOCIETY MUSEUM, Main St., 1853. One of only six early grist mills surviving in the state has been converted to display local artifacts, photographs, manuscripts, letters, and farm implements. Located on the site of a canal built in 1818, the mill, once operated by lumberman Jonathan Farrar, is a two-story shingled frame building with a gabled roof and one-story porch. Its interior remains virtually unaltered. NR. June 15-Sept 15, M-Sa 1-5 and by appointment. Donations accepted. 924-6936.

Dover-Foxcroft

BLACKSMITH SHOP MUSEUM, Chandler Road, 1863. Much of the original equipment of this Civil War-era shop is still in place: the anvil, bellows, oxlifter, and other pieces are on view. Operated by the Dover-Foxcroft Historical Society. Apr-Oct, daily 8-8. Donations accepted. 564-2549.

Fort Kent

FORT KENT MEMORIAL, Block House St., 1839-43. Built as a result of the boundary dispute with Canada, Fort Kent was

abandoned just after the signing of the treaty ending the altercation. In the early winter of 1838-39, a local militia company began construction of the hewn log blockhouse with a second-story overhang, narrow horizontal loopholes, and heavy plank door. By September 1840, Federal troops relieved the militiamen and built barracks and officers' quarters, but in vain, as the fort saw no military action. The state maintains the fort and a small museum with displays of lumbering artifacts and equipment. NR. NHL. Memorial Day-Labor Day, daily 9-sunset. Free.

On Market Street stands the former **Bangor and Aroostook Railroad Station,** now operated by the Fort Kent Historical Society, with exhibits on the area's economic and social history, emphasizing lumbering and agriculture. April 15-Labor Day, Sa-Su 10-4 and by appointment. Donations accepted. 834-5143.

Greenville

"KATAHDIN", Village Cove, 1913-14. One of the few remaining lake boats once so common on Maine inland waters, the "Katahdin" was the last and biggest steam vessel operated by the Coburn Steamboat Company on Moosehead Lake, where such service began in 1836. Built at Bath Iron Works, (see Bath listing), she was de-livered in sections and assembled the following year. As originally constructed, she carried two enclosed passenger decks with covered open promenade areas, a pilot house, and large entry ports on the lower deck for passengers and vehicles. As modes of transportation changed, the "Katahdin" ceased to be economically feasible, and from 1940 until the mid-1970s she served as a towboat for hauling lumber. Recently acquired by the Moosehead Marine Museum, the boat is to be restored to her original configuration. NR. June-Aug, M-F and holidays 10-4. 50¢ 🚹

On Pritham Ave. stands the **Eveleth-Crafts-Sheridan Historical Home** (c. 1889), maintained by the Moosehead Historical Society, which contains a Victorian kitchen exhibit, local artifacts, and memorabilia. June 1-mid-Oct, M-F 10-4. Free.

Houlton

AROOSTOOK HISTORICAL AND ART MUSEUM, 109 Main St., 1903. This is a handsome Colonial Revival building (also known as the White Memorial), with exhibits of Aroostook pioneer tools, military uniforms and arms, and Indian artifacts housed on the second floor. Municipal offices currently occupy the ground floor. NR. May 27-Sept 26, M-F 10-12, 1-5 and by appointment. 50¢. 532-3050.

On Garrison Hill (US 2) stand the **Hancock Barracks,** named for John Hancock. When manned from 1828-46, the barracks comprised the second most northern Federal outpost in the U.S. Even further north (one mile from the U.S.-Canadian border), one of Maine's ten remaining covered bridges spans the Meduxnekeag Stream. **The Watson Settlement Bridge** (1911), reaches 150 feet across the stream. It is still serving this agricultural area.

Madawaska

ACADIAN LANDING SITE AND TANTE BLANCHE MUSEUM, on the St. John River off US 1, 18th century. A large cross on the riverbank marks the original settlement of French-Canadian Acadians ousted from New Brunswick by the British in 1785. (The sufferings of the Acadians are recounted in Longfellow's *Evangeline*.) The museum, including a 19th-cenutry schoolhouse, features Acadian and local artifacts commemorating the struggle which took place over the northern U.S. boundary. NR. June 8-Labor Day, M-F 9:30-4:30, Su 1:30-4:30. Free.

The nearby **St. David Catholic Church** and its companion church, **Our Lady of Mount Carmel,** several miles down US 1 in Grand Isle, are excellent examples of the bold, outsized construction, very French in feeling, typical of turn-of-the-century architecture in this border area. NR.

Madison vicinity

LAKEWOOD THEATER, NE of Madison in the town of Lakewood, 1882. This eclectic 2½-story frame landmark, situated beautifully on the shores of Lake Wesserunsett, was built as a Spritualist meeting hall and was converted to a theater in 1898. Reputedly the oldest summer theater in America, it developed into a preview theater for potential Broadway productions.

New Portland vicinity

NEW PORTLAND WIRE BRIDGE, off ME 27 and 16, 1841-42. Spanning the Carrabasset River, this unusual suspension bridge measures nearly 200 feet in length, but only 12 feet in width, thus permitting only one lane of traffic to cross at a time. Two large Sheffield steel girders support the bridge between its high, shingled frame towers which are themselves reminiscent of a much more famous span—New York's Brooklyn Bridge. NR.

New Sweden

NEW SWEDEN HISTORICAL SOCIETY MUSEUM, off ME 161. A replica of New Sweden's 1870 community hall is the home of farm and lumbering equipment and other artifacts of the early Swedish settlers of the region, along with various handcrafted household pieces. June-Aug, M-Sa 11-5, Su 2-5 and by appointment. Donations accepted. 896-3018.

Old Town

OLD TOWN HISTORICAL MUSEUM, N. Fourth St. Extension. The former waterworks building houses artifacts depicting historic Old Town. Exhibits pertaining to the logging industry and the Penobscot Indian tribe are included. June-Sept, W-Su 9-8. Free.

The nearby Penobscot Indian Reservation (descendants of the Algonquin Federation) maintains the **Penobscot National Historical Society** whose museum details the complete history of the tribe in exhibits featuring artifacts, photos, and religious items. Open all year, daily 12-8. Free. Two nearby churches, one Catholic and one Episcopal, are located in the vicinity. **St. Anne's,** off ME 43 (1828), was built on the site of two missionary churches and is considered to be one of the oldest established Catholic parishes in New England. **St. James,** on Centre Street (1892), is a graceful frame Gothic Revival style building designed by Henry Vaughn, the noted architect who was co-designer of Washington's famed National Cathederal. NR.

Orono

UNIVERSITY OF MAINE, 1868. Originally established as a college of agriculture, as were many state universities, the campus of more than 200 acres borders a branch of the Penobscot River. The 1904 Carnegie Library, of Tusco-Doric design, houses the **Art Galleries**, with collections of modern and historic Maine art, contemporary American art, and graphics. Open all year, M-F 8-4:30. Free. 581-7165. In **South Stevens Hall** is located the University's **Anthropology Museum** with exhibits on weapon and tool development, fossil man, and American Indians. Special sections cover Maine Indians and American pre-history. Open during university sessions, M-F 9-3:30, and by appointment. Free. 581-2746.

Patten

PATTEN LUMBERMAN'S MUSEUM, Shin Pond Road, ME 159, 19th-20th centuries. 2,000 artifacts are housed in eight buildings and trace Maine's lumbering history. The diverse exhibits include steam and gasoline log haulers, an 1820 logging camp, a blacksmith shop, and the working model of a sawmill. Memorial Day-Labor Day, Tu-Sa 9-4, Su 1-4; Labor Day-Columbus Day, Sa and Su 12-5, and by appointment. $1 adults, 50¢ children. 528-2650.

Stockholm

STOCKHOLM HISTORICAL SOCIETY MUSEUM, Main and Lake Sts. The museum building served as the town's first store and post office and now contains exhibits of household items, farm and lumber implements, and a local history collection including photographs and memorabilia. July-Sept 3, daily 1-4, and by appointment. Donations accepted. 896-5672.

Van Buren

ACADIAN VILLAGE, ME 1, 18th-20th centuries. A collection of sixteen reconstructed and relocated simple frame buildings have been assembled here to demonstrate aspects of Acadian culture. They include houses, barns, a railroad station, school, shoe shop, blacksmith shop, general store, barber shop, and church. All are furnished with period pieces. NR. June 15-Sept 15, M-Sa 10-5, Su 12-5, and by appointment. $1.50 adults, 50¢ children. 895-3401 or 895-3522.

Lodging and Dining

THE following list of inns and restaurants, by no means exhaustive, has been chosen with the intent of demonstrating the broad range of historic accommodations available throughout the state of Maine. These range from 18th-century private homes with only four or five guest rooms to the grand shingled resort hotels of the late 19th and early 20th centuries which attract guests for stays of a month or more during the summer. They have in common the loving care with which they have been restored and the love with which they are cherished by innkeepers and returning visitors alike.

Many of the inns listed have played their part in the history of Maine and the nation— hosting such famous figures as William Howard Taft and Ernest Hemingway, or witnessing important events such as the first public poetry reading of Edna St. Vincent Millay.

The hospitality of Maine's inns often includes fine dining, with fresh seafood *de rigueur* along the coast. Space does not permit listing the many other attractions available to the traveler— from fresh and salt-water fishing in fair summer weather to skiing and skating in winter.

Bar Harbor

ATLANTIC OAKS-BY-THE-SEA, ME 3, 04609. (207) 288-5218. Sonny Cough. All year. The 1905 former estate of Sir Harry Oakes has 84 rooms, all with ocean views. Expensive. MC, V, PC.

CLEFTSTONE MANOR, 92 Eden St., 04609. (207) 288-4951. The Jackson Family. May 1-Oct. 30. This 1894 house was the summer residence of the Blair family of Washington, D.C. President Taft and other notables once stayed here. 19 rooms. Afternoon tea. Moderate. AE, MC, V.

MANOR HOUSE INN, 106 West St., 04609. (207) 288-3759. Jan & Frank Matter. May-Oct. Built by a Col. Faster in 1887, this Victorian mansion was enlarged in 1897. 10 rooms; cottages available. NR. Moderate, MC, V, PC.

Bath

GRANE'S FAIRHAVEN INN, N. Bath Rd., 04530. (207) 443-4391. Jane Wylie & Gretchen Williams. Open all year. 1790 country home built by Pembleton Edgecomb for his bride; surrounded by woods and meadows; overlooking Kennebec River. 9 rooms. Inexpensive. PC.

Blue Hill

BLUE HILL INN, Union St., 04614. (207) 374-2844. Jean & Fred Wakelin. Open all year. Built in 1832, the Blue Hill has been an inn since 1840. There are many lovely historic homes nearby. 9 rooms. Moderate. MC, V.

Brunswick

STOWE HOUSE, 63 Federal St., 04011. (207) 725-5543. Peg & Bob Mathews. Open all year. It is fitting that this home, originally built as an inn in 1804 and made famous by Harriet Beecher Stowe should once again serve the needs of the traveler. The house serves as the home of the innkeepers and as a restaurant. Rooms—55 in all—are located in a motel unit. NR. Moderate.

Camden

CAMDEN HARBOR INN & RESTAURANT, 83 Bayview St., 04843. (207) 236-4200. Jim & Loureen Gilbert. Open all year. Has been an inn since it was built in 1874 to accommodate steamship passengers en route from Boston to Bangor. 18 rooms. Moderate.

WHITEHALL INN, 52 High St., 04843. (207) 236-3391. The Dewing Family. May 30-Oct. 15. Edna St. Vincent Millay first recited publicly in this 1834 former sea captain's home. Later additions. 45 rooms, MAP, moderate.

Castine

THE PENTAGOET INN, Main St., 04421. (207) 326-8616. Natalie Saunders. 1894 home with 14 rooms, in a town that was governed by Dutch, English, French following its founding in 1630. Revolutionary battles took place in the nearby harbor. Public restaurant. Moderate. AE, MC, V, PC. Apr.-Nov.

Center Lovell

CENTER LOVELL INN, ME 5, 04016. (207) 925-1575. William & Susan Mosca. May 30-Oct. 15, Dec. 10-Mar. 15. 1805 home with wrap-around veranda. Its own garden provides much fresh produce. Public invited for dinner. MAP, moderate. MC, V, PC.

Damariscotta

THE BRANNON-BUNKER INN, ME 129, 04543. (207) 563-5941. Dave & Char Bunker. May-Oct. Late 19th-century barn, which served as a dance hall during the 1920s, is connected to an 1820 Cape style house. 6 rooms. Kitchen privileges. Inexpensive. MC, V, PC.

Dennysville

LINCOLN HOUSE COUNTRY INN, Dennysville, 04628. (207) 726-3953. Mary & Gerald Haggerty. All year. Georgian Colonial with attached ell and woodshed built by an ancestor of Abraham Lincoln in 1787. 6 rooms. NR. Moderate. MC, V. ¶

Five Islands

GREY HAVENS INN, Reid Pk. Rd., Box 82, 04546. (207) 371-2616. The Hardcastle Family. June 1-Labor Day. Built as an inn in 1901 by Walter Reid, who later donated nearby land for Reid State Park. Deepwater anchorage, and beautiful views. 15 rooms. Moderate.

Kennenbunkport

CAPTAIN LORD MANSION, Pleasant St. (P.O. Box 527), 04046. (207) 967-3141. Bev Davis & Rick Litchfield. Open year-round. One of Kennebunkport's most handsome residences has been sensitively restored for today's enjoyment and comfort. There are fourteen working fireplaces, eleven of which are found in guest rooms. NR. Expensive, PC.

ENGLISH MEADOWS INN. RFD #1, ME 35, 04046. (207) 967-5766. The Kelly Family. Apr. 1-Oct. 31. This 1860 Victorian farmhouse with attached carriage house rests on 6 country acres boasting century old lilacs and flowering fruit trees. 14 rooms. No pets, no children. Moderate.

THE OLDE GRIST MILL, Mill Lane, 04046. (207) 967-4781. David F. Lombard. One of a handful of tidewater grist mills in the country, this 1749 building, now a restaurant, has been owned by the same family since its construction. NR. Moderate. AE, D, MC, V.

Monhegan Island

ISLAND INN, Shore Road, 04852. No phone until mid-'83. Robert A. Burton. Reachable only by ferry from Port Clyde or by private boat. A rambling informal inn built in 1850 (with early-20th-century additions). No children or pets. 45 rooms. PC. Mid-June-mid-Sept. ¶

Moose River

SKY LODGE (and Motel), ME 201, Box 99, 04945. (207) 668-2171. Rita Nadeau. May 15-late fall. 1929 log lodge on 200 acres; much handwrought pine furniture. 17 rooms. MAP, moderate. AE, V. ¶

Newcastle

THE NEWCASTLE INN, River Rd., 04553. (207) 563-5685. George & Sandra Thomas. All year. Circa 1900 inn with attached carriage house overlooking Damariscotta River. 20 rooms. Moderate. PC. ¶

Ogunquit

CLAY HILL FARM, Agamenticus Rd., 03907 (207) 646-2272. R. Perkins & R. Maurais. Open all year. This c. 1820 farmhouse on 27 country acres is a noted restaurant. Expensive. AE, MC, V.

THE OLD VILLAGE INN, 30 Main St., 03907. (207) 646-7088. Frederick L. Thomas & Alf. B. Kristiansen. Mar.-Dec., closed Mondays off season. An inn since its construction in 1837; recently renovated and decorated with antiques and original art. 6 rooms. Moderate. MC, V, PC. 〖¶〗

Portland

BOONE'S FAMOUS RESTAURANT, 6 Custom House Wharf, 04112. (207) 774-5725. Thomas & Emily Stratis. Year-round for lunch and dinner. Boone's has been in continuous operation for 84 years. Noted for its seafood. Moderate. AE, D, CB, MC, V.

Sargentville

OAKLAND HOUSE, 04673. (207) 359-8521. Sylvia & James Littlefield. May-Oct. A relative of the innkeepers was born in the original farmhouse on the island in 1776; additions made it an inn in 1889. 10 rooms; cottages. MAP, AP, moderate. 〖¶〗

Scarborough

ATLANTIC HOUSE HOTEL, Box 467, Kirkwood Rd., 04074. (207) 883-4381. Dino W. Giamatti. June 1-Oct. 1. Large frame summer hotel thought to be Maine's oldest summer resort (1850). 90 rooms. Lunch open to the public. NR. MAP, moderate. PC. 〖¶〗

Searsport

THE CARRIAGE HOUSE, East Main St., 04974. (207) 548-2289. Louise & Jack Fernan. Open all year. Built in 1849 by a Yankee clipper ship captain; once owned by Maine painter Waldo Pierce. Ernest Hemingway was a frequent guest here. 7 rooms. Moderate. AE, MC, V.

THE HOME PORT INN, Main St., 04974. (207) 548-2259. Dr. F. George & Edith M. Johnson. Open all year. An 1863 sea captain's home, appointed with period antiques. 7 rooms. Inexpensive. AE, MC, V, PC.

South Bristol

COVESIDE INN, Christmas Cove, 04568. (207) 644-8282. Barbara & Mike Mitchell. June 15-Oct. 1. The 1894 inn with detached motel is on Christmas Cove, discovered by Captain John Smith in 1614. Good harbor facilities. 15 rooms. Moderate. 〖¶〗

South Brooksville

BREEZEMERE FARM INN, Box 290, 04617. (207) 326-8628. James & Joan Lippke. June-Oct. An 1850 farmhouse and cottages on 60 acres overlooking Orcutt Harbor and Penobscot Bay. 7 rooms (inn). MAP, moderate. MC, V, PC.

Stonington (on Deer Isle)

CAPTAIN'S QUARTERS INN & MOTEL, Main St. (Box 83), 04681. (207) 367-2420. Bob Dodge. Open all year. Several connected 1880s buildings with various past uses (barbershop, old post office) make up this 14 room inn on the water. Moderate. MC, V, PC. 🍴

E. Waterford

THE WATERFORD INNE, Chadbourne Rd., 04223. (207) 583-4037. Barbara & Rosalie Vanderzanden. May 1-Feb. 28. Original 1825 home and later barn and wood-shed in same family until 1970s. 9 rooms. Moderate. PC. 🍴

Waterford

THE ARTEMUS WARD HOUSE, ME 35 and 37, 04088. (207) 583-4106. Lynn Baker. Closed Easter-May 29, Oct. 15-Nov. 15. This 1805 home was later owned by Charles Farrar Browne, a humorist known as Artemus Ward. 4 rooms. NR. Afternoon tea open to the public. No children under 12. Moderate. PC.

Yarmouth

HOMEWOOD INN & COTTAGES, Drinkwater Point, Box 196, 04096. (207) 846-3351. Fred & Colleen Webster. June 11-Oct. 12. The historic house at the center of this complex, and appropriately called the Maine House, was built c. 1742. Some of the 42 rooms available there; most in cottages. Moderate. AE, MC, V, PC. 🍴

York Harbor

DOCKSIDE GUEST QUARTERS, Harris Island Rd. (Box 205), 03909. (207) 363-2868. David L. Lusty. Late May-mid-Oct. Central house was built in 1880; there are also modern cottages; all situated on a small island in York Harbor. 20 rooms. MAP, moderate. MC, V. PC. 🍴

YORK HARBOR INN, US 1A, 03911. (207) 363-5119. Open all year. Noreen Linehan. This 17th-century inn was originally located on the Isle of Shoals, but was floated ashore c. 1700. 12 rooms. NR. Moderate. MC, V. PC. 🍴

Index